BIG
WORLD
Small Sasha

ISBN: 979-8-218-37328-3

First Edition, 2024

Cover photo: Félix Bédard-Bruyère

Cover design: Tio & Sasha

Contents

Author's note

To write this book, I dug into my memory, read through the notes, journals, and emails I've kept over the years, consulted several people in this book, and fact-checked every fact I've included about our world. There are no fictional events or characters in this book. Some names and character details have been changed to protect identities. Dialogues did not happen exactly as they are written. Most dialogues did occur, but I cannot remember the exact words that were used. Some dialogues are drawn out to explain my point of view to the reader.

Thank you for your interest in my journey.

Prologue

September, 2017

I've been traveling around the world for over ten years. I don't have a house, a city, or a particular country to come back to when I run out of money. I find having an ordinary life with a "home" and a "career" boring and unnecessary.

For me, home is our entire planet Earth, and I think it is time for us to analyze what we're doing on it.

People often ask me how I can afford to travel so much. I've never had much money, and I don't think that I ever will. Nobody gives me money or funds me in any way. When I run out of money, I work any odd job, usually in hospitality because it's easy to get hired, make quick cash, quit, and move on.

I don't value working for money. I do it because I have to in order to live in society. I've never had one consistent job for more than seven months. I don't work very much compared to most people, but when I work, I work my ass off and I save almost every penny I earn.

It's not so hard to save when everything you own has to fit into one backpack.

Currently, I'm in Siberia. I flew to Moscow then took the Trans-Siberian Railway to Irkutsk with a friend, making stops along the way. I wasn't planning to live in Irkutsk before I came here, but once I got here, I decided that I liked it. So I found an apartment and I unpacked my backpack. I will stay here until I decide that I want to leave.

Railway tickets added up to about $150. A decent hostel, on average, costs $8 per night (but you can even find some for $4 or $5). There are also hospitality exchange websites where you can find like-minded people who you can stay with for free.

If you stick to things like rice (or buckwheat), vegetables, and beans, you can survive on about $20 per week for food.

What else do you really need? *Water*—here, you can drink from the lake.

Altogether, I spent about $300 on an entire month of traveling across Russia, including railway tickets and accommodation. That's one night out in Sydney or New York for some people.

Seeing the most beautiful places on Earth is usually either free or cheap. To get to Olkhon Island (a remarkable place on Lake Baikal), for example, cost less than $10 by bus and ferry from Irkutsk. When I got there, I talked to a local woman in a market who offered me accommodation for about $5 per night. It wasn't the prettiest, but I didn't come there to sleep in a nice room, I came to see the national park. If you don't speak the local language, you can still find cheap deals online. The most expensive thing I paid for was a whole day four-wheel drive tour of the island, which cost about $17, including lunch and vodka. *Worth every penny.*

If we want to get into expensive countries—I once came to Switzerland with $500 and stayed there all winter season, snow-boarding and babysitting, then traveled to Italy, got robbed of everything but one credit card, got a replacement passport, back-packed Turkey for a month on that credit card, then flew to Australia—where I found an illegal job in a café to pay back my debt.

All in all, it is a misconception that money is what stops people from traveling (for those who come from privileged countries anyway). The reality is that money is just an excuse.

Don't get me wrong, this lifestyle is not for everybody, and there are some big things to sacrifice. But if you do dream of it, don't let *money* hold you back. What you need to survive on Earth is not money, but food, water, and (sometimes) shelter.

When you have little to no money, you end up hitchhiking, couchsurfing, and budgeting any way possible. Through this, you experience local life and culture all over the world—*real people,* and experiences you would never even know to dream of. You also don't rush, you take your time and get a closer and longer look at the most spectacular places on Earth. *Dramatic, pristine beauty.*

Through all of this, you come to realize what's really important in life.

You learn to understanding what it means to live, and that we are all part of this Earth and everything on it.

And you see the flaws in our society.

The system we live by—the money system—is just a big scam. Think about what money is. It is a human-made entity that only exists because we believe in it. It represents nothing (not gold, nor resources), yet it controls all of our lives—and now is dominating most other life and resources on our planet. Banks are legally allowed to lend out ten times the amount of money they actually have. So they are lending you a fictional thing that they don't even have, and if you don't pay it back, they can take your things—real things. What a lie. The whole system is crooked, this is just the tip of the iceberg.

Most people revolve their entire lives around making some kind of career, usually for the money. I bet most people don't even know why they get stuck in one job or career, they just do it because that's what they've been taught, and that's what other people keep on telling them to do.

I never listened to what people told me was important. I sought to question everything and figure it out myself.

It took ten years for my family to finally stop arguing with me about my lifestyle.

I don't believe in any of this bullshit and—for as much as I can —I will not live by it.

—

I wrote this book to show you that you don't have to either.

Part 1

1

The Job Game

I was surfing in Nicaragua last time I realized I was running out of money and would have to go back to slavery to continue to live on Earth. I considered staying in Central America and getting an English teaching job at first. I even applied and was accepted to work at a school in Honduras, but then I mulled over the nine-month contract I would've had to sign and dismissed the idea. I knew it would be much easier to just go back to the US, work in a bar for a couple of months, save money, quit, and then travel around the world without being tied down to a job.

I had two options in mind: Vegas and Hawaii. Vegas would be dreadful, but I was sure I could score a bartending job there. Bar work in places like Vegas pays so well in tips that I could easily save a few thousand dollars in just two or three months of slaving. Hawaii is expensive and not as promising for work, but it's like a playground for me—*beaches, mountains, jungles, surf, hiking, diving, climbing, and a lot more.* Plus, my best friend from high school lived there.

I looked at flights. There was a cheap one to Hawaii.

Fuck it. Three days later I was all Aloha.

One thing to note is that I've never revolved my life around making any kind of career for money. I recognize that I need money to live in society. I know that I need to work in order to get money. So for me, work is simply a means of getting money. Nothing else.

I've never even considered merging my life (the stuff I like to do) with a long-term means of making money. I don't even know if that could have been possible... *Could I have become a professional snowboarder, perhaps?* Well, that would have taken a lot of effort and probably would have ruined the fun of snowboarding. *How about a professional photographer? Maybe it's not too late, even now?* But then I would have to take pictures of what other people tell me to take pictures of, not what I want to take pictures of. I'd also probably have to stay in one place for a long time or go where other people tell me to go. I'd much rather just make money as quickly as possible, quit, and then live without trading my time and energy to some "job."

So I try to view work as a game. *Let's play the "job game" for a couple of months so I can get it over with and continue to live on Earth.*

July, 2016

I flew to Honolulu then caught a bus to the North Shore. I was determined to get a job there. I didn't want to live anywhere else on Oahu and I couldn't afford a flight to another island. As soon as I arrived, I heard that a fancy beachfront hotel called Turtle Bay was opening a new restaurant called Roy's. Everybody said this would be the best work on the North Shore. I even met people who wanted to quit their manager positions just to serve tables there.

I immediately filled out an online job application. Under "position wanted," I ticked two boxes: bartender and server (although last time I served tables, I told myself it would be the *last time*). My application was accepted that night. Next came the interview.

I dressed up in borrowed clothes and asked a friend named Scabies to drive me to the interview. It was held in the lobby of that luxurious hotel. I tried to make it look like I belonged there. I was clean, calm, and ready to recite the story inside my head (only if asked, of course)—*I worked in a bar in Australia for five years, then I moved to Hawaii, where I worked as a server and bartender.*

I want to live here on the North Shore and work in this restaurant for the rest of my life. I don't like lying or holding back the truth about myself, but you gotta do what you gotta do in a world where you need money to survive. If they know you're a nomad, they won't hire you.

A manager named Chris Pirrone scanned my application and then squinted at my face. "I remember you." He laughed. "You worked at Breakers."

"Ah, yes, Breakers," I said. *He remembers me, that's good, I hope. He thinks I'm a local. Great.* We talked about Breakers and what a mess of a place that was, and how great Roy's was going to be. We talked about the North Shore and the North Shore people we both knew. *It's good to be a local.* He agreed to hire me.

"Training will start in four weeks," he said. "See you then!"

"Mahalo!" I would never usually wait that long for the "job game" to start, but so many people assured me that Roy's would be a goldmine and that it would be worth it, so I waited.

Four weeks in Hawaii... Zero dollars in my bank account. What to do? I had to borrow money to buy a van to live in. The van cost nine hundred dollars but it drove and had no back seats. I acquired a mattress from Craigslist then sanded down and painted the ceiling of the van. The headliner was so worn out that it had deteriorated into a brown moldy gunk. I thought it would be ironic if I worked in a fancy restaurant at Turtle Bay and lived in a gunk van.

August, 2016

I showed up to training four weeks later. The place looked nice. It was right on the beach, there was new wooden furniture and a beautiful bar facing the ocean. I had never been part of a restaurant opening before, but I could tell that Roy's was serious business. They gave us a binder as thick as a brick—half filled with recipes, half with "front of house" business. Roy came in. We all introduced ourselves, then we started learning the "Roy's ways."

The training was intense. It went on for six to seven hours each day for three weeks and we were paid minimum wage during this time (about eight dollars an hour). After a few days of training, the managers separated the "front of house" staff into sections— bartenders, servers, food runners, and bussers were told to go to different corners of the restaurant. Since many of us didn't know which position we'd be assigned, the managers called us out name by name.

"Natalie Boutilier—section one," said Pirrone. A beautiful girl with long brown hair and green eyes stood up and walked over to the bartending section. "Sarah Lewis—section one." Another beautiful bartender. They all seemed to know each other. "Jade Eckardt —section two." A pretty blonde girl walked over to the server section. "Sasha Davletshina—section four," Pirrone continued.

"What? Was that me?" I jumped up. "Section four—the busser section?"

"Yes, Sasha," said Pirrone. "Section four."

What? Me? A busser? I almost had a panic attack. *I applied to be a bartender! Not to clean tables! I just wasted over a fucking month failing at this stupid "job game," waiting for this stupid training to start. What the hell kind of money could I make bussing tables?*

Someone else who was called to the busser section put down his apron and walked out. I kept it cool, tried not to tear up. Went through the training, learned how to pick up dirty dishes and pour water into water glasses. At the end of the day, I talked to Pirrone and calmly explained that I applied to be a bartender, not a busser. He then told me that I could train with the servers the next day and "see how I go."

See how I go. OK. No hope for bartending then. I was devastated, but at least there was hope for serving tables. *Fuck.*

We spent the next few weeks tasting and learning about all of the food on the menu, which was some of the best food I've had in my life. The servers and bartenders had to learn what was in every dish, how each dish was prepared, and how to "spiel" everything on the menu. I stayed up until five in the morning each night, learning every single ingredient in every dish, every spice, exactly how it was cooked, how it was served, and what wine it "paired" with. I learned about the origin of every fish on the menu, I learned how it lived, where it lived, what it was fed, and what its mother's middle name was. I learned that masago was caviar from a small forage fish in the smelt family which grazes on plankton at the edges of ice shelves in the North Atlantic, North Pacific, and Arctic Oceans. Yes, it has scales. I learned all the ingredients in shichimi, I learned that hoisin sauce has MSG and that soy sauce is not gluten free. I learned the definition of nori, namasu, browning, braising, blanching… Ask anybody in that place if my spiel made them cum. *It sure did.* I aced every test. I made sure I would be a fucking waitress.

And I got it! *Yes.*

September, 2016

The restaurant opened. I messed up a few times. Everybody did. *It's okay.*

I worked more and more. Wasn't making much money. We (servers) had to split about fifty percent of our tips with the other staff, so I was making about fifty dollars per lunch shift and about a hundred dollars per dinner shift. That's very little for restaurant work in Hawaii.

After three months in Hawaii I was still in debt. *Roy's was a mistake,* I realized. *I could have saved plenty of money by now working somewhere else.*

I couldn't turn back now. *Work harder. Work more!*

I did. The more I worked, the faster I got, the more tables I could handle, the more tips I made. That's the thing about hospitality jobs in the US—the more you can handle, the more money you make.

Serving tables really is hard work. You need to have a good memory and be very organized inside your head. Little things like "Can I have some ketchup?" can easily throw off your organization when you're slammed. You need to keep a constant list of priorities in your head, and this list is continuously changing, every few minutes or so. If you know how to manage the list, you can be a good server. Double check everything and you won't make mistakes. Calm yourself and don't get overwhelmed in stressful situations. *Don't forget that it's just a game.*

October, 2016

I worked a lot. I worked well. I won every single competition in that place—I won bottles of wine, money, beer, gift certificates, I even won a costume contest once.

On Halloween, Roy's offered a hundred-dollar prize plus a bottle of wine for the best costume. At that point, I lived in a share house across Keiki Beach with a bunch of friends. It was the kind of house where a lot of people come and go all the time (surfers and hippies stay for a few months and then leave, leaving their crap behind), so there was a lot of crap—clothes, shoes, toys, and other stuff that didn't belong to anybody.

I was determined to win that contest. The night before Halloween, I found a cardboard box, duct tape, clothes, shoes, and a giant stuffed panda. I turned the clothes into a little body and placed it in the box, which I turned into a cage using the duct tape. Then I found a black fluffy sweater. I put it on and stuffed the panda into the back of the sweater so that the panda's head popped out above my head. Then I made a hole in the back of the box and inserted my head into it, making my head look like the head of the little body inside the cage. My real body then looked like the body of the evil panda, whose face I painted with "blood."

I was pleasantly surprised that it actually turned out as I had hoped—it was a giant evil panda holding a miniature captive (me) in a cage.

So Roy's is a pretty high-end restaurant. The kind that people with little bow ties and sparkly dresses go to. The meals cost about fifty to sixty dollars, the appetizers cost twenty to thirty. We had to properly present and serve bottled wine and we were supposed to "spiel" every table.

My first table on Halloween was a party of seven rich people celebrating something. A couple of them laughed at my costume, but I could tell that some of them were not very pleased at having an evil panda and miniature captive spiel them and serve them expensive food and wine. I spieled them good. I told them all about the melt-in-your-mouth ahi with the soy-mustard butter sauce and the smooth, earthy red wine that complemented its exquisite taste. They bought in.

Once I brought the wine glasses to their table, however, I realized I had a problem—I couldn't reach the table in my costume. I was able to reach the corners of the table, but when I tried to set a wine glass between two side-by-side chairs my hand stopped short. The cardboard cage was in the way. I considered turning my body ninety degrees and extending my arm from the side of my body, like a pregnant waitress may do, but unlike a pregnant waitress, I wasn't able to turn my head and see where my hand was. I didn't think to make holes in either side of the cage, so the only direction I could see was straight ahead of me.

One man smirked. "Just give me all the glasses," he said, "before you break something."

I handed him the wine glasses, then returned with their hundred-dollar bottle of Pinot Noir. "This is a two thousand ten Domaine Serene Cuvée, from Willamette Valley." I added a small touch of miniature captive tone to my voice, just to match my costume. The evil panda opened the bottle. "Would you like to have a taste?" I asked the white-haired woman who ordered the wine.

"Yes," she said. Her chair was not at the corner of the table.

I walked over to her, held the wine bottle at the very bottom, extended my arm as far as it could go, and tried to pour her a "taste."

"Wait, wait, Sasha!" My manager grabbed the bottle right before I spilled its earthy contents all over this woman's sparkly dress.

The rest of the night went kind of like that. I couldn't hold a tray, I couldn't see anywhere but straight ahead, I was sweating profusely, and I needed a ton of help from my coworkers. It wasn't a very productive night but it was totally worth it.

I was *$100 up.*

December, 2016

I continued to slave away through November and December. I worked many doubles which ran from 9:45 a.m. to up to 1:00 a.m., usually with no break. After a double (and I often did two or three doubles in a row), I would need an entire day of bed rest just to recover. After one day of rest, I would have to come right back to work again. I basically ate nothing but Roy's employee meals, which were usually tasty but not the healthiest, and I had severe back pain that I could not get rid of because of the stress of the job. By the end of December, I started to feel depressed.

What am I doing? I asked myself.

I took a day off and went into the jungle. I always liked this quote from the film *The Power of One*: "Any question you have, the answer you will find in nature."

I walked around the jungle barefoot and alone. Felt the mud slip between my toes.

Think.

Five months in the job game and I have little to show for it. I've paid back my debt, saved a few thousand dollars but not nearly what I would expect from five months of work. I wasted two months —one month waiting for the stupid game to start, one month training, getting minimum wage. I have serious back pain. I'm not happy.

Come back to reality. *What am I doing?*

I am a little person on a giant sphere that we call Earth, moving through a vast infinity of wonder we call the Universe. I am so insignificant. This "job game" is so meaningless.

I felt deep empathy for those who don't see it as a game, but allow it to engulf their entire lives.

How can you just live and accept this? How lost and confused must some be...

It doesn't have to be that way.

*I have to **do** something about this!*

But what?

I grabbed a guava tree. Looked at its intricate beauty. The interwoven shapes of its bark. The colors—red, pink, brown, even blue! The colors were weaving.

Think.

I spent the last nine years of my life traveling all over the world. If I died today, I wouldn't regret a minute of it. I don't believe in the system we live in, I have no desire to settle down and join it. I know I will quit this job soon.

Why am I so confused then?

When I left Nicaragua, I broke up with Chris. *He was so perfect. So beautiful inside and out. He understood me deeply. He was funny, witty, sexy, and smart. I miss him.*

Was that a mistake? It didn't feel like a mistake. I couldn't handle it anymore. We spent two and a half years traveling around the world together—three months in one country, two in another; three months together, four months apart. We had four passports between the two of us, but none that allowed us to live in the same place for more than a few months. I couldn't be torn apart anymore. I needed to be on my own for a while. It felt right.

What is it then?

I'm just overworking myself. I don't have a plan. A date. Where am I going next? What am I doing?

What am I doing?

I thought about the last few of years of traveling—*Australia, Sri Lanka, Indonesia, the Caribbean, Lake Tahoe, Europe, Russia, Ukraine, Nicaragua.*

I need more. Not more places or more adventures, but more purpose. *More depth in my life.* I started to feel guilty. Guilty for taking advantage of the system and just having fun, knowing that the whole world was going to shit.

Look at these people. Look at what we're doing to our planet. We're killing it all for the job game! Can't they see that it's just a game?

No. *They can't.*

Think.

I struggled with university, but managed to finish in 2014. I graduated with a degree of International and Global Studies from the University of Sydney. The degree spanned from studying international political systems, to international business, to cultural issues, international conflicts, war, environmental problems, and so on. The core subject analyzed global and international problems and looked at how different types of institutions dealt with different types of problems. For example, how organizations like the UN or various NGOs tried to solve issues like deforestation, climate change, the abuse of human rights, and more. Through my studies, I realized that all of these organizations were failing and that our global problems were only getting worse.

My conclusion to the entire degree was that our whole system needed to be completely dismantled and recreated in order to solve any global problem. Gaining this kind of perspective from a "prestigious" institution only confirmed my belief that there was absolutely no point of joining our fucked up society, building some kind of career for money, or living a boring ordinary life.

I thought about this and stared into the guava tree.

It is so beautiful.

How could I live without this guava tree? Without the forest, without the extraordinary biodiversity of our oceans, our Earth. We cannot live without life on Earth.

*I have to at least **try** to do something. But what? And how?*

Perhaps... The Venus Project. This was the only organization I knew of that proposed an in-depth, holistic plan for how to redesign the entire global system and culture starting from the very core—human values, mentality, and behavior. Any other form of activism seemed pointless to me because the hard effort would eventually be wiped out by the money game.

I picked a guava.

How to join the Venus Project? I had been wondering that for years.

On my way to Nicaragua in spring of 2016, I flew to Florida to meet one-hundred-year-old Jacque Fresco, the founder of the Venus Project (TVP). While I was at the TVP research center, I also met co-founder Roxanne Meadows and a volunteer named Saso. I told them that I spoke Russian, and they said that the Russian-speaking team was the biggest TVP team in the world, but they had some communication issues and needed a good Russian-English link.

That was my chance. *I could be the missing link!* I thought, jokingly. I immediately volunteered to help and gave them my contact details. Saso told me they could use my help. He even said I could become a point of contact for the Venus Project, but I'd have to go through an "orientation process" first. And the next orientation process wouldn't start for a few months. He said they'd email me when they were ready.

OK. I cleared my head. Dropped the squashed fruit from my palm.

I just had to wait. *TVP is in my near future. For now, get a grasp of reality. Don't lose it. Don't let the "job game" get to you. Remember your insignificance in the vast universe.*

Make a deadline: March first—I quit no matter what. Bust it out, save as much money as possible, quit, and go. It doesn't matter where, just quit the stupid game!

I walked out of the jungle.

2

The Hawaiian Islands

Waves the size of houses crashed on the North Shore of Oahu. I'd seen many waves in my life, but I had never seen waves like these. Across the street from our house was Keikis—the heaviest shore break on Oahu. You could feel our house tremble on a big day.

I'd go straight to the beach after work, just to stare at the waves under moonlight. The energy was so powerful that it frightened me sometimes. So much weight coming down at once, crashing, bursting, vibrating, resonating, then being sucked back out to sea like air through a vacuum.

I need these moments alone in life. To think and not think. To sit on lumpy sand between monstrous waves and the shadows of mountains. Kaena Point in the distance. The Universe above my head. The Milky Way was staggering—you could see thousands of stars from the North Shore. *Each star—another sun. An entirely different world.* I closed my eyes and felt heavy. I was so small, yet so big. I felt powerless and powerful at the same time. I saw myself as this bundle of atoms, sitting on a bundle of sand, on a little island in the middle of the great Pacific Ocean, on little Earth, orbiting around our very own star, *one of hundreds of billions of stars in our galaxy—one of hundreds of billions of galaxies*. And all of this— was bundles of atoms.

In the mornings I would come back to the beach to watch humpback whales breaching close to shore, right in my backyard.

On my days off work, I'd explore Oahu's volcanoes, jungles, and waterfalls.

Everything changed after that day in the jungle. I was rejuvenated. I knew exactly what I was living for: I had two months to save as much money as possible and then I'd be a free slave again.

Now I really got down to business. I worked so much that I was getting in trouble for how much overtime I was building up (because Roy's had to pay us something like eleven dollars an hour for overtime). I was no longer depressed. I was excited, happy, and enthusiastic. I met interesting people at the restaurant, like Jack Johnson and John Jackson.

I got into intriguing conversations with my guests. I shared my travel stories with them, my ideas about the world, the Venus Project, everything. One older couple was so impressed by me that they tipped me two hundred dollars three nights in a row on a ninety-dollar bill, and five hundred dollars on their last night in Hawaii. Unfortunately, I had to tip out half of that money, but those moments inspired me not only for the money, but because they made me realize that I was actually able to influence people. *If I can impress somebody enough to give me a thousand dollars just by telling them a few stories between courses, maybe I can do something much more important*, I thought.

In the two months between that day in the jungle and my final quitting date, I made more money than anybody else in that restaurant, bartenders and managers included. I saved over ten thousand dollars in just two months of serving tables. This was the first time in my life that I earned that much money and I was planning to make these savings last for a long, long time.

March 1, I quit.

I sold my van and moved out of my house. I bought three things that were important for what I wanted to do: a good camera, a good backpack, and a lightweight hammock. Altogether, this stuff added up to a bit under a thousand dollars, so you could say that I traded my van in for these things. I had no concrete plans for the future so I decided to simply live out of my hammock and explore the Hawaiian Islands for the next few months.

14

My good friend Emma flew in from Australia to join me for my first two weeks of freedom. Emma is one of the most badass chicks I know, and one of the best influences of my life. I met her when I was eighteen years old, in Whistler, Canada, and she basically showed me how to be a strong, independent woman and pay no attention to what other people say you can or can't do. Emma's originally from the Northern Territory, Australia, and she used to ride bulls. Now she works as a fitter and turner in a diamond mine.

Once Emma flew to Oahu, we heard that the Big Island's active volcano, Kīlauea, was erupting and that it was possible to see lava flowing into the ocean.

"Shall we?" I asked.

The next day we were on the Big Island, driving to Volcanoes National Park in a small rental car. We parked the car at the Jaggar Museum and walked to the observation platform. The land around us was dry and barren. Beyond the platform we could see a collapsed pit crater with a flaring lava lake.

I gazed through a telescope. I could see the lava churn, splash, and burst out of its pit.

"Check out the name of this crater," said Emma. "Ha-le-ma-uma-u."

"Hard to pronounce, eh?" I smiled. "It says here that according to Hawaiian mythology, Halema'uma'u is the home of Pele, the goddess of fire, lightning, dance, wind, volcanoes, and violence."

"Yep, I can see why!" Emma chuckled as a burst of lava spewed toward the sky.

After a walk through the museum, Emma and I took a long drive through the national park, from the summit of Kīlauea all the way to the Pacific Ocean. This was a powerful sight—a steady mountain slope of dried up black lava met the bright blue endless ocean. We drove for hours, gazing at black dusty rivers of Pāhoehoe (smooth, unbroken lava) over steep slopes covered in 'A'ā (rough lava blocks).

Toward the end of the day, Emma and I drove to Kalapana, a small oceanside town beneath the volcano. There, we rented bicycles and rode down a long dirt road that led to the lava flow. The ambience of this place was magnificent. There was dark volcanic rock all around us; to the left was the Pacific Ocean, to the right was a picturesque sunset, and up ahead was a volcanic vent.

I couldn't stop smiling as we pedaled toward the smoke. Once we arrived at the end of the dirt road, we put our bikes down and walked over the dry, uneven clumps of hardened lava to the edge of the cliff.

"Whoa!" I caught sight of the lava meeting the ocean. The mix of energy was incredible—red hot liquid rock flowed directly onto ocean waves as they crashed against the steep black cliffs.

"Wow, it's like a waterfall of lava," said Emma. We walked closer and stood still for a few minutes, mesmerized by the sight.

"Isn't it just magical to see the island grow with your own eyes?" I said as I stared into the falls.

We rode our bikes back after dark, then got into our rental car and drove to a nearby beach. Emma and I decided not to book any hostels or hotels, but to camp on different beaches instead. This would give us the ultimate freedom to explore the Big Island. Instead of wasting money and having to come back to the same place each night, we camped wherever we wanted and went wherever we wanted, whenever we wanted. This wasn't exactly "legal," but it was warm and safe enough to sleep outside without a tent, so we figured it would be unlikely for us to get a camping fine.

The first night, we slept on a beautiful black-sand nudist beach. We made a fire, roasted potatoes, and slept beneath the stars. The next day, we drove up Mauna Kea (Hawaii's highest volcano), then down to another beach on a different part of the island.

Once we made it to the west side, Emma and I were eager to do a night dive with manta rays. We didn't want to pay a hundred dollars each for the standard snorkel tour, so we came up with a better plan: we rented dive torches for about eight dollars and asked our friend Aaron to join us. Aaron is a lifeguard I had met on Oahu. He's tall, he's strong, and he knows the ocean better than he knows his own truck.

Aaron met us the next afternoon. "We'll have to swim to the dive boats," he said, "the ones with the big lights that attract the mantas. I'm not sure where they are exactly, but we'll find out."

Next, we talked to some locals and found the dive site: big jagged rocks led to the dive boats just behind the Sheraton Hotel in Kona. After dusk, the three of us walked over these rocks with nothing but torches and dive masks in our hands.

I looked down at the water. The swell frightened me as it moved up and down, crashing against sharp stones in the darkness. I jumped in when Aaron said, "Go!"

And there we were in the black ocean.

Stars above. Dive boat eighty meters away.

I tried not to think about sharks. That wasn't too hard as the current and swell were distracting enough.

Just swim, I thought.

Got to the dive boat!

This was *spectacular!* There were several huge manta rays sweeping gracefully from the deep black ocean to the fluorescent boat lights. The guys in charge of the dive boat noticed us and started yelling something, but luckily we couldn't hear much underwater! I dove down to get a closer look at the mantas. I don't know what I was thinking as one large manta ray was gliding toward me (probably just "aaahh"), when all of a sudden, I realized that I was way too close and directly in front of this sweeping giant, and the manta rammed straight into my arm! The poor thing was terrified, it squiggled up like a worm and swam upward. I had to go upward too. *That hurt!* I had a massive bruise on my arm for the next few weeks.

*　　*　　*

Since Emma and I didn't pay for any tours or hotels, our Hawaiian adventures didn't cost much money. We paid about twenty dollars per day for the car rental (with no insurance). We slept on beaches and bought food from supermarkets or farmers markets. Apart from that, we paid for gas and a drink here or there—the same stuff you'd probably buy at home. I wasn't paying rent anymore, so traveling at that point was even cheaper than living in one place.

One night, Emma and I went to the Kalapana Night Market to sell Wacky Whistles (funny sounding whistles from Australia) and earned about a hundred dollars. What can you do with a hundred dollars in Hawaii? Not much, right? *That's why it's best not to need much.* You can buy a bag of rice, a bag of beans, and thirty dollars of fresh fruits and vegetables—this can last you several days. Spend the other fifty dollars on gas—that will get you more than halfway around the Big Island. *What else do you really need?* Car rental, I guess. I usually don't like to rent cars but Emma was short on time and it happened to be cheap so it was most convenient. On a side note, I speculate that car rental companies actually make money through selling insurance, not through renting cars. If you already have a vehicle insured somewhere in the US, your insurance policy might cover the rental vehicle and this can save you a lot of money.

If somebody had paid for a week of accommodation in a five-star resort for me in Hawaii, I probably would have slept there one or two nights at most. I think that staying in a hotel highly restricts you because you waste so much precious time going back and forth from your hotel room and "getting ready." I never realized how much time I wasted in life just "getting ready" until I lived in a van. "Getting ready" mostly means just organizing your crap. Remember, a hotel room is just a place where you can sleep and store your crap.

For me, the feeling of "freedom" is at its highest when I don't know where I'm going to sleep at night and I don't care because I'm too excited about where I am and what I'm doing.

* * *

Once Emma and I got back to Oahu, we continued our adventure. We climbed Pu'u Manamana and Ka'au Crater, surfed, snorkeled, camped at Kaena Point and Makua, jumped off a fifteen-meter cliff by Hanauma Bay, climbed to the Makapu'u Tide Pools, paddle-boarded to the Kaneohe Sandbar, sailed in Honolulu, and danced to Tavana (an amazing Hawaiian musician). None of this cost much money. Hiking, surfing, snorkeling, camping, and cliff diving is free. The paddleboards and sailboat belonged to friends. Tavana's show is also free—and awesome! So even Hawaii can be cheap if you don't waste your money on tours or hotels.

Maui & Molokai

Once Emma returned to Australia, Aaron and I flew to Maui, where we bought an old Honda Accord wagon for six hundred dollars. Aaron and I spent the next month living out of that wagon and exploring every corner of Maui, from the top of its remarkable volcano to the foot of every waterfall we could find. We didn't always know where we'd sleep at night, but we always managed to find at least one tree to hang our hammocks on.

At the end of the month, Aaron and I sold the wagon for twelve hundred dollars, then took off for the island of Molokai.

We had heard that Molokai was home to a peculiar little town called Kalaupapa. This town sits on a flat peninsula that's separated from the rest of the island by staggering six-hundred-meter cliffs. Its geographical location gave it an interesting history: from the 1870s to 1969, people with leprosy were forced into exile and quarantined on this peninsula. A few patients (who are now cured) still reside there. The settlement now has about 120 residents and allows visitors, but only through tours. Children under sixteen are not allowed on Kalaupapa.

Neither Aaron or I were big fans of spending lots of money on tours, so we figured out a cheaper plan: I looked up a few people on Couchsurfing and there happened to be a host in Kalaupapa. At the time, Couchsurfing was a decent hospitality exchange platform. People used to use Couchsurfing to host travelers for free or to meet different people from around the world. I used this platform for many years, but unfortunately, Couchsurfing has morphed into a horrible profit-driven company in recent years so I no longer use it or recommend it to anyone.*

Back in 2017, however, I logged into Couchsurfing and contacted a guy named Tim from Kalaupapa. I asked if he wanted to host or meet up with Aaron and me. Unfortunately, he said he wasn't available to host or meet us, but he did give us some useful advice on how to visit the peninsula:

You could look up Damien Tours and take a walking tour of Kalaupapa on your own. I'm not sure of the cost but we do get a lot of people that like to do that as it is cheaper than the guided tour. They will give you directions to get to the bar as your first stop and you will get your pass and instructions about the walking tour from Gloria Marks. She is a patient and owns the bar and Damien Tours. Just a thought!

    Much Aloha,

    Tim

We called up Auntie Gloria and found out that the walking tour was thirty dollars. The flight from Maui to Molokai was fifty dollars. That was a bit pricey for me, but it was worth it. The plane was the size of a van; it fit about twelve passengers and I was able to speak to the pilot. We took off to the most incredible views of

Maui, then crossed the channel and flew alongside the highest ocean cliffs in the world. Molokai's cliffs were covered in jungle—there were no roads, no visible paths, all you could see was dense foliage and colossal waterfalls pouring directly into the ocean.

We circled around the majestic cliffs then landed in Molokai Airport. From there, Aaron and I hitched a ride to the largest town on the island, Kaunakakai (not to be confused with Kalaupapa), and searched for some local info. To find local info, we didn't look for a tourist information center; we looked for the local bar: Paddlers. That was the only bar in the dusty little town of Kaunakakai.

We found the bar, ordered a couple of Bloody Marys, and talked to a friendly bartender named Mike. Mike explained that there was no road from "mainland" Molokai to the Kalaupapa Peninsula, so the only way to get there was by plane, boat, or a two-hour hike down some steep cliffs. Mike also said that there was a campground at the top of the cliffs that led to Kalaupapa. "Follow the road back toward the airport, make a right on Kalea Highway, and keep on going toward Pālā'au State Park. You'll see the campground on your left just before you get to the Kalaupapa Lookout. If you guys wanna head down the trail in the morning, I'd camp there," said Mike.

After a couple more drinks, Aaron and I stepped back onto the road and hitched to the campground. It was easy to hitchhike on Molokai. We never waited more than a few minutes for a ride and everyone who picked us up was extremely friendly. The population of the entire island was about seven thousand people so everybody basically knew each other.

We got to the campground just before sunset. It was located in a dark green forest of tall winding trees. There were no other people around and the wind was so strong that it made the forest howl. I was relieved that I wasn't alone. Aaron and I had some canned food for dinner, then hung up our hammocks and tried to get some sleep.

It was hard to sleep. The moon was bright but barely lit up the clearing in the forest. The towering trees creaked and cracked all night, and shadows appeared left and right. My hammock swung from side to side as I tried to fight my nightmares and irrational fear of the forest. *Just sleep,* I thought. *It's just a forest and some wind, nothing to be afraid of.*

I didn't sleep much that night, but I was ready for the big hike in the morning regardless. Aaron and I had breakfast and hid our large backpacks in the forest, then took off for the trail.

The Kalaupapa Trail is only about 3.5 kilometers long, but has an elevation change of around six hundred meters, so it's a bit harsh on the knees. By 10:00 a.m., we were dripping with sweat but happy to meet Auntie Gloria. She was a nice lady with no noticeable signs of leprosy. The "bar" wasn't really a bar, it was a tiny convenience store with a couple of tables and benches. *No chance for Bloody Marys!* Auntie Gloria gave us a visitor's pass and a map of Kalaupapa, then sent us on our way.

Kalaupapa seemed a bit eerie as well. It was an old little town on a beautiful peninsula surrounded by staggering green and brown cliffs. It was sunny, hot, extremely windy, but somehow stagnant and quiet. Something felt strange about the place.

Aaron and I walked around for hours, going from building to building and picking mangoes along the way, then we latched onto someone else's tour for a bit. We couldn't eavesdrop for too long, so I bought a book called *Olivia: My Life of Exile in Kalaupapa*, to feel less guilty about the vital information we may have been missing by being too cheap to pay for a real tour of the settlement.

The book described a firsthand account of a girl who was sent to Kalaupapa in the 1930s, after being diagnosed with leprosy at age eighteen. According to the book, Kalaupapa became a wonderful home and community for her, and she continued to live there even after the patients were cured and free to leave. Olivia died in Kalaupapa at age ninety-two. Her biggest battle seemed to have been the stigma associated with leprosy, along with the control that doctors, nurses, and the State had over patients.

I didn't read any gory details about the history of Kalaupapa in this book. Maybe the gore happened before the 1930s, or perhaps the history wasn't as brutal as some people had claimed. One guy who picked us up hitchhiking told us that they used to throw patients out of the boats they were sent on, far from the shore, to watch some of them drown or get eaten by sharks as they tried to swim to Kalaupapa. I can't say whether that really happened or not, but humans seldom surprise me with gore anymore.

Aaron and I ripped open a few coconuts for lunch, drinking the juice and adding fresh mango chunks to the meat. After lunch, we took a dip in the ocean then trekked back up the cliffside. It was dark by the time we made it back to the campground. We managed to find our backpacks in the forest, but once we put them on, we started walking around in circles. It took us about twenty minutes to find the road even though we were only a few meters away from it.

Since there were no cars around, we had no choice but to spend one more night in the creepy campground. For dinner, we fried coconuts over a fire, cooked buckwheat, and mixed it all with the mangoes we had picked in Kalaupapa.

The next day, we hitched a ride back to Molokai's main town and somehow ended up at the bar again. We put our backpacks in the corner, sat on the high chairs, and chatted with Mike over some bourbon and cokes. A few hours went by and the bar started getting busy. A live band showed up and so did Mike's beautiful wife, Lauren, and a few of their friends.

Once Mike finished his shift, he invited Aaron and me to a barbecue and offered us a place to stay for the night. Mike and his family were so warm and welcoming that it felt like we were a part of their family too. They treated us with delicious local food and the best mangoes I've had in my life—the *Mapulehu*. This variety of mango was bred on Molokai; it is as smooth as vanilla mousse cake and as juicy as a ripe tangerine. Mike and Lauren had planted several Mapulehu trees in their backyard and each tree was rich with fat, beautiful mangoes. In fact, Molokai was rich with many varieties of tropical fruits and nutritious vegetables.

The people of Molokai seemed proud of their culture and homeland. They spoke the Hawaiian language, practiced Hawaiian traditions, danced the hula, picked flowers for leis, cooked Hawaiian dishes, and traded fruits and vegetables with each other. Aaron and I stuffed our faces with mangoes as Mike explained the true meaning of "aloha" to us.

"Aloha is when you do something for someone else and you don't expect anything back. If you're expecting something back, it ain't *aloha*!" he said.

"Beautiful," I said. *Aloha is trade-free.*

Although Molokai seemed like a true paradise, this island was far from problem-free. Mike and Lauren explained that Monsanto (now owned by Bayer) has been using the Hawaiian Islands as a testing ground for new chemicals. They spray who-knows-what on big chunks of land on the islands and this has had serious effects on the local people and the land. Monsanto was causing big problems on Kauai, then it reached Maui, and now the company came to Molokai. Mike and Lauren were upset that they hadn't been able to get the community to stand up against this corporate giant.

"Standing up against Monsanto is important," I said to Mike and Lauren, "but I don't think it will be enough to stop the problem in the long term. If you stop one company from exploiting your land, another one will come along sooner or later. You can continue to fight them but if they have enough incentive—enough profit to gain—and enough power, they'll figure out some way to get what they want. I think the problem is much bigger than these evil companies. The problem is the entire structure of our society— that's what brings these companies into existence in the first place." I dug my knife into a fat mango. "In this system, every company's aim is to make a profit, regardless of how much they waste, pollute, hurt people, or destroy the environment. Sustainability and people's long-term needs will only ever be secondary to profit gain in this system—and *that's* what needs to change."

I told Mike and Lauren about Jacque Fresco and his idea of a resource-based economy. "That's an idea that the economy should be based on resources and the carrying capacity of the Earth, rather than on profit-making. If we continue to plunder our planet for profit, we'll have no chance to assure sustainability for future generations. And if we want to solve problems like land exploitation, we have to think bigger." I stuffed the mango into my mouth.

* * *

The next day, Aaron and I hitched to the west side of Molokai. We hung our hammocks by a big empty beach and swam in the ocean. It was rugged and windy but nice to spend a few days camping on

24

the beach. After that, we wanted to check out the east-side jungles. We hitched back to Kaunakakai and randomly ran into Mike on his way to work. As soon as we told Mike where we were heading, he handed us the keys to his truck, saying it'd be easier to drive there. Thanks to Mike, we not only got to see the winding cliffside road and the east-side beaches, but we also got to explore the north coast of Molokai, where you can find the highest sea cliffs in the world.

This was surreal. We lay on top of these kilometer-high cliffs and watched birds fly beneath our bodies.

At the end of the day, we filled Mike's tank with gas, thanked Mike, and bought another fifty-dollar flight back to Maui. This flight was just as incredible as the last and the pilot was so nice that he picked us up hitchhiking on our way out of the Maui airport.

Aaron and I hitched across Maui then took a ferry from Lahaina to the island of Lanai. We spent a few days camping on Lanai, then flew to my favorite island, Kauai.

*Instead of Couchsurfing, you can use Bewelcome.org or Trustroots.org.

Kauai

I had been to Kauai once in 2015, but only for one week when I hiked the Kalalau Trail with Chris. The Kalalau Trail is an eighteen-kilometer point-to-point trek along the northwestern part of Kauai. It goes up and down the rugged sea cliffs of the Na Pali Coast and leads to the most jaw-dropping beach I've seen in my life, Kalalau Beach. This perfect patch of baby-soft sand is nestled between aqua-blue water and staggering lush green mountains; it is surrounded by jungles and caves, and features a stunning waterfall. Around Kalalau Beach you can find tropical fruit such as guavas, mangoes, passion fruit, avocados, noni, and much more. There are several trails that go from the beach to Kalalau Valley, leading to cascading freshwater pools and waterfalls, breathtaking views of the mountains and ocean, extraordinary flora, and an enormous garden. There are also some caves and semi-permanent campsites where hippies reside for months or years at a time.

The Na Pali Coast is a twenty-six-kilometer stretch of Kauai's coastline. It starts from Ke'e Beach in the north, passes by Kalalau Beach, and extends down to Polihale State Park on the west side of the island. "Na Pali" means "high cliffs," as the cliffs along this coastline rise up to 1,200 meters. The Kalalau Trail that I did in 2015 only covers about half of this coastline, because the other half is accessible only by helicopter, boat, or kayak.

Lucky for us, Aaron had a friend on Kauai who happened to own several ocean kayaks. This friend's name is Mel. She's an ocean kayaking guide, a big wave surfer, and a super nice person.

Once we got off the plane, Aaron and I hitched to the southern part of Kauai, where Mel was surfing. After the surf, Mel brought us to her place and not only offered her kayaking gear to us, but immediately set us up with everything we needed to kayak up the Na Pali Coast for several days. She gave us maps, dry bags, all the information we needed, drove us to a shop to stock up on supplies, then loaded her truck with a two-person ocean kayak and drove us to Polihale State Park, about an hour away from where she lived.

"Remember what Mike said about aloha?" I said to Aaron.

"Yep. Mel is a hundred percent aloha," he said.

Mel dropped us off at the end of Polihale Beach, where the dirt road ends and the sand meets the Na Pali Coast. This was our first peek at the coastline's towering reddish-brown cliffs. We arrived after dark and decided to sleep on the beach and take off kayaking first thing in the morning. Mel helped us unload the kayak, gave us kayaking directions to a local secret beach, and told us that she and her friends would meet us there in three or four days. She drove back home and we spent the night listening to the sound of big ocean waves, smelling the salt, and just getting mesmerized by the sight of the Milky Way above this gigantic shadow of a rock wall.

The adventure begins tomorrow, I thought. *Real adventure.*

Aaron and I lay on the beach with no tent and no cover. We gazed at the stars all night. I was so excited that my entire body was shaking. *This coast, this island, this magical planet, the Universe!* It was just overwhelming! I couldn't dream of being anywhere else.

"Aaron, guess what?" I whispered.

"What?"

"I'm a free slave now!" I felt like it had just sunk in, even though I had been out of the job game for over two months. "Aaron, I'm free again! Free for as long as I can make my savings last. My life is back in my own hands!" He smiled and gazed into the fire. I couldn't sleep at all that night.

In the morning, the weather was nice but the waves were a bit big for my liking. Our mission was to break through the waves on our kayak and enter the open ocean, then paddle several kilometers north until we reached a big empty beach where we had to ride a wave in. I was a bit nervous at first, but I trusted Aaron and his knowledge of the ocean. Let's just say I was about seventy percent sure we would be all right... And maybe about ninety-seven percent sure we would be alive after.

I hopped into the front seat, then Aaron pushed the kayak onto the whitewash. I had only kayaked a handful of times in my life (and last time I almost died) so I was by no means an expert at this.

I tried to keep my balance. Aaron jumped in the back. Little waves were pushing us left and right, splashing onto the kayak and blinding me for a second or two. Aaron controlled the steering and voiced commands. Now the waves looked huge!

"After this next one, paddle for your life!" said Aaron.

"This next one?" I screamed back, "But the one after it looks massive!"

Three, two, one, "PADDLE!" yelled Aaron.

"*AHHH!*" I paddled for my life!

Twelve steady hand movements up this huge rolling hill and we almost got sucked back to shore but we made it! *I knew I could trust Aaron!*

Now we were in the ocean. "Wow, this is exciting," I said. After a couple of steady breaths we were ready to paddle up the Na Pali Coast.

"Hold up," said Aaron. "Take a look ahead."

"Holy crap! Fins!" There were dozens of them splashing toward us.

"It's a pod of dolphins!" I grabbed my mask and jumped straight out of the kayak to swim with them. They were everywhere, splashing and playing, swimming so gracefully. I swam right up to them and was able to see their faces and beautiful body movements in the water.

Once the dolphins swam away, I got back into the kayak to paddle up the coast. We paddled north, against the current, and admired Kauai's enormous cliffs, caves, and incredible rock formations. We paddled for about four hours before we spotted the secret beach that Mel had told us about. It wasn't hard to find because it was the first big beach we came across and there were some small wooden pavilions and markers on the land.

The waves looked a bit smaller there but they still made me nervous when it was time to land. We had to follow two markers to land safely and avoid being thrown onto shallow reef. One red and white rectangular sign post was placed behind another one. Once you had these two rectangles lined up so that one was hiding the other, you knew you were in the channel. You had to keep this alignment the whole way going in to avoid hitting the reef, which can be challenging when you factor in the ocean current and breaking waves. We lined up the markers then Aaron studied the ocean for a minute or two.

"When I say, paddle, paddle as hard as you can," said Aaron.

"Okay."

"OK. Ready? GO! PADDLE! PADDLE! PADDLE!" We paddled for a wave, caught it, kept our balance, rode it in, paddled left and right to keep the alignment of the sign posts, and landed safely on the soft white sand. *Whew!* We pulled the kayak up onto shore and got ready to explore.

This beach was stunning. The landscape was much more arid than in the Kalalau but at the back end of the beach stood a dramatic 750-meter-high rock wall. The gigantic cliffs were a reddish-brown color. There were a few small shrubs and some trees here and there, but no lush vegetation or tropical fruit that you'd find farther up the coast. There was drinking water though; Mel told us there was a valley that led to a freshwater spring.

Aaron and I took our gear out of the kayak, walked around for a bit, and found a perfect camping spot—an empty pavilion on the grass a few meters away from the sandy beach. The pavilion had a table, some benches, and enough space to hang up four hammocks. Plus, there were trees nearby for additional hammock space.

We unpacked our stuff, hung our hammocks, made some sandwiches for lunch, and took a long relaxing nap. I felt like I was in a dream before I even dozed off, swinging in my hammock, listening to the sound of waves crashing along the shore of this secret beach, surrounded by astounding cliffs. *Sleep for a little while. Doze.*

We woke up to the sound of a strange groan. It was a monk seal pup and its mother! We walked to the edge of the beach to have a closer look at them. The seal pup was black and about one meter long. The mother was the size of a couch and had some big scars on her body. They lay in the same spot all day and didn't move much, apart from when I accidentally came a little too close and the mother rose up and threatened to kill me. I ran away quickly. I'd been told that monk seals are more dangerous than sharks in

Hawaii. They don't look so graceful or scary on land, but I could sure as hell imagine what they could do in the water. So just in case I wasn't scared enough of hitting the reef and being thrown off our kayak while getting pounded with waves, now I also had to worry about Hawaii's most dangerous animal tearing me to shreds while all of this was happening.

Aaron and I hiked up the valley Mel told us about, found the freshwater spring that ran beneath two stones (as she had described), and filled up on the best tasting water I'd had in a long time. We continued to walk up the rocky valley and eventually ran into a tall waterfall at a steep and narrow dead end. We climbed up some rocks and splashed around in the waterfall, then walked back down the valley and picked taro leaves along the way. We had learned from Mike that taro leaves were healthy and delicious if you boil them for a very long time—and time was all we had on the Na Pali Coast. Aaron also spotted some shrimp, made a spear out of a stick, and caught one for dinner.

We cooked over a fire and slept in our hammocks. There were no people around, just us, cliffs, the ocean, and the Milky Way.

* * *

The next day, a few kayakers and local boaties showed up. Everyone was nice and basically kept to their own corners of the beach so it still felt like Aaron and I were alone in this magical place. The ocean looked calm so we took the kayak to explore some ocean caves and revisit the Kalalau.

Getting the kayak out was easy this time. We aligned the markers and smoothly entered the open ocean. We paddled slowly up-current, stopping along the way to check out the coastline's beautiful rock formations. After about a two-hour paddle, we found a big open ceiling cave. The silver-streaked cave walls rose high above our heads and led to an opening where rays of sunshine flooded in. The water was dark blue but deep and crystal clear. In the middle of the cave, there was a big gray rock. I put on my mask and snorkel and jumped into the water. It was so transparent that I could see almost the entire cave from beneath the surface.

After a couple more hours of exploring the coast and entering different caves, Aaron and I spotted Kalalau Beach. The view was as staggering as I had remembered.

"Wow, there's nobody here," said Aaron.

"That's strange," I said. "Last time I came to Kalalau, it was busy as hell. There were hikers, boaties, and hippies everywhere. We could barely even find a camping spot. Sometimes we even had to stand in line to get under the waterfall!" This time, Kalalau was completely empty.

What happened? It felt like there had been an apocalypse or something.

We pulled the kayak onto the beach and explored the caves and surrounding area. All the best camping spots were empty. Some stuff was left around, clearly abandoned. There was a huge pile of garbage in the middle of the beach. In the pile there were plastic containers, torn-up tents, clothes, cans, and old fish bones.

We walked past the garbage and followed a path through the vegetated area behind the beach. "Check that out," I said. A spiderweb-like net hung between five trees. Inside the net lay a sleeping bag and some pillows. Below, there were books, pots and pans, clothes, and freshly picked fruit.

Aaron poked at the fire pit. "It's still warm."

We wandered around the area, then crossed a river and walked up the Kalalau Valley trail. Eventually, we ran into a little old man. He looked a bit rugged, had a long beard and messy gray hair. He was carrying something in a metal container. We asked him what happened.

"They raided us," he said, "day in, day out. Everyone without a permit got kicked out. Rangers came in on helicopters and arrested people without ID, even handcuffed some and brought them to jail."

"Oh damn." I had heard about these raids but I didn't realize they would be so hardcore. "How'd you get away?" I asked.

"I went farther up the valley. Eventually they caught me too and gave me a fine. Hah!"

"A fine? That's funny," I said. *As if a piece of paper with some scribbles means anything to a man who lives in the jungle.*

"Good fire starter, right?" said Aaron.

"Not even! I used it to wipe my ass!" The little man cracked up and continued walking.

Aaron and I went farther up the valley to try to find the garden. Back in 2015, I met two hippies who lived in the Kalalau Valley. Their names were Steve and Mowgli. Steve was just enjoying spending a year or two in the jungle, hanging out with friends, playing music, and having a good time. Mowgli lived in a cave in the back of the valley and maintained the Kalalau garden, which was enormous. He was a very bright guy who seemed quite displeased with our society. Back then, he said he was planning on building an irrigation system for the garden. That was two years ago, so I was excited to see what this place looked like now. *Would it be abandoned?* I wondered. *There's no way these rangers would have found Mowgli, he's way too smart. I bet he's around here somewhere!*

Aaron and I walked up the valley for a while, couldn't find Mowgli or the garden. We took a dip in the cascading pools to cool off. I tried to remember where this place was. We found the biggest bush in the world, the rope swing, and the ancient stone that marked the spot where Hawaiians used to meet to trade goods. Then after two or three hours of wandering around the valley, we finally found the garden. It was in perfect shape—and the irrigation system was complete! It ran through the entire garden and had been built with stones.

I remembered what Mowgli said back in 2015, *I'm working on the garden because I like the idea of anybody being able to come here and take anything they need for free,* so I didn't feel bad about taking some food. Aaron and I picked a big zucchini and a bunch of mangoes, papayas, and different types of bananas.

We walked back down the valley feeling rejuvenated and stoked about our new fruit and vegetable supply. Then we waved goodbye to the little old man, got back into our kayak, and paddled down-current. We made it back to our secret beach just on time to watch the sunset over the ocean. For dinner, we roasted green bananas and papayas over a fire, then topped them off with canned beans. For dessert, we had mangoes.

* * *

Mel and two of her friends showed up in their kayaks a couple of days later. They told us about a beach with seven-hundred-meter cliffs and a giant X that marked the spot of an ancient Hawaiian burial ground. The X had been formed by two intersecting lava tubes, while the burial ground was one of the most well-preserved archeological sites in Hawaii.

When the ocean was calm, the five of us paddled to this beach. We tied our kayaks to some buoys and swam onto shore to check out the sacred site. The X looked dramatic as it towered over the ancient burial ground. Snorkeling in this place was spectacular too. There were many types of colorful corals, big schools of fish, and an abundance of sea life. Aaron managed to spear three lobsters and a big crab with his spear gun. We boiled them up for dinner and ate them with more fire-roasted green bananas and our giant zucchini.

The five of us spent a few more days on the Na Pali Coast, relaxing, snorkeling, kayaking, and snoozing in our hammocks. Life was just precious. Aaron and I could have easily stayed there all summer long, but it would have been rude to hog Mel's kayak for too long. Plus, I had a big flight to catch now.

After a few days, we packed our stuff and kayaked back to Polihale Beach, where Mel's truck was waiting for us. The ocean was calm and it was easy to paddle down-current. Once we landed, we stacked the kayaks together, tied them down, and drove back to Mel's place.

Aaron and I flew back to Oahu the next day. The Venus Project contacted me then, saying they were ready to start their online orientation process. They said if I wanted to become a point of contact for the Russian-speaking TVP team, I could join their discussion group the following week. Believe it or not, I was more excited about this than I was about Hawaii.

I think most people would have been sad to fly away from these islands, especially after such an adventure. I said goodbye to Aaron and to the rest of my friends, took off in a big airplane, and watched the sunset over big puffy clouds. Strong emotions came over me. I felt both happy and sad for everything that was, that is, and that will be. I thought about Hawaii, the ocean, the jungles, the mountains; the adventures, the people. *My mission was complete—* the job game was over. *At least for a while.* I had almost forgotten that that was the reason I came to Hawaii in the first place.

I felt a deep feeling of relief and satisfaction. I had about eighteen thousand dollars in my bank account. That was more money than I ever had in my life. About triple the amount, actually. *I could live on that for years,* I thought. After ten years of traveling, I was confident that I could go almost anywhere in the world and do almost anything I wanted on a budget of five hundred dollars per month. After doing the math (18,000/500), I realized that I had enough money to travel around the world and live job-free for the next three years. *Not too bad for just seven months of serving tables!*

3

The Journey

I got off the plane in Newark, New Jersey. My mother greeted me with a big smile and a long warm hug. *I didn't come here to stay...* I just flew in to join a family party. My stepbrother's "graduation." It seemed important to my mother and her husband.

The party was fun but I wasn't sure where to go after it was over. I originally wanted to use my savings to explore South America—to backpack through the Andes, to drink maté and dance tango in Argentina, to traverse Patagonia, and to just get lost. This had been my dream for a long time, but at that point in my life there was something pulling me toward a different direction.

While I was at my mother's house, I began to volunteer for the Venus Project. I joined their online discussion group and began the orientation process to become a point of contact (a more or less official volunteer). I was also introduced to the Russian-speaking TVP team, which was somewhat disconnected from the main English-speaking TVP organization.

The Russian-speaking team had been created in order to translate and promote the work of Jacque Fresco in the Russian-speaking region of the world. The problem, however, was that the team had not been in close contact with the main TVP organization (or so I was told). My task was to fill in that gap and become their communication link. So, while I was at my mother's house, I was pulled into their online chats and began communicating.

I knew I was in for something when I first joined TVP, but *this* I did not expect. I was thrown right into the middle of a huge conflict. There were problems upon problems upon problems. I spent hours on my computer every day, talking to many people from TVP and trying to thoroughly understand what was going on.

At that point, I didn't know any other organization that looked at global problems the same way that I did. I also admired Jacque Fresco so much for his life's work that I couldn't imagine anything more gratifying than to work toward making his life's work a reality.

I decided that I should settle in one place for a while to try to work out these problems or do something else in the same direction. I also wanted to slow myself down and study for a while. I don't mean that I wanted to attend some kind of institution, I just wanted to study on my own to get a better understanding of the world we live in. I think everybody should do this.

So... Settling down was the next long-awaited adventure! But where to settle, I wasn't sure. *It would have to be somewhere cheap so I could live off my savings and not have to work,* I thought. *Well, I joined the Russian-speaking team, right? So naturally, I should go back to Russia. I haven't lived in Russia in twenty years!*

I decided to buy a flight to Moscow. I made that decision because, for one, I have a Russian passport, so I'm legally allowed to stay in Russia as long as I want. The only other places where I can live indefinitely are the US (because I also have a US passport) and Svalbard (the only entirely visa-free zone on Earth), but the cost of living is very expensive in both of those places. Secondly, I wanted to improve my Russian language skills; clearly, Russia was ideal for that. Lastly, a friend I had met in Hawaii was planning to travel across Russia on her own for all of August. Her name was Maricruz, she was from Costa Rica, and she asked if I wanted to join her on this adventure.

How can I say "no" to an adventure? It's simple, I can't! I told Maricruz I would meet her in Moscow. From there, we planned to take the Trans-Siberian Railway across Russia, making several stops along the way. I thought this would be a great opportunity to explore Russia and decide where, exactly, I wanted to "settle down."

The Russian Railway

I arrived in Moscow on August 1. Soon after, Maricruz showed up with her big backpack, big curly hair, and big friendly smile. I didn't know Mari too well before this trip, but she seemed like a beautiful person both inside and out. We stayed at my father's apartment in Moscow and he showed us around the city. We visited the city center, the Red Square, Moscow University, and a few beautiful parks and old churches. My grandma treated us with her delicious soups and homemade pies, my cousins took us for walks around the Moscow River, and my aunt even bought us tickets to a ballet.

After a few days, Mari and I took a train from Moscow to Kazan with my dad. The three of us stayed in a hostel in the city center and visited the beautiful city and its surrounding area. My dad had a friend who lived in Kazan and was happy to give us a city tour. She also brought us to a charming hilltop village by a riverside and to her mother's dacha (country house) where we had a big meal, cakes, and tea from a samovar.

After a few days in Kazan, my dad went back to Moscow and Mari and I took a bus to my other grandmother's home in Tatarstan. This Tatar grandmother of mine, Baba Zoya, is one tough babushka. She's the kind of babushka that comes to mind when you hear the word *babushka*. She has no hair and few teeth, and she may actually kill you if you don't eat enough food. Every time I visit her, she gives me a gigantic plate of food, piled with potatoes, meat, dumplings, fried pastries, pig fat, and so on, which I will eat slowly. Then when I'm completely stuffed and on my last bites of food, she tries to stack more fried dumplings or meat pie on my plate and yells stuff like, "What, are you not gonna eat anything at all?" When I say that I really can't eat another bite, she smiles, pours me a big cup of tea and hands over an enormous piece of Tatar pie filled with rice, raisins, sugar, and eggs. She's so crazy about food that the only words I know in the Tatar language are, "Yes, Grandma, I am eating, I am eating!"

Baba Zoya is so obsessed with feeding everybody that she has a schedule for feeding ducks, pigeons, and stray cats and dogs. The pigeons recognize her when she comes out of her apartment in the morning, they follow her to the park across the street and wait for her to feed them there. Sometimes they sit on her head. Next, she feeds the ducks in a nearby pond. These ducks are so well fed by Baba Zoya and other babushkas that they barely react when you throw food at them, even in winter. Baba Zoya purposely buys seeds for pigeons, bread for ducks, and cat food. Yep, she also walks around with cat food, even though she doesn't have a cat.

When I visit Baba Zoya, I usually go to the banya with her. A banya is a Russian bathhouse which features a sauna. I enjoy the sauna aspect of it, but sometimes it gets awkward when Baba Zoya hits me with a bouquet of dry leafy branches. Hitting yourself (or others) with these dry branches inside the hot sauna is a Russian bathing ritual which is meant to open up pores and improve blood circulation. This is how it happens: I stand naked in the middle of a hot sauna packed with eighty-something-year-old women, Baba Zoya yells at me to spread my arms, then she smacks the shit out of my entire body, from my arms, to my back, to my boobs, to my legs. One time, she told me to spread open my legs and then she smacked me directly in the vagina! *Yeah, babushka, it's important to have good circulation there too!* Thankfully, she didn't do that to Maricruz.

Mari and I left Baba Zoya's place feeling absolutely stuffed. Not only did we eat enough food to be able to fast for the next month, but we were also handed such a huge bag of "take-away" food that we basically didn't need to go grocery shopping for the next three weeks.

The rest of the route across Russia was decided by Mari because she was short on time due to her one-month visa restriction. We took a thirty-six-hour train from Tatarstan to Chelyabinsk, where we spent just one night but had a good time with some random locals. Then we took a twenty-four-hour train to Novosibirsk. It was raining in Novosibirsk and I had a lot of TVP work to catch up on, so I basically spent the whole time studying in a café while Mari cruised around the city.

At that point, I still didn't know where I wanted to live. I knew that I wanted to live in a city as opposed to a village because I wanted to talk to open-minded people and there was a much bigger chance of finding them in cities. I didn't want to live in Moscow; it was too big, expensive, and overcrowded. Kazan was pretty and conveniently close to Moscow, but it somehow didn't feel right. Chelyabinsk seemed boring and Novosibirsk was also too big. *I want a nice medium-sized city with a bit of culture and beauty,* I thought. Next was Krasnoyarsk.

Mari planned on just one day in Krasnoyarsk. We got to the city in the morning and planned to leave that same night. I don't usually like to travel that fast, but this was a result of Mari's visa restrictions, so we didn't have much of a choice. We stored our backpacks in a hostel by the train station for 100 rubles (about $1.50) and took a public bus to a park called Stolby. Stolby means "pillars" in Russian. There were a lot of boulders and rock formations in this park, some of which looked like giant pillars. The park was green and mountainous, and had some amazing viewpoints.

We showered off in the hostel and got back on the train. Fortunately, the Russian railway is very comfortable. Every passenger gets their own bed with a mattress, blankets, and clean sheets. There's always boiling water available for free, so you can drink tea, coffee, or soup all day long if you want. I like to spend the day in the top bunk, relaxing and gazing through the window for hours at a time as the train rocks back and forth. I love seeing hours and hours of taiga moving by—rivers, hills, small villages, raindrops, and sparse rays of sunshine softening the dense forest. Seeing so much untouched forest makes me regain some hope for the future of our planet.

There's no way we could destroy ALL of that, right? I'd stare and ponder.

Everything is slower but somehow more notable on the train. I take my time with meals. Chew slowly, taste every bite. Sip my coffee. Smell. Listen. Think for a while. *Slow it down.*

Our next stop was Irkutsk, the gateway city to Lake Baikal. The railway station in Irkutsk was old and rugged, but seemed to have some character to it. We took a tram to a hostel and glanced at the old city center on the way. I liked it. It seemed to be what I was looking for—a city, but not too big, it was cheap and had nice architecture that gave it a cozy atmosphere.

I knew one person in Irkutsk, a girl named Tanya, who was in our Russian-speaking TVP chat. I had never met her in person and I hadn't spoken to her much, but when she heard that Mari and I were coming to Irkutsk, she offered to give us a tour of the city and to take us to Lake Baikal.

Tanya showed Mari and me two big riverside parks, a beautiful island on the Angara River, the old city center, and a number of charming old churches. I was already considering staying in Irkutsk after Tanya's city tour, but once I saw Lake Baikal, I made my final decision.

The three of us took a minibus to Listvyanka, a lakeside town about an hour away from Irkutsk. We walked up a narrow footpath, climbed a small hill, then looked out onto the open ocean. Oh wait, *it was a lake!* Lake Baikal looked endless, like the ocean but calm and crystal clear.

With a surface area of 31,722 square kilometers and a depth of 1.6 kilometers, Lake Baikal holds about a fifth of the world's fresh surface water. It is considered to be among the world's clearest lakes and is the most ancient lake in geological history, aged at approximately 25 million years.

"I can't believe this entire thing turns to ice in winter!" I said to Mari. "I *have* to see it frozen." And so, I decided to stay. I figured it would be cheaper to rent an apartment and stay in Irkutsk until winter than it would be to go somewhere else and then come back to Lake Baikal when it was frozen. And I mean, at that point I really made up my mind that I had to see this lake covered in ice.

Mari flew from Irkutsk to India and I stayed in a hostel for several days while searching for a place to live. I used a website called Avito.ru to find a flat. Avito is similar to Craigslist or Gumtree, where individual people post anything they may want to sell or rent. I searched through the classified ads for a few days, then moved into the first place I came to see. It was an old one-bedroom apartment next to a riverside park in the historical city center of Irkutsk. In the apartment there was a separate kitchen, a bed, a couch, a dirty old bathroom, and a big desk. The rent cost about 250 dollars per month for the entire place. No roommates, no bills. *Perfect.* This was the first time I lived completely alone, since I could never afford my own place in the past.

* * *

It felt a little strange at first. Maricruz was gone. Tanya was nice but I didn't know her too well and I didn't feel like she could really understand me. Few people can, so that's okay, but sometimes that can make you feel lonely. Everyone else I knew was thousands of kilometers away.

I set up the internet and took out my laptop. *Now I have my own space, my own time,* I thought. I used this time to focus on the Venus Project. I did my best to try to solve their internal problems. I spent almost every minute of every day writing and translating messages, contacting different people from TVP, and digging into as much information about the organization as possible.

I tried my hardest to be this "missing link." I worked nonstop; I wrote and translated over one hundred pages of texts and documents. But nothing worked. I tried harder and harder but it still didn't work.

Eventually, I started to feel hopeless. The only goal I saw worth working toward—a resource-based economy, a global social system based on the carrying capacity of the Earth—was diminishing in front of my own eyes. *If we can't even manage to fix these little internal problems, how the hell are we going to change the world?*

Maybe we are hopeless.

I may have been on the brink of getting back to a confused and depressed state, feeling completely alone, in the middle of Siberia, detached from everything and everyone, losing hope in the one thing I really cared about. Losing hope in humanity again, and in

41

the future of our species. I've gone through moments like this before. In the past, I've coped with them by digging into documentaries, articles, and information about the world, to find out more about how it actually works, and to understand why it's so fucked up. Through this, I've realized that I should never feel sorry for myself. I have everything I need in life. Others don't. Others are starved, enslaved, and abused. I have power and resources that they don't. *I need to use this to make things better for them.* But not knowing how, I'd simply pack up my backpack and hit the road in search for answers.

This time, something different happened. Before I hit the tipping point, somebody sent me a book called *Morality and Ethics*, published by a project called TROM.

It pulled on my heartstrings. *What is this project?* I wondered.

There was a documentary on their site. It was fourteen hours long. I spent the entire night watching the whole thing, from start to finish, no break. I fell asleep as the sun came up, feeling renewed, as if my crumbled hope had been reshaped.

I woke up and dug back into the site. There were books—tons of them. I started going through them. Every page I read was like a reflection of my own perspective—my thoughts, values, and conclusions about the world, but there were links, sources, evidence —for everything! It was so well organized!

*This must have taken a **massive** amount of effort. Who's writing all this stuff?* I wondered.

Tio...Tio...Tio... Every book was signed by a person named Tio.

I found his personal website and read a few of his blogs. I saw myself in him. He used to volunteer for the Venus Project full time. He worked side by side with them for years. He created TVP Magazine, managed TVP's social media, worked on their website, made videos, articles, memes, and much more. But he also had problems with TVP. After many years, these problems escalated and he moved all his work to his own project—TROM: The Reality of Me. It sounded like a tough breakup.

I learned that Tio was broke most of the time and went through a lot of trouble with his family because his project was not the least bit focused on making money. Instead, it was focused on gaining an understanding of our global problems and society. *Who the hell can profit from that?* I could relate to this because I was also broke most of the time since I rarely focused on making money. I never saw the point. I had big arguments with my family over this too.

I felt a deep appreciation for this person and great respect for his work, especially after learning how much he struggled to keep this project going.

I decided to go out of the city to clear my mind. I had heard about a music festival called Baikal Live, located in a small village about three hours from Irkutsk, by an island on Lake Baikal. I took my hammock and a sleeping bag, then bought a minibus ticket to this village. I didn't pay to enter the festival, I just walked in and listened to the musicians; then I wandered the hills that overlooked the lake. They looked like giant fingers caressing the glassy water.

The next day, I took a ferry to Olkhon Island, then hitchhiked to a village called Khuzhir. I found a room for five dollars per night and a four-wheel drive ride that took me to the northernmost tip of the island. In the north, I walked up gigantic rocky cliffs that overlooked Lake Baikal. There was nothing, not a single boat, no people swimming, no seabirds, nothing but endless blue water beyond the cliff face.

I shared a few photos of Olkhon Island on social media and got the typical response from my friends: "HOW are you doing this? Where do you get so much MONEY?" I get these comments all the time because I've been traveling consistently for over a decade, so people see that I'm moving around a lot and I guess it confuses them. I never bothered to give them an in-depth explanation of what I was doing before, but I guess Olkhon Island slipped me the last straw.

I started writing then and there, in this little hut on the island, and I couldn't stop. I had never written much in the past because writing took so much time and effort, but now the words were just flowing to me. I came up with the long comment I have as the prologue to this book. I posted it on social media with a collection of my best photos from the past few years of traveling. I got a big response. Dozens of comments, many re-posts, hundreds of "likes."

I never cared much for "likes" but it was interesting to know that people responded to this post. They seemed to understand, agree, or at least appreciate what I was writing. Even my *brother* said he was proud of me. He had *never* said that before.

Next, I decided to start a blog. I had considered writing a travel blog for many years but never got around to it, mostly because I didn't see much purpose to it. *What could be the purpose of a travel blog? To share photos and stories? I can just do that through email or social media. To get sponsored? Make money? Eh. Probably not worth the effort, plus, that would probably change me and my lifestyle. Restaurant work is not all that bad after all.*

But now I saw something more important: the parallel connection between my life and the TROM project. Almost anything I wrote could be connected with the bigger, more important picture— what we're doing on Earth, how we're harming ourselves and the environment that we depend on, and what we can do about this. *If people enjoy my travel stories, then maybe, at least some of them would listen to the other stuff I have to say.*

I hitchhiked back to Irkutsk with some hippies.

Made a website. Wrote some blogs.

And then I decided to write a book.

Part 2

4
1989-2007

I was born in Moscow, Russia, two years before the collapse of the Soviet Union. Both of my parents were biology graduates of Moscow State University. My mother came from a long line of scientists. Her father was a neurophysiologist and the head of laboratory at the Moscow Brain Institute, her grandparents were well-known neurologists, and her mother translated scientific papers from Japanese to Russian. My father came from a small city in Tatarstan. His father was an engineer by training, and worked for an oil company. My father's mother (Baba Zoya) was a food inspector.

My parents met in university, married young, then had two kids—my brother in 1987, followed by me, two years later. Our childhood in Russia was precious. My brother was my best friend, we were almost inseparable. He protected me from everything and everyone. In the summertime, we used to go to our dacha, where we ran around the forest, chased cows, burned earthworms, and built tree houses. In winter, we lived in a small apartment in Moscow. We never fought back then.

My father worked as a junior scientist at my grandfather's institute at first. Sometimes he also shoveled snow or swept the streets outside our apartment for extra money. After the fall of the Soviet Union, however, he managed to create a business. He set up a firm for importing powdered drinks and other foreign goods into Russia. The business grew so well that by 1995, we became millionaires.

Having a lot of money was both good and bad back then. On one hand, it bought us goodies and opportunities that other people didn't get—trips to Europe, clothes from America, candy from all over the world; on the other hand, it wasn't always safe and peachy. Russia was a dangerous place in the 1990s. Since my father had a business, he had to deal with the mafia (meaning, he had to pay the mafia for "protection" against themselves). He had friends with businesses, some of whom had "disappeared." My parents witnessed somebody getting shot and killed on the street and my mother even developed a habit of inspecting our car for bombs before driving. My parents were worried about our safety, so my father did what he could to get us out of Russia.

He managed to get a US working visa through his business, and with the help of an American lawyer, he eventually got a green card. Once he received the green card, he bought a house in a town called Tenafly, New Jersey, and moved my family there soon after.

Tenafly is a suburb on the outskirts of New York City. It was very different from Russia. Every house was so neat, every shrub was trimmed flawlessly. There were so many laws and rules, so many pretty lawns, and so many fake smiles. I didn't like it.

Once we moved into this new house, my dad left. I think I didn't realize what was going on at first. He had a business to take care of in Russia, so he couldn't exactly move to the US with us. At first, he came to visit us quite often, every few weeks or so. When he came, my mother would get into huge arguments with him. She would cry hysterically and smoke cigarettes. My brother and I would try to calm her down, not knowing what was going on. Then my dad would leave again and we would all cry. Every time he left, it hurt. It hurt our entire family. And it happened over and over and over again. It shattered me every time.

And I guess one day I realized that we were never going to be a family again. I felt heartbroken and abandoned.

Business? I thought. *How could **anything** be more important than our family?*

My mother coped with her depression by getting a series of operations—her lips, her boobs, nose, maybe more. I can't say if it helped or not. My brother started drawing weird pictures, and I learned to protect myself. I didn't want it to hurt anymore, so I hardened up. I became tough. I learned to live in defense-mode. I pushed everyone away, especially the ones who were closest to me. I became mean. And I turned my best friend into my enemy.

I didn't care about anyone back then. I hated America. I hated the stupid American kids in school. They made fun of me when I didn't know English. Some teachers made fun of me too, in front of the whole class. I hated them all. I shut everybody off. I even pretended not to understand English after I had learned it fluently.

It wasn't my mother's idea to move to the US, but she understood the benefits that it was meant to bring us. My mother eventually came to grips with the situation, learned English, took a computer programming course, and got a job at a big tech company (her "dream job," in fact). My dad lost his business and most of his money a few years later, when an economic crisis hit Russia, but my mother managed to keep us in the US because of her new job.

My mother drowned in her work. The company paid her a salary for a full-time job, but she must have worked over double the hours without being compensated for them. She was highly stressed all the time, and constantly afraid of losing her job, since the company made cuts almost every year and outsourced a ton of work for cheap labor.**

As the years went by, I grew from a mean little kid into a reckless teenager. At age eleven, I went to a summer camp where I met an older girl who taught me how to steal. We were both kicked out of the camp for stealing clothes from a shop, and when I came back home, I turned this new hobby into an addiction. I made friends with other troubled teenagers. We stole thousands of dollars of items—clothes from stores, jewelry, money from people's pockets, you name it. When my mother noticed how much stuff I had, she tried to accuse me of stealing, but I lied and I screamed at her. I ran away any time she tried to punish me.

My best friend's name was Chili. Well, that's what we called her because she came from Santiago, Chile, and she ate hot chili peppers by the handful. When Chili was just thirteen years old, her mother moved back to Santiago and left Chili and her two teenage brothers alone in a house in Tenafly. Their mother paid the rent and sent them about a hundred dollars per month for food. Chili didn't know her father, so she basically spent most of her teenage years without parents. Meanwhile, one of her brothers was already into heavy drugs by age fifteen.

Chili and I drank alcohol by age thirteen; smoked weed and got our first body piercings and tattoos by age fourteen; tried ecstasy, cocaine, magic mushrooms, and PCP by age fifteen; had big parties where people smoked crack and shot up heroin by age sixteen; and by the time we were seventeen, we were picking up drugs from New York City and selling them to rich kids in Tenafly. (Or maybe that last one was just me. Me and some older kids, not Chili.)

But let's rewind just a little bit and go through a few stories from my teenage years. I think I can best describe my adolescent experience by sharing some old diary entries.

The following paragraphs are real, unedited notes from my diary. Please don't judge me by them now, as I am an entirely different person today.

September 26, 2003 (age 14):

Lemme just say some things that are going on right now. Like 2 or 3 months ago I got arrested for shoplifting. 2 or 3 weeks ago I started getting into smoking reefer. Right now I'm doing community service in Harlem because of the shoplifting crap. On the first day I walked in and I was the only white girl, everybody else was all ghetto. So I thought they'd be mean to me cuz I'm white, but they treated me no different from anyone else and now I'm friends with them. Now I'm chillin with them every Saturday in the hood. This is getting me into shit. Last Saturday, me and my friend Jay and two other guys smoked some purple haze in like this guy's basement of his apartment. Then me and Jay left and smoked more haze on one of those lil' paths next to the fucking highway.

Yesterday, he took me to his apartment and we smoked something else. I don't know what it was. We smoked it with two other guys he knew on the stairs going up to his apartment. His whole house is like the size of my room, maybe even smaller. It's all just one big room with 2 beds and a tiny stove and small fridge. I felt so... I don't even know the words for it.

We lied down on his uncle's bed, I was about to pass out, and he starts feeling me up. I think I actually kind of liked it but I didn't want to kiss him because my mouth felt so dry from the pot.

He would have fucked me.

I had my period.

I was so high.

Thank god I had my period.

I was so fucking high.

I think I gave him head.

At least we used a strawberry flavored condom. I think I sucked. It was so weird.

Next week, he's gonna want to have sex with me. The only reason he didn't this week was because of my period. He wanted to put it up my ass but I told him no.

I don't know what to do.

I know I'm not a good writer but I just want to express my feelings, I have no one else to say this to, not even my best friends. I can't tell them I'm about to have sex.

I don't even know if I want to have sex.

I don't know what to do.

My life feels so fucked up right now.

I want to feel like somebody cares for me.

November 7, 2003 (age 14):

The next week after all of that happened with Jay, I was ready to have sex with him. I knew that I wasn't ready and that I wasn't in love with him, I knew that I needed my first time to be special and that it wouldn't be special with him, I knew all of that, but I wanted to do it anyway, I just wanted something exciting in my life and I wanted to feel better about myself, I wanted to feel like somebody loved me, even though I knew that that wouldn't happen with Jay, he just wanted to have sex because he hadn't for a month. Jay just wanted money and sex.

So me and him went to his apartment on 125th street and he smoked some trees that I paid for. His apartment was locked and he didn't have the key so we couldn't go inside and fuck. When he was high he just wanted to do it right there on the stairs. Imagine that, my first time having sex and it was right out in the open, in Harlem, NY, on the plain gray cement dirty stairs with piss on every corner, that smelled like shit, with a guy I met 3 weeks ago.

I left and nothing happened. The weekend after was his last week of community service and I didn't hang out with him then. And I probably never will.

Right now this is Jay's life: he has no home because he had lived with his uncle before who had recently died, so he stays at his friends houses between Harlem and the Bronx. His parents are both hustlers. He's been locked up 3 times in his life and arrested too many times. He makes money by selling crack and he's having a baby because his ex-girl doesn't believe in abortions. This boy is 16 years old! I do not want to get in on him with this shit.

January 3, 2004 (age 14):

Last December, I went to Cancun, Mexico with my family. I got weed from a flee market and then I got my first tattoo. It was great, I smoked weed while getting a tattoo.

A few weeks ago I snorted up some Xanax pills with a guy who has recently dropped out of high school—Mitch, and another guy—Luke.

January 10, 2004 (age 14):

I snorted cocaine with Mitch and Luke at Chili's house. We only did a line each—for $5. But my friend Jennifer is trying to get me to do more. I'm gonna try not to be stupid about it, I don't wanna fuck myself up.

January 16, 2004 (age 14):

My best friend overdosed on taking fucking 20 pills of Benadryl, we were all smoking at the time too and it was the scariest thing that I've ever seen in my life, she had a seizure. She was all shaking, going crazy and shit, then she just stopped. Stopped everything, laid her head on her arm and stopped breathing. Everyone was running around the house and screaming. We called the ambulance.

But everything's all done and better now, she stayed in the hospital for a few days, her mom even flew in from Chile because of that.

March 26, 2004 (age 15):

Vince hung himself today.

I don't understand... They think it was the chemotherapy that did it. All of that medicine that they've been giving him. He had blood cancer, the kind that you can never get rid of.

I feel like my life is so fucked up right now. All anybody ever does is use me for my house. I've been hanging out with people that do so many drugs, all older people, even people that have dropped out of high school.

April 10, 2004 (age 15):

I was in my "soon to be" bathroom in my room alone with Mitch and I accidentally knocked over my lamp and it fell on the floor and broke into little pieces. I was really fucked up and depressed so I just sat down on the floor with Mitch, took a piece of broken glass, and cut myself. It was bleeding so much all down my arm.

Later that night (after I cleaned myself up a little) a bunch of guys from Englewood came to my house—including this guy Shawnsey who tried to fuck me last time I was high at his house (I didn't let him). This time I was drunk. He took me in my mother's room. I don't remember everything 100% but I remember he put me on my mom's bed, I tried to get up and run away but he held me down. He was kissing me and shit and I started hysterically crying and screaming that Luke was gonna kill himself (cuz me and Luke kind of liked each other, but he's really depressed, on all these drugs, and keeps on talking about killing himself). All I was thinking about was Luke so I tried to run away from Shawnsey but he just kept on holding me down on the bed. He kept on pulling down my pants (I was pulling them back up) his big black dick was out and he already had a condom on. I still wouldn't fuck him so he pinned me down and started fingering me. I pushed him away and ran to the door, he ran after me, he pinned me down against the door and fingered me like that, holding me down. I don't really remember what else happened with him, but I did get out somehow...without him fucking me.

April 15, 2004 (age 15):

My friend Oliver died in a car accident.

Being "good" doesn't do shit for you... Live your life however the fuck you want to cuz you have nothing else. Oliver was like an angel, always smiling beautifully, always singing and dancing, he didn't drink, smoke, do any drugs or anything. People say, "He didn't deserve to die," that is true, but you know what? **Shit just happens.**

I stopped writing in my diary for a while after that, but I'll just mention a few more points and I think that will be enough:

A few people from our "crew" died by committing suicide and/or overdosing on drugs.

One time I convinced my mother to help out a homeless friend by letting him live in our basement for a few weeks. I don't know how I convinced her to agree to that, but after he moved in, we not only found out that he was a heroin addict, but also that he was selling heroin to a lot of my friends. Then he stole a thousand dollars from my mother and he ran away.

My mother also agreed to let Chili live in our house during our last year of high school. My mom was always busy with work and rarely home on weekends, so Chili and I had huge parties when she wasn't around. These parties were filled with cocaine and cocaine dealers, loads of alcohol, many other drugs, and people from all sorts of Jersey ghettos.

My brother was a quiet person and of course, he *hated* all of this, and he hated me for this. But I didn't give a shit. He'd yell at me, hit me, call me a slut, and renounced me as his sister. I'd yell back, hit back, call him a freak, and renounced him as my brother.

I remember wanting to patch things up one day by telling him I loved him because he was my brother. His response was, "Fuck you. You're *not* my sister anymore!"

So I became tougher. *Fuck him,* I thought. *I don't need to be accepted by my family, not like I have much of a family anyway.*

I was terribly mean even to my mother, and my mother is like the nicest person in the world. As you can probably tell though, my mom was extremely kind but also a huge pushover because of that, so I was able to bully her around like crazy. She had absolutely no control over me in my teenage years.

My dad still visited (or took us on vacation) from time to time, and my brother and I took trips back to Russia once we were legally allowed to do so. Those trips didn't change my behavior though, because my friends in Russia were basically doing the same thing as my friends in the US—tons of drugs and alcohol. The only difference was that they had a different mentality toward certain cultural ideas. What was "cool" in the US may not have been "cool" in Russia, what was "good" in one country may have been "bad" in the other, the clothes were a little different, as was the music, the food, and cultural ideas about things like the roles of men and women. I wanted to be accepted by all the teenagers around me, so I quickly learned that there was no unanimous "cool," "good," "bad," "right," or "wrong"—it was all about people's perceptions, and this perception was different in different parts of the world.

At one point in the early 2000s, I was coming back to Russia every summer for up to two months at a time. This was before the rise of the internet and social media, so my life in Russia wasn't the least bit connected to my life in the US. In Russia, I spoke Russian, hung out with Russian kids, and lived in a Russian environment. In the US, I spoke English, hung out with American, Israeli, Latino, and Korean kids, and lived in an American environment. Since my "Russian life" wasn't connected to my "American life," I kind of felt like I was living in two different realities. This allowed me to understand that my own reality and perception of the world was not the only reality or "truth" that exists, and it allowed me to understand that I could change my reality and my perception if I wanted to.

* * *

OK so how did I get out of this huge drug mess? you may wonder.

Here's a diary entry I wrote on June 2, 2008:

I guess what really saved me from fucking up my life with all this shit at age 14-15 was Dan Freisure.

I fell in love hard. I don't care what anybody says, I was 15 and I was in love with Dan. Mentally insane. I would do anything for him. I spent the whole summer of 2004 in a daze, ecstatic when I was with him. When I wasn't with him I would cry hysterically because I thought I was going to lose him in the fall when he was supposed to go to college in Boston. Instead of letting him go, I spent my whole sophomore year of high school traveling to Boston. I spent every weekday of 10th grade studying and saving up money to get to Dan on the weekends. I could not stand to be without him. Every Friday I would get out of school and run straight to the bus stop, I would take the 166 Bus from Tenafly to 42nd st, then the subway down to Chinatown, then I would walk from the west side of Canal St. to the east side and catch the 4 to 5 hour Chinatown Express bus from NYC Chinatown to Boston Chinatown. Then two more subways to get to Dan's apartment in Boston, around Fenway. I would spend Friday night, Saturday, and Saturday night with him before doing that whole trip back again to New York each Sunday. I definitely spent at least 12 hours each week on buses and subways just to spend about 32 hours of the week with Dan. I don't regret it because those few hours I spent with him were like a fucking fantasy to me.

I lost my virginity to him when I was 15, I think it was sometime around his prom. It was awesome, the best way to have sex for the first time by far. It hurt but it didn't hurt so much because I felt so many emotions come out of my body and I knew he enjoyed it.

He didn't take me though. He made plans to go to prom with one of his friends, but then left her for some gorgeous Spanish chick that he sort-of knew. I remember when he was trying to decide what to do about his prom dates. He came up to me once in school saying, "I wonder if I could take two dates to the prom?" I got all happy and excited thinking one of them would be me, but no, he was talking about both of the other girls.

Moments like that convinced me that he wasn't in love with me. I'm sure he loved me, but there's no way he was mental for me like I was for him. I mean, he had a car in Boston, it would have taken him only 4 hours to drive back to Jersey on weekends, and he had few classes in Berklee College of Music. He probably drove back like 2 or 3 times in the whole year, and I don't think that I was ever the only reason.

I think I was pretty much lost in the world of Dan Freisure until the end of my junior year of high school. I ignored my friends a lot and pretty much everything else but Dan and schoolwork. I don't like that I neglected my friends, especially Chili—she had so many problems at that time with her mom leaving her...

But anyway, I think I did gain a lot of independence in those two years, and that made me mature hella fast. I also worked hard in school and smartened up in general.

So by the time I let go of Dan, I was able to walk on my own two feet and resist all of the bad shit that was flying at me when I was a freshman. I was still with the bad crowd—some that shot up heroin and shit, but I wasn't so young and naive anymore, I was my own full person now and I think I got a lot of respect from some people. If I hadn't been in Dan-world for two and a half years, I could have ended up in dope-world for way longer.

The weird thing was that I didn't mind letting go of him—my feelings kind of just disappeared and it was all OK, and I was a much different person—in a good way.

By traveling to Boston to be with Dan, I also learned to manage my money well. My mother gave me twenty to forty dollars per week for lunch and whatever else I needed, and I found a part-time job in a deli. I got free food from the deli and I saved every penny I earned to make sure I could get to Boston to be with Dan. I realized that the only stuff I needed money for was transportation and food, and the reward for managing my money right was incredible—it was *love,* or love-making.

I broke up with Dan in my last year of high school, I suppose just because my feelings for him disappeared. Soon after, I replaced those feelings with a new healthy passion: *snowboarding.* I had always loved skiing, but when I got onto a snowboard, my entire life changed. I became obsessed with this sport! I thought it was so cool and that any guy on a snowboard was hot.

I got a driver's license and an old Honda Civic when I was seventeen years old, thanks to my dad. I also got my first waitressing job, where I was paid in tips instead of an hourly wage. I never received a paycheck from this restaurant, but I made about a hundred dollars per five-hour shift in tips. That meant that I was earning about twenty dollars an hour—*not too bad for a seventeen-year-old.*

I used my money to drive north to snowboard in New York State and Vermont. I even drove to Quebec once. I usually slept in my car and instead of buying lift tickets at the ski resorts, I just "borrowed" day passes from people who were leaving the mountain after midday. This was easy to do back then. I'd hang out in the parking lot of a ski resort until I saw somebody packing up to leave, then I'd come up to them and kindly ask for their ski pass. Since I was just a cute little girl, they would usually smile and agree. Then I would take out my nail clipper and carefully clip the zip tie or aluminum tag holder that the ski pass was attached to. I'd grab the ski pass, say, "Thanks!" and head up the mountain.

Nowadays, most ski resorts use much more advanced technology. Most resorts use electronic passes that include photos, names, and information like age and gender. Some may use facial recognition technology or other tools that make it very difficult to "borrow" someone else's ski pass. Back in 2006, however, each daily ski pass was just a long sticker that you would fold over these cuttable little holders to attach to your ski pants. It was just like stealing a shirt—cut in the right spot (where it's barely noticeable), take out the sticker, then re-attach it to your own ski pants. I did this in many resorts all over North America.

At first, I sucked at snowboarding. My balance was not good. I fell a lot. It hurt a lot. I struggled, but I was determined to get better. I had fun nevertheless, and I met many interesting people on the slopes. I remember watching an old guy jump off a huge cliff in Vermont. He landed gracefully and yelped out a big "Whew!"

Wow! I thought, *I want to be like **him** when I'm sixty!*

I talked to him later that day on a chairlift and realized that he was so full of life! And he *approved* of what I was doing! Rather than telling me that I should be in school, he said that he was impressed that I had driven all the way from New Jersey to Vermont by myself. When I came back to my car at the end of the day, there was a note from him on my windshield. It said, *Always enjoy life and never give up skiing or snowboarding!*

I met other old people who were having the time of their lives. I met Brazilian people who were living in Vermont for the winter season, I met snowboarding bums and all sorts of college kids, and I just had a lot of fun.

One time, I met a group of guys who invited me to stay in their college dorm. They had a big party and I remember somebody telling me that if I see police on the campus, I should run into the forest. Next thing I knew, I was in a car with one of the college guys and we were pulled over by police on the campus. *He* was driving, but *I* was drunk.

Being drunk is illegal for me, I thought, *I'm only seventeen!* So as these cops were talking to the driver, I bolted toward the forest. I sprinted as fast as my drunken legs could move, but a big fat pig caught up to me, grabbed my legs, and tackled me to the ground. Then they brought me to jail.

I spent one night in jail, just "sobering up," then the cops finally let me go when the breathalyzer hit zero the next day. I was relieved to be released, but the way they let me go was just wrong. This jail was located a good thirty-minute drive away from the college campus. My car was at the college campus. All of my stuff —my keys, phone, wallet, and everything that was in my pockets the night before—had been *brought to a different police station,* about another forty-minute drive away—in the opposite direction. *And the cops didn't offer to give me a lift!*

So basically, the police just opened the jail cell and let me "free" in the middle of nowhere, with no car, no money, no keys, no phone, or anything else that I previously had in my possession. *That ought to teach me a lesson!*

I hitchhiked to the college campus and found a person who helped me break into my own car, where I had a spare key hidden. Then I drove to the other police station, got the rest of my stuff, and drove home.

The Hustle

This little car gave me other opportunities. By the time I was seventeen, I was already good at saving money and keeping my priorities straight. I also knew a lot of big drug dealers and rich white kids. I knew different people from all over Bergen County, but the town I lived in mostly had two classes of people: middle class and super rich. Our high school was very "cliquey," so the schoolkids separated themselves into different groups. The biggest groups were:

- JAPs "Jewish-American Princesses" (rich cool kids).
- [Middle class] cool kids.
- Nerds (not cool but smart).
- Geeks (not cool or smart).
- FOBs "Fresh off the Boat" ("fresh" Korean immigrants who didn't speak English).
- Koreans (second generation Korean kids).
- Israelis (speaks for itself).
- And us… I'm not sure what everyone else called us, probably "druggies" or "skaters," though not all of us skated.

There were other cliques in Tenafly High School, but those were the main ones. Some kids (like the Israelis) intermingled with the different groups, but most kids kept to their tight little circle of friends. All, except the nerds, smoked weed.

In my last year of high school, I got the hook up to get large quantities of good quality marijuana from New York City. I'd drive my little Honda Civic across the George Washington Bridge to Washington Heights (arguably the worst ghetto in NYC), meet some dodgy-looking black guys in the basement of a housing project, hand them a stack of cash, they'd hand me an ounce of weed, then I'd drive back across the bridge, weigh it out, divide it, bag it up, and sell it to the cliques. Word spread fast that I had the best weed in town.

I made a bit of money doing this, but those drug dealers in New York usually ripped me off, so I didn't make all that much. What I got from them was great quality weed—purple skunk, blueberry haze, you name it—the best stuff you could find at the time in Tenafly, but when I weighed it out, it was rarely the whole ounce I had paid for. Sometimes there was so much weed missing that I couldn't even make a profit, even when I made each gram a little skimpy. And it's not like you could change the price of weed. The standard was set: $20 per gram, $10 per dime.

There wasn't much I could do about getting ripped off. Every time I went to Washington Heights to buy weed, I was scared as shit. I usually went there with a male friend of mine, but there were a couple of times when I actually did this alone. Imagine that: *a skinny 5'1" seventeen-year-old white girl driving alone to the most dangerous ghetto in NYC to buy an ounce of purple haze from somebody who looked like Biggie Smalls.* I guess getting a little ripped off was not too bad, I'm lucky nothing worse happened.

I stopped selling weed when a "friend" of mine came into my house when I wasn't home and stole my entire stash along with the profit I had made. Needless to say, we were no longer friends after that.

I knew back then that this lifestyle was toxic. I didn't really want to be all drugged up. I didn't want to end up in jail or kicked out of the country, but it was the situation I lived in that pushed me to do these things. I suppose the benefit I gained from this was the bravery I picked up. *If I could handle picking up ounces of weed alone from big scary drug dealers, I could probably handle almost anything, right?*

* * *

Once I turned eighteen, I broke my wrist snowboarding. This devastated me because all I wanted to do that winter was take snowboarding trips up north. I had to wear a cast for about two months and as a result, I missed almost the entire winter season. That was disappointing, but I wasn't going to give up then. I decided that I *will* go snowboarding as soon as my wrist healed and I finished high school. I was meant to graduate in May, 2007, and then go to college in September. That meant that I had June, July, and August to snowboard.

I searched the web. *Where can you snowboard in June, July, and August?* I found two options: South America or Whistler, Canada. I took a long look at the map and actually considered driving to Argentina, but decided that I probably wouldn't make it there by August. But *Whistler* was doable! I did the calculations—my longest trip, so far, was from New Jersey to Quebec. That took two days. Whistler was about five times the distance. *Ten days—not too bad!*

I set this goal and told all my friends about it. They wanted to join! *Five* of us started to plan this trip together. But of course, as it always goes, one friend abandoned the idea, then another one made his excuse, then another one made hers, until the very last week when I was supposed to leave with one friend and he bailed out too. I wasn't going to let that get me down though! I packed my car with everything I needed—a snowboard, clothes, sleeping bags, pillows, a tent, food, water, and a paper atlas. Yeah, there were no smartphones in 2007.

I saved some money from waitressing, lied to my mother about leaving alone, and took off as soon as I graduated high school.

*There were several reasons why my father never moved to the US with us. His business was a big factor, but my parents also had relationship problems. As a child, I wasn't aware of these relationship problems; I only remember being told that our father had to go back to Russia to take care of his business.

**My mother also claims to be a workaholic; she may say that she's always loved her job (and that she enjoyed working overtime and accomplishing projects), despite the stress it gave her.

5

The Road, 2007

Once I left, I knew I would never come back. I left, and I left it all behind. All the harmful drugs, all the harmful people, all the toxic situations. I drove far. I drove for hours and hours, all alone. *I changed my reality.* The past was now in the past and I had no idea what was ahead of me. But it didn't matter. All that mattered now was my little car and my paper atlas.

I took the fastest route across the country: Highway 80 going west from New Jersey to Chicago, then up to Minneapolis, Fargo, and across North Dakota. I didn't have enough money for hotels and I didn't even know that hostels existed back then, so I slept in my car or in my crappy little tent, wherever I could camp or park the car. I bought huge sugary ice coffees from McDonald's for one dollar, that kept me up and driving for a while. For food, I mostly made sandwiches. I bought bread and whatever else I needed from supermarkets along the way. I had three CDs in my car: *Because of the Times*, by Kings of Leon, *Pablo Honey*, by Radiohead, and *The Best of Led Zeppelin*. I didn't need anything else.

The first spectacular place I came across was the Badlands in North Dakota. I stopped at a vista point and was approached by two bison. Their shaggy heads towered over my car. I got out, tiptoed around the bison, and admired the wide open scenery. There was a desert with yellow shrubs, small hills, and a shallow lake. White puffy clouds roamed the sky as far as the eye could see. I breathed it all in. *Freedom!*

I drove west and hit Montana. I remember the feeling that overtook me once I started driving through big mountain passes. I slurped on my giant ice coffee as the song "Gallows Pole" blasted through my speakers. I clenched my steering wheel, trembled with excitement, and kept on driving.

There's nothing that transformed me more than mountains. The farther I drove, the bigger, more dramatic, and powerful they became, the more enlightened I felt, the more free, more excited, and filled with adrenaline. Idaho was *amazing*! There were huge HUGE mountains! I couldn't wait to get to Whistler and go snow-boarding!

After over a week of driving, I made it to the Pacific Coast. I stopped in Seattle to check out the city, then made my way up to Canada. *Got through the border without a problem!* Next was Vancouver.

I thought that the drinking age in all of Canada was eighteen, so I was excited to go to a bar legally for the first time in my life once I was in Vancouver. I parked my car somewhere near the city center and found a busy street with some pubs. I stood in line to get into one place and started talking to the people around me. I told them that I was eighteen and was excited to drink legally. They told me that the drinking age in British Columbia was nineteen!

"What?" That took me by surprise.

"Yeah, it's nineteen in every other Canadian province," one girl explained.

Lucky for me, this group of people snuck me into the bar anyway, hung out with me all night, and even let me crash on their couch at the end of the night. That was my first introduction to friendly Canadians.

The next day, I drove to Whistler. This was the most mind-blowing drive of my life! I saw towering rock walls and gigantic mountains emerging from water. There were glaciers in the distance; endless, timeless hilltops all around me. I couldn't stop glancing at the mountains! I was *literally* shaking with excitement. I was in *awe*, I was *in love*, I was *ecstatic!* And then the car in front of me hit the breaks at a yellow light and I smashed directly into it.

I got out. "It doesn't look too bad, right?" I said as I looked over the two cars. It was just a small bump. "The mark is barely even noticeable."

Then the driver and his wife got out with their baby and started cursing at me, saying that it *was* bad, saying something about a neck injury. "You'll have to pay for all of this!" they yelled.

They called the cops, took the baby away in an ambulance, gave me a fine, did some paperwork, then everybody left.

I got really upset then. *What the fuck—an ambulance? That was such a little bump. A fine? Money? I don't have any money! I'm just a kid. What the fuck did I just do?! Where am I? How the fuck did I get so far?* I realized where I was—on the other side of North America, about five thousand kilometers away from home. I was all alone. A piercing rush of fear and detachment overtook me. I started crying hysterically.

I tried to calm myself down, then walked into a gemstone shop to ask for a phone. There, I broke down crying again, hysterically. The two ladies who worked behind the counter came up and hugged me straight away. They didn't let go until I could speak again. I told them what happened.

They said not to worry. "Just go to Whistler and find a job! There's so much work over there," one of the ladies explained. "And don't you have car insurance? I'm sure your insurance will cover the accident, the important thing is that you're okay!"

I wiped my tears as the ladies told me about staff housing. "You can live in a dorm in Whistler for a hundred and thirty or so dollars a month in the summer. Ski instructors live there in winter, but in summer it's open to anybody—and it's cheap. Just go and settle in there for a few weeks! You'll have fun, I'm sure!"

OK. I calmed down, thanked the ladies, got back in my car, and drove carefully the rest of the way. I found the staff housing and had enough cash to pay for one month of rent. The next day, I poached lift tickets and went snowboarding.

Whistler

I rode up several ski lifts to get to the glacier. I spotted black bears and deer along the way. At the top, I was above the clouds. I felt ecstatic all over again. I never even imagined mountains like this before! Their peaks poked out like islands on a sea of clouds.

One of the first people I spoke to on a chairlift was a good-looking Australian snowboarder. I asked him what he was doing and he said he was just traveling around the world and snow-boarding. After the summer in Whistler, he planned to go to Europe and snowboard in the Alps.

Um... Can I come with you... Please? I imagined asking him.

He asked what I was doing, and I told him I was just there for the summer. "I have to go to college in New York in September," I said.

"What are you gonna study?" he asked.

"Business," I replied, knowing how dreadful that sounded.

He looked disappointed. I was disappointed too. Then I told him that I drove from New York to Whistler by myself and the look on his face changed immediately! He was impressed.

I talked to more people and told them about my road trip, and it turned out that they were all impressed! This surprised me because I didn't think that driving across the US was such a big deal. It was amazing, yes, but it's not like it was difficult.

Once I realized that people were impressed by my driving-across-America story, I started purposely bringing it up, and maybe even bragging about it. But this had the opposite effect. People were not impressed by braggers, and soon I realized that the more I tried to impress people, the less impressed they were—and vice versa.

I moved into a cramped and dirty old dorm room in the staff housing building. The place reminded me of a college dorm, but without the college. I shared a bunk bed with a girl from Toronto and a kitchen, bathroom, and living room with two other flatmates. One of those flatmates was a funny French-Canadian guy named PL. He introduced me to his favorite crew of people—Tom, Scott, Max, Sean, a girl named 34, and a few others. We got along straight away, they were all zealous skiers and snowboarders. They told me all about the mountain and the amount of snow it gets in winter, and what it's like to venture out on their snowmobiles and freeride all day. They told me there was so much snow the previous winter that they even built a half-pipe in their own backyard.

I loved these guys! And Tom, my favorite, happened to be selling magic mushrooms, which were also my favorite.

One day, a few of us decided to take mushrooms and go on a hike to a lake. The hike was Scottie's idea, he made it sound like it would just be a walk in the park leading to a nice beach where we could swim and relax.

We started the hike with seven people. All of us had summer clothes and swimmers on, some of us wore light sneakers, some only wore flip-flops. We took a few beers and headed for the trail.

Tom brought a huge bag of magic mushrooms with him. I grabbed a big handful and put it in my mouth. *They kicked in fast!* I had no idea how much I ate.

The trail began at a narrow opening in the middle of some dark green interwoven leaves and branches. It looked like a creepy fairytale. The branches surrounded and weaved around the trail entrance in snakelike motion. I was already hallucinating.

I took one beer with me and nothing else.

We walked through the bushes and up the trail. We followed the markers through lush green forest, past big rushing rivers, and over beautifully carved wooden bridges.

The farther we walked, the more intense the trail got. We climbed uphill through steep narrow passes, hopped over huge boulders, and sometimes used both hands and feet to make it up the trail.

I found a tiny precious flower. I stared at its intricate beauty. The interwoven shapes of its leaves. The colors—red, pink, brown, even blue! The colors were weaving. I looked straight ahead, there was the most beautiful river in the world! To the left—the most beautiful forest! There was hair-like moss growing on all of the trees, it was slow-dancing, mingling, and intertwining with the branches. The whole forest was breathing! I looked to the right—I could have died right there. The open view of the Coast Mountains was out of this world! The mountains were shimmering, weaving, and changing colors. I was ecstatic! I was one with it all.

We climbed higher and higher, and the views got more intense. My trip also got more intense. I clenched the beer tightly in my hand and never took a single sip. We hopped through a pond using stones as our steps. The pond was covered in gigantic lily pads. Each lily looked like it was the size of a hippo!

We climbed even higher and passed by a few hikers on the way. Everyone we saw on the trail had real trekking gear on— hiking boots, jackets, tents, camping equipment, the whole deal! A group of Japanese hikers stopped when they saw us, didn't say anything, and simply pointed at our shoes and laughed.

After several hours, we noticed a sign that said, "5 km to go!" We kept on walking. An hour later, another sign: "5 km to go!" Another hour—the same sign again! *Were we tripping or what?*

Three out of seven people turned around. Scott, Tom, Sean, and I kept on going. *Gotta get to the lake and go for a swim! That's the mission!* You always gotta have a mission when you're tripping on mushrooms.

Eventually, we did it! The four of us made it to the top of the mountain and there it was—a lake. Rainbow Lake, it was called. It was half-covered in ice and on the other side of the lake there was a glacier.

Since our goal was to swim in a lake, we clearly *had* to jump in. The four of us dove into the freezing cold water for a split second then ran out as quickly as possible. *Refreshing!*

Then, all of a sudden, a gust of cold wind ran across our bodies.

The light dimmed.

We glanced across the valley.

The sun dipped just below the adjacent mountain.

We realized then that we were in danger. Two of the guys were in flip-flops. We had no flashlights, no jackets, no sleeping bags, no tent, nothing warm at all. We didn't even bring a camera. All we had was wet swimmers and beer! We were standing right next to a glacier on top of a mountain and *it took us like ten hours to get here!*

Tommy offered me more mushrooms. I grabbed another handful and put it in my mouth.

That was a mistake.

We moved swiftly down the trail. We didn't speak once or stop walking on the way down. *Now the mission is to make it home!* It got dark. I got scared. I tripped hard. *I shouldn't have eaten more mushrooms.* We moved fast but with caution. We climbed over huge stones in pitch black. The narrow passes, the lily pads, the hills, the rocks, everything was so much harder in the dark.

My mind was going nuts. *Are we gonna die out here? I don't want to die, I just started living! Just move. Don't think, just move. Move! Move!*

It felt like it was never going to end. We got lost twice but Scottie managed to find the trail with his flip-phone light. Then finally, after walking around the forest in the dark for hours, we found the road! We all thought it was another river at first. The four of us cheered as we stepped onto the concrete. We walked back to the guys' house feeling absolutely relieved to be back.

"Whew!" I took my first sip of beer as we stepped into the house, then I collapsed into the couch and slept for the next twelve hours.

* * *

I spent the summer of 2007 having the time of my life. I went snowboarding, hiking, exploring, swimming in mountain lakes, and meeting a lot of different people from all over the world. I met people from many different parts of Canada, Europe, South America, Japan, Africa, Australia, New Zealand, you name it! And they were basically *all* having the time of their lives. Everyone was really nice and they were all absolutely stoked about living in Whistler and just being alive.

Most of the people I met who were genuinely happy and passionate about life were those who were completely immersed in their favorite hobby, whether that hobby was snowboarding, biking, art, music, whatever. They didn't make their favorite hobby just their hobby, they turned it into their lifestyle. Most of them had to work every once in a while to support their lifestyle, but their jobs didn't seem important to them because their jobs were not their "career," lifestyle, or identity.

While I was in Whistler, I found a cash job cleaning houses for sixteen dollars an hour. I didn't work a lot but I made enough money to buy food, pay for rent, and save up for gas. I didn't need much else.

Across Canada

At the end of August, it was time for me to pack up and leave. I had less than two weeks to make the drive back to New York City to start university on Wall Street. I didn't want to do the drive alone again, so I went to all of the dorm rooms in staff housing and looked for a companion to join me on this trip. By going around to all of the staff housing rooms, I met even *more* cool people, and I *really* didn't want to leave then!

Unfortunately, I felt like I had to. I was a stubborn and uncontrollable kid, but I still cared about my parents. University seemed to be the most important thing in the world to them. I would be a *complete* letdown if I didn't go. Plus, I grew up with the idea that you *had* to go to university if you didn't want to be a failure in life. *It was just a thing that you had to do.*

As I was packing my last few belongings the morning I was due to depart, I heard a loud knock on my door. I opened the door and in came a loud and excited British guy. "YOU HAVEN'T LEFT YET!" he said.

Oh yeah, that's Tom, I met him last night in one of the dorms.
"Nope, I'm about to head out," I replied.

"CAN I COME WITH YOU?" he asked.

"Of course!" *Yes!* And I got my companion!

You see, the drive from New Jersey to Whistler was amazing to do alone, and I think the effect that it had on me would have been different if I had been with somebody else, but sometimes it was scary. Sometimes I drove for ten hours straight and I would almost start hallucinating at night on the big five-lane highways. I was terrified of big trucks and deer crossing the road. Sometimes I didn't know where to sleep and I would be scared of people breaking into my car or tent.

Because of that, I was stoked to have Tom join, even though he didn't have a driver's license or even know how to drive a car. Tom needed to get to Toronto and he didn't have a US visa, so we had to drive through Canada without crossing the border. I saw this as a great opportunity to check out a new route across North America.

Tom and I said goodbye to our friends and took off through the winding roads of British Columbia. The drive was absolutely spectacular. The mountains got bigger, the scenery turned wild, and we were spellbound. We stopped in little towns like Banff, checked out caves, lakes, and local pubs. We slept anywhere we could set up my tent. It was a crappy tent that I had already used a lot, so it was in very bad shape during this road trip. At one point, we had to tie one end of the tent to the car to keep it from collapsing, and I think Tom's feet stuck out of the other end.

After a couple of days, we drove out of the mountainous region of Alberta and through endless flatland. The speed limit was lower in Canada than in the US, and after mid-Alberta, there wasn't much scenery apart from farmland. From then on, the drive seemed to take *forever.*

We stopped in cities like Calgary, Regina, and Winnipeg. One night, we stayed in a trailer park campground in Winnipeg and met a group of locals. They were *real local.* We made friends with them and were invited back to their house, where we drank beer and smoked weed out of a gas mask bong. It was literally a gas mask with a bong attached to the mouthpiece—I found it hilarious.

That night, these guys gave us a hallucinogen called peyote. Peyote can be used as a traditional medicine in some Native American cultures, but clearly, we were not in the right state of mind to take it properly.

As soon as I took a big puff, I felt like the air around my body turned into a solid state. The air began to vibrate in thick solid waves and I thought that little people were going to steal the table. I felt a swarm of little people vibrating and picking up the kitchen table to take it away. I grabbed the table and screamed, "Don't let the little people steal the table!" A couple of minutes later, the drug wore off and I had the worst headache of my life.

The next day, I bought one of those gas mask bongs and drove on to Ontario with Tom. The road through Ontario sucked. It constantly weaved back and forth and the speed limit was about ninety kilometers per hour the entire way. I was also terrified of hitting deer since there were a lot of forested areas in Ontario. Eventually we got to Toronto, where we stayed with a friend of Tom's for a couple of days. It reminded me of New Jersey, so it didn't impress me much.

I left Tom in Toronto and drove the rest of the way alone. After another day or two of driving, I finally arrived in New York City. I was a few days late for university but I really didn't care. I *really* did not want to be there.

6
NY to CA, 2007-08

I was supposed to attend Pace University in downtown Manhattan. I left my car at my mother's house, then she drove me to a college dorm near Wall Street. As soon as I walked in, I felt like a train had hit me. *What the fuck am I doing here?*

I unpacked my stuff and tried to make sense of the situation. *Why am I here?* I looked out the window and gazed at the concrete below me. There were business people everywhere, roaming around like zombies with briefcases. They all looked so stressed, all running around, rushing to get somewhere, rushing to do something. *What are they running around for?* They looked miserable. *What are they living for? Do they even know?*

Everyone's rushing around here to make money. But for what? They want money—to buy stuff? Why buy stuff? To be happy? Stuff doesn't make you happy—MOUNTAINS do! And whatever your favorite hobby is. I felt like everyone on Wall Street was lost.

I couldn't be there. It was killing my soul. It felt like torture, like my spirit was getting hushed and my entire life was being suppressed.

Why the hell would I study business?

No. I can't. I just can't.

I dropped out within the first week. I wrote a long letter to my mother, explaining that I just had to go back to Whistler this year and that next year I promise I will go to university. I will not go back to this business institute in New York City, but I'll attend a different university, somewhere in the mountains. *I'll start applying now, I promise!*

Her reaction wasn't as bad as I expected. Lucky for me, she's the nicest person in the world. My dad accepted as well, as long as I promised to apply to another university.

The greatest feeling of relief came over me as soon as I left that campus. I felt like I was freed from slavery! At least temporarily. Now my goal was to get back to Whistler and snowboard all winter long. That was the only thing I wanted to do and NOTHING was going to stop me now.

I had no more money left so I moved back to my mother's house and got two full-time jobs in two restaurants. I wanted to leave by October, before it was too dangerous to drive over those huge mountain passes in my Honda Civic, so I only had one month to save as much money as possible.

I worked at the Tenafly Diner in the mornings and at a fancy Mexican restaurant called Mama Mexico in the evenings. The morning shifts absolutely sucked. I had to do *so* much work—take orders, bring food to the tables, make coffee, make dessert, clean it all up, and run around like crazy! And the place was cheap so people barely even tipped. Sometimes I'd walk away from an entire breakfast and lunch shift with only about twenty dollars in my pocket. I would have quit but I didn't have enough time to look for another job—I had to leave in four weeks!

Mama Mexico was a bit better. I was the only white person that worked there. Everyone else was from Mexico or some other part of Latin America. Seventy-five percent of the staff didn't speak English—the cooks, bussers, and food runners only communicated in Spanish. The only people who knew English were the waiters, bartenders, and managers. Even our staff meetings were in Spanish. Luckily I did know a bit of Spanish from studying it in high school, so I could somewhat comprehend what was going on most of the time.

I was able to make about a hundred dollars per shift at Mama Mexico, sometimes more, sometimes less, and I loved working with Latinos. They're such hardworking, open, and friendly people. All the guys are a bunch of pervs, sure, but I found that their catcalls and dirty talk was just for show, so if you know how to deal with it, it just becomes funny rather than offensive or irritating.

I worked about ninety hours per week in September of 2007. Each week, I did six to seven shifts at the Tenafly Diner and six to seven shifts at Mama Mexico. Half a day off was what I considered to be my weekend at the time. I ate food only at those two restaurants and I saved every penny I earned. At the end of the month, I bought a season pass for Whistler Mountain, quit, and hit the road.

Road Trip #3

This time, I took a friend with me. His name was Clark. He was one of the guys I had met in the college campus where I was thrown in jail the year before. He wanted to go Out West to ski, so we decided to drive out together. When he first contacted me about this trip, he said that he wanted to go to Mammoth. I looked up "Mammoth" on a map and found it somewhere in the northwestern part of the US, directly on my way to Whistler. *No problem!* I thought. But when Clark stepped into my car in October, he told me that Mammoth was located in the middle of California.

"*California?*"

"Yeah, I was surprised you agreed to drive me so far out of your way. You said you knew where it was?" Clark said with a bit of a worried look.

I checked the map again. Apparently, there's more than one "Mammoth" in the US! *Oh well.* I couldn't back out now, so this just meant that I had an even *bigger* adventure ahead of me.

Clark and I took a new route across the country—Highway 80 through Pennsylvania, Ohio, Indiana, Illinois, Missouri, Kansas, Colorado, Utah, Nevada, and finally to California. We drove long distances, this time Clark helped me drive whenever I let him. We mostly slept at his friends' houses in random cities across the country. We still didn't have a GPS or a smartphone, but somehow, we managed just fine.

I dropped Clark off at Mammoth Lakes, California, and prepared for another two-thousand-kilometer drive alone. I decided to take the scenic route going north—Highway 101 along the Pacific Ocean. I drove up a narrow winding road on top of beautiful cliffsides that overlooked the ocean. I was captivated by the scenery. My emotions were amplified by the song "Stairway to Heaven" blaring from my stereo. *I chose the right road,* I thought. I was more excited than *ever* to be alive!

I drove through the redwood forest and touched the Pacific Ocean for the first time. I slept in my car in Fort Bragg, then in a hostel in Oregon (I finally found out about hostels then). After another beautiful serpentine drive through the mountains of Oregon and Washington, I finally made it to the Canadian border! There, I had my very first troublesome encounter with border police.

I wasn't expecting to have any problems at the border. I mean, I wasn't doing anything wrong, I didn't have a criminal record and I wasn't breaking the law in any way. I was just an eighteen-year-old kid that wanted to live and snowboard in Whistler. But when I tried to drive into Canada, they didn't want to let me in! They searched my car and noticed that I had *everything* in it. Blankets, clothes, cooking utensils, anything that I may need for life.

The border policeman said, "It looks like you just packed everything up from your house to go and live in Canada."

Not realizing that this was the very *wrong* thing to say, I replied with, "Yeah! I want to live in Whistler!"

The man explained to me that as a Russian citizen, even with a US green card, I was not allowed to live in Canada. And now, because I told him that I was planning to live there, by law, he was not supposed to let me in.

I must have had an absolutely devastated look on my face. I almost cried. I begged him to let me in. I told him all I wanted to do was snowboard in Whistler, "I just want to snowboard, please! I promise I won't do anything bad!" He suggested for me to go to a different ski resort in the US, but I begged and pleaded him, saying that there's *nothing* better than Whistler.

Perhaps I was lucky to have stumbled upon this particular border policeman. By law, he really was supposed to send me back to the US, but he had kind eyes, he was a snowboarder himself, and I could tell that he felt bad about this situation. I was just a kid that wanted to snowboard, that was the truth. He would have killed my dream just because I had the wrong piece of paper in my hands.

"Okay, drive in," he said quietly. "Just don't tell anyone it was me that let you in."

Whew! Relief! *And a new lesson learned!*

Winter in Whistler

I drove up to Whistler and asked my friend Alfie to crash on his couch for a few days. Alfie was an interesting South African guy I had met in staff housing during the summer. He was already crashing on someone else's couch at the time, but he managed to temporarily squeeze me into the place as well. I told him I just needed a few days to find my own place to live.

It turned out this wasn't as easy as I had expected. Whistler was *crazy* when it came to housing in winter. There simply was not enough space for everybody. Rent was extremely expensive and every house was stuffed with as many beds as possible. Sometimes people even rented out closets or bathrooms to sleep in.

I searched for housing for a while and couldn't find anything. I started getting desperate after a few weeks; I looked for anything— a room, half a room, a quarter, a closet, anything! I *really* wanted to live in Whistler. There were a lot of other people looking for housing and not so many rooms available, so I basically had to compete with others to try to get into any place I went to check out. *Whatever potential roommate seemed the coolest got to move into the house!*—That's how it went in Whistler.

This made it tough for me because I was so young. *Nobody wants to live with an eighteen-year-old!* After being denied several times, I showed up to check out a room in a fancy apartment right in the center of Whistler. It cost eight hundred dollars per month to share a big bed with a chick named Emma. That was a bit pricey for me, especially to share a bed, but I was basically ready to take anything at that point.

Hmm, I thought. *How do I get these people to like me?*

There were four people living in the apartment: two twenty-something-year-old Australians named Danny and Emma, a big Belgian guy named JB, and an eighteen-year-old Australian guy named Toby. Toby was planning to move out in a few days, so if I got to move in, I would be his replacement.

I remembered what I had learned in the summertime: *the less I try to impress people, the more impressed they are—and vice versa,* so I tried my hardest not to impress these people.

I suppose it worked... I impressed Toby so much that he wanted to have sex with me. *But I didn't need to impress Toby! Toby was leaving! I needed to impress Emma, the person I could potentially share a bed with!* I was attracted to Toby but I didn't want to have sex with him because I thought these guys wouldn't choose me as a roommate if I did that.

Pretty soon, Toby told Emma to lie to me saying that I got the room, so that I would sleep with him. Next, I don't particularly remember how the sequence of events unfolded, and I don't particularly remember Emma ever telling me that I got the room, but basically, all five of us got drunk together several nights in a row, I slept with Toby, and I never left the apartment. When Toby moved out, all my stuff was already there, so I moved in.

I had the best winter of my life with these guys. Emma, Danny, JB, and I bonded like family. We snowboarded together, cooked meals together, went out together, and had big parties in our apartment. The parties usually ended in pillow fights, food fights, and/or crazy water fights. We were like uncontrollable children running around this fancy apartment, throwing pots of water, burritos, and curry at each other. Once, Emma cornered me in the bathroom, grabbed my hair and tried to stick my head underwater, then rammed my face straight into the bathtub fossette, giving me a massive black eye. It was all about laughs and fun though, none of us ever had a real argument in that apartment.

I was never able to get a working visa for Canada, but I found several cash jobs that winter through friends and notice boards. At first, I shoveled snow and did some housekeeping jobs here and there, then I worked in a cookie factory. The factory made delicious organic cookies of many varieties, and I was able to eat or take home any broken or overcooked cookies. I usually came home with a giant plastic bag of cookies after each shift, so my roommates loved me then.

Eventually, thanks to Alfie, I got a consistent job bussing tables at an Indian restaurant. The manager made an agreement to pay me one dollar less than minimum wage, since I was working "illegally," but gave me some tips and a big meal at the end of each shift. The meal was a huge plate of rice, delicious curry, and naan bread.

Life was easy and sweet back then. I had a season pass for Whistler Mountain, so I went snowboarding almost every day. I improved a lot, learned to ride powder, hit big jumps, and shoot off cliffs and cornices. I worked from about 5:00 p.m. to 10:00 p.m., so I had enough time for both snowboarding and partying with my roommates. I got free food and earned enough money to pay rent. Plus, I had *love* in my life—my newfound family, and I even had a fuck buddy at one point.

All of us were stoked about life in Whistler. "We're all broke as hell," said Emma, "but we live like millionaires!" We even had a jacuzzi tub in our apartment building.

My roommates and I made friends with the security guard in our building. He was a young French-Canadian guy named Jeremy. He didn't speak much English, but we invited him up for parties and he gave us the key to the building's hot tub when the place was closed. One morning, I stole the hot tub key while Jeremy was asleep on our couch. I brought the key to the locksmith and made a copy before Jeremy woke up and noticed it was missing. We didn't tell Jeremy, but from then on, we had twenty-four-hour access to the hot tub, that is, until Emma ate the key! *On purpose, yes.* A few days later, we got it back and I had sex in that hot tub. I also had sex in an elevator that winter and in a gondola that went up the mountain.

Life changed, however, when my roommates talked me into joining them on an epic road trip to South America. They had been talking about this trip for a long time. In summer of 2007, Emma, Danny, and JB bought a van in Montreal and drove it across North America together. After the winter season, they planned to drive it down the West Coast, to Mexico, and beyond. They said that there was enough space for a small Russian like me. I wasn't interested at first though. All I wanted was to stay in Whistler and continue snowboarding. But after getting to know these guys and having such a great time with them, I began to contemplate this road trip.

Then one fine morning, I woke up and I asked myself, *Am I fucking crazy? How the hell could I **not** go on such an epic adventure with these amazing people that I absolutely love? This is an opportunity of a lifetime!*

Unfortunately, it wasn't as easy as that. In order to make this trip happen, I needed to make some changes in my life. Since I was working for less-than-minimum-wage as a busser, I was barely earning enough money for rent and food. I couldn't work legally in Canada so it was tough to find work with decent pay. I knew that I needed at least a couple of thousand dollars for such a big trip to South America, so I felt like my only option was to go back to the US, where I could work legally, and save money.

In March, I quit my busser job, packed up my stuff, and took off for California with Jeremy. Jeremy had always dreamed of driving from Quebec to California, and had made it as far as Whistler, so he saw this trip as an opportunity to complete that dream. He was also planning to join the rest of our crew on the epic road trip to South America.

In short, the idea was that Jeremy and I would drive to California, where I could find a legal job. I would work for a couple of months and quickly save some money, then when Emma, Danny, and JB drove down the coast (at the end of April), I would quit this job and go with them to South America. That was the plan.

The Border

My plan was smashed as soon as we hit the border. I really wasn't expecting problems this time. I mean, I had US residency, I wasn't doing anything illegal. *They **have** to let me in, right?*

I had bought some beer and whiskey at the Canadian duty-free shop at the border, since I was nineteen now and legally allowed to do so. I didn't think that simply *possessing* alcohol under the age of twenty-one was illegal in some states, since it wasn't in New Jersey. I also still had that gas mask bong in my car, but I hadn't smoked out of it since I had cleaned it and I didn't have any weed with me. I knew that smoking devices on their own were not illegal, only the drugs were.

The cops took the gas mask bong out of my car and asked me what I used it for.

"Tobacco," I replied.

They didn't like that reply. They wanted to confiscate my bong *and* my alcohol. That pissed me off. I was rude to them because I thought they had nothing on me. *I'm not doing anything illegal! I'm a US resident! Just let me into the freaken country!*

They were rude back. "Hand over the bong and alcohol or you're getting arrested," one fat cop said.

"Arrested? No." *Arrested for what? This pig just wants my beer and whiskey—he's bluffing.*

"No?" he replied. "You have three seconds to change your mind."

"No." I crossed my arms.

"Three... Two.... One..."

What the hell can this pig do? I'm not doing anything illegal!

"OK," he said, "you're arrested for being a minor in possession of alcohol." He took out a pair of handcuffs and locked them onto my wrists, symbolically, it seemed.

"Minor in possession of alcohol?" I was baffled. "I'm nineteen years old!"

"In the state of Washington it is illegal to carry alcohol until the age of twenty-one."

"But I wasn't drinking it! In New Jersey you can bartend at eighteen."

"In Washington—you cannot." Apparently, these laws vary from state to state—*another lesson learned.*

I tried to be nice now. I tried to talk him out of it, saying that he can have my alcohol after all, but it was too late. He said that I was already arrested and now I would have to go to court. Then he filled out a bunch of paperwork as I sat there, handcuffed, on a hard plastic chair.

After an hour or two, he took off the handcuffs, handed me a piece of paper, and said that my court date was set for April. "See you then!"

I was angry and perplexed. *How could I be arrested for having a closed bottle of alcohol in the trunk of my car? Now I have to go to court in April—in Washington State? Fuck!* I couldn't not go to court because I *had* to clear my record. I didn't have US citizenship yet. If I had anything on my record, I could be denied citizenship and that would change the course of my entire life.

God damn it.

I took the stupid piece of paper, walked back to my car with Jeremy, then drove into the US. I drove for hours and hours, calming myself down with music and beautiful scenic views of forests and rolling hills.

We drove through Washington State and the stunning mountains of Oregon, then down to California. Clark was the only person I knew on the West Coast, so we decided to drive to Mammoth Lakes, hoping that Clark could hook me up with a job there. We got stuck in a massive blizzard on the way, did a 360-degree turn in my Honda Civic, and almost skidded off the road. After about three days, we finally made it.

I didn't have enough money to pay for rent anywhere, so I had to find a job that would also give me accommodation. This was common in ski areas and Mammoth Lakes did have this option, but we quickly learned that it wouldn't work for Jeremy and me. Mammoth wasn't hiring many people at the time, they paid something like six or seven dollars an hour (which was a lot less than what I was getting "illegally" in Canada), and Jeremy wouldn't have been able to live there because he didn't have working rights in the US and the accommodation was strictly for staff only.

Clark suggested for us to go to Lake Tahoe instead, an area four hours north of Mammoth Lakes. Jeremy and I arrived there the next day and were stunned by the beauty of the crystal-clear, gigantic blue lake and the striking surrounding mountains.

There were several ski resorts around Lake Tahoe, so we drove around and talked to people to find information. Eventually, we found out that a resort called Kirkwood was hiring people and provided staff housing. We drove through an incredible mountain pass to get to Kirkwood, and once we arrived, I talked to a manager and was hired straight away! I got a job as a ski lift attendant, which I soon realized was the worst job in a ski resort. I was also given a room in a disgusting old four-bedroom apartment with six male flatmates. Luckily, there was one empty bed in my room where Jeremy was able to hide out.

My new flatmates were nice, but they did a lot of cocaine and they were messy as hell. The kitchen was piled with about three feet of dishes, there were old chunks of food and dust everywhere, and I don't think anybody had ever swept or vacuumed the floor in that place.

I chose one cup, one plate, one fork, one knife, and one spoon. I washed and used only those utensils and kept them in my bedroom. The lifty job got me a ski pass to Kirkwood Mountain, so I was able to snowboard on my time off, but I usually had to work all day and the mountain was closed at night. They paid me seven or eight dollars an hour, which was less than what I was getting "illegally" in Canada, they charged me for the shitty staff accommodation, and they didn't provide any food. Soon I realized that this entire situation was a big mistake. *I should have just stayed in Whistler...* Unfortunately, it was too late to turn back now.

I worked as a lift attendant for a few weeks, made a lot of new friends in Kirkwood, and had fun anyway. Kirkwood was an amazing mountain to snowboard on. It got a lot of fresh snow and had great terrain—there was a huge cornice, many different cliffs and shoots, and some fun tree runs.

When it was time for me to go to court in April, I took a few days off work and drove back up to Washington State (1,400 kilometers away). I assumed it would be easy to settle this "minor in possession of alcohol" case. *I'll show up to court,* I thought, *the judge will take one glance at this case and see how stupid it is—a nineteen-year-old was arrested for having a closed bottle of alcohol (that she bought legally at the Canadian duty-free shop) in the trunk of her car—and he/she will dismiss the case and let me go. Right?*

I was wrong.

I showed up to court and pleaded not-guilty. Astonishingly, the judge couldn't settle this stupid case in one day. They didn't throw me in jail, but they told me that if I wanted this case off my record, I would have to come back to court AGAIN on May 14.

REALLY? I thought. *I'm nineteen years old. I wasn't drinking and driving. I wasn't even drinking at all! At nineteen, it's legal for me to make porn, to be a stripper, to own a gun, to go into the military and kill people or be killed myself—but I can't have a fucking closed bottle of alcohol in the trunk of my car?*

I guess not.

I told them I would come back to court on May 14. *What an idiotic waste of everyone's time and energy.*

I gave up on the idea of the epic road trip from California, since Emma and the crew were planning to leave in April, but I still considered the possibility of flying to meet them somewhere after this bullshit court case was over with.

I drove back to Kirkwood and decided to quit the lifty job and make some real money in South Lake Tahoe. I gave my boss a one-week notice, during which time *everything* went wrong. I wrecked my car that week by driving over some big rocks that had fallen off a cliff. There was about 1,700 dollars worth of damage, so the car was totaled. I got fired for selling my "freebie" lift tickets to some random people, so I couldn't ask for my job back and I could no longer live in staff housing. Jeremy left to catch up with Emma and the crew, and on top of it all, I broke my hand in two places.

So that was me at nineteen: all alone with no job, no home, no car, almost no money, a court date, and a broken hand.

I felt that piercing rush of fear again—loneliness, detachment, stress. *Where am I? How the hell did I get here? What the hell am I doing?*

The scariest part was losing my car. This car had been my best friend and safety net throughout all my adventures across North America. I had always felt safe with my car because I knew I could drive away from a dangerous situation and sleep in the car if I needed to. Without it, I felt exposed and vulnerable.

I thought about Emma, Danny, JB, and the epic road trip, then I pulled myself together somehow. I found a bed in a share house in South Lake Tahoe for about a hundred dollars per month. The bed was in an attic of a small house that was shared by about twelve people, but that didn't matter to me.

I sold my totaled car for 650 dollars, then I went to every single restaurant, bar, café, and shop to find a new job. This was in 2008, during the recession, so work was not easy to find.

I spent all day, every day looking for work. I got so desperate that I even applied at McDonald's, Taco Bell, and some supermarkets. *But still no!* Taco Bell told me I was too pretty to work there. *WTF?!* I took off my cast so that hiring managers wouldn't know I had a broken hand. When they shook my hand, it hurt, but that was what I needed to do in order to get a job.

After about two weeks of nonstop job hunting, I finally found a job at a sandwich shop. This meant that I only had three weeks left before I had to leave for court again. I worked at the cash register for about eight dollars an hour, got some free food and a little bit extra in tips. I gave the shop a one-week notice before I quit, after which they fired me on the spot, saying that that was too short of a notice. *Another lesson learned.*

After I got fired, I went into Bank of America to open a bank account on the West Coast. While opening a checking account, the banker offered me an eight-thousand-dollar credit card! *Imagine that.* I was nineteen years old, unemployed, and basically homeless, *and they want to give me an eight-thousand-dollar credit card?* I accepted!

Then I convinced three of my old flatmates from Kirkwood to drive me to Canada. I'm not sure how I convinced them to do that, but we ended up having a great road trip. We stopped in some ski resorts along the way, poached lift tickets, and explored new mountains.

On our way up the coast, we met a couple of girls at Mount Hood, Oregon. One was really fat, the other was cute and skinny. Apparently, I made out with the skinny one, and then Alex, our seventeen-year-old driver, lost his virginity to her. My other flatmate screwed the fat one, and then she gave him a hundred dollars the next day!

After Mount Hood, the boys drove me to the courthouse in Washington State. I went in, pleaded not-guilty again, and this time, they told me that I had to come back to court AGAIN in two weeks!

What the fuck? I was enraged. *How can they do this? "Minor in possession of alcohol?" What a stupid fucking crime! I'm nineteen years old! I bought the alcohol LEGALLY in Canada! It wasn't open! I wasn't drinking it! What is wrong with this fucking system? It's like these laws hurt people a lot more than they help anybody!*

I was pissed, but at least I was only about a two-hour drive away from Whistler, where I knew I had friends I could stay with.

We got into Alex's car and headed toward the border. Now I wasn't sure what to expect, but this time I had no bong, no alcohol, no blankets, no pillows, no kitchen utensils, almost nothing at all. *I will never again tell them that I want to live in Canada. And I will be extra nice!*

Of course, we were all denied entry. The border policeman questioned us individually and made his conclusion that the three boys didn't have sufficient funds to enter Canada, and that I didn't have sufficient "ties to the United States."

Now I was in complete rage over all these bullshit laws, countries, and all their stupid regulations. *Can't I just fucking live on Earth?*

Now what? The boys have to drive back to California. I have court in two weeks. *I have* to go to court. I can't go back to Tahoe, *it takes two to three days to drive there and I can't afford another trip. I don't know anybody in Washington State. I no longer have a car and I don't have enough money for a hotel.*

***I have** to get into Canada.*

I took my snowboard and backpack out of Alex's car and told the boys to leave me there at the border. They drove back to California. I walked to a town called Blaine and found the local library. I used their computer and checked the last message that Emma had sent me. She said they were in Cancun, Mexico. *That was one week ago. Who knows how long they'll stay there... They may have left already.* I had no way to contact them, since these were still the days before smartphones.

I don't need "ties to the United States," I thought. *I need to prove to Canada that I won't live there.*

I looked up flights. *Five hundred dollars from Vancouver to Cancun.* That was nearly half my money. *Fuck it.* I booked a one-way ticket for June 3.

I printed this ticket, took my backpack and snowboard, and walked to the Canadian border. There was no pedestrian sidewalk there, so I walked down the drive-through checkpoint. The border policemen waved me into the station, then questioned and searched me again. I showed them the flight and told them the truth, "I will fly from Vancouver to Mexico on June third. Until then, I have nowhere to stay but Whistler. Please let me in."

A police officer stapled a piece of paper into my passport, saying that if I didn't leave Canada on June 3, there would be a warrant out for my arrest. "You can enter Canada for three weeks only. If you overstay, you will be deported," he said.

"Thank you, I understand." I took my backpack and snowboard, then walked into Canada.

I hitchhiked from the border town to Vancouver and made it to the main bus station right after the last bus to Whistler had left. I slept in the bus station that night with a bunch of homeless people and took the first morning bus. Once I arrived in Whistler, I felt like I was home again. Emma, JB, and Danny were no longer there, but I had many other friends in Whistler and I still had my season pass for the mountain.

I spent the next three weeks staying at friends' houses and snowboarding as much as possible. On May 28, I went back to court for the third time and the judge *finally* dismissed my case.

7

Mexico, 2008

After May 28, I was "free" to go. *Go where?* I wasn't sure. I had about five hundred dollars and a one-way ticket to Mexico. Emma had messaged me saying they were all the way in Guatemala by that time; but she also said that Toby, the young Aussie guy I had replaced in their apartment, was in Cancun. I contacted Toby and he told me to take the flight and then come to an island called Isla Mujeres, just off the coast of Cancun.

I was a little nervous to get on a one-way flight to Mexico with only about five hundred dollars in my bank account, but I was comforted by the thought of my new eight-thousand-dollar credit card.

Once I was in Mexico, I started writing in my diary again:

June 8, 2008

Isla Mujeres, Mexico.

I spent today selling Piña Coladas out of coconut shells on the beach. We bought an old machete, pineapple juice, ice, straws, and a bottle of rum, then chopped down coconuts, made cocktails, and walked around the beach selling them to tourists and rich Mexicans. Made about $30 between me and sexy Aussie Toby.

Life is sweet here, staying in a hostel without paying, living on the land, coconuts and fires, half-naked always.

I've only got about $400 right now (and a credit card) but I think it could last me a little while in Mexico if I continue to sell coconuts.

June 10, 2008

I got kicked out of the POCNA hostel last night/this morning so I'm in this little hostel alone now but I like it... The four of us: Toby, Sam, Sarah, and I are planning on heading to Tulum tomorrow. I am pretty much over this little island now and very excited to move on.

This trip ended up being my first backpacking adventure. Toby and I moved from city to city on public buses, stayed in hostels and crappy hotels, and checked out ancient ruins, beaches, and other interesting sights everywhere we went. While in Mexico, I realized that although my car had been my safety net throughout all of my great adventures, it had also been restricting me quite a lot. Back in the US and Canada, I was willing to drive great distances, but I wouldn't consider flying anywhere because I felt vulnerable without my car. I was afraid of getting stuck somewhere with no place to sleep, or of getting trapped in a dangerous situation that I couldn't get away from. But once I was in Mexico, I realized that avoiding dangerous situations was much easier than I had thought. There were hostels and cheap hotels everywhere, public buses were cheap and abundant, and now, I didn't have to worry about that giant hunk of metal I had been hauling around all these years!

I felt liberated, as if I had been freed from my possessions! I didn't have much stuff in general back then. I had a small backpack, some clothes, a toothbrush, a passport, a credit card, and a flip-phone. That was about it.

June 12, 2008

Tulum was alright. It rained a lot while we were there and the hostel was too expensive for what it was. After 2 or 3 days, Toby and I decided to head straight to Palenque to see the crazy ruins and waterfalls.

Toby's a bit of a nut, crazy in the same way that I am. He's the only guy that can actually make me cum. I fucking love it. We took a 12-hour bus ride from Tulum to Palenque. It was dark and we had blankets around our bodies, so we got a bit frisky. It was really erotic because the bus shook a lot and went over a lot of speed bumps. Hopefully we can take another night bus sometime.

So we were pretty drunk that night on the bus. Hammered, actually. In fact, we were so drunk that I didn't remember arriving in Palenque or finding a hotel room, and when I opened my eyes in the morning, I shrieked because I thought I was in jail. I looked to my right and saw Toby, then I realized that this wasn't a jail cell, it was just a *really* crappy hotel room.

Palenque was amazing. We stayed in the town itself, rather than in the touristy area, and it felt like real Mexico. We ate the best fire-roasted chicken I've ever had, played pool, and just roamed around the town talking to Mexicans. Palenque is located in Chiapas, a poor region with many indigenous people. We took a trip to some stunning waterfalls and noticed tiny little kids selling bananas. We bought one bunch of bananas from a little girl, then over a dozen more little kids came running at us, screaming and crying, "Compra banana! Compra banana!"

We can't buy all the bananas, I thought. *I'm sorry.* These kids must have been four or five years old and they literally had tears in their eyes over selling bananas to tourists. *What a way to spend your childhood...*

Toby and I also took a trip to the Mayan ruins in the jungle near Palenque. This was a powerful sight—a towering ancient city that dates back to 226 BC. *How did they move such enormous stones?* We were both stunned.

Neither Toby or I planned our trip or had much of an objective in mind. We were just two nineteen-year-olds having fun in this Mexican playground. After Palenque, we took buses to San Cristobal, Puerto Escondido, Acapulco, Zihuantanejo, and Mexico City.

August 28, 2008

Almost every time we got to a new city in Mexico, we would walk around for a while looking for a $5/night place to sleep while it was pouring down heavy rain, and one of us would have no shoes. But it always worked out, we always managed to find a shitty $5/night cockroach infested room to sleep in.

The worst $5/night hotel room we stayed in was in Acapulco. The shitty hotel was actually located somewhere outside of Acapulco, in the ghetto. The ceiling leaked when it rained. The bathroom was outside, and it wasn't really a bathroom, it was just a hole in the cement wall with a showerhead sticking out of the top and cockroaches big enough to rape you. The sink was just one of those big plastic buckets that you would normally use for washing your dog or dirty child.

We got a couple of body piercings in Zihuantanejo. Toby got his nipple pierced and I got the side of my stomach. It hurt and eventually my body rejected it by slowly pushing it out of my skin... And now I'm getting this big scar from it.

The piercing place we went to was not very professional. They had old and dull piercing equipment and cheap body jewelry with plastic ends. Toby's experience was the worst—the piercer grabbed Toby's nipple and stuck a dull needle halfway through it, then swirled the needle around the nipple and tried to jam it through the other half. It took a few attempts for him to break the skin on the other side of the nipple. Then the piercer attached a long plastic tube to the needle and slowly wiggled and jammed it through the nipple. The nipple ring followed. Toby said this was the worst pain he had felt in his life.

August 28, 2008

About two or three days later, I started feeling really sick. At first it just hurt to pee, but then one morning I woke up and I started puking and crying from nausea. Toby ran out to find a doctor, then walked me 7 or so blocks to the doctor's office. The doctor was so happy and jittery that it looked like he was on crack. He didn't do any tests on me, didn't take my blood pressure or heart rate. He asked for my symptoms and had a translator tell me that I had a urinary infection. Then he injected a bag of antibiotics into my arm.

After an hour or so of lying there with a needle in my arm and Toby next to me, I felt a lot better. The doctor charged me about $240 and sent me off with vaginal pills for a yeast infection, cream for a yeast infection, and some kind of $20 pills for Toby—saying that Toby gave me the infection. He also gave us this word of advice: no spicy food, no sex, no alcohol, no smoking... Basically no fun.

When Toby took the mysterious pill that the doctor gave him, he immediately got sick and threw up. It was a good thing that he didn't take another one because when I got back to my mom's house in Jersey and saw my regular gynecologist, she told me that it was parasite medication.

Also, I didn't have a yeast infection, so there was no need for the pills or cream that he gave me.

We bought flights to New York soon after we came across those health problems. Since I was nineteen years old, I was still covered under my mother's health insurance and I was able to go to a good doctor in the US. It turned out that I was fine, it really was a urinary infection and it was all better by the time I saw my doctor. But now I had a new problem in my life: *round two of university.*

8

Utah to Australia

All I wanted to do was continue to explore the world and enjoy my life, but I had promised my parents that I would go back to university in September of 2008. This time, I enrolled in the University of Utah, where I knew there were big mountains nearby.

Toby took a bus from New York to Montreal and I flew to Salt Lake City, Utah. Once I got to Utah, I felt ready to let go of Toby and give this university thing a try.

I didn't know what I wanted to study, but I didn't have to choose yet, so I just picked some random classes that I thought were interesting or easy: Biology 101, Environmental Studies 101, Spanish 101, French 101, and Russian 101. I knew Russian fluently and my Spanish was not too bad either, so I took those classes just to get some easy credits.

I moved into a dorm in the main university campus in Salt Lake City. The room was small and plain. There were two single beds, two small desks, and not much else. I shared this room with a girl from Korea who barely spoke a word of English. She seemed nice but I couldn't really communicate with her.

I met some of my dormitory neighbors, but I felt like I couldn't really communicate with them either. I felt weird and out of place, as if I were ten years older than everybody around me. I mean, I *was* one year older than most of my classmates, but these eighteen-year-old kids acted like they were eleven or twelve! They ran around playing tag and hide and go seek, they didn't curse, drink, smoke, talk about sex, or watch rated R movies. They didn't even drink coffee. And they didn't know *anything* about the world!

I kept on hearing them talk about their "missions." Everybody seemed to have been on a "mission" somewhere and this was like the most exciting thing in the world to them. I thought, *Jeez, you guys have all been in the military? That's weird.*

Soon I realized that they were all Mormons and they had all been on "missions" to spread their Mormon religion around the globe. This religion claims that Jesus came to America and that dark skin is a result of the sins of your ancestors. Mormons are not allowed to curse, drink, smoke, have sex, watch rated R movies, drink coffee, or even jerk off. But it turned out they did anything they could to twist their way around all of these rules.

This was a diary entry I wrote in 2011, as I was looking back at my experience in Utah:

I ended up going to the University of Utah because I wanted to snowboard there. I often say that this was the biggest mistake of my life and an enormous waste of my 19th year. But at least I learned something: never live in a small, religious—especially Mormon—city. The snow was the driest and fluffiest snow I have yet felt—the mountains were amazing—definitely some of the best. The people— unbearable. Sheltered. Backstabbing. Just so fake.

Describing these people in further detail would really just make me angry and frustrated (by "these people" I don't mean *everybody* in Salt Lake City or every single Mormon, but the majority of the people I communicated with while studying at the University of Utah—the majority of which were Mormons from Salt Lake City).

Anyway, here is just one situation that I mention to people from time to time: by Mormon rules, Mormons are not allowed to have sex before marriage. So since it is a natural animal urge and force of nature, young adults, who have reached the age of puberty obviously have strong sexual desires. So Mormons figure out ways to get around these rules—for example, they'll drive down to Vegas, get married, fuck for a night, and then get divorced after! Or they'll put the penis into the vagina without moving it so that it "doesn't count" as sex! Or my personal favorite—now I really thought this was one of those ridiculous rumors that could not possibly be true, but apparently it is true! Of course, I am talking about anal sex—so I asked one Mormon kid who went to school in Salt Lake City, "Is it really true that Mormon kids will fuck in the ass to avoid going to hell or whatever it is they believe?" And the kid answers, "Well, some people really take it to the limit"...

TAKE IT TO THE LIMIT?! ...These people actually believe that anal fucking is BEFORE the limit! I mean, I have nothing against anal if that's what people want to do, but it is weird to consider anal sex as some kind of foreplay to regular intercourse. And what the hell kind of "God" is this Mormon perv anyway?!—He'll punish you if you have sex in the vagina! But he's okay with anal :) He also accepts "written permission" from Vegas :D or when you don't move it too much!

Jesus Christ.

Toby called me a couple of weeks after I moved to Utah. He said that he missed me and that flights from Montreal to Salt Lake City were cheap.

"Would you consider moving out of your dorm and renting a room together in Salt Lake City?" he asked. "I have a six-month tourist visa for the US, so I could live with you in Utah until March. And maybe we can go somewhere else together after that, if you want."

I was already sick of the Mormon kids and their childish behavior, so I happily agreed. Toby came to Utah a few days later and we rented a room in an apartment close to my university. The room was cheap and decent but we had to share the apartment with a Mormon guy who I eventually punched in the face.

For work, I found a job as a salesperson. I had to stand in shopping malls, sports stadiums, and other public places, and persuade people to talk to me. Once they started talking to me, I had to persuade them to show up to a hardcore sales presentation where another person would try to sell them a timeshare property. The company I worked for was called Worldmark by Windham and this was the worst job I've had in my life. The job, however, was based on commission so the pay was pretty good if you worked hard.

From time to time, I worked with an extremely religious Mormon salesman who drank Red Bull nonstop. I once asked him why he thought it was okay to drink Red Bull but not coffee, and he replied with, "Well, coffee has so much *bad* stuff in it!"

The truth was that Red Bull simply did not exist back when Joseph Smith was writing the Book of Mormon, so that made it "OK," *kind of like anal sex.*

* * *

I hated the next few months of my life. I hated the University of Utah, I hated the Mormons, and I hated my job. I withstood two semesters in this place before I quit in spring of 2009.

Rules and Roos

I quit my job and the University of Utah, bought a 1989 Toyota Corolla for 420 dollars, and hit the road again. First, Toby and I drove this old little car from Salt Lake City to Las Vegas, LA, San Diego, all around the Grand Canyon, Arches National Park, and back to Salt Lake City. After Toby's US visa expired, he flew to Canada and I drove from Utah to Vancouver alone. The Corolla was in such bad shape by then that it wouldn't go faster than about twenty kilometers an hour uphill and I had to keep the window open to keep myself from dying of carbon monoxide poisoning. Once I made it to Vancouver, I sold this car for the same price I bought it for—*$420.*

At that point, I had paid back the credit card debt I had accumulated in Mexico and I managed to save two or three thousand dollars from working in Utah. Next, Toby and I decided to take a trip to his home country, Australia.

I didn't have a problem getting into Canada this time because I packed lightly and showed the border police my University of Utah student card. For the Canadians, this student card was enough proof that I had "sufficient ties to the United States." Now, however, I had a much greater challenge: getting a tourist visa for Australia. I still didn't have US citizenship back then, so I wasn't allowed to enter Australia without a visa.

I went to a travel agency to minimize my chances of getting denied. I wasted hundreds of dollars on this agency and had to spend several weeks sending them endless amounts of paperwork. Most of the paperwork was documents that proved that I was "tied to the United States." I had to prove that I had US residency, that I was going to university in the US, that I had a car in the US, that my mother had a house and a job in the US, on and on. I also had to prove that I had enough money to travel to Australia, that I didn't have any health problems, that I wasn't a criminal, and so much more. I even had to send them a letter from my mother, stating that she took responsibility for my trip to Australia. I had to do all of this just to get a two-month tourist visa!

This world is so unfair, I thought. *Most people have no idea how unfair it is. It's like a fucking prison—if you don't show the guards the right piece of paper, they won't let you into their territory. It's even more unfair than a prison, actually, because you're assigned a piece of paper the minute you're born. As if you get to choose where you're born!*

I was born in Russia, so I was assigned a "Russian" piece of paper (or "passport" as they call it). Many countries (like Australia) won't let me into their territory with this piece of paper. They say that I need a "visa" too. Another bullshit piece of paper that requires a ton of money, time, and effort to get—and there's no guarantee that you'll ever get it. Even after going through the exasperating process of applying for the visa, the authorities can easily deny you entry, especially if you're poor. But if I had been born in the US or Western Europe, I wouldn't need to go through any of this! Australia and almost every other country would just let me straight into their territory, no questions asked!—All because I was born in the "right" place.

How is this not considered racism? I wondered. *I mean, most countries preach for equality and "human rights," but they see no problem with assigning human beings a piece of paper according to where they were born—and then discriminating against the humans with the "wrong" pieces of paper.*

What a primitive society.

After over a month of paperwork, the Australian government finally approved my tourist visa. Toby and I flew from Vancouver to Brisbane, visited his father and some relatives, then took a bus to the Gold Coast. Both Emma and Danny were living on the Gold Coast at the time, and JB happened to be visiting them, so Toby and I decided to settle there for a few weeks. The five of us couldn't all live together this time, but it was fantastic to see the entire Whistler crew on the opposite side of the planet. Emma, Danny, and JB told us all about their epic road trip to South America. It sounded no less eventful than our adventure in Mexico.

Toby and I spent the next few weeks with our friends on the Gold Coast, then we backpacked up Queensland with JB. We took buses from the Gold Coast to Cairns, making several stops along the way. We snorkeled at the Great Barrier Reef, tried scuba diving for the first time, visited the "whitest beach in the world," and got to pet kangaroos and emus in an animal sanctuary. The trip wasn't too expensive because we cooked all of our own food and often snuck into hostels without paying. The most expensive part was the flight to Australia and the buses that we took up the coast.

At the end of August, Toby and I flew from Cairns to Sydney, and then from Sydney to New York. At this point, I was finally eligible to get US citizenship so I scheduled an appointment for the great "citizenship exam."

9
NYC, 2009

The day after our arrival in New York, I went straight to an official US government office to perform the final US citizenship ritual. I didn't care to be a US citizen per se (or a citizen of Russia or any other tribe for that matter), but I knew that having a US passport would be mighty handy in this world.

Holders of a US passport are allowed to enter 186 countries and territories without a visa; this includes Australia, New Zealand, Europe, Japan, and many other places that citizens of poorer countries aren't allowed to enter without permission. I knew that with a US passport, I wouldn't have to waste all that time and money on visa applications to visit rich countries; all I'd have to do is present my US passport to the border control people—and they'd let me straight in! Like magic. Or like a privileged person in an unequal world.

I accepted this privilege, however wrong it may be. I passed the citizenship exam, passed the English test, repeated some words after a human in a business suit, and I became a US citizen.

But I wasn't free yet. I had promised my parents that I would go to university...

This time, I tried out City College of New York. Toby and I rented an old basement studio apartment on 91st Street and I signed up for college classes on 125th Street. My mother was over the moon about me studying in New York. She had missed me a lot while I was traveling and now she was elated that I would live nearby. "Now we can see each other on weekends and you can join us for all the holidays!" she said as she gave me a long hug.

My mother helped Toby and me move into our new flat and bought us bedsheets, cooking utensils, and other appliances that were missing from the place. She was so happy about our move to New York that she even offered to pay for half our rent! This helped a lot since the cheapest apartment we could find cost 1,500 dollars per month.

After Toby and I moved in, I went up to City College and began round three of university.

Soon I began dreading all of this. *This is almost worse than the University of Utah,* I thought. Everyone in this college was so ghetto and the classes were easier than the ones I took in high school.

I took one "music appreciation" course where we learned to appreciate classical music and operas. In one section of the exams, all we had to do was listen to a song and write down the title and composer of that song. For the essays, I reworded Wikipedia pages and got an A+ every time. I also took algebra, history, English, and other high-school-style classes that were boring as hell.

For work, I found a job in a comedy club in the West Village. I was one of those annoying people who passed out flyers on the street. I was paid ten dollars an hour plus one dollar extra for every person who entered the club with my flyer. Every once in a while, I'd walk away with over a hundred dollars in a night.

I probably should have quit in order to find a better paying job, but I had a lot of fun working in that comedy club. It was a small club with a lot of interesting people, and every comedian was so passionate. None of the comedians came to the club to make money, they just *loved* making people laugh, and they worked so hard on their acts. I realized then, that stand-up comedy was a true art.

Chili lived in New York at the time and worked in a restaurant in the East Village, so we would meet up frequently. She was doing pretty good those days, working hard, studying hard, and staying away from all the crap we were exposed to in high school. I think she always had it rough though, having to basically grow up without parents. Overtime, this made her a very strong and independent person, but it definitely wasn't easy.

Toby and I enjoyed living in Manhattan but I couldn't stand City College so I quit after one semester. This time, however, I had good news for my mother: "Don't worry, mom," I told her. "I quit City College but I applied somewhere else! At the University of Sydney —it's the 'Harvard' of Australia. It will be much better than City College of New York!" This was actually Toby's mother's idea. She tried to get me into Sydney University because she lived in Sydney and wanted Toby to come back home.

"Toby's mom sorted through the classes I took at the University of Utah and City College and she found a degree that's compatible with what I've already studied," I said. "It's called International and Global Studies. It's supposed to be a great program and Sydney University ranks as one of the best universities in Australia." My mom cared about that kind of stuff. "Maybe even one of the best in the world!" I hyped it up a notch. "If I get in, I'll be able to transfer the credits I got from my previous studies to Sydney University, so they won't be completely wasted."

My mother was a bit disappointed that I wanted to leave New York so quickly, but she loved the idea of me going to a "high ranking" institution, so she was happy about this decision. "All right," she said, "but you have to promise not to quit this time!"

I smiled, patted her on the head, and gave her a big hug.

The Trap

Before I left New York, I met up with Chili and told her about my new plan. "I quit City College," I said. "I can't stand it." We were sitting at a cheap sushi joint near West 4th Street. It was a small place with hard plastic furniture and colorless walls, but they served warm sake and accepted my fake ID. "I applied to Sydney University instead, so I'll move to Australia if I get in."

"Hah!" Chili grinned. "I could've guessed you wouldn't stay around here too long! Okay girl, you do you. Maybe I'll come visit you one day." She picked up the warm porcelain bottle and poured the sake into our little cups.

"That'd be great!" I gestured a "cheers."

"Can I ask you a question though?" said Chili. "How are you paying for all of this? Isn't Sydney University gonna be really expensive?"

I took a sip of sake. "Yeah it's expensive, but Sydney Uni is actually a lot cheaper than most colleges in the US, especially the ones that "rank" on the same level. But there is no way in hell that I would pay for university no matter how cheap it was! I don't want to study in these bullshit institutions in the first place. I'm being forced to do this."

"So your mom's paying the fees?"

"Well originally, my dad planned to. Back when he had a lot of money, he bought a big house for us to live in. The idea was that my mom, my brother, and I would live in that house until my brother and I finished high school. Then, since my mom didn't need such a big house to herself, she was meant to sell it, buy a smaller place, and use the difference to pay for our college tuition. That was my dad's thinking. All of that didn't work out exactly as planned, but my mom is still so insistent about us going to these bullshit universities. Now she's happy to pay for it even if it gets her into debt."

"Wow your mom's so nice," said Chili. "Damn, you should be grateful that your parents wanna pay for your studies. I wish my parents did that."

"But why? Think about it, what's the point of all this? What's the point of studying in a university?—It's to prepare you for a career! I don't want a fucking career. I just want my parents to leave me alone and let me live my life like I want to.

"I don't *ever* want to be a zombie business person or a slave. I don't want to live like my mom, working nonstop, constantly stressing out, and only having two or three weeks of "vacation" time per year. I just want to travel around the world and enjoy my life. I don't need much money or a "career" to do that, so I don't need a university degree. But my parents won't accept that! They *need* me to go to college. They want me to study "who knows what"—any bullshit—just for the sake of getting a fucking diploma. *Another stupid piece of paper.*

"That's like the most important thing in the world for them so if they want to pay for it, then I'll go through with it. I'll sacrifice three or four years of my life for them but there is no way in hell that I would get into debt and ruin my *entire* life over their demands." I finished off the sake and stared into the white wall. It came to me then, that all of this was a great big trap.

You grow up with this idea that there's no option but to build a career in order to have a good life on Earth, so you get out of high school, confused as hell because you have very little information about the world—no one ever teaches you about money or about how this whole system works—and you're immediately thrown into university because you're already convinced that this is what you *have* to do. You go through the four years or so and prepare yourself for a career, then (in the US) you leave university with TONS OF DEBT, so you're already trapped in the system! Now, because of your debt, you HAVE TO participate in the system. You have to build that career and make that money so you can pay off your debt and then finally be able to afford a house and a good life, if you're lucky. But most likely, you'll be in debt for a long time, maybe for the rest of your life, once you get a mortgage for that house and start popping out children.

NO THANK YOU! I'D RATHER SNOWBOARD!

As you can probably tell, I was a little bit angry back then. I always got along well with Chili, but sometimes I'd get drunk and have horrible fights with Toby. I'm not sure why he continued to put up with me. Maybe it was just for the sex.

10

Europe, 2010

I finished that semester of City College with a 4.0 GPA, packed up all my stuff, and booked a flight to Europe with my new American passport. Round four of university wasn't meant to start until August, since it was in the Southern Hemisphere, so I had about seven months of freedom ahead of me.

Toby wanted to learn French at that time and I just wanted to snowboard, so we made a compromise: "Let's go to the French-speaking Alps!" That meant either France or Switzerland. I didn't have much money after living in New York and I knew that both of those places would be expensive, but we couldn't think of a better place to go. We *had* to leave the US by January because Toby's US visa was expiring.

I'll just find a job or something, I thought. *And worse comes to worst, I still have that eight-thousand-dollar credit card!* I was relieved that I wouldn't need to apply for a visa this time. Traveling with a US passport seemed so easy—all I had to do was book a ticket, get on a plane, and present my US passport to the airline and border control people. *No visas, no hassle!*

The cheapest flight Toby and I could find was to the Netherlands, so we decided to go on a little backpacking adventure on our way to the Alps. We flew to Amsterdam in January, passed through border control without a problem, then made our way to the city center. We decided to spend a few nights eating space cake and

111

exploring the squares and canals of Amsterdam before heading south.

We booked into the cheapest hostel we could find, which cost thirteen euros per night. It was old, dirty, cockroach infested, and stuffed with people. Toby paid for one bed in a twelve-person dorm, then snuck me into the hostel without paying for a second one. *We'll share a bed anyway,* we thought, *so why pay for two beds?*

After eating our first space cake, Toby and I walked around the city, checking out the canals, hookers, and pretty old buildings. After over an hour, we still didn't feel anything from the space cake so we assumed we were ripped off and nothing was going to happen.

We went back to our hostel and I started to feel a buzz as soon as we entered the room. Then, all of a sudden, I quickly felt myself getting higher and higher as the people around me started talking to me. Well, one guy wasn't actually talking, he was miming! He kept his mouth closed and mimed information about the other people in our dorm.

'This guy's feet stink!' He waved his hands around and dramatically pinched his nose with two fingers. 'This guy snores!' He mimed a sound coming out of the guy's mouth. 'This guy's hot!' and so on. This strange person was not using sign language, he was literally miming.

I wasn't sure how to respond. *Do I mime back? Do I speak? He could be deaf, maybe. I don't even know what language he understands—I'm in Europe!* I nodded and smiled as he put on makeup and a dress.

Later on, Toby and I met up with some Dutch friends who took us to a few bars and a place where you can get food from a wall. It was kind of like a vending machine but with warm burgers and fries. Toby and I also visited the Heineken factory and saw a live sex show. It was basically two people having sex in a circular room surrounded by booths where people pay money to peek through little holes. Apparently, we had just missed the orgy.

* * *

While Toby and I were in Amsterdam, I started to get some kind of bumps on my body. They looked like insect bites at first, but then swelled up like a poison ivy rash. We thought that this had to have been an allergic reaction to something because Toby and I were sleeping in the same bed and he didn't have a single bump on his body. I dismissed the idea of bedbugs and continued to sleep in the same place.

After a few days, the bumps grew exponentially both in size and number. I started thinking about bedbugs in the middle of the night. *Maybe they're not biting Toby for some reason, or maybe he just doesn't get a reaction to them.* I tightly covered my entire body in blankets and had terrible nightmares about being attacked by bedbugs. In the morning, my face was covered in huge sores.

"They went for my fucking face!" I screamed out.

I used the internet to look up information. *Yep, my skin looks just like that!* One website said to look for small shells and bloodstains on the sheets. *Found them!* Then look for the bedbugs themselves hiding in corners of the mattress and fabric indents of curtains. *Found them! Fuckers!* There were so many of them! *Fuck!*

We immediately packed our stuff, informed the hostel staff, and left. We had already booked bus tickets to Switzerland—we were meant to take an overnight bus to Paris, spend one day there, and then take another overnight bus to Zurich. That was our way of saving money—sleep on buses and don't pay for accommodation.

It rained in Paris so we spent almost the entire day walking around the Louvre in agony from the bedbug bites and the shitty situation. We could only deal with the problem once we got to Zurich. We learned that bedbugs die from heat, so we had to put everything we owned through a dryer.

Once we made it to Zurich, we put all of our clothes directly into a high heat washing machine and then a dryer. Then we carefully examined every single item that we couldn't put under high heat: electronics, books, toiletries, everything. Luckily, bedbugs are not microscopic, so you can spot them if you look carefully. We found and killed three or four of them. If there was any item we were uncertain about, we threw it away. We carefully inspected every little corner and crevice of our backpacks, then bought a special bug spray and sprayed them down in a park. We spent the entire day and over thirty Swiss francs on this process, but at the end, we were bedbug free.

The Swiss Alps

Switzerland was extremely expensive and I only had about five hundred dollars left when we got there. Toby had about twenty thousand dollars that he had gotten as inheritance from his grandmother; he had been using this money to trade Forex while we were together. Toby didn't earn much through trading, but it was enough to hold him over and not dip below the twenty grand. We kept our money separate through our entire relationship though, so this didn't matter to me.

Toby and I found only one hostel in the entire French-speaking Alps. It was called Chalet Martin and was located in a small town called Gryon, Switzerland. We arrived by tram and met a big group of friendly people from all over the world. There were people from Australia, New Zealand, the US, Canada, Ireland, and many other parts of Europe. The hostel itself looked nice, it was a wooden chalet with a big kitchen, two cozy living rooms, a movie room, and a pool table. It was located right across a ski lift and there were beds available for about five hundred dollars per month.

"I don't think we'll find anything cheaper than this in the Swiss Alps!" I said while handing over my last five hundred dollars to the hostel.

Toby and I decided to stay in Chalet Martin for the rest of the winter. I bought a season pass for the mountain on my credit card, borrowed an old snowboard from somebody at the hostel, and got to go snowboarding every day. Luckily, I also managed to find a job pretty quickly.

One night, a local woman came by the hostel and asked if anybody wanted to work for her babysitting company. "I need a babysitter for tonight, from eight p.m. to two a.m.," she said. "We pay twenty-five francs an hour."

Twenty-five Swiss francs an hour for babysitting? I thought. *That's about the same as twenty-five US dollars an hour!* I immediately volunteered and she hired me for random last-minute babysitting jobs from then on. She didn't ask for any working papers, documents, or anything. She paid cash and didn't even care that I didn't speak French or German.

Considering the amount of money I was paid, this was one of the best jobs I've ever had. Of course, sometimes I had to deal with horrible whiny children, sometimes I had to change diapers, which was absolutely disgusting, but oftentimes, I would babysit at night, when the kids were asleep and I had to do nothing at all.

One night, I showed up to babysit for a group of people who wanted to go out after their house party. The kids were already upstairs and asleep. The party was over and there was a huge amount of fancy food, Swiss cheese, nice wine, and champagne left over. The parents were very nice, they gave me the TV remote and told me to help myself to anything in the kitchen. So I was paid twenty-five francs an hour to watch TV, eat crab cakes, and drink champagne. *Not too bad!*

I didn't work a lot that winter but I didn't really need to. I needed twenty hours of work per month to pay for rent and perhaps another fifteen or so hours to pay for a month's worth of food. That's about thirty-five hours of work per month for food and rent. I let my credit card debt linger for a little bit and I didn't have any other expenses.

Food was pricey in Switzerland, but just like anywhere in the world, you were still able to buy a bag of rice, beans, and some vegetables for a reasonable price. That's the kind of stuff I've always lived off and I never needed much else. Delicious Swiss cheese and chocolate was also surprisingly cheap in the little town we lived in, so that was a nice addition. And so was beer and wine, believe it or not, though that was not always a nice addition.

Remember that anger I mentioned before? It came out in a rage whenever I had too much to drink.

On my twenty-first birthday in Switzerland, my new friends and I played King's Cup with shots of Jaeger and then I punched a tall Canadian guy in the face and gave him a bloody nose. Then I screamed at Toby, even though he did nothing wrong, and I punched a door, even though it did nothing wrong. The only person who was able to calm me down that night was Chris, a tall and handsome Australian snowboarder who I had a huge crush on.

Needless to say, this "crush" was a big problem since I was already in a relationship with Toby. Toby was such a nice and easy-going guy, he was not only my boyfriend at the time, but also my best friend. We had gone through so much together. But at the same time, I never really felt like I was in love with him and I never really wanted to be in a romantic relationship with him for so long. I cared about him a lot and we had a lot of fun together, especially while traveling, but I felt like that was all it was—just fun.

I had already fallen in love once in the past (with Dan Freisure) so I knew what I was missing. I was missing that state of mental insanity, when you're in complete euphoria in the presence of your loved one. All you care about is that person and you long to be with them whenever they're away. Your mind goes crazy over this, but it's the most incredible feeling in the world when you're together. Sex is out of this world, you feel really and truly alive, and everything feels absolutely perfect, or irrelevant, as long as you're together.

I don't think this feeling ever lasts forever and I don't think there is only *one* person you can fall in love with, but I do think it'd be a shame to live your entire life and never experience such a state of mind. So I never imagined that I would prevent myself from ever being able to experience this feeling again just for the sake of staying with Toby. But at the same time, I couldn't break up with him! He was my best friend. *How could I hurt him?* He was so nice and he never wanted to argue or even disagree with me no matter how crazy I got.

So instead of leaving him, I would get drunk and crazy and pick fights with him. The next morning, we would have make-up sex, go snowboarding, and everything would be all right again. That is, until we had one too many après-ski drinks and I would go over the edge again.

I started to question whether I had a drinking problem or some other psychological problem back then. I did, of course, but I couldn't quite pin-point it just yet.

Euro-Trouble

Toby and I left Switzerland in spring, once the snowboarding season was over. We bought a two-month train pass for all of Europe and decided to just go backpacking.

"How much money do you have saved up now from babysitting?" Toby asked me as we were packing our backpacks.

"About a thousand francs." I pulled out my big stack of cash. "That's like seven hundred euros. I think it'll be enough for two months if we sleep on the train as much as possible."

"Yeah and let's avoid expensive hostels. I think we need to get out of Switzerland ASAP and go somewhere cheaper and warmer," said Toby.

"Wanna go to Spain?"

"Um, okay!"

We took a tram from Gryon to Geneva and then tried to get onto the next long-distance train to Spain. France, however, was in the way and the French train employees happened to be on strike that week. We made a last-minute decision to go to Italy instead, but the next train to Italy wasn't until about 5:00 a.m.

"Shit, so we're stuck in Geneva?" I said as we scanned the timetable.

"Unless you wanna go to Germany instead," said Toby.

"No, I don't think that's a good idea. Germany's gonna be expensive too. Let's just take that five a.m. train to Milan and then go south from there."

"Okay. But what are we gonna do until five? The cheapest hostel in Geneva is like forty francs a bed."

"Forty francs? So eighty francs for the two of us?—Just to sleep in a dorm bed for a few hours. That's insane. What if we just stay up and walk around the city until five? We can sleep in the train in the morning," I said.

"Yeah okay, we can do that. Just be careful with all that cash," said Toby. "I'm sure Geneva's safe but who knows, it still sounds like a bad idea to walk around all night with a thousand francs of cash in your handbag."

"I'll stash it in my socks!" I grinned.

I put some cash in one sock, some in another, some in my pants pockets. Then I put one of my passports into one jacket pocket, the other passport into another one, my train pass into a third, and my little camera into a fourth. I kept an empty wallet and an old sweater in my handbag.

"If someone tries to rob us, I'll just give them this handbag and run away!" I said to Toby.

"Let's just try not to get robbed, okay," he replied.

Toby and I wandered around the city until we were too tired to walk. We were too broke to get a drink or even a small bite to eat in Geneva, so we strayed away from the bars and late night cafés. We tried to sneak into some hostels, but had no luck. After several hours of walking, we were cold and absolutely exhausted.

"I don't think I can walk any longer," I said. "I just want to lie down and sleep, even for an hour or two. I'm so tired." I leaned my backpack against a building and looked around. We were on a quiet street filled with back-to-back parallel-parked cars. *All of these people must be at home and asleep,* I thought. *Lucky them.* In front of me was an old Honda Civic. *Just like the one I used to have.* I glanced down at the vehicle. *What if...* I gently touched the handle of this old car and quietly pulled it toward me.

It opened!

Toby looked at me wide-eyed, then chuckled. "Okay let's get in quickly!" he said. "Before anybody sees us!" We stuffed our backpacks and bodies into the back seat of this random car and slept in it until about 4:00 a.m. We locked the car doors, thinking how funny (and uncomfortable) it would be if the car's owner showed up to find us there. *Would he or she be scared? Or angry? Maybe both... Let's just hope they don't call the cops!*

Luckily, we left before anybody noticed us sleeping in this car. At 5:00 a.m., we caught the train to Italy.

Toby and I slept in the train for several hours, then got off in Milan. We explored the city center and were reassured that we were now safe. Milan looked so clean and rich that it felt like nothing bad could ever happen there or anywhere else in Italy, for that matter. I took all of my bundles of cash, my two passports, camera, wallet, train pass, and everything else that I had stashed in different pockets, and put it all back into my small handbag.

Toby and I didn't have a plan or objective for Italy, and since we made a last-minute decision to go there, we didn't get to look up any information about where we were heading. We randomly decided to go to Naples next, just because there was another overnight train between Milan and Naples.

I felt safe on the train to Naples and was not too worried about my handbag with the thousand Swiss francs and all of my valuables. Little did I know, Naples was known to be the capital of thievery, and when I woke up in the morning, my handbag was nowhere to be found.

"Um, Toby, where's my bag? Have you seen it?" I searched around the cabin.

"No... Did you look under the seat? Or behind your jacket? Or maybe in your big bag?"

"Yeah I looked everywhere. Where the fuck can it be?" I searched frantically and then realized what had happened—I fell asleep with it on my lap, and somebody came into the cabin and stole it.

"Shit!" I felt so dumb. "How could I put all that stuff back into my handbag? I *just* had it hidden! *Fuck!*"

I felt like a bomb had just dropped on me. "One thousand Swiss francs! I wasted so much time earning that fucking money! *Both* of my passports! My camera! My wallet! My driver's license! Bank cards! Train pass! Cell phone! Everything!" All of my valuables were gone! *Stolen!* I had nothing else, just some old clothes in my big backpack. Every single thing that was worth anything was in that little handbag and now it was gone. Every single thing, except... *My lucky credit card!* That was in my pocket!

I felt a bit of relief. I was still upset, mostly at myself, but I looked at Toby and I looked at myself, and I realized that we were both just fine. Nobody had hurt us, we were both healthy, and we were exploring the world. *Shit happens.* After a few big breaths and a bit of time, I felt much better.

"I'm fine, Toby!" I said as we walked around Naples looking for a hostel. "We're fine! That stuff was just money, documents, and "stuff." I don't really need any of that crap anyway! *Fuck it!*"

I felt a huge feeling of relief and freedom when I realized that nobody could rob me again because I had nothing. I was free from "things" and from the idea that my life would collapse without those "things." We even went out for beers that night and celebrated. *Lucky I still had that credit card...*

We booked into the cheapest hostel we could find, which cost about five euros per night, then I filed a police report and applied for a new passport at the US embassy. This was surprisingly easy to do, but the embassy said that the passport would take about one month.

Hmm... One month in Italy... Zero dollars in my bank account... What to do?

Naples, Italy

Luckily, Toby and I knew one nice guy who lived close to Naples. He had stayed at Chalet Martin just one week before we left Switzerland. The guy's name was Romelo, his family was Mexican but he grew up in Texas and was serving in the US military in Naples.

We called him up and told him what happened.

"Oh damn guys!" he replied. "Didn't you know that Naples is world-famous for purse snatching?"

"Well, we know now," I said, laughing.

"You guys can stay with me while you sort your stuff out. I have two free rooms in my place. Usually my dogs sleep there, but I'll kick them out for ya."

It turned out that Romelo lived in a fancy three-bedroom, two-story house right on the outskirts of Naples. He was such a nice guy that he let us stay at his house for the entire month I was waiting for my replacement passport.

Romelo lived by himself and spent most of his days at work, so Toby and I spent most of our time roaming around the neighborhood and cooking meals. At night, we went out with Romelo, his military buddies, and their Italian girlfriends.

One girl we met in Naples was particularly memorable to me. She had fake tits the size of bowling balls, a fake ass, liposuction in various places, puffed up lips, and god knows how many other plastic surgeries. The only thing she ever talked about was her body and how to "improve" it even more, and she was extremely insecure even though she was praised by every man she ever walked by.

I once had to spend an entire day with this woman and she literally spent the *whole* day repeatedly asking me whether I liked her tits and ass.

"You like my tits?" she asked.

"Yes, yes, they're nice tits," I replied. *What the fuck else am I gonna say?—No, they look like bowling bowls!*

"You like my ass?"

"Yes, yes, nice ass," I replied.

"You like my legs?"

"Yes, nice legs."

"You like my tits?!"

Is she fucking mad? Maybe she is actually mentally insane. How many times can you repeat the same stupid question?

"Maybe I should make them even bigger!"

There is literally nothing else in her head, is there?

Then she asked me, "Why don't *you* get a boob job?"

Well, let's see, since I live and travel around the world with little money, I have to make sure that I keep my priorities straight. I don't consider big boobs to be a priority because I can't eat them, ride them, or live in them. I also don't feel the need to try to impress anyone. If someone likes me for who I am, that's great. If they don't like me, that's fine as well. Out of the seven billion people in the world, somebody's gotta like me no matter how small my tits are.

Besides, if someone liked me just for my gigantic knockers, that wouldn't mean anything to me. That kind of attraction wears away quickly and what you're left with is your fake personality and your little brain. So if I were to invest into anything that would attract people, I'd rather invest into the stuff that's long lasting— my brain. Read a book, for fuck's sake, learn a musical instrument, do something meaningful.

I probably didn't say all of that to her. I probably just said I don't want a boob job, that's all.

11

Turkey, 2010

Once I received my new passport, Toby and I were ready to continue our adventure. The only problem was that I had no more money left and I couldn't afford to buy another long-distance train pass. Since I was now digging myself into debt and we knew that we had to be in Sydney in August, Toby and I decided to make our way toward Australia. The cheapest Australia-bound flights we could find were out of Istanbul, Turkey, so we decided to go there next.

"I still have my train pass," said Toby, "so I can take the train through Eastern Europe and meet you in Istanbul. There's no point of wasting money on a flight when I can still use my pass."

Oh right, your pass wasn't stolen. "Okay well I would take the train too if it was cheaper, but it's like three times the price of a flight. Isn't that weird?" I said. "Let's go to Rome and I'll fly from there, then I can just meet you at a hostel or something in Istanbul."

We took a tram from Naples to Rome, visited the Colosseum and the old ruins in the city center, went to the Vatican for one day, then I flew to Istanbul. Toby took a forty-hour train from Rome to Turkey.

Once I got to Istanbul, I found the cheapest hostel in the city. It was dirty and cockroach infested, but it only cost about four dollars per night. I knew to check for bedbugs this time, so at least it was clear of those. The hostel provided clean sheets, but the kitchen and bathrooms were absolutely disgusting and the living area was dusty as hell. All the rooms in the hostel were covered with stacks of thin straw carpets and it seemed like nobody had ever swept or vacuumed the place.

"Maybe instead of vacuuming, they just top up the rooms with a new straw carpet every once in a while," I joked with my new hostel roommates.

Toby arrived after a couple of days. We spent some time together in Istanbul, strolling by the Golden Horn waterway and eating delicious fresh fish kebabs by the old bridge. We visited some big mosques and churches, the Grand Bazaar, and the impressive Basilica Cistern. We basically had no money so we weren't planning on buying anything, but we walked around some old shops just out of curiosity. Soon, we realized that Istanbul was no place for window shopping. The salespeople in these little shops were so hardcore that we couldn't go near a store without being nagged about buying random crap. They tried so hard to sell us stuff that it actually upset me at one point.

"This old man literally looks like he's about to cry," I said to Toby as we walked out of a shop empty handed. The man was frail-looking, with hollow cheeks and deep wrinkled lines on his face, his eyes just barely alive with the hope that we would buy a souvenir. *What a sad way to live,* I thought as I glanced back at the old man. *To be forced into selling shit all your life. To cry over not being able to sell some stupid souvenirs—because if you don't sell this useless shit, you might not be able to feed yourself or your family.*

Some people in this world really have it hard. They can't just play the job game like me, they were already born with a losing hand.

Toby and I went back to the dusty hostel and talked to a few travelers. One guy showed us photos of a fascinating place called Cappadocia.

"It's a UNESCO World Heritage Site," he said. "You guys gotta check it out!"

"Wow! Is that real?" I asked, eyeballing the photo. "I've never seen rocks like that! They look like gnome homes, or giant penises. Wow and look at that little window! Toby, we gotta check this out!"

Toby and I were so intrigued by this guy's photos and explanation of Cappadocia that we decided to take an overnight bus to the middle of Turkey to see this place. Luckily, public buses in Turkey were relatively cheap. Once we got to Cappadocia, we booked into the cheapest hostel we could find and bought a disposable camera. The next day, we rented a scooter and went exploring.

We drove the scooter up some dusty streets and to the top of a deep canyon filled with the strangest rock formations I had ever seen. "This place is surreal," I said as we gazed into the canyon. Some rock formations looked like pillars, some like giant mushrooms, others looked as if they came straight out of a fairytale. Dry sandy wind whisked gently across my face as I recalled what I had learned about this place.

Cappadocia stands on a high plateau amid several volcanic peaks. The unique rock features on the plateau were formed from volcanic ash that had coated the region millions of years ago. This ash was compressed and eventually formed into soft, malleable rock called "tuff." With time, the tuff was eroded by wind and water, leaving harder rock in the form of domes, pillars, and penises up to forty meters high. The famous mushroom-shaped caps in Cappadocia are a result of a tougher layer of basalt that formed over the tuff. Since basalt erodes slower than tuff, unique shapes were formed through weathering.

The best part, however, was that there were little doors and windows carved into these giant penises! *During the Roman period, prosecuted Christians fled to Cappadocia and soon realized that these unique domes and pillars were very malleable. They built homes, churches, stables, and storehouses by carving into the rock. Underground cities were also carved out and used as hideouts for up to twenty thousand people!* Toby and I were only able to see the first five levels of one underground city, but there are many underground cities in the region and some are over ten stories deep.

We drove to the Love Valley, Fairy Valley, Pigeon Valley, Rose Valley, Urgup, and many other incredible places. Since we could only afford to rent a scooter for one day, we tried to make the best of it. We explored many fascinating rock formations and walked deep into some of the most spectacular canyons we had ever seen. At the end of the day, we watched the sunset over the dimly lit gnome homes of a town called Goreme.

"This place is just precious," I said as I scanned the valley in the fading light.

"And so are you," Toby smiled, grabbed my waist, and kissed me.

* * *

After a few more days of exploring Cappadocia on foot, Toby and I decided to move on. We went to Antalya, in the south of Turkey, then took a long bus ride through a tropical forest, down a mountain, and into a narrow rock-faced valley that met the sea and the ancient ruins of Olympus. This was a truly awesome sight. It looked as if the rocky mountain had been sliced open to create this narrow valley. Towering rock walls and dozens of wooden tree houses stood on either side of the path to the ancient city. Most of the accommodation in Olympus was in tree houses and most of the visitors we met were rock climbers.

I would have loved to give these walls a go myself, but I wasn't a climber back then and I had negative money so it didn't work out. Toby and I didn't have enough money to stay in a tree house either, so we camped in the forest. We took a public bus back to Istanbul the next day, then finally flew out to Sydney.

12
Sydney, 2010

Toby and I arrived in Sydney around June. We stayed with Toby's family for a few days, then moved into the cheapest apartment we could find. The apartment was cold, cockroach infested, and located in North Sydney, the business district of the city. It was "cheap" for Sydney, but extremely expensive for my budget. I realized then, that it was a mistake to go to Australia so early. Sydney was insanely expensive and I still hadn't gotten my student visa so I didn't have legal working rights in Australia; plus, I still had about two months left before I needed to start university.

It was too late to turn back now, so I found a cash job in a café across the street from our apartment. The café was run by a Chinese man and the job absolutely sucked, but I was paid about fifteen dollars an hour just for cleaning tables. Fifteen dollars an hour is less than minimum wage in Australia but it was enough to hold me over and pay back some of my credit card debt.

After several weeks in Sydney, the Australian government finally issued me a student visa to study at Sydney University. This visa also gave me the right to work in Australia, so I quit my "illegal" Chinese café job.

"Fuck cleaning tables for less than minimum wage," I said to Toby. "I'm gonna find a job as a bartender."

"But you've never bartended before," he replied. "Don't you need to take a course or something? Or have some experience?"

"I'll just lie on my resume. How hard can it be, really?"

I made a good-looking resume filled with lies about bartending courses and experiences, then applied at different bars all over the city. The first offer I got was a trial in a big bar in King's Cross.

I showed up dressed up and ready for work. Once I got behind the bar, I felt a bit less confident.

There was a very serious-looking manager and a lot of different bottles of alcohol. "Here we have the house spirits," the manager explained. "Gin, whiskey, bourbon, vodka, rum, and tequila."

Okay, I know all of those, I thought.

"Here's our top-shelf liquor: Grey Goose, Bombay, Patron, Gentleman Jack."

Yes, I've seen most of these.

"Here we have the Campari, Midori, Vermouth, Cointreau, Chambord, things like that. Here's the wine. Are you familiar with wine?"

"Yes." I lied.

"And our beer—we have twenty beers on tap. You know how to pour beer, right?"

"Yes." I lied again.

"Okay, you can serve this gentleman," he said as a little old man approached the bar.

"Yes, sure," I stuttered. "How can I help you, sir?" I asked the man.

"G'day! Can I have a Forex please?"

"Sure," I said, trying to figure out what type of alcohol I was supposed to look for. I scanned over a few bottles and didn't find anything with the word "Forex." Eventually, the manager signaled to a beer tap with the letters XXXX. *Ah! Four-X—got it!*

"Right," I said. *Hmm, let's see how this thing works.* I grabbed the beer tap handle and slowly pulled it toward me. A lot of foam came out. *Oh shit.* I tried not to panic as foam inundated the beer glass. *Just keep it cool.* Foam was everywhere! *Where the hell is the beer?*

I turned off the tap, then tried to hand the glass of foam to the customer, but the manager snatched it from my hand and re-poured the beer.

"Six dollars and twenty cents, please," he said to the man.

Once the little man walked away, the manager taught me how to work the beer tap. "For most Australian beers, you do two pours," he said. "Pull the tap all the way until the glass is about half full. Then you let it settle and you pour again. You always wanna get at least a couple of centimeters of head on the beer, but not too much."

I poured a few more beers and got the hang of it.

Then another customer came by and asked for a "Bundy and Coke."

I looked around the bar. *I understand the "Coke" part but what the hell is a Bundy?* I couldn't find anything with the word "Bundy" on it. Eventually the manager pointed to a bottle of rum.

"Bundaberg rum!" he said. "Australia's best."

I sloppily poured the rum into a large glass and reached for the coke.

"No, no, stop!" said the manager. "You have to measure the liquor! You can't just pour rum or any other spirit into a glass like that. And you poured way too much! Look, pour it into a shot glass first, then into a rocks glass. Use this rocks glass unless the customer asks for a tall or a double."

Oh fuck. I wonder if he's figured out that this is my first time behind a bar. I followed his directions and continued to make amateur mistakes all night. Fortunately, he was there to correct and teach me. That night, I learned all about pouring beer and mixing drinks. I learned how to make some cocktails and some popular shots. I learned about all kinds of liqueurs and mocktails. I learned some bartender lingo, the names of the different glasses used in New South Wales, and a few other relatively important bar terms.

I spent about ten hours behind the bar that night. I didn't get paid and I wasn't offered a job after this trial, but I realized that this was a great experience for me regardless.

"I told you I didn't need to waste money on a course!" I said to Toby. "This was way better than any bartending course I could've taken—and it was free!"

I felt confident about lying to the next bar. Next, I applied at a pub called Three Wise Monkeys, in the city center. It looked like a cool place. It had a big bar, some nice rustic furniture, and some friendly-looking bartenders. By chance, I walked in about an hour after somebody had quit their bartending position. I spoke to the manager, got a trial that night, and passed like a pro.

From that day on, Three Wise Monkeys became my second Sydney home. I really enjoyed working there at first. It was fun and easy. The bar had a pub, a cocktail bar, and a nightclub. I only worked in the pub and nightclub at first, so I didn't even have to make cocktails. I poured pints and schooners of beer, mixed simple drinks, and served shots. *Easy.*

About half of the Three Wise Monkeys staff were from Nepal and they were the nicest people I had ever worked with. In fact, everyone who worked in this pub was kind and friendly to each other, and there were no "cliques" or drama of any sort, even though there was a lot of staff.

The pay was great too. I was paid twenty-three dollars an hour from Monday to Friday, twenty-six dollars an hour on Saturdays, thirty on Sundays, and about fifty dollars an hour on holidays! Plus a little bit extra in tips and free food during the shift. The only thing that sucked about this job was the horrible pop music in the nightclub, the dumb customers, and the late hours. Sometimes I would start work at 10:00 p.m. and finish around 5:00 a.m. This screwed up my sleeping schedule and made it difficult to attend university.

Oh yeah, speaking of university, that was the reason I came to Sydney in the first place, wasn't it...

The University of Sydney was extremely challenging. Since I had transferred some credits from my previous studies, I was considered to be a second-year student from the get-go. I also started attending classes at the start of the second semester, rather than the first semester of the year. This made it extra difficult because all of my classmates already knew what they were doing and I was clueless since the University of Utah and City College of New York had basically taught me nothing. Not to mention that all of these Sydney Uni students were geniuses! I had basically snuck my way into this institution, while every Australian student at the University of Sydney was at the top of academia and had worked very hard to get there.

My core subject was called International and Global Studies. I didn't really know what it was meant to be about since Toby's mother had chosen this degree for me. On the first day of class, the lecturer introduced the title of the course.

"International and global," she said. "What does that mean?"

"In simple terms," she continued, "*international* refers to the activity that goes across national borders, while *global* refers to a holistic outlook of our entire planet and civilization."

OK this is important, I thought.

I realized that this "International and Global Studies" course was different from the stuff I was studying before. It was challenging, but it wasn't *just bullshit* like most of my previous courses. It wasn't really aimed at a particular career either. A few of my classmates wanted to work for the United Nations, but that seemed more like a dream rather than a definite career plan that they were preparing for.

On top of the core International and Global Studies course, I also had to choose a "major." Somehow, I ended up with two random majors: Spanish and international business. I suppose those majors aligned with the courses I had taken previously. However, since I was a lot more interested in science than I was in Spanish or business, I also took some environmental studies and sustainability courses.

I ended up studying a huge array of subjects at the University of Sydney: from business, to Spanish, to science, to international and global studies. For the next four months of my life, I basically did nothing but study and bartend. I completely drowned in my university studies and I still almost failed.

This degree wracked my brain. We discussed international conflicts and international laws, indigenous land rights, culture, and development. We looked into the global problems of climate change, deforestation, sustainability, and sustainable development. In my environmental studies course, we looked at how industry was affecting the environment, for example, by cutting down huge chunks of rainforest for palm oil. In the business course, I learned nothing but how to make a successful business; so I basically learned how to create all of those problems I was studying about, by focusing on nothing but making profit.

I barely made it through that first semester, but managed it somehow. I probably would have quit again if I didn't have a big holiday ahead of me. Since the University of Sydney was in the Southern Hemisphere, my summer holidays ran from the beginning of December until the end of February, so I had three months of freedom before the start of the next semester.

I bought a flight to New York and broke up with Toby the night before I left. It was really hard but I had to do it. I just couldn't stand living like a "normal person" anymore, renting an apartment with my boyfriend, going to school and work every day. I hated the entire situation and I wanted out.

It also bothered me that Toby seemed indifferent to the problems of the world. He didn't care about sustainability, climate change, or any of the huge problems I was studying about. He didn't care about the slaves we saw in Turkey or the children who were crying while selling bananas in Mexico. He once showed a poor begging child a hundred-dollar bill and then laughed about it! I almost punched him in the face for that. He didn't want to discuss anything interesting because he didn't want to "argue" about anything. All he seemed to care about was having a beer and a good time, and that was no longer fulfilling enough for me.

I had some drinks after work and came home just a few hours before my flight to New York. I sat next to Toby on the couch, blasted Arctic Monkeys from my speaker, cried, and told him that I had to end our relationship.

"I'm sorry," I said. "When I come back to Sydney, I don't want to live with you anymore. I can pay for my part of the rent and give you money for whatever you need but I won't come back here. I'm sorry."

"You don't wanna live with me?" He looked upset.

"I don't want to be with you anymore. I'm sorry. I just can't do this anymore." I cried.

"How long have you been thinking about this?"

"I don't know. Maybe since Switzerland."

"That long?"

"I'm sorry." I cried and blasted the music, then I packed up my backpack and left the apartment. I knew this was a bad way to break up, but I just didn't have the guts to break up with him any other way.

I'm such an asshole, I thought. *How could I hurt him like that?* It tore me up, but I still felt like it was the right thing to do. *If you don't want to be in a relationship with someone, it's wrong to force yourself to be in that relationship. Our relationship would have only gotten worse, and the longer I would have waited, the worse the breakup would have been. I did the right thing.*

A few hours later, I flew away. I flew for hours and hours and left it all behind me. I thought about all of the good times and all of the bad times we had together. *Canada, Mexico, Utah, Queensland, New York, Amsterdam, Switzerland, Italy, Turkey, Sydney...* It was over now.

I felt a bit of relief. I wanted to be on my own. I wanted to travel alone. To think, to learn, to experience, to analyze the world, and to just be me. Me and only me.

Finally.

Part 3

13

Break, 2011

Where should I go next? I wondered.

I really should have stayed in Sydney and bartended at Three Wise Monkeys for an extra three or four weeks to save money, but for some reason, I decided to spend my last few hundred dollars on that one-way ticket to New York. Maybe I just missed my mother. It was great to see her, of course, but I didn't want to stay at her house for more than a few weeks and that flight brought my savings back down to about zero.

Maybe I should go to Spain, I thought. *I need to improve my Spanish so I don't fail next semester. But I'll need some money...*

I decided to get a job for the next three weeks. *I'll save money quickly while I'm at my mom's house, then I'll quit and fly to Spain!* That was my new plan.

I created a new resume filled with new lies, then I applied to work in every bar and restaurant I could get to. If anybody asked, I'd tell them that I had been living at my mother's place all of my life and that I was planning to stay there for the rest of my life.

Luckily, I found a job straight away! A crappy restaurant in a New Jersey shopping mall agreed to hire me. The restaurant was called Ruby Tuesday.

"You can come in tomorrow at nine," said the manager.

I quickly learned that this was a very bad deal.

"Here's the coffee," the manager explained in the morning. "Make sure it never runs empty! Here's the cleaning equipment. Make sure you wipe down the tables with this spray after every customer. Here's where you pick up the food. Here, you make the desserts. Here are the ice cream scoopers. The whip cream. Cakes. Here's the cash register, I'll show you how it works."

I had to do *everything* in that place—take orders, bring food to the tables, clean the tables, clean the floor, make coffee, tea, desserts, and run around like crazy! I was paid about six dollars an hour by the company and the customers barely tipped! Plus, the managers expected us to stay at the restaurant for an extra one or two hours to do sidework like cleaning glasses, sweeping the floor, and vacuuming the carpets. We weren't paid extra for this "side-work," so we were basically working for nothing.

Wow, I really appreciate Three Wise Monkeys now, I thought, *and Australia in general.* I had to do sidework there too, but I was paid a decent wage for it.

The worst thing about Ruby Tuesday, however, was dealing with the staff. Everyone was so fake and competitive. The few people who I actually managed to have a conversation with looked at me like I was insane when I told them about my life and future plans. They couldn't imagine going to Australia or even Canada, and they probably thought I was making this stuff up.

I don't give a shit, I thought. *Fuck this job. Fuck these people.*

I worked at this restaurant for one week before I blew up at the manager, saying that I wasn't going to spend an hour vacuuming the floor for free. "If you want me to vacuum the floor, then PAY ME!" I said. Then I quit, giving him a two weeks' notice.

He smiled and said, "You're smart!" Then told me that he would recommend me to a better restaurant.

Fortunately, I didn't need his recommendation because I was off to Spain after those three dreadful weeks.

Spain

I only had a few hundred dollars saved up from Ruby Tuesday, but I found a cheap flight to Portugal and some contacts in Spain through my friend Alfie, from Whistler. Alfie's friend recommended a full-time Spanish course in Granada for an affordable price, saying that the accommodation there was cheap as well.

I said goodbye to my mother and flew to Portugal in the beginning of January, 2011. I spent one fun night in a hostel in Lisbon with some random travelers, then decided to try couchsurfing for the first time. I had hosted a few couchsurfers in Sydney while living with Toby, so I already had a Couchsurfing profile with a few positive references. This, I was told, was important for finding a couch. Next, I looked up hosts in Seville (a city between Lisbon and Granada) and sent a couchsurfing request to a few different people.

To my surprise, a host named Sam replied within a few hours and said that I was welcome to stay with him and his girlfriend, Ana. After confirming my stay, I took an overnight bus from Lisbon to Seville, then walked to the city center to meet Sam and Ana.

How did I know that these two random strangers weren't planning to rob or kill me? some might ask. Well, I wasn't one hundred percent sure, but I was willing to take the risk—because it was extremely low. The platform I used to find a host included a reference system. This meant that whenever somebody hosted or stayed with a host, they left a reference on that person's profile. Sam and Ana had many positive references from both hosts and couchsurfers, and zero negative ones. I read through their profiles and references, then decided that they were trustworthy (and interesting) people.

And I was right. In fact, I was blown away by Sam and Ana's kindness and generosity. Not only did they offer me a completely free place to sleep, but they picked me up from the city center, showed me around Seville, and shared delicious Spanish meals and churros with me. They treated me as if I were a long-lost friend, even though we were complete strangers.

As we were chomping down churros, Sam and Ana told me about their travel stories. Sam was American but had lived in a small village in Tanzania for over a year and spoke fluent Swahili. After living in Tanzania, he met Ana and hitchhiked around Europe with her. They said that they spent only 4,000 euros between the two of them in an entire year of traveling, including three weeks in Norway on only 140 euros!

Even though I had already spent almost four years traveling around the world with very little money, I don't think I realized what I was doing at the time, so Sam and Ana's stories about traveling through Europe on such a tight budget inspired me a lot. They told me about how they hitchhiked, couchsurfed, stayed with gypsies, and in random squat houses. I had never heard of squats before, so Sam and Ana introduced me to a lot of new insight.

"A squat is an abandoned place that people occupy," explained Sam. "You can find them all over the world. Sometimes people occupy a piece of land, an old house, or even entire buildings that have been left abandoned."

"Interesting. So people just move into an empty building and live there until they get kicked out? Don't they get kicked out quickly?" I asked.

"It depends. Some squats have been around for years, others only last a little while. A friend of mine squatted an apartment building in London for several years before the cops came and kicked out the entire community. The funny thing was, when they asked the cops what they were gonna do with the place after kicking everybody out, the cops said they planned to turn the building into a homeless shelter! Hah!"

"So they made people homeless in order to make a homeless shelter?"

"Yeah, exactly."

"Wow, that's ironic. So what kind of people live in these squats? Is it dangerous?" I asked.

"That also depends. Of course you can find drug addicts and weirdos in some squats, but I've also stayed in places full of super cool and interesting people. Artists, musicians, programmers, all kinds of creative people that just wanna do what they love but can't manage to make a "living" out of it. At least not enough to pay rent in expensive cities. So they just squat and continue doing whatever they love. Some squats even have electricity and internet, usually stolen from the neighbors." Sam grinned.

"We stayed in one squat where we basically had everything we needed for free," said Ana. "We had electricity, internet, nice furniture that people threw away, and two fridges that were always full of food."

"Like free food?" I asked.

"Yeah, thrown away by supermarkets and big food vendors. These companies throw away SO MUCH food every day. Most of it is still perfectly good to eat. So we would just go to the back of supermarkets right after they closed and we'd pick up all kinds of thrown-away goodies. Fruits, vegetables, canned stuff, cheese, pastries, precooked meals, basically anything! A lot of it is wrapped in packaging so it's still clean."

"It's so crazy that they just throw this stuff away," I said.

"Yeah well, if they gave it away for free then they would lose customers!" said Sam.

"Yeah," I said, "and the name of the game is to make profit so it's better to waste food while people starve than it is to give it away. I think globally, we throw away something like thirty percent of our food, while more than twenty thousand people die of hunger EVERY DAY."

"I think it's actually closer to fifty percent as far as I'm aware," said Sam. "Clearly, there's something wrong with the way we distribute resources on this planet."

"Yeah, there's gotta be a saner way."

We agreed.

* * *

141

After a couple of days with Sam and Ana, I took a bus to Granada. I absolutely loved Granada from the beginning. It was a small and beautiful Spanish city surrounded by mountains. I loved its narrow cobblestone streets, its authentic Spanish vibe, its tapas bars, its whitewashed caves, and its passionate musicians. Between the music venues, tapas bars, and cave homes were speckles of dry shrubs and giant cacti.

I walked around the picturesque squares and listened to musicians strumming their guitars and singing flamenco music. People gathered around, clapped their hands, and sometimes sang along or danced. In the distance, I could see the emblem of Granada —the Alhambra, an enormous thirteenth century castle that overlooked the entire city.

Sam and Ana had told me that there was a squat house in Granada. I found it after a couple of days of wandering around, but hesitated to go in. The squat was behind a big metal fence in a shady-looking part of town; there were anarchy symbols and graffiti all over the fence, and loud heavy metal music playing in the background.

I felt a bit intimidated. *I'm just a small blonde girl. They might not like the way I look,* I thought. *But if they judge me by my looks then they're fakers!* I thought again. All of the clothes I was wearing were used clothes, given to me by other people, but they looked pretty ordinary. Apart from that, I only had one small tattoo, no makeup, no accessories, no dreads, or anything "badass" or special.

Most of the clothes out there look "normal," okay, I thought, *and I take what I can get. If I wanted to look more "badass" then I would have to spend money on black clothes, dark makeup, tattoos, and other "accessories," but by doing that I would only be contributing to the system. Isn't that ironic?! What's the point then? In the end, I'd still be the same person on the inside, but I'd have even less money left over for food.*

I didn't really know if they would judge me or not, but I decided to try to find some information about this squat before attempting to go in. I contacted over a dozen people on Couch-surfing and asked if they knew anything about this place. Almost everybody I contacted replied back and said, "No, I don't know this place, but if you want to hang out, let me know!" So I didn't end up staying at the squat, but I made a lot of new friends and connections through Couchsurfing.

I ended up couchsurfing the entire month I was in Granada. Most of the time I stayed with a friendly guy named Fernando. Fernando considered himself to be multi-sexual; he had a transvestite girlfriend and some very fun flatmates. Neither Fernando nor his flatmates spoke a word of English, so this place was perfect for me. I got to stay for free, I met some great friends, and I got to practice a lot of Spanish. Fernando also showed me some awesome natural hot spring pools and some great flamenco shows.

While I was in Granada, I took the intensive Spanish language course that Alfie's friend had recommended. This set me back a few hundred dollars, but it was worth it. The course, combined with my couchsurfing experience, allowed me to learn more Spanish in those four weeks in Granada than I had learned in my entire six years of studying in school and university. In addition, I met even *more* fun people at the language school!

I had a lot of fun in Granada. I never paid for dinner, instead, I bought two-euro drinks and ate the tapas that came with the drinks. I didn't pay for accommodation or anything else except some snacks and the Spanish course. I saw dozens of amazing live music performances for free and I made friends with about half the city in the short time that I was there. I loved everybody from the language school, I loved Fernando and all of his friends, and I met so many other people from having contacted them on Couchsurfing. By my fourth week in Granada, I could barely go anywhere without running into somebody I knew.

I didn't want to leave at the end of the month, but I had already booked a big flight and I was back down to negative money. *Luckily, I still had that credit card.* I flew to Moscow, visited my family, then flew back to Sydney for round five of university.

14

Sydney & NZ, 2011

Round five was hard. I learned about more problems, more abuse, more conflicts, more laws and regulations, and more about how none of these laws or regulations were working.

I just couldn't get it. More than half of the population is being exploited, the "Global South" they call it. Enslaved, basically, to work in horrible conditions in factories, mines, farms, and wherever else. Our *planet* is being exploited. We have no global control over anything, no global limits to deforestation, no global limits to fishing the oceans, we have all the technology we need to solve climate change, but not the international or global cooperation that's needed to put this technology in place. The best we have today are some international agreements, which seem to be completely useless.

Then these courses promote the need to develop third world countries in the same way that rich countries have "developed." This is what really bugged me. Don't get me wrong, I don't want people to suffer, I don't want human beings to live in poverty, and I don't want anyone on our planet to be exploited. But I couldn't help but wonder, *How is developing these places through trade possibly going to be sustainable in the long run?*

I mean, if your goal is to "develop" poor areas by helping them sell more and more shit—that just can't be sustainable. Sure, you might give some poor people new business opportunities and perhaps their businesses will thrive and they will do better, but businesses require resources, so the more successful businesses there are, the more resources we will need. There's no global control over the resources we use, so this will inevitably lead to more and more exploitation of the land and therefore, to more problems. That means no sustainability. **Real sustainability has to be global.**

And then I went to my business class which taught me how to make more and more money. *That's the goal!* That other stuff—exploitation, limitation, sustainability, whatever—was not even *mentioned* in the business class. *And that's what most people study today.*

I almost failed that semester too, but at least I did OK in Spanish.

I lived in a crappy share house in a suburb called Newtown for those four months and continued to work at Three Wise Monkeys. Bartending was basically my only "break" from studying at university, so I worked a lot, paid back my debt, and saved some money.

After that semester, I was horrified and basically depressed, but I was willing to continue university after a one-month break snowboarding in New Zealand.

New Zealand

I found out that the best places to snowboard in New Zealand were around Wanaka and Queenstown, two towns in the South Island. I had plenty of money saved up this time, but I decided to get onto Couchsurfing anyway to see if I could meet some locals. I scanned through a few profiles and found one interesting host—Enzo, a Brazilian guy who worked as a skydiving instructor in Wanaka.

That sounds so cool, I thought. *I'd love to meet a skydiver!*

I sent him a message asking if he wanted to meet up when I come to New Zealand. He replied one day later saying that he was not in New Zealand at the time because he was skydiving in Aruba to escape the winter. That was disappointing, but he also added that he read my profile and was curious to meet me because there weren't a lot of "us" in this world. He also wrote this:

Enzo. June, 2011

I am returning to the North Island in September and then will be sailing around the island for 3 months on my yacht, stopping at all beautiful islands on the coast and enjoying that most beautiful playground that Aotearoa is... That's my kind of life!!!

If living out in the wild, in basic conditions, surviving every day to watch the sunset is something that interests you, then let's stay in touch and I will take you sailing to the islands in the spring...

I almost fell off my seat as I read that message. *Sailing around New Zealand?* I didn't know a thing about sailing, but this sounded like an opportunity of a lifetime! As long as the captain wasn't a creep, that is. I read through Enzo's Couchsurfing profile some more and checked his references—they were all positive. He seemed like a genuine person; and not only that, he seemed like a real adventurer—someone who skydives and sails and builds his own boat and chases sunsets and—*Damn it. I'm supposed to be back in university in August.*

I thought it over and decided not to quit university for this sailing trip just yet, but to stay in touch with Enzo, get to know him better, and see if he was really serious about taking me on this journey. Over the next few months, Enzo and I exchanged long letters about life, philosophy, and adventures. He was very interesting to talk to.

In July, I flew to Christchurch, New Zealand. There, I witnessed the aftermath of the 2011 Christchurch earthquake and I began to write in my diary again:

July 3, 2011

While hitchhiking and talking to people in the Rollerstone Tavern, I realized the devastating effect that the earthquake had had on the local population.

"I have a completely different respect for the Earth now," said a man who had seen giant waves of cement in a parking lot basement when the earthquake hit.

I talked to people who had lost their family members in the earthquake. One woman told me that she witnessed a busload of people getting squashed by a falling building. I walked around the outside of the fenced-off, crumbled city center and observed the shattered infrastructure.

Entire buildings had collapsed. The entire city center was in ruins. One hundred and eighty five lives had been lost. Many more were wounded, shocked, and shattered.

It was devastating. This just goes to show you that no matter what you aim for in life, it can all be crumbled down and destroyed within seconds.

I slept in a hostel that night and got ready to hit the road the next morning. I decided to hitchhike to Queenstown, which was about five hundred kilometers away from Christchurch.

Before coming to New Zealand, I had only hitchhiked a handful of times, and only when I had no other option. This time, I could have taken buses to get around, but the buses were so ridiculously expensive in New Zealand that I couldn't bring myself to pay for them. Besides, I knew that New Zealand was a very safe country, so I wasn't worried about hitchhiking alone.

I stuck my thumb out on Highway 1 and was picked up straight away! A friendly Kiwi couple drove me to the next town, a few kilometers down the road. We had a nice chat, then they dropped me off on the south side of town.

I stuck my thumb out again and was picked up by a beautiful Maori woman who was going a few more kilometers down the road. She had a powerful-looking tattoo on her chin. She explained that the tattoo was called a moko kauae and represented survival, resilience, and her true cultural identity. Unfortunately, I didn't get to speak with her for too long before she dropped me off again.

Next, I caught a lift with a chubby truck driver who was going over a hundred kilometers in the direction I needed to go. This guy was extremely friendly. We chatted about our lives and hobbies, and he even bought me lunch on the way! I tried to pay for both of our lunches, but he wouldn't let me.

After the truck driver dropped me off, I caught a few more short lifts with more friendly New Zealanders. Unfortunately, I didn't make it all the way to Queenstown that day, but at least I didn't get stranded at night. I caught my last lift to a pub/hotel in a small town. I tried to hitchhike farther as it was getting dark, but the people in the pub noticed what I was doing and became increasingly worried about me. Eventually, the owner of the hotel told me to stay put and gave me a discount for a room. She seemed like a very caring older woman.

I slept in the hotel room and got back to hitchhiking the next day. It turned out that hitchhiking in New Zealand was awesome! I never waited more than a few minutes to catch a lift and everybody that picked me up was extremely kind and friendly. Everyone seemed to be concerned about me hitchhiking alone, since I was just a small girl, so they wanted to "save" me before something bad happened. Because of that, I was picked up by families, senior citizens, and people that had never picked up hitchhikers before.

One time, a middle-aged couple even brought me to their home for lunch. At first I thought this would be an awkward situation because they also invited their daughter and son-in-law for lunch, who were not in the car when they picked me up hitchhiking. *How are they going to introduce me?* I wondered. *'This is Sasha— a random hitchhiker we just picked up...'* But it wasn't awkward at all. Their thirty-something-year-old kids didn't question why their parents were picking up hitchhikers and the entire family welcomed me into their home with open arms. They made delicious turkey sandwiches and great cappuccinos, then the couple dropped me off at a bus station, telling me to catch the bus because hitchhiking was dangerous.

I thanked them and continued on. I made it to Queenstown just before dark, then booked into a hostel and got a good night's rest.

The next morning, I went up the mountain. The view above Queenstown was out of this world. Towering snow-capped mountains emerged from Lake Wakatipu, an enormous sky-blue body of fresh water. The lake was so huge that it resembled a giant river flowing between the staggering Southern Alps of New Zealand.

The ski slopes, however, were quite small and barely had any snow on them. Since the snowboarding season hadn't kicked off yet, I decided to hitch farther south and explore some more of New Zealand. The next destination I had in mind was a town called Dunedin, on the southeastern coast of the island.

July 5, 2011

I was dropped off in a small town right behind another hitchhiker who was also holding a sign that said "Dunedin." We laughed and started talking. I think this guy is a totally awesome and free person. He's 36 years old and hitching around the world with a bald head, a huge beard, and an even bigger smile. We talked while holding up our signs for about 20 minutes until we got picked up by a big truck.

It was a beautiful ride over to Dunedin. I parted with Mike and the truck driver and made my way to the couch I planned to crash on. I am now lying on a mattress in my own room in the house of 4 nice kiwi boys—all for free! Oh how I love hitchhiking and couchsurfing!

July 7, 2011

The next day I met up with Mike again and we spent the whole day walking and hitching to the Otago Peninsula—the wild, easternmost part of Dunedin.

At first, we went to the information center to find some info about the place. They said that the only way to get on/around the peninsula was through an organized tour, the cheapest of which was $120! They said that there was no other way, so Mike and I decided to prove them wrong.

Hitching not only got us exactly where we wanted to go, but also gave us a chance to talk to the local people—three different people that were lucky enough to live on that beautiful peninsula. An old guy, an old lady, and a young guy in a Mustang.

Mike and I hitchhiked to the end of the Otago Peninsula, climbed around the grassy hills, stopped at the steep rocky cliff-side, and gazed over the Pacific Ocean. There, we watched royal albatrosses spread their enormous wings and take off using powerful gusts of wind. These giant seabirds have an average wingspan of over three meters and are estimated to fly 190,000 kilometers each year! They soared high above our heads and far out to the ocean. Right before sunset, Mike and I also spotted a *little penguin*, the smallest penguin species in the world. The little penguin was extra cute—he had a blue coat and was only about thirty centimeters tall!

Perhaps the best part of the experience, however, was talking to Mike. Mike and I had such a great journey to the Otago Peninsula and we barely spent a penny on it. We hitchhiked to Dunedin, couchsurfed, and hitchhiked to the very end of this scenic peninsula. The only thing I had to pay for was food. So at that point, I really understood that I didn't need much money to travel anywhere I wanted, but I wasn't sure if this kind of lifestyle would be "sustainable" or desirable in the long run. Mike, however, was thirty-six years old and had been traveling like this for over a decade. He seemed so humble, happy, and fulfilled in life. He was from South America and he didn't have working rights in New Zealand, but he managed just fine finding cash jobs as a barista. He explained how he loved traveling around the world and had no interest in settling down, finding a job, or raising kids.

After talking to Mike, I understood that life can be simple, yet so much more fascinating and extraordinary than most people even imagine.

July 20, 2011

I hitched back to Queenstown the following day because I heard that there had been a big dump of snow and the mountain I had a pass for was opening.

Got two nice and easy rides, went snowboarding, then Emma came and stayed with me for a week. That was definitely the best part of the trip. I very much love and respect Emma.

We had a couple of 19-year-old boys tag along with us on snowboarding trips (Steve and Jacob) they were pretty fun but totally useless. Couldn't even put chains on the tires. Me and Em did everything.

The day after Em left, those two boys, plus Erik from Belgium and I went skydiving! It was such an epic day—skydiving over Lake Wanaka in the day, snowboarding at night. Falling from 15,000 feet was incredible—such an amazing feeling—indescribable!

Soon after skydiving, my New Zealand vacation was meant to come to an end. I was supposed to fly back to Sydney for another dreadful semester of university.

I talked to Erik late at night before I left. He had been traveling for a long time, snowboarding, and enjoying his life. I told him about my university studies, how they were killing me, and how I was only studying to get my parents off my back. He said that was a poor reason to spend so much time doing something you don't like. I agreed. I thought about the sailing trip around New Zealand.

Life's short. I might never get such an opportunity again...

15

Outback Australia, 2011

I flew back to Sydney then wrote another long letter to my mother, saying that I just had to go sailing around New Zealand, but that I will come back to university one year later and I will finish my degree. *I promise!*

She was on the opposite side of the planet now and there wasn't much she could do about this. I submitted all of the paperwork to defer my studies for one year and then tried to figure out how to manage my time, money, and new visa situation.

Once I deferred my studies, I lost my student visa. The Australian government gave me about one month to leave the country (until the end of August). Enzo told me to meet him in New Zealand around mid-October so we could sail from October until the end of December.

This meant that I *had* to leave Australia at the end of August, but that I could not fly back to New Zealand yet. Legally, I could only be in New Zealand for three months at a time, so I didn't want to enter New Zealand earlier than October because I would have had to leave earlier than December, which was when we were meant to be sailing.

Confused? I was too.

"Okay so I can't be in Australia after August. And I can't be in New Zealand before mid-October. That means that I have to spend September and some of October somewhere else. Somewhere that's not Australia or New Zealand but isn't too far away so that plane tickets don't cost a fortune," I said to my friend Kristina.

"You wanna go to Asia?" she replied.

"Hah. Well, I might have to. I'm not sure where else I can go."

"Can I come?" she asked.

"Sure!" I smiled. "You wanna join me for the whole two months?"

"I don't know, maybe. I want to do something different with my life. I'm sick of being in Sydney. I don't even know why I'm here. I came to Australia to experience something different but all I'm doing is working all the time."

"Yeah well, if you want to make a real change in your life, you need to change your *lifestyle* not just your location or your job," I asserted.

Kristina was a Russian-Lithuanian girl who lived with me in that crappy share house in Sydney. She grew up in Vilnius, where she was a top mathematics student and later a successful worker bee for an insurance company. She wasn't particularly happy with her life in Vilnius so she decided to make a change by moving to Australia. The problem, however, was that Kristina changed locations drastically, but she didn't really make a change in her lifestyle. She came to Sydney and worked just as hard as she had worked in Vilnius, except now she did random housekeeping and café jobs, rather than office work for an insurance company. *I can't say which of those options is worse...*

So Kristina wasn't particularly happy with her lifestyle in Sydney either. When she heard about my past adventures and future plans, she decided to quit her lifestyle and join me for a bit.

"What do you think about traveling through Australia just for a week or two before we go to Asia?" she asked. "I'd love to see more of Australia."

"It's so expensive here though," I said. "It'd be so much cheaper to just buy a flight from Sydney to Bali or something."

"Yeah but don't you wanna see the Outback, or Tasmania? Or the Great Ocean Road? What if we do it cheaply?"

"Yeah I do. But how do we do it cheaply?"

"We can try relocating a campervan. I heard that you can basically rent a campervan for free if you drive it from wherever it's located to wherever the campervan company needs it to be. There are a bunch of websites where you can find deals like that. Or maybe we can find a rideshare on Gumtree."

Kristina and I spent a couple of days looking for campervan relocation deals but couldn't find anything decent. At the same time, we kept an eye on the classified ads on Gumtree.

"Hey, check this out!" Kristina found something after a few days. "There's a guy offering a ride from Katoomba to Alice Springs. Katoomba is just west of Sydney. What do you think?"

I glanced at the ad.

Date Listed	07/08/2011
Address	Katoomba NSW 2780, Australia

Driving from Katoomba to Alice Springs on 18.8.11. Looking for 1 or 2 people to share costs and fun times in Landcruiser 4x4. Im a safari tour guide so I can share much knowledge. Departing 18/19.8. BUT you will have to take train to meet me in Katoomba (3 sisters town in Blue Mountains).Email me. Sorry No mobile ph where i am now. Cheers. Eddie.

Visits: 138

"Oh he's a safari tour guide! That could be cool," I said.

We emailed the guy, then met him in person at the Blue Mountains one week before his departure date. He impressed us from the start.

"Call me Manu," he said. "That's my native name." We met in a café in Katoomba, then strolled to a beautiful walkway that peered over a sea of eucalyptus trees. Manu had tan skin and black hair tucked into a neat ponytail. He pointed out three large rocky pillars and smiled as he told us all about the Blue Mountains National Park and the Aboriginal tales that accompanied the misty scene.

Manu also told us about himself. "I grew up in the jungle, in Papua New Guinea. But I've lived all over Australia for many years, in lots of different Aboriginal communities. So I have a lotta stories to share." He winked.

We liked him. His four-by-four even had the word "spirit" on the license plate. We agreed to meet one week later and drive *spirit* to the middle of Australia.

* * *

Before our departure (and before we even met Manu), I worked as many shifts as possible at Three Wise Monkeys. I worked so much that I managed to pay for all of my expenses using just my tips and I put entire paychecks into my savings account. I did many doubles in a row, so it was extremely tiring, but it was worth it because I knew what I was working for: *one year of freedom.*

When the time came, Kristina and I moved out of our house, packed up our backpacks, and drove off into the desert with our new friend. I was thrilled to start our new adventure and to be free from work and university once again. The three of us drove hundreds of kilometers each day and happily chatted for hours on end.

Toward the end of the day, Manu would simply turn off the paved road and into the bush, then park his four-by-four anywhere that looked like a good camping spot. We spent our first night sleeping on top of a beautiful green hillside that overlooked the ocean in South Australia. There, I saw one of the most breathtaking sunsets of my life. Red and orange sunrays appeared through a thin opening between thick violet clouds and periwinkle hills. The ocean shimmered blue and a perfect layer of yellow appeared in the sky above. The shadow of a eucalyptus tree stood still and black as we gazed in awe and silence.

After sunset, we made a campfire, grilled steak and roasted sweet potatoes, then slept in a bed of blankets beneath the stars.

The next day, we drove through hours of flatland. We talked, laughed, and got to know each other even better. In the evening, we camped on red desert sand and Manu played the didgeridoo for Kristina and me. He explained that Aboriginals use the didgeridoo to tell stories, rather than as a traditional musical instrument. One person would narrate the tale, while another person played the didgeridoo to accompany the spoken words and help the listeners visualize the story. Manu played us the sounds of a hopping kangaroo and a dingo sneaking around the bush.

That night, he also talked about energy. He believed that certain special places in the world hold an incredible amount of energy. Places like Uluru, the Grand Canyon, and Machu Pichu, places that native people have regarded as sacred for thousands of years.

"I have a lot of energy too," he said, smiling. "You can take as much energy from me as you want, I have plenty to give!"

I stared into the fire, listened to the didgeridoo and Manu's stories of kangaroos and Aboriginals, and imagined breathing in Manu's positive energy. *He sure is a fascinating character,* I thought.

The three of us slept on the same big blanket on the red sand, with nothing between our eyes and the brightest stars I had ever seen.

"In the desert, you don't have to look up to see the stars," said Manu. "Just look straight ahead and you will see them all around you."

It's true. They twinkled in every single direction.

In the morning, I opened my eyes and sprang out of bed as soon as the sun came up. I felt so energized and excited that I immediately sprinted a few laps around our campsite. This was strange because it normally takes me at least a half hour to drag myself out of bed in the morning, and I rarely move faster than a sloth before 10:00 a.m.

Kristina grinned at me as she took a sip of coffee. "Wow, you really did take his energy!" she teased. We giggled, then Manu gave me the nickname *Mulari,* which is an Aboriginal name of a small desert mouse.

As the three of us drove farther north, Manu told us about his past. His father was a British marine who had settled in the rugged lands of Papua New Guinea; his mother was a native princess, covered head to toe in tattoos. He explained what life was like growing up in the jungle.

"If we were hungry, we'd pick fruit or go hunting. If we were thirsty, we'd collect water from the river," he said. "We had no concept of shops or money." Manu told us a crazy story about being stalked and chased through the jungle by cannibals. He said that after that incident, his father decided to bring him and his siblings to Australia. "We had a hard time moving to this so-called civilization. We knew English because of our pop, but we didn't know a thing about society. It was confusing, you see, to go from the jungle, where we had everything we needed, to a place where you have to work to get money—and then trade this money for food that's already been killed, prepared, and stored for you in a shop.

"I didn't like being forced into this system. I was used to just catching the food and making the stuff myself. Hell in this society, you even gotta pay for a place to sleep! Imagine how that sounds to a jungle boy.

"I didn't like it one bit. I got angry. Ran away, joined some Aboriginals. Eventually, I came back to society, tried work again. Got angry again. Ran away again. I battled with this for years. Years and years."

"It must have been hard for you," I said.

"Yeah. I've moved around a lot," said Manu. "Lived in different Aboriginal territories and walked the land. Now I work in national parks whenever I have to, but I try to stay away from society as much as I can."

"Yeah I think the best thing you can do in this life is minimize the amount of time you spend slaving for money," I said. "I also try to work as little as possible. I'll work for a few months or so, then quit and travel around the world on my savings. I can't stand when people tell me I should get a "real job." They're basically telling me to become a full-time slave, as if there's nothing better to do with my life!"

"Yeah, there's nothing worse than being a faithful slave," said Manu. "You're doing the right thing, Mulari."

* * *

After a few more days of driving and camping in the bush, Manu, Kristina, and I made it to Alice Springs. Kristina was so impressed by Manu and so eager to see more of Australia that she decided to stay with him in the Red Centre. Next, they planned to drive to Uluru, the giant rock in the middle of Australia. I was happy to see Kristina so excited and full of life. This was her chance to explore the kind of Australia she was looking for all along. I would have continued this journey with them too if it wasn't for my stupid visa restriction.

By law, I had to leave the country in just a few days, so I hitched a ride from Alice Springs to Darwin, then caught the cheapest flight I could find out of Australia: Darwin to Denpasar, Bali.

16

Indonesia, 2011

September 14, 2011

I arrived in Bali on Friday, August 26.

I spent the first few days alone, wandering the busy streets of Kuta and thinking over the inspirations of the past week.

Eventually I made friends with some local people that worked around the hotel I stayed in. We hung out, went surfing, and had lots of fun together.

I ended up riding a motorbike around practically all of Bali with one of the guys, a Sumatran boy named Moza. He was really nice and knew a lot about the island.

The motorbike rental cost about five dollars per day and every hotel we stayed in cost between five and ten dollars per night. We stopped at local spots for food, which cost between one and three dollars per meal. We didn't have a plan, objective, or any obligations, so we drove anywhere we wanted and simply explored the island.

We went to the Monkey Forest in Ubud, the mountains in Bedugul, the enormous lush green rice fields in Jatiluwih, many amazing temples, beaches, waterfalls, and hot springs all over Bali, and of course, to Uluwatu, the temple on the sea.

I loved this feeling of sweaty freedom. Nothing really mattered and you were salty almost all the time. We lived for the road, the sea, the spicy dishes, and the sunsets in the distance.

After a couple of weeks of exploring Bali, Moza offered to show me his home village in Sumatra, an island over a thousand kilometers west of Bali. I considered it but was a little worried about his intentions. *What if I get stuck in a weird situation in some rural village in Sumatra? How would I get out of it?*

I flipped a coin and it told me to go east instead.

Lombok

September 20, 2011

I left Moza in Bali and set off to new wild, eastern lands.

During my first day on the island of Lombok, I rented a motorbike and drove up the beautiful mountainous coastline in search of a possible (and cheap) method of climbing Gunung Rinjani, a 3,700-meter volcano.

It turned out that it was "impossible" to climb this volcano without paying for a tour (and actually would have been very dangerous), so after bargaining a lot, I booked a 3-day package for around $100 and set off on this trip the following day.

It was a *very* hard trek.

The first day we climbed for about 8 hours, starting on a nice steady hill-climb, ending on a seemingly never-ending vertical slope. We started with 5 tourists, 1 guide, and 3 porters, ended with 3 tourists, 1 guide, and 2 porters (a Swiss couple just could not make it!).

The poor porters not only carried all of our gear on a stick on their shoulders, but cooked all of our food and went on further treks to get drinking water. They looked so skinny, tired, and worn out. Some porters hiked in flip-flops, some (in other groups) had no shoes at all!

We went to bed right after sunset, completely exhausted, and woke up at 3:00 a.m. the next day to hike to the highest rim and watch the sunrise above the volcano.

We set off for the rim under moonlight with rented flashlights. We stepped through extremely loose volcanic rocks and soil on the steepest slope on the trek. For every two steps up, we slipped one step back. It seemed never ending! I felt myself moving forward but could not see myself getting closer to the top. Our group separated as every person needed to go at their own pace.

As I was alone, I saw the sun begin to creep up from below the volcanic mountains. I looked up at the challenge ahead of me. I knew I needed to catch that sunrise.

This was when I started to think about Manu's words: "The energy, it's real. It exists in places like Uluru, Machu Pichu, places that indigenous people have regarded as sacred for centuries."

This is one of those places! I thought. *The entire island of Lombok was created from this one volcano! And the energy, it's here!*

I stopped walking, closed my eyes, took a deep breath in, and visualized the energy flowing into me.

When I opened my eyes, a strange hand appeared in my face. At first I thought it was our guide, but it wasn't, it was some random young guy. He took my hand and pushed me forward. It felt as if we were flying up the mountain. When we were just a few meters from the top, he turned around to go help someone else, asking for nothing in return.

I made it. I reached the top about 25 minutes before anybody else in our group and I got to watch the sunrise over a sea of clouds that lay below Gunung Rinjani.

The view was absolutely mind-blowing. The feeling, incredible.

*While I was climbing this incredibly steep volcano, the idea of "energy flowing from Gunung Rinjani to me" was a great motivator, but I was aware that this was a play in my imagination. There is a lot to learn about energy, but the only way to truly understand such a phenomenon is through science.

After a bit of rest, we descended into the inside of Gunung Rinjani, to the dark blue crater lake. I jumped into the lake, immersing myself in the cool water, and then went off with my group to the hot, volcanic waterfalls for relaxing natural water massages.

There was a perfect natural rock pool just below the thermal waterfall. We sat there like kings and queens while the warm spring water massaged our backs.

We slept by the crater lake, then spent one more day hiking up and out of Gunung Rinjani. At the end, I felt like my legs were going to fall off, so I decided to spend some time relaxing on the tiny Gili Islands off the west coast of Lombok.

The Gilis are beautiful little islands with no automobiles and little air pollution. This was nice. What came next was a bit of trouble.

Sape

September, 2011

As soon as I left the Gilis, I went to the dirty, overcrowded city of Mataram to extend my visa. From Mataram, I planned to head to Komodo.

This was when I really started to get fed up with the local people and Indonesia in general. In touristy areas, the hassling is annoying but easy to ignore, in not-so-touristy areas it is just overwhelming.

I could not take one step without somebody trying to get my attention, always wanting something from me—selling a hat, a car ride, a hotel room, anything at all! In Mataram, a 6-year-old girl snatched money straight out of my hand (only about 20 cents but it made me so angry).

I bought an overnight bus ride from Mataram to Labuan Bajo (the nearest city to Komodo). Got ripped off on the way to the station, ripped off on the ride, tossed and turned on a broken bus seat for 10 hours, grabbed at from all angles, made fun of and laughed at in my face. By the time I got to the destination—which was actually a village called Sape, still an 8-hour ferry ride away from Labuan Bajo—I had had it to the point of freaking out in front of a huge group of people, cursing at the bus driver, and even crying eventually.

Looking back at the situation, I should have planned shorter bus trips, making at least one stop between Mataram and Labuan Bajo. But because Mataram was so chaotic and *everyone* was out to get money from me, I just wanted to get out of there as fast as possible. I bought the last seat on an old, hot, overstuffed bus. I was exhausted both mentally and physically by the time I sat down. The seat I paid for didn't stay upright, it kept falling down onto the person behind me, so this person kept on kicking my seat forward. I closed my eyes for one second and a teenage boy who was sitting in front of me grabbed my boob! I was *pissed!* I shoved my flip-flops into my seat to stop it from falling back, shoved my backpack between the two seats in front of me to block the teenager, then I sat in this position for about ten hours, sweating like a pig.

I didn't even want to get out of the bus at the rest stops because I was afraid that somebody would steal my backpack. Eventually, I couldn't hold it anymore and went into a disgusting public toilet and peed into a hole in the ground while wearing my sixty-liter backpack. It was an incredibly uncomfortable situation and I was outraged because I knew that I had paid about double the price that everybody else had paid for the same bus ride. That was why I freaked out at the bus driver and made him give me back some money once we arrived in Sape.

Once I got some money back from the bus driver, I took a deep breath and just walked. I put my 20-kg bag on my shoulders and walked for 6-8 kilometers down the one straight scorching hot road in Sape. I walked and it was all okay.

I found a hotel room in Sape for a very cheap price.

It was so cheap that I got scared at night.

This hotel room is nice and clean, I thought as it was getting dark. *It even has towels and a shower. Why did they only charge me two dollars? Could they be planning something?*

I started thinking about how I cursed at the bus driver in front of that big group of people and made him give me back my money.

This is a small town. They probably all know each other. What if they want to take back this money or punish me for my behavior?

I panicked. There was no window in the hotel room, just one way to get in or out—the door. I blocked it with a cabinet.

That's not really gonna cut it if they really want to come in here.

I didn't sleep or leave the room all night. Someone knocked on my door, but I didn't open it or say anything. Instead, I blocked it with more furniture. They knocked some more and called my name, but I stayed still and silent. I didn't have a smartphone back then and this hotel didn't offer WiFi so I had no way of contacting the outside world. I stayed put and hoped for the best.

In the morning, I realized that I had been safe all along. The room was so cheap because the hotel manager thought I was only planning on staying there for a couple of hours, before the departure of the night ferry. He was knocking on my door to tell me that the ferry was leaving!

"Oh, sorry about that!" I said to the manager, feeling extremely embarrassed. "I wasn't planning on taking the night ferry because I would have ended up in Labuan Bajo alone in the dark, and I wouldn't know where to stay."

"Don't you have hotel reservation?" he asked.

"No, I just find hotels when I arrive. I find cheaper rooms like that. But I don't want to walk around looking for a hotel at night, especially with all of my stuff."

"Yes, better you stay safe," he said. "The next ferry is at nine a.m., it arrives at five p.m."

"I'll catch that one, thank you!"

The ferry ride to Labuan Bajo was an interesting experience. I was the only white person on this ferry, so the locals were very curious about me. Kids pointed at me, yelling "bule" (white foreigner), as their mothers and fathers stared me down, examining my face and hair, and pointing at my nose. As soon as I sat down, about fifteen people surrounded me and just stared. It was very awkward. I smiled and tried to speak some Indonesian, but I didn't know many words so I couldn't say much. After five or ten minutes, I stopped attempting to communicate, but the people continued to stare at me. I wasn't sure what to do next. *Should I just ignore them? That seems kind of rude. But staring back at them is really awkward too!*

I felt like a celebrity or an alien. Eventually I picked up a book and ignored everybody that was staring at me. A few hours later, I arrived in Labuan Bajo.

Labuan & Komodo

Labuan Bajo is a small coastal town situated on a beautiful piece of land. There were meandering hills and islands all around, and the water would have been spectacular if it wasn't filled with garbage. Every bit of coastline around this little town was absolutely trashed. There were soda bottles, candy wrappers, food containers, plastic bags, and all kinds of garbage floating as far as the eye could see.

How could you turn such a remarkable place into a dumpsite? I wondered as I caught sight of a man throwing an entire bag of trash into the sea.

I walked around Labuan Bajo for a while, looking for the cheapest hotel in town. Eventually, a local woman offered me a room for about six dollars per night. The room was basically just a slab of concrete with four cement walls, a fan, a small bed, and a mosquito net. There were no tiles on the floor or paint on the walls, but I was happy about the mosquito net. I put my stuff down, went to a local eatery for some rice and curry, then walked around to find information about the Komodo dragon and national park.

I learned that Komodo National Park spans across twenty-nine islands, the largest being Komodo, Rinca, and Padar. Almost all of the Komodo dragons live on those islands, so I realized that I needed a boat ride to see these legendary lizards.

I walked around Labuan Bajo some more, talked to boat captains, and bargained for the cheapest price I could find. There was a set price per boat, so after I found a boat, I roamed around and looked for fellow tourists who could split the cost with me. I found one couple from Canada and a nice French man. The next day, the four of us took off on a two-day boat tour of Komodo National Park.

September 28, 2011

I found paradise.

We swam through aqua blue seas spotted with truffle-shaped hills. We dove to see colorful coral, swarms of fish, turtles, and manta rays the size of houses! Finally, on the islands of Rinca and Komodo, we spotted the dragons.

They looked like big, lazy, oversized lizards. Actually, they are the biggest species of lizard in the world, growing up to three meters long and weighing up to seventy kilograms. And it turns out they're not as lazy as they look. Previously, people believed that Komodo dragons made a sneak attack on their prey, taking a small nibble and then stalking the prey until it died from the bacteria in the dragon's saliva, but it turns out that Komodo dragons actually attack to kill on the spot. They charge at their prey and aim for the throat. Sometimes, they can even take down an animal with their powerful tails. Komodo dragons will stalk their prey and wait for it to die if the prey escapes their attack, but this is not intentional. Also, it's most likely not bacteria that kills the prey, but venom secreted from the dragon's lower jaw.

Large Komodo dragons feed on anything from water buffalo, to Timor deer, carrion, and smaller Komodo dragons. They can eat up to eighty percent of their body weight in one meal and can survive on twelve meals per year. If the prey is small enough (such as a goat), the dragon will try to swallow it whole. If it's hard to swallow, the dragon may ram the carcass against a tree to force it down its throat. Some dragons use so much force that they end up knocking the tree down.

Clearly, I was excited to see this animal in the wild. We spotted several small dragons as soon as we arrived in Komodo National Park. They were calmly lying beneath the deck of the information center. Apparently, the people that worked there fed them chicken from time to time.

Our group hiked around Komodo Island with a guide. The island was very beautiful, dry, hilly, and rugged. The views of the aqua-blue crystal water and the hazelnut islands in the distance were spectacular. We spotted some bigger dragons by a river, one that was stalking a water buffalo.

After the hike, we came back to the boat, where an amazing meal was prepared for us by the captain and his crew. We had rice, squid, fresh fish, all sorts of spicy Indonesian dishes, salads, and tropical fruit. The captain and his crew were relaxing on the boat, smiling, sunbathing, and eating mangoes. They seemed calm and happy.

After lunch, we got to explore an entirely different world. The captain moored his boat and all of us (including his crew) plunged into the water. We dove down to see vibrant coral reefs, massive schools of colorful fish, sea turtles, and six-meter-wide manta rays. This absolutely blew my mind. I watched these gargantuan gentle giants sweep right beneath my body and I just couldn't believe my eyes.

This is incredible! I quivered as I floated in the water.

At the end of the long and gratifying day, we watched the sunset over the sea and observed hundreds of flying foxes sweep over the islands. We moored the boat in a quiet corner of the national park, took one last look at the moon and the shadows of the nearby islands, then went off to bed. There were a few cabins in the boat but I decided to lie on the deck and fall asleep to the sound of the wilderness and the water crashing on the distant shores. The boat rocked back and forth and swayed with the wind.

I felt so alive, so bewildered and captivated that I couldn't sleep. I thought about the incredible wildlife in this national park. *The Komodo dragons, the manta rays, the fish, the turtles, the coral.* Then I thought about how it was all endangered. *The coral... It will go extinct, probably within my lifetime.* I thought about the beautiful truffle-shaped islands and the color of the water beneath our boat. *How incredible.* I thought about the trash in Labuan Bajo, and the trash all over Indonesia. All over the world, for that matter. I thought about the captain and his crew, and the other people I had met in Indonesia. I remembered the guide and porters that slaved on Gunung Rinjani.

That was such a tough hike and I barely carried anything. The porters carried the tents, water, food, pots, everything! They didn't have backpacks, they carried up to thirty kilos of supplies on a stick on their shoulders, and some of these guys didn't even have shoes. The Rinjani guide had told me that they go up and down the volcano nonstop, sometimes they go for weeks without a single break. They all looked tired as hell. When I asked the guide if the hike gets any easier with time, he replied with, "No, it hurts. Always hurts."

As I lay on the boat, I thought about how lucky I was. I realized that people rarely ever "choose" what they do in life. *You don't choose where you're born or how you're raised, so you don't really choose your lifestyle—you're just pushed into certain circumstances. You're forced to trade most of your life just to survive, so most people end up having to take whatever slave job they can get.*

If you were born near Gunung Rinjani, you might be forced to take a "job" as a porter or a guide. If your family is poor, you probably won't have many other options. If you were born by Komodo, you might be forced to take a "job" on a boat, if you're lucky. If you were born in Australia, you might be forced to wash dishes for sixteen dollars an hour or bartend for twenty-five dollars an hour. You probably won't survive for long unless you trade your time and energy for money, but at least in Australia, you'll have access to good healthcare, education, running water, and a lot of other perks. If you were born in Indonesia, you won't even be able to enter Australia without a visa, and you won't get a visa unless you have a ton of money. So it's not really about choice, it's about where you're born—*it's all about luck.*

Becoming Loca(l)

Once we got back to Labuan Bajo, I got into a craze about money. My budget was meant to be ten dollars per day, but I just blew a hundred dollars on Rinjani and another forty or fifty dollars on Komodo National Park. It was definitely worth it, but now I had to be extra careful with money to make sure I would have enough for the sailing trip in New Zealand. Enzo said that I'd only have to pay for food and personal items while sailing, but I didn't know exactly how much that would cost and I still didn't have a flight to New Zealand or anywhere else.

I realized that locals lived on less than ten dollars per day in Indonesia, so I decided to put myself into the shoes of a local. I only ate in local places for about one dollar per meal, I roamed around for hours looking for the cheapest accommodation I could find, and I wouldn't spend any extra money on anything that I didn't absolutely need. My shoes had holes both at the toes and heals from the trek to Rinjani. My sandals were so worn down that I could almost see through them. They gave me foot cramps, but I still wouldn't spend an extra five dollars on a new pair.

The Canadian couple from the Komodo tour asked if I wanted to join them on a drive to a waterfall outside of Labuan Bajo. There were motorcycles for rent for five dollars, but no scooters. I tried to ride one of the motorcycles, but realized that it was too big for me and would have been dangerous to drive around the hilly island. A guy at the bike rental shop offered to drive me for an extra five dollars, but since that was half of my daily budget, I told the couple to go without me. I suppose five dollars was not a big deal for the Canadian couple though, so they offered to pay for my driver.

I accepted the offer and we took off for the waterfall. We had a great day trip through the serpentine jungle roads and saw a beautiful waterfall, but at the end of the day, the couple forgot to pay my driver!

I paid the ten dollars for the motorcycle and driver, then I panicked because I knew I had just blown another day's worth of money on something that was not exactly necessary. I should have just brushed it off, but in my mind, I was a local and five dollars was *a lot* of money to me. In my mind, it wasn't even about saving money anymore, now it was about *survival*.

I walked around the town looking for this couple, since they told me they would pay for my driver. I went to their hotel—they weren't there. I walked around the one and only busy street in Labuan Bajo—not there either. Then I went looking for them in different cafés and restaurants. *I found them!* Having a nice dinner-date in a somewhat fancy restaurant. They looked so nice, the girl had a pretty dress on; they were drinking wine and enjoying some appetizers. And they *were* so nice! They looked surprised but happy to see me, even though I looked like a dirty street kid.

I ran up to them, asked them for the five dollars, and then left the restaurant, feeling excruciatingly embarrassed. *They must think I'm fucking nuts!* I thought. *Fuck it. I'll probably never see them again. I just need to survive!*

At that point, I felt like I could identify more with the local Indonesian people than with the other tourists I ran into. I decided to keep on going east, where there were no tourists. The next destination I had in mind was Bajawa, the closest city to a number of interesting-looking native villages. There weren't many buses around, however, so I caught a ride with a tour guide for the price of the local bus. It was that cheap because the guide was going to Bajawa anyway.

The drive from Labuan Bajo to Bajawa was incredible; we drove through lush green mountain passes, weaved around the side of the ocean, and up and down colorful hills. It's no coincidence that the Portuguese colonizers called this island "Flores." The jungle was covered in flowers!

We stopped at the guide's mother's house, in a small village in the mountains on the way to Bajawa. She gave us some snacks and a fresh cup of coffee, then the guide explained some things to me.

"When I was kid," he said, "there was no road here. If you want go to Labuan Bajo, you walk for four days on this path. Now the path is road.

"Things change too fast here in Indonesia. Look at my mother, I gave her a cellphone so I can call her, but she don't understand. I call her and it rings but she don't know how pick it up. I explain but she don't get it.

"Environment is changing so quickly, but the people's minds can't keep up."

I thought about this for a while. *I suppose that's why there's so much garbage everywhere you look. Forty years ago, the only garbage these people had were banana peels and coconut shells. It wasn't a problem to eat a banana and throw the peel anywhere you want, but now big companies have replaced those bananas with Snickers bars and the peels with plastic. The environment changed quickly, but the people's minds haven't changed.*

After another four or five hour drive, we made it to Bajawa.

There, again, I could not escape the constant attention. Every few meters I walked in a public area someone would yell "bule" at me. What bothered me the most was that I felt like I could not relate to anybody. I was always on the other side, always the "bule," never another human being. It seemed like everybody just wanted something from me, that I could not talk to another human being on a straight and honest level, and that nobody could be trusted.

I was angered by this and did not want to give my money away to anybody. Because of this, I refused to pay for a tour or even a motorbike ride to the traditional villages. Instead, I walked. I walked for 20 kilometers and reached the village of Bena—where they asked me for money to enter the village...

It was an interesting-looking village. The houses had thatched roofs and there were graves in people's front yards. There were also big stones and little thatched-roof shacks and umbrellas on their territory.

The next morning, I woke up feeling fed up. I decided that I should no longer venture farther east to my next destination, Kelimutu (the volcano with three different color lakes), because it was too frustrating to deal with the people here.

I decided to spend one more day in Bajawa, visit one more traditional village or see the hot springs, then head back to Labuan Bajo and eventually back to Bali (from where I could fly).

However, I felt like it would be a shame to leave these traditional villages without learning much about the people and their ways. I read a small bit of information in my guide book and tried to find more on the internet but was quite unsuccessful. Then I decided that it may be worth it to pay for a tour as long as the guide was very knowledgeable. There were several one-day tours available and also an overnight tour where you can sleep in one of the traditional villages.

The overnight tour seemed ridiculous to me—paying over $100 to sleep in someone's house is not what I would call a meaningful experience. If you are paying to be a guest, you are still very much on the other side, and still learning very little. Finding an intelligent, English-speaking guide for a one-day tour also seemed unlikely, I got the feeling that these "tours" were actually more like expensive methods of transportation rather than enriching guides.

So I walked again. I walked until my feet ached and then flagged down a bemo (minivan). I asked where it was going, looked at my paper map, and said "Okay, take me there!"

As I left the van, something miraculous happened—the driver declined my money, saying, "I'm just helping you out." This was the first bit of genuine kindness shown to me by a local person in a long time.

I was dropped off at a vibrant market, walked around it for about 15 minutes, and then bumped into a young girl who started speaking to me in English (this was surprising because most people around Bajawa don't know a word of English). After about a one-minute conversation, she invited me to visit her village. At first, I was a bit skeptical, thinking that maybe she wanted something from me as well, but she seemed very nice so I decided to trust her.

East Nusa Tenggara

October, 2011

This was (and still is) a truly amazing experience. Right when I had had it and was about to give up on Indonesia, I was accepted and brought into the other side.

My friend's name is Asry. She showed me her village, introduced me to her family, fed me, and invited me to sleep in her house. *Really* funny and ironic isn't it? Her and her family are the traditional Ngada people, from the same background as the people of Bena and Wogo, the villages people tour and pay big money to sleep in.

The entire family is very kind to me, they accept me and tell me that I am a part of their family. They feed me enormous amounts of food and ask for nothing in return.

On my second day in Malanuza (their small village), I was invited to a huge family celebration. This was something I had never expected. Asry's family dressed me up in their traditional black cloth and told me to carry the gift for the party on my head—rice in a traditional basket. Then we walked from one thatched-hut village to another. When we arrived at the scene, swarms of people surrounded me. There were about two hundred people at this party and I think most of them had never seen a white person before. They dressed me up even more, adding a yellow band, beads, and a headband to my outfit. Then they crowded around and observed me, making comments about my nose and white skin. No one except Asry knew a word of English, but it was easy enough to understand what they were talking about.

They gave me rice and grilled meat, then commented about the way I eat. They were surprised that I liked rice and that I could eat with my hands. It was a bit difficult to pick up the rice, but I didn't really have a choice since there were no utensils at the party.

After they fed me, they sent me to not only watch the traditional ceremonial dance, but to participate in it! They shoved me into a circle of people in the middle of the ceremony and I tried my best to copy their dance moves. I shuffled my feet to the beat of the drums and waved my hands around in circular motion like the other dancers. I felt honored and awkward at the same time.

I snuck off the dance floor after a few minutes, then the drums got louder, as did the powerful yells to the ancestors. And the animal sacrificing began.

Asry led me to a small room in the middle of the big house that this party surrounded. The room had a small door and was elevated above all of the other rooms in the house. Asry explained that this was the spiritual room, where the family prays to their ancestors. The door is small so that you give respect by bowing your head when you enter.

Next, I heard a scream and loud banging drums—a large pig was sacrificed outside. I looked out and saw its neck split open and blood dripping into a bucket.

Asry explained that this party was a celebration of the building of the new house we were sitting in. This house will be the "main house" of a small village, the place where family members meet, have celebrations, and pray together. Animals are sacrificed on this day and their blood is smeared onto large sheets of metal which are then placed on top of this elevated spiritual room to create a special trapezoid-shaped roof. The blood of the sacrificed animals is an offering for their ancestors.

Asry left the spiritual room and I sat there with ten very old people that gave me more rice and grilled meat.

I sure hope their ancestors don't like human blood, I thought.

I knew it was crazy to think that they might want to sacrifice me too, but I couldn't fully get that thought out of my head, especially since I had only met Asry two days before this ceremony and everything seemed so wild! The banging drums, the black cloths, the yells, the dancing, the blood!

But at that point, I figured if they did want to sacrifice me, it was already too late to do anything about it now, since I was god-knows-where and outnumbered by about two hundred people. I chuckled and continued to munch on my grilled meat.

The second animal I saw being sacrificed was a dog. The tribal leader gave it three smacks on the head and it fell dead and was hung from a rope tied to a large wooden pole. A few minutes later, they tied a second dog to this pole while the dead one still hung in the air. As you could imagine, the living dog was absolutely shitting itself.

I didn't see whether the second dog was sacrificed or not. I saw it tied to the pole for several minutes, panicking, and emitting so much fear that I could practically see it, then a man untied the chain and led it away.

Asry's family cooked and ate every part of every animal that was sacrificed, including the dog. During this celebration, thirty kilograms of rice were cooked, everybody ate a lot, and each family unit took home a goody-bag of rice and meat in the same traditional basket they came in with.

Later, they put up the thatched-roof shacks and umbrella-like structures that I noticed in Bena. These structures are called *ngadhu* and *bhaga*, and they commemorate the male and female ancestors of each family unit.

* * *

No one attempted to sacrifice me during this party, so I ended up living in Asry's village for over a week. I felt honored to be there and to have this experience.

Asry's house was made out of bamboo. It didn't have running water, a kitchen, much electricity, or much furniture, but it was nice and cozy, especially in the mornings.

Each morning, I would wake up slowly as faint sunrays shined through the misty air. Sometimes it felt a bit damp and chilly at first light, since this village was in the mountains. The smell of smoke, fire, and coffee filled the air. I'd stretch out my arms, take a deep breath, and slowly make my way to the family room. There were always five or six family members crowded around a fire pit inside the house in the morning. Somebody would always hand me a fresh cup of home-grown coffee, the best coffee I had ever had. Then I would sit quietly on a small stub of wood, sipping the coffee, and getting lost in my thoughts and the crackling sound of the fire.

In the day, Asry and I walked around her village and met with more family members. They were all very nice and they fed me A LOT. They showed me their cows, their pigs, gardens, rice fields, and coffee plantations. They showed me how they made their own knives, their own furniture, weaved clothes, and crafted many other products.

179

While I met with Asry's family members, they mostly talked about food, my white skin, and my "long nose." At first, all the attention that my nose got in Indonesia made me feel bad. Ever since I was a kid, I never liked the way my nose looked and I hated when people pointed it out. While backpacking through Indonesia, I started to feel even more self-conscious about this because *everybody* kept on pointing at my nose, talking about it, and sometimes even grabbing it! But after some time with Asry's family, I realized that most of these people paid so much attention to my nose because they thought it was beautiful. They called it "long nose" and compared it to their "ugly" flat noses, which I thought were beautiful.

Everyone also seemed to be obsessed with my white skin color, constantly telling me that I was beautiful because I was "white." I tried to tell them that people from my part of the world spend tons of money and do harmful things to their bodies in order to make their skin look browner!

That was when I realized that there is no such thing as beauty. It's all about perception, and each individual culture (and person) has their own perception of what is or isn't beautiful. So what you consider to be your worst qualities may actually be your most beautiful qualities to somebody else. After coming to this conclusion, I stopped caring about my nose and how I looked in general. I threw away my last piece of makeup, realizing that the cosmetic industry is a huge scam. *If beauty is all about perception, they really do the world a disfavor by marketing an unattainable image of beauty just to sell more shit.*

Truckin' Indonesia

I decided to leave Asry's village after her brother and cousin came by in a big cargo truck and invited us to go on a road trip with them. They were delivering heavy equipment between Bajawa,

Maumere, and Larantuka (the eastern end of Flores) and were happy to bring family and friends along.

Seven of us squeezed into this giant truck—Asry, her brother, three of her cousins, me, and for some reason, a five-year-old kid. I don't remember whose kid he was, but I don't think he was the child of anybody in our truck. That didn't seem to be so important to them though, since everyone in the family took care of all the children.

Larantuka is only about four hundred kilometers away from Bajawa, but since the road was not well maintained and weaved around the mountains like crazy, the drive took several days. It was a beautiful drive, nevertheless, and Asry and I had front row seats in this big truck. We drove up and down big mountain passes, through flowery hillsides, past black volcanic beaches, rice terraces, and lush jungles. We took breaks by the ocean and stopped to eat rice and curry in local eateries.

Everywhere we went, I was greeted with excitement and curiosity. Since I was now with Asry and her family, people didn't seem to attack me for money like before, now they wanted to give me stuff instead!

We slept in the houses of Asry's aunts and uncles in other villages in Flores. Her family members took us in and fed us until we could barely move.

October 8, 2011

Now I am in Moni, a small village below Kelimutu, the volcano with the tri-colored lakes. Tomorrow I am meant to see this volcano (leaving at 4:20 a.m. to watch the sunrise above it!).

I am not sure exactly what will happen next, but I feel that it is time to leave Indonesia and move on to new lands... Plus, my friend is calling me to join him on his yacht in New Zealand on a two-month sailing trip! So as long as they let me back into Aotearoa, I shall soon be writing of grand adventures in open seas.

I did the short and easy hike up Kelimutu the next morning, watched the sunrise over the three different colored crater lakes, said goodbye to Asry and her family, and then made my way all the way back to Bali. The trip back to Bali was much easier now that I knew a bit more Indonesian and I felt like I could understand human beings better. I stopped getting annoyed at everybody that was hassling me on this trip. People continued to yell "bule" at me, point at my nose, and try to get money from me, but I wasn't bothered by this anymore. I understood that it was the circumstances that the people grew up in (the environment) that caused them to behave the way they did. If I had been born in their place, I would behave just the same way.

I took buses back across Flores, to Labuan Bajo, Sape, Sumbawa, and Lombok. I rented a motorbike in Mataram and drove around the south of Lombok by myself, then I took a ferry to Bali and flew out to my next adventure: a two-month-long sailing trip on the North Island of New Zealand.

17

Sailing NZ, 2011

I flew to Auckland at the end of October. It was much chillier in New Zealand than in Indonesia, but I had one pair of leggings, one light sweater, and one good-quality purple jacket. That was enough to keep me warm.

I was meant to meet Enzo at a marina about two hundred kilometers away from Auckland. I knew that everything was extremely expensive in New Zealand so I didn't even bother trying to find public transportation to this place. Instead, I tried my luck hitchhiking. I walked from the airport to the road going southeast, then realized that it was a busy highway and there was no safe place to stand. It was too late to go back now, so I walked down the ramp and pulled out my thumb. To my surprise, somebody pulled over straight away!

"What the hell are you doing there?" said the driver as soon as I hopped into his car.

"I'm trying to get to the Bay of Plenty. I can't afford to take the bus. I know that was a bad spot, sorry. And thanks a lot for pulling over!" I said.

"That was a very dangerous place to stand," he said in a thick Kiwi accent. "You better be careful. I'm not going far out of the city but I'll drop you off somewhere safer."

He dropped me off at a petrol station, where I immediately caught a second lift. A few lifts later, I made it to the marina.

This was exciting! *What a change from Indonesia!* Everything felt so *different* at this marina. I took a big breath of air. It was fresh and salty. There was a parking lot, a small building, and a dock with many sailboats. The boats bobbed up and down in their little spaces and a few people roamed around the marina.

I had never been on a sailboat before and had always assumed that sailing was just for rich people, but here, none of the boats looked too fancy and the people didn't look particularly rich either. I was excited to discover this sailing lifestyle! I was also excited to meet Enzo. He seemed like such an interesting person. He had told me that he was born in Brazil but had immigrated to the US when he was around seventeen years old. There, he started skydiving. He had lived in New Zealand for several years and had worked as a skydiver in various drop zones all over the world. I was very curious to learn more about this skydiving lifestyle, thinking that perhaps I could try it myself one day.

After a few minutes of wandering around the marina, I found Enzo. He was standing next to a charming little baby blue and white sailboat. He was tall, with long brown hair and a nice smile, but was not as good looking as he was in his profile pictures. *That shouldn't matter, right?* I was excited to talk to him not only about sailing and skydiving, but about everything! I had read so much about him before my arrival that I was sure he'd be a person I could learn a lot from. Plus, I had just spent the past two months basically in my own head since most Indonesians I came across didn't speak English, so I was dying to have a real conversation with someone.

I gave Enzo a big hug. "Nice to finally meet you!" I said.

"Likewise, darling! Come on, I'll show you your new squat," he said. "Her name's Selena. She's thirty-seven foot long and made of steel." He knocked on the hull.

The yacht was tied to a berth at the very end of the wharf. On the deck and all around the boat there were all kinds of ropes, drills, hoses, buckets, pieces of equipment, and power tools. "She's my baby," he said. "I bought her a few years ago, hollowed out the hull, cleaned and painted everything, and made all the furniture inside. Come on, I'll show you the cabin down below."

I slid my backpack off my shoulders then followed him down a little stairway to the cabin beneath the deck. "It looks really cozy," I said.

Inside the yacht there was a booth with two seats, a sink and a water system that brought up ocean water, cabinets filled with canned food and freshwater tanks, one pretty big bed at the end of the boat, and a toilet seat over a bucket of cat litter.

Enzo laughed about his toilet then gave me the keys to the bathroom and shower at the marina. It was clean, private, and had proper plumbing.

"Make yourself at home, darling," he said. "We might be stuck at the marina for a few days. I just need to fix the self-steering and a few other things, but it shouldn't take too long and then we'll sail into the sunset as promised!"

It was obvious that Enzo wasn't ready to take off sailing yet, but he did warn me about this before my arrival and I told him I was happy to help with the work that needed to be done.

"No problemo, Capitan!" I said, "Let me know what I can do to help."

"Okay princess, let's put you to work then!" He laughed, then handed me a couple of books. "Have you ever been on a sailboat?"

"Nope," I replied.

"Okay, read this." The first book he gave me was called *Sailing for Dummies*. "You should at least learn the basics of sailing in case I get thrown overboard." He grinned. "And if you're gonna live on my boat, you also have to read this book." The second book looked a bit more intimidating. It was black, about eight centimeters thick, and was titled, *The Culture of Make Believe*. "I have a buddy from Jersey who's never read a book in his life. Someone gave him this book and he actually managed to read *half* of it! This book will change your life."

"Looks intriguing," I said. "I'll give it a read, thanks!"

I spent my first few days hanging around the marina and reading *Sailing for Dummies*. I tried to get my head around the anatomy of a sailboat and all of the sailing lingo. I had no idea there was an entirely different language based around sailing! And so much to know!

Enzo spent all day, every day working on fixing parts of his boat. I wasn't sure what he was doing exactly, but I told him that I was always happy to help. From time to time, he gave me work like cleaning out shelves or painting inside the cabin. At night, we cooked dinner inside the boat and chatted a bit.

From reading Enzo's Couchsurfing profile and messages, I had assumed that he would be a very happy, calm, and humble person. I thought that Enzo and I would bond straight away and become great friends, but as time went on, it became evident that reality did not meet my expectations. The more I talked to Enzo, the more I realized that he wasn't the person I had imagined him to be. We didn't have as much in common as I had expected and he wasn't really interested in having a conversation with me. He acted like the happiest person in the world when we were around his neighbors at the marina or in front of random people in grocery stores, but when we were alone in his boat, he seemed miserable and highly disturbed.

The more time I spent with Enzo, the more outrageous and offensive things he would say. He claimed, for example, that there was not a single intelligent American on Earth and that all women were "whores" and they ruled the world.

I tried not to get offended by what he said. I was a guest on his boat, staying there for free, so I didn't want to fight with him. Instead, I stayed calm and tried to understand what he was talking about and why. I thought of this as an interesting psychological challenge for myself.

"What do you mean by that—all women are whores?" I asked. I kept my emotions to myself and tried to understand what he was trying to say. If I didn't agree with what he said, I calmly explained my thoughts. If he didn't agree, I would leave it at that. After a while, I ended up bubbling up my thoughts and keeping them to myself, since I had no one else to talk to.

I probably should have left the marina as soon as I saw this bright red flag, but I was so curious about sailing that I just couldn't leave yet. The environment around me was so exciting—the salt, the boats, the ocean, everything! I just wanted to go on one sailing trip before abandoning this adventure. Plus, I realized that although Enzo was a bit crazy, he still had some positive attributes.

He's not the person I was expecting to meet, I thought, *but he's still an interesting person. He's a skydiver, he travels around the world and lives on a sailboat. He hand-built his boat, he's hand-crafting his own self-steering, and he believes that you can achieve anything you want if you work hard to do it.*

I admired his passion and determination, and I liked that he wasn't a "normal" person. I also loved living out of the sailboat even in the marina. I loved cooking there, I loved cleaning and painting the boat, I loved reading and smelling the ocean, playing guitar on the deck, and watching the sunsets in the evenings. Everything was so simple, yet exciting on Selena.

* * *

One night, Enzo and I came back to the boat when it was storming outside. There was strong wind, heavy rain, lightning, and thunder. The boat was rocking up and down and banging around like crazy. It was dark inside the cabin. I got into bed and listened to the powerful sounds of the wind, thunder, and the steel boat hammering against the wharf.

Most people would probably be terrified right now, I thought.

I was enticed and excited. Then Enzo rolled his body on top of mine and said, "What the hell have you gotten yourself into?

"Aren't you scared?"

"No."

Then he kissed me.

I wasn't particularly attracted to Enzo but I was very attracted to the situation. The boat, the storm, the ocean, this life. *I just love life.* I love having fun. I love physical pleasure and emotional stimulation. And I love *feeling alive.*

He undressed me and went down on me, saying that was all he wanted. But I wanted more. I wanted it all. And I got everything I wanted, that night and every day after.

After that night, our relationship improved a little. Enzo and I still couldn't have much of a conversation, but we had great sex, and a lot of it. It was the only way we really connected. But this was also a problem because it was distracting for him. He grabbed me any chance he could, but then cursed himself out for not being able to finish his boat work on time. He also got into a crazy defensive state of mind. He constantly talked about other girls, commenting about how hot they were and how he would like to have sex with them, or telling me all sorts of sex stories from his past and how great those girls were. I wasn't sure how to respond to those comments, so I mostly ignored them or replied with my own stories. I didn't take any of this too seriously, I was just a twenty-two-year-old girl having a bit of fun. *Not like I was planning to make him my boyfriend or something.*

I realized that most people overcomplicate sex and relationships. Sex and nudity have become extremely taboo because of our insane culture and religions. This has made sex, boobs, and vaginas almost like scarce resources, which makes our society go even more insane. Men chase women around for their resources, women play games and run away because their resources are taboo. Sometimes women force men into possessive relationships in exchange for these scarce resources, and oftentimes, both people end up possessing each other rather than simply enjoying each other's company.

Because sex, boobs, and vaginas are so taboo, women are also looked down on in our culture for wanting to have sex or flaunting their taboo resources. In reality, these cultural ideas and taboo mentality are absolutely ridiculous. I mean, you have two people: a man and a woman, they are attracted to each other and they have sex. They perform the same act together—one act—yet a man is supposed to enjoy this act while a woman is looked down on if she enjoys it? WHY? What's so bad about having sex in the first place? Are we hurting each other or anybody else?

In our society, it seems that sex and nudity are more taboo than murder and violence. Have a think about that.

Personally, I have no interest in playing any fucking games or accepting the insane ideas of our culture and society. If I want to have sex, I will do that given the right situation. If people look down on me for wanting to have sex, that's fine with me. There are over seven billion people on Earth, I'm sure somebody will understand me. If not, well, at least I got to have some fun in my life.

So Enzo and I spent several more days at the marina, mostly having sex, before we took off on our first sailing adventure.

Enzo gave me one duty before we left: make the grocery shopping list for a week-long sailing trip. I took a look at the cans that were already in the boat, found a pen and small piece of paper, then scribbled down a list that looked something like this:

- Beans x 7
- Canned veg x 7
- Eggs
- Pasta
- Rice
- Cabbage
- Canned fruit x 7

I didn't take this list too seriously because I wasn't a very organized or responsible adult at the time, plus, I didn't think it was a big deal. We were only planning a one-week trip to a nearby island.

Enzo didn't ask to check my list before we left for the shop, but once we got to the supermarket and I was a little bit confused about what, exactly, to put into the shopping cart, he completely freaked out on me.

"I GAVE YOU ONE EASY AS FUCK TASK, AND YOU COULDN'T EVEN DO THAT?" he yelled. "YOU'RE A FUCKING FAILURE. WHAT THE FUCK IS THIS LIST?"

He grabbed the list and scorned me in the middle of the grocery store, making me feel embarrassed as hell. He acted like our lives depended on this list, as if we were planning some dangerous journey across the ocean.

"If this list was so important to you, then why didn't you check it before?" I asked. "You knew this was my first time planning something like this."

"BECAUSE I THOUGHT THAT YOU HAD A FUCKING BRAIN, YOU DUMB BLONDE!"

I walked away and bought the stuff that I had on my list. *Don't get upset,* I told myself. *These growls are just a manifestation of his personal crisis. Let's just go on this one-week sailing trip, then I'll leave Enzo alone and travel around New Zealand by land. It's not a good idea to continue to put up with this shit.*

Enzo bought a separate basket of groceries, then he calmed down and we drove back to the boat. We had sex later and things were back to kind-of okay, then we took off for the sailing trip the next day.

We untied all the ropes and left the marina using just sails and no engine. I had no idea what we were doing but I was very excited at first. I tried to remember what I had read in *Sailing for Dummies*, but everything happened so fast that I couldn't keep up with the action. Enzo yelled commands at me, some of which I didn't understand, then he cursed me out and scared the shit out of me. After that, I sat quietly in the corner of the cockpit as he managed the boat on his own.

Once we were out at sea, he was calm and quiet. Everything changed then. We sailed all afternoon, past the sunset, and into a brilliant starlit night. There was a big swell that night, about two meters or so. Selena crashed into the icy cold waves with immense power. I was absolutely terrified, yet incredibly excited. The sound of the wind, the sound of the sails getting hampered and turned, the waves crashing against the hull, weaving, swirling, churning, and disappearing into the dark obis. Reappearing again, crashing, weaving, churning, disappearing.

Down below it was the worst. I had no idea you would hear such sounds inside of a sailboat! The sound of crashing waves was magnified tenfold, as if the boat was getting beaten down by the ocean. There were vicious clanking sounds from the steel hull, as if some giant was hitting the boat with a hammer. It sounded like the boat was going to fall apart any moment! I couldn't be down below for more than ten seconds. You couldn't even stand down there as the boat rocked you from side to side, back to front. I also felt this intense heaviness down there, as if the mass of my body had suddenly doubled, and the mass of my head had tripled.

On the deck it was calmer—ride the boat up the wave, roll it down the wave, then crash into the next wave. Ride the next wave up again, down again, crash again. *Stay in the cockpit and hold on; if you fall out, you're dead within thirty minutes.*

Each crash was spectacular! There was bioluminescent phyto-plankton in the water—plankton that light up like stars when agitated. Every time the boat crashed into a giant wave, the little plankton appeared like a galaxy on our deck, then rolled down and vanished like shooting stars. I was mesmerized by this sight—stars above, stars below, the wind, the elements, the waves, the ocean. *This is what life should be about! Not learning how to make some business plan in university!*

I remember this moment perfectly because I fell deeply in love right there and then. Not with Enzo, but with sailing, and with life.

When the waves got bigger, Enzo made me go down below and sleep. I was absolutely terrified down there, but that heaviness pinned my body to the bed and knocked me out cold and fast.

I woke up a few hours later to the sound of calm waves and easy rocking. We were anchored.

Enzo took my hand and said, "Come here. I want to show you something."

We walked onto the deck; the night was calm and dark. I could see a half-moon bay and black mountains in the distance.

"Do you believe in magic?" he asked.

"Sure." I smiled. Then he took a stick and crashed it along the water. The ocean lit up like the Milky Way.

* * *

In the morning, I stuck my head out the hatch. I felt cool wind hit my face. I smelled salt, dirt, and lush vegetation. I heard birds diving into the water and the sound of small waves crashing on sand. I looked ahead and saw a perfect bay. No people, no other boats in sight. Just a deep dark green forest of interwoven trees and vines reaching out toward an empty beach and crystal blue water. We had breakfast then took the dinghy to shore to explore the rolling hills and fantastic views of Mayor Island.

Enzo was in a much better mood now and I was beaming with excitement. We climbed around some logs and big rocks, then up a small path through the forest and to a beautiful lookout. On the way, birds flew by so closely that they almost hit us in the head.

"They're not scared of us because they rarely see humans," said Enzo.

There was nobody on the island. Just the two of us.

Back on Selena, everything was perfect. It was warm and sunny, we had no need for clothes, and we were stocked with delicious food and great books. There was a light breeze that swayed the boat from side to side as it calmly bobbed up and down around its anchor.

Everything was somehow slower but more meaningful on the boat. I sat in the booth down below, next to Enzo's crochet "Home Sweet Home" sign, and gazed at the Pacific Ocean through a little window. I held a book in one hand and a cup of tea in the other. I took a sip and attentively listened to the sounds around me. Every breeze, every wave, every bird call, every drop of water that hit the deck was so notable. I took another sip. *So sweet.* Every taste was so powerful. Every touch, so distinct. And time stood still on Selena because nothing really mattered.

Enzo and I spent a few days in this spot then decided to sail to the other side of Mayor Island. Once we got there, we realized that we hadn't been completely alone on the island after all. There were two caretakers on the big beach—two big Maori brothers. Enzo and I were supposed to pay to land there, but instead of paying, we offered one of the brothers a bottle of wine.

"All right, sure guys." The big guy accepted. "Just don't tell my brotha!"

"Sure thing, bro!" said Enzo.

"You guys wanna drink it with me later tonight?" he asked.

"Why not?" said Enzo. "We can even bring some rum!"

"All right!"

And that was how we made a new friend. I don't remember this guy's name, but Enzo and I called him Bubba. Bubba was a real big Maori guy with some cool islander tattoos and a big smile. He seemed very calm and friendly. Enzo and I rowed the dinghy to his part of the beach around sunset, then the three of us made an enormous fire using wood from a few cabins that had been knocked down by a landslide. Bubba and I chatted for a while, while Enzo was mostly silent. It felt great to finally have a real back-and-forth conversation with someone. After an hour or two, we noticed a fishing boat in the bay.

Enzo stood up and stared at the boat. "I bet you they have lobster," he said. "Sasha, you should go over there and ask them for lobster!"

"Do you *really* think they would just give me lobster?" I said.

"Yes! Take the dinghy, paddle over there, and ask them for lobster! Actually, they call it crayfish here, so ask for crayfish."

Lobster is one of my favorite things to eat but I rarely eat it because it's so expensive, so I took the dinghy and decided that it was worth an ask. *The worst thing that could happen is they say no, right?*

It took about ten minutes for me to row to the fishing boat alone under moonlight. The bay was calm and quiet. On the boat there were two fishermen, one older Kiwi guy and one younger one. They looked surprised but happy to see me pop up from the dinghy.

"Hey there! How are you guys doing?" I leaned my head over the side of their boat. "I'm just coming from the beach over there and I live on that sailboat." I pointed to Selena. "My friends told me that you might have some crayfish! Do you happen to have a lot? Would you have any extra crayfish to spare?"

The younger guy looked annoyed but the older one was clearly the boss and he was extremely friendly. He looked around and told me they hadn't caught many crayfish, but then he said, "Aw, but it's not every day that such a sweet young girl paddles up to our fishing boat in a dinghy! How many are you there on the beach?"

"Three." I smiled.

He opened his cooler and pulled out three lobsters! I couldn't believe it! Especially since it really looked like they hadn't caught many and these things are expensive. I felt really bad that I had nothing to offer them in return.

I thanked them a lot and rowed back to the beach with our three lobsters. Bubba and Enzo were overjoyed at my "catch" and Bubba offered to cook us a big Maori breakfast with these lobsters the next morning.

Enzo and I slept in the sailboat that night then rowed back to Bubba's beach in the morning. As we approached the picnic table, Bubba was already setting it with freshly boiled lobster, fresh beer-battered fish, bread with butter, orange slices, fresh sea urchins, and a few Maori dishes. This may have been the best breakfast of my life.

* * *

Enzo and I spent a few more days at Bubba's beach then sailed back to the marina. The sail back was calm and dolphins followed us along the way as they played in the wake of our boat. I almost touched them as they leaped in front of us! We also trailed a line from the back of the sailboat and caught a fish for dinner.

When we came back to the marina, I had the best shower of my life. I realized only then, that a hot shower is pure luxury—and the best kind. After the shower, we made some fish and chips, then resumed our marina lifestyle.

The autopilot was now broken and there were several other things that Enzo needed to repair before we could take off to explore more islands farther north. Enzo had been pretty calm and respectful while we were on Mayor Island, so I decided to continue this adventure with him. After we came back to the marina, however, he fell back into his strange and crazy mood.

He started talking about other women nonstop, he constantly blamed me for anything that went wrong, and he randomly screamed out the word "whore" dozens of times a day as if he had Tourette's syndrome. When we went to the grocery store, he told random people that he was "living the dream!" but back on the boat, when we were alone, he was angry and miserable. He'd say things like, "Sex is very bad unless it's for making babies," then he would come on to me. He talked about how important it was to wear makeup and to be "fashionable," yet he didn't have many "fashionable" clothes of his own. He also once told me that he thought women were almost never raped, and if they were, it was their fault.

I could never really tell whether Enzo actually believed what he was saying, or whether he was just testing my response. I coped with his behavior by staying calm again. I understood that something traumatic must have happened to him in the past, and that this trauma manifested through his behavior. I tried to understand him, rather than get angry at the things I disagreed with. Our sailing trip to Mayor Island was so incredible that I didn't want this adventure to end yet, even if Enzo was crazy. I would have left his boat if he had asked me to, but he didn't, so I just stayed and waited until he was ready to take off sailing again.

I dug into the big book that Enzo had recommended when I first arrived: *The Culture of Make Believe*, by Derrick Jensen. Once I started reading it, I couldn't put it down. It started off exploring hate, culture, and the reason behind the lynching of colored people in the early twentieth century in the US. It went on to examine horrific events of the past and the present, detailing cases of rape, murder, genocide, slavery, environmental destruction, and atrocities such as the Bhopal gas tragedy.

The book made some very important points. *Slavery is bad— almost everybody agrees with that now. The transatlantic slave trade of the sixteenth to nineteenth centuries was horrifying. But what about what's happening today? Is it really that different?* Derrick Jensen points out that it's actually more expensive to own a slave than it is to rent one. If you own slaves, you have to provide them with food, water, clothing, and shelter. When they become old or sick, they become a burden to your wallet. However, if there are a lot of slaves available, you don't have to own them!—And that will save you money. You can pay them just enough to keep them alive while you need them, and when they get old or sick, you don't have to continue to pay them (or provide them with food, clothing, and shelter), you can replace them with other slaves!

Think about it. Providing a slave with food, clothes, and shelter would probably cost more than two dollars per day, so why not just give the slave that two dollars per day of work and have them get their own food, clothes, and shelter? That way, you can make them disposable and also make them believe that they are "free." As a result, you can maximize your profits and simultaneously make the slaves believe that it's their own fault when they don't have enough to eat or feed their children.

That's exactly what happens all over the world today. *Today, nearly **half** of the human population lives on less than $5.50 per day and over half a billion people live on less than $1.90 per day.*

Apart from pointing out these very harsh facts, Jensen also highlights the reason behind these horrifying behaviors. He explores "hate" throughout the book, realizing that it's not some inborn "hate" or "cruelty" that causes humans to enslave or abuse one another. Companies don't choose to set up factories in Cambodia and pay their "employees" the lowest possible salary because they are "bad people" or because they hate Cambodians, they do this simply because it's the most profitable thing to do. *Exactly what I learned about in my business class! That's the **right** thing to do in this system! Because the most important thing for a business is to make as much profit as possible.*

After reading this book, I realized that the *whole* system was the problem. All of these businesses, these huge incentives to make profit at the expense of everything else—that's the problem! That's *global*. And all of the solutions I learned about in university are just band-aids attempting to patch up this cancerous profit-driven system. *That's why they're not working.*

This book gave me all the more reason to have absolutely no desire to participate in the system, to build some kind of career for money, or to have a child.

Fuck this system! Let's just go sailing!

* * *

As we lived at the marina, I talked to our seafaring neighbors and learned more about the sailing lifestyle. It turned out that sailing was not at all just for rich people! In fact, most people living in that marina were pretty broke. Our neighbor Dave, who was one of the nicest Kiwi guys I had met, barely had a penny to his name, yet he lived for sailing. He dreamed of sailing to Antarctica and around the world one day. He lived on his boat year-round and worked odd jobs to pay for food and boat maintenance.

I talked to many older people, sailors that had been all around the world, and I decided that if I ever grow up, I'd like to be just like them.

Through Enzo, I learned a lot about communication. I learned to stay calm and listen. The less emotional I was, the better our communication was. I learned to calm myself in general, to focus on the positive things, and to block out negativity. It turned out that the grocery items I had bought for our first sailing trip were perfect —we had enough of everything, plus several canned food items left over for the future. I didn't make a fuss over this, but the second time around, I made a spreadsheet on my laptop to organize exactly what we needed. Enzo seemed pleased with it.

Enzo and I took off sailing again after a few weeks. As we sailed, Enzo was calm and peaceful, he taught me how to steer and work the sails a bit. We had a good time fishing and exploring some islands and beautiful beaches along the Coromandel Peninsula. The most memorable island was the Great Barrier Island. It was larger than all of the other islands we visited and it had a population of around one thousand people. There were some paved roads, cute houses, and a very expensive ferry that went to Auckland once a day.

Enzo and I came to shore and hitched around the Great Barrier Island. The first car we thumbed at always stopped to pick us up; the driver always smiled and asked us who else we had caught a lift with, since everyone on the island knew each other. We found one art/pottery shop with an "honesty jar" and no shopkeeper. If you wanted to buy something from this shop, you'd simply write down your purchase on a paper pad and drop the cash into the honesty jar.

"It goes to show you how trusting people can be, given the right environment," I said to Enzo.

Later we found some incredible white-sand beaches with perfect waves and pointy hills in the distance. I never saw more than two surfers in the water at once.

We hitched back to the boat and spent a few nights anchored in a beautiful bay. Enzo was relatively nice most of the time, but every once in a while he'd say something outrageous and I just couldn't hold myself back any longer.

He once laughed as he told me a story about his Brazilian friends "buying" a hooker for someone's birthday, "But the birthday boy's dick was so big that even the hooker refused to fuck him! So they fucked her anyway AND took her money! Hah!"

I don't think my reaction was quite what he expected. "You're laughing about your friends raping and robbing a woman? How can you laugh about that?"

He replied with something like, "You can't rape a hooker anyway."

I walked away and made my final decision to get off the boat as soon as we made it back to the mainland.

The next day, we took off for the mainland. We sailed straight through the bay at full speed with two sails perpendicular to the boat and the wind directly behind us. We were flying! I smiled as the wind frolicked my hair and the sun caressed my skin. Then, all of a sudden, Enzo sensed that something was wrong. He muttered something that I didn't get, so I replied with, "What?"

Then he violently yelled, "SHUT THE FUCK UP!"

Two seconds later, we ran into a reef. Lucky for Enzo, his boat had a steel hull so we didn't capsize. The boat was stuck on top of this reef at about a forty-five-degree angle, flapping up and down and clanking against the rocks with every little wave. It was a bit frightening but I wasn't too worried since I knew I could swim to shore if I needed to.

Two local guys came up on a power boat. "What the hell are you doing here?" they yelled at Enzo. "Didn't you look at the charts?"

Enzo's face turned bright red. "Yeah I looked at the charts. It was a mistake."

"Well your mistake destroyed the reef here, mate. Learn to read the charts!" They helped us pull the boat off the reef, then Enzo motored it to a wharf where he could have a look at the hull at low tide. I didn't say a word to him. As soon as we were tied to shore, I went for a long walk on the land. I thought it over and decided that it was time to leave. *I don't need to wait until we get back to the mainland, I can get off right here.* There was a hostel on the Great Barrier Island and a daily ferry to Auckland, so it was a safe place to leave from.

I came back to the boat after a few hours and started packing my stuff. Then Enzo took my hand and said, "I have to apologize." But instead of apologizing, he made many excuses for the way he had been behaving. He said that he was very stressed, he had to do a lot of work to the boat, he was low on money, et cetera.

This wasn't the apology I was looking for but I decided to sail back to the marina with him anyway, since it would save me an expensive ferry ticket.

Enzo inspected the hull at low tide and confirmed that it was fine, there were just a few small scratches on the surface. At high tide, we left the bay. The sail was calm and beautiful; dolphins followed in our wake again. A few hours later, we docked at the marina, then I packed up my stuff, thanked Enzo for the experience, and left.

* * *

I hitched north to a town called Whangarei and stayed with a nice couchsurfing host. This guy had a big house and three other couchsurfers staying with him. He drove us all to the northernmost tip of New Zealand, then we skimmed around the beach dunes in his four-wheel drive and visited some awesome North Island hot springs.

I thought about the experience I had with Enzo. *He was an asshole but he was very special in some ways, and I learned so much from the journey he shared with me.*

I loved the feeling of living that sailing lifestyle and being so different from other people. I remembered the time we went to a local bar together:

December, 2011

I remember looking around and seeing ordinary people who lived ordinary lives. I thought about what they probably did all day and what they would probably do when they got home. Then I thought about our lives, and what we would do when we get home. And what home was, and what it all meant to us.

It was so real. So passionate. Most people may not even understand it. I loved being unordinary.

I decided to send Enzo a card with a picture of me on his sailboat, thanking him for the valuable experience. After that, I bought a flight to New York. My next plan was to visit my mother for the Christmas holidays, then make my way to the Rocky Mountains, where I would snowboard for the rest of the Northern Hemisphere's winter season.

18

USA, 2012

I had spent about four months traveling Australia, Indonesia, and New Zealand since I left Sydney in August of 2011. Both Australia and New Zealand are expensive countries, but I managed to keep my budget pretty low. I spent less than two hundred dollars on food and petrol during our road trip through Australia, about two hundred dollars on a flight from Darwin to Bali, probably about six hundred dollars on two months of backpacking through Indonesia (I paid for accommodation, public transportation, food, and a couple of tours); I spent another five hundred seventy dollars on a flight from Bali to Auckland, around two to three hundred dollars for all expenses on the North Island of New Zealand (the only expense was food), and a whopping one thousand dollars on a flight from Auckland to New York.

This means that I had spent around two thousand dollars on a fantastic four-month-long adventure in the Southern Hemisphere, plus another thousand dollars on a big flight to the other side of the planet. I had roughly five thousand dollars saved when I left Sydney, so once I got to the US, I still had about two thousand left. At the time, the Australian dollar was pretty much equivalent to the US dollar.

I knew that two thousand dollars would not get me very far in the US, so I decided to get a job for a few weeks while I was visiting my mother. I searched through the classified ads on Craigslist and found a job offer for a daytime bartender in a pool hall. The place was called Castle Billiards Lounge and was located in a town called East Rutherford, New Jersey. I showed up with a great new resume and a lively smile, and was hired straight away!

"We pay ten dollars an hour," said the boss. "We only need a daytime bartender, just so you know, but maybe you'll be able to pick up some night shifts from time to time. We don't get a lotta customers in the day, that's why I'm paying ten an hour."

Usually bars in the US pay nothing-an-hour because bartenders rely almost entirely on tips, but here in the pool hall, it was clearly a different story. I came in the next morning.

"Here's the bar." The manager took me over to the big square in the middle of the pool hall. The bar was lined with all kinds of bottles that I was pretty familiar with.

"Here are the beers, the house spirits, some liqueurs. Coke, Sprite, Fanta, all that stuff. Bloody Mary mix. Now I did tell you we don't get a lotta customers in the day, right?"

"Yeah, no problem." *Should I quit now?* I wondered. *At least they pay ten an hour. Let's see how it goes.*

It turned out that this bar got about five customers per day, so I wasn't quite sure why they needed a daytime bartender in the first place, but I ended up loving this job! I barely had to do anything in that place. I came in around 10:00 a.m., made coffee, drank the coffee, and read poetry. When I got bored of reading, I played some pool. A few regulars came in and taught me how to aim and shoot properly, so I improved a lot at pool. The regulars didn't buy many drinks but they all had funny personalities, so I enjoyed talking to them. They made me feel like I was living in an episode of *Seinfeld*.

"You know that every other daytime bartender quit from boredom?" said Scottie, a one-armed professional pool player. He had lost his arm after getting a staph infection. He was in a coma for a while, almost lost his life, and ended up getting one arm and one leg amputated. I watched as he adjusted the custom-made bridge cue that replaced his left arm. "All the other girls would just stay in the bar all day, watching television! After a few weeks they'd quit cuz they'd get too bored!" Scottie chuckled. "Now the guys are making bets on how long till you quit!" Then he burst out laughing.

That's funny, I thought, *I'll quit in about four weeks, but not because of boredom!* I enjoyed playing pool, reading, and chatting with the people at this pool hall. Castle Billiards even had WiFi so I was able to bring in my laptop and surf the web while I was "working."

One morning, I received an email from Enzo as I was sipping coffee by the pool tables.

Enzo. January 5, 2012

The year didn't start well if I must say... on the fourth jump of the day, just before landing, I was caught by a very rare mini tornado which makes the parachute don't work and you immediately go back in freefall... my instincts were to save my passenger so I slid as much as I could under him and he landed right on top of me...

The outcome is that I am in Intensive Care Unit in Christchurch writing to you and paralyzed from the hips down... have gone through surgery, went real real well... now only time can tell... It's a new adventure for me and amazingly there are no more worries.

I have lived an awesome life... gone to the ends of the world and bla bla bla... whatever your future plans are my dear, please don't do what society says!!! Do what's in your heart...find assholes like me and keep traveling...

Something like this happened to me and now I can make everyone at the hospital laugh at my morbid jokes because I smile at life... but I guess it is only because I never lived according to the rest...

I almost dropped my coffee. *He's paralyzed?*

I offered to fly back to New Zealand and see him, but he said not to just yet. He said that he was just fine and very lucky to be taken care of by the New Zealand healthcare system. He said that he would be in the hospital for a while and it would be better for me to visit him once he was out.

205

We exchanged several letters over the course of the next few weeks and he ended up telling me that he was in love with me and wanted to start an adventurous life together after he got out of the hospital. I ended up telling him exactly how I felt about everything he did and said. I wrote that if he wanted me to love him, I needed explanations for the name calling, the yelling, the contradictions, the blame, the ridiculous statements, everything.

He still didn't apologize for his behavior but he did admit that almost everything he did was due to his own insecurity, and that now, he had changed.

I left it at that and stayed in contact. I quit the pool hall job after about a month, said goodbye to my mother and the regulars at Castle Billiards, then flew to Florida with my snowboarding gear. This time, an old friend from high school was waiting for me in Jacksonville.

I spent a couple of nights in Jacksonville with my friend Colin, then we drove to New Orleans for Mardi Gras. Once we got to New Orleans, we met up with friends, ate some jambalaya, flashed some people, got some beads, and danced to some blues.

After a few days in New Orleans, I parted with Colin and took a bus to Albuquerque, New Mexico. I spent one night in a hostel in Albuquerque, then hitchhiked to a town called Taos.

* * *

Taos is a peculiar little town located at the southern edge of the Rocky Mountains, where the mountain range meets the desert. The ski resort, Taos Ski Valley, is big, steep, and gets a ton of very dry snow, as well as a lot of sunshine. I decided to come to Taos because I knew somebody who worked at the resort as a ski instructor. This guy's name was Dean. He offered me a couch for a few days and said he could help me get a job as a snowboarding instructor.

When I showed up to Taos, I loved it straight away. It felt like the Mexican Wild Wild West but with a big snowy mountain on the side. I admired the adobe houses, the clay pottery, and the beautiful landscape. There was a lot of delicious Mexican food and a huge variety of chili peppers, beans, and rice in the shops—all for an affordable price.

The people that picked me up hitchhiking seemed a bit strange but were all very nice. They had funny accents and used a lot of Spanish words in their slang. More than half of them were drunk though. That seemed to be what the locals did on their days off, they just drove around drinking and picking up hitchhikers. Half of them didn't even know where they were going so they would just drive me wherever I needed to go. This wasn't the safest way to get around but I didn't have enough money to buy a car and there wasn't much public transportation available in Taos.

I didn't have enough money to buy a season pass for the mountain either, so I was set on getting an instructor job so that I would get a pass for free. I turned in a job application and then looked for a place to live.

I searched for shared accommodation on Craigslist and found an awesome wooden cabin in the desert right below the mountain. It was a bit out of the way since I didn't have a car, but the place was stunning. The cabin was new, it had a huge kitchen and living room, a balcony, a jacuzzi tub, beautiful views of the desert and surrounding mountains, and it only cost four hundred dollars per month for my own room, including bills. There were six other people living in the cabin but it was very spacious and they all seemed friendly.

I decided it would be worth it to live in this cabin and hitch-hike to work every day, since hitching seemed easy in New Mexico. I handed the landlord one month's rent, unpacked my backpack, then hitched back up the mountain to beg for a job.

Taos Ski Valley didn't want to hire me at first, maybe because I didn't have any instructor certificates, but I was extremely persistent. I came to the ski school office every single day and talked to the managers until they got annoyed enough to hire me. Once I got the job, they trained me as a kid's snowboarding instructor and gave me a season pass.

Perfect! That was all I really wanted. Not the job, just the ski pass.

I was a shitty instructor because I didn't really want to work, I just wanted to snowboard. Whenever there was a powder day, I would show up to work about a half hour late (after doing some runs), then I would make my students follow me as I carved around the fresh snow on the sides of whatever slopes they could somewhat handle. I did enjoy seeing some kids improve their skills and get really excited about snowboarding, but mostly, I just wanted to snowboard without them.

I was paid less than ten dollars an hour as an instructor, while the resort charged two hundred dollars per student for a six-hour lesson. Sometimes I had up to ten students in one group, so this means the resort received two thousand dollars for the lesson that I taught, while I only got about fifty-four dollars. Maybe I would have cared more about this job if they had treated their "employees" more fairly.

On my days off work, I'd spend all day riding the beautiful mountain. Snowboarding has always been like therapy or meditation for me. I'd plug in my music and glide down the fluffy light blankets of fresh powdery snow, ducking around trees or doing little jumps along the way. I adored the breathtaking views and the peaceful nature of being deep in the mountains.

As I worked for Taos Ski Valley, I also got to know a lot of people. I met most of the ski and snowboarding instructors, some of the park guys, some ski patrol staff, and many other people who worked for the resort. Everybody except the managers seemed to be there just to have fun and enjoy life.

One night, I went out with a bunch of instructors to see a live band at a local bar. There was one lesbian ski instructor who seemed to check me out every once in a while at the ski school. She was about five years older than me, blonde, and pretty good looking in a bit of a manly way. We took a few shots at the bar and she started dancing with me and getting pretty close. I was curious about this whole lesbian thing so I let her take me home that night. I don't remember how the sequence of events unfolded but somehow, I ended up in her bed, she went down on me like no one ever had before, and I did the same to her except I had no idea what I was doing.

I didn't think I was very good in bed, so I felt a bit insecure and said something really stupid to her the next morning. I told her, "I'm just kidding. I'm not really a lesbian." Then I left her house and never talked to her again, feeling horrible and horribly embarrassed for having said that.

I ended up falling for one Native American pro snowboarder guy who worked in the park. His name was Ryan. I don't know what it was about him, maybe just that he was so damn good at snowboarding, plus he was super sweet and free-spirited. He had tan skin, long black curly hair, and a great smile. He liked me too at first. We had a great time snowboarding together, going to different hot springs and parties, hitchhiking around, and climbing mountain peaks. Once the snowboarding season was over in Taos, we decided to hitch to California together.

"Tahoe doesn't close for another month!" said Ryan. "We can go there and chase the snow."

"Let's do it!" I grinned.

In April, I moved out of the nice cabin, packed up my backpack, then realized that I had *too much* stuff for hitchhiking.

"Jeeesus!" said Ryan when he saw my bag. "Girl what the hell you got in there?"

I had a fully loaded sixty-liter backpack, plus my snowboard, boots, and a guitar that I almost never played. Ryan basically just had a toothbrush, a snowboard, and boots.

"Yeah I know, it's too much," I said. "But the thing is, I don't know what to do with this stuff. You left your stuff in Taos because you'll come back here. You're family lives here. I'm not planning to come back, I'm just going in one direction. This is all the stuff I live with."

He rolled his eyes and pulled out his thumb. We hitched a few lifts, got stuck for a while, then made it to Colorado just before dark. We spent a couple of nights at Ryan's friend's place, then hitched farther and got stuck even worse. Someone dropped us off in the middle of nowhere, on a ramp leading onto an interstate highway. Behind us, there was nothing but a field. Few cars came by and none of them stopped for us. We stood on this ramp for over six hours, staring at the long straight road running through that flat open field.

Eventually it got cold. We didn't have a tent, sleeping bags, or much winter gear. I got frightened when I realized we only had about twenty minutes of sunlight left. *Nobody will pick us up in the dark and we'll freeze here at night!* I panicked inside my mind.

About a minute later, a random guy appeared out of nowhere. We didn't notice him until he was directly behind us. He was an old traveler with long hair, a dog, and a raggedy old backpack. It looked like he came straight out of a movie. He was obviously hitchhiking and hopping freight trains.

He walked right by us and didn't say anything.

"Hey man!" Ryan yelled out. "How do you get a lift around here?"

"Walk the highway," he replied. "Just walk the highway."

He continued on his way.

We grabbed our backpacks and walked down the ramp onto the five-lane highway. The old guy was already gone.

Next, we walked the highway. Cars zoomed by us at 150 kilometers an hour. We stuck our thumbs out and walked straight.

Just keep walking. My backpack was heavy. The snowboard and guitar were a burden.

Zoom! Each car shed a deafening sound.

It'll be dark in about ten minutes.

Don't panic.

Don't think. Just walk. Walk straight.

All of a sudden, a big cargo truck stopped for us.

Whew! Right before dark!

We ran up to the truck and hopped in fast. It was a nice new truck and the driver was heading all the way to Salt Lake City, Utah, where I knew some people. The truck driver was a nice young guy.

"Make yourselves comfortable," he said. "You look tired. Been a long day?"

"Yeah, we've been hitching for a while," I replied, "standing out in the cold."

"Go to sleep if you want. It'll be a few hours before we get to Utah."

I felt safe in this truck. I took off my shoes and lay down in the driver's bed behind the seats. Ryan stayed up for a little while chatting with the driver but eventually dozed off too. After a few hours, we made it to Salt Lake City.

Ryan and I decided to take a small break in Utah. We stayed with some of my old university friends and went snowboarding. We didn't have ski passes for the mountains in Utah, but the ticket checkers weren't too strict since all of the snow was melting anyway. We snuck past the mountain staff and got to ride the last of the Utah spring slush.

After the ski resorts in Utah closed, we continued hitchhiking. We walked the highway again and caught a lift with a cargo truck that was going all the way to Reno—exactly where we wanted to go next. Ryan had some friends in Reno who said we could crash with them and catch a lift to Tahoe in their car the next day. The catch was that those friends happened to be in a strip club the night that we arrived.

After a long ride in this cargo truck, we made it to Reno. Ryan and I thanked the driver, took our snowboards and backpacks out of the truck, then ordered a taxi from the truck stop to the strip club. We must have looked funny walking into this strip club with our raggedy clothes, a huge backpack, and two snowboards. The staff didn't seem surprised or annoyed though.

"Welcome!" They kindly greeted us as we stepped into the strip club. "You can put your stuff back here, we'll take care of it."

I put my stuff down then went into the bathroom to try to comb out my messy hair. I couldn't be bothered digging into my big backpack for a change of clothes, but at least I had some deodorant at hand.

I felt a bit underdressed wearing ripped jeans and an old T-shirt in this fancy strip club, but the girls seemed to like me anyway.

Maybe they sense that I'm an experienced lesbian now, I mused. *Or maybe they just want my money...*

I was pretty impressed by their ability to climb up and down the strip pole. That must take a lot of strength and endurance. Unfortunately, I still had no money to give them.

Ryan's friends were nice. There was one guy and one couple. The girl that was with us used to work in this strip club. Now she was completing her master's degree in psychology.

The five of us slept in a cheap motel that night, then drove to Lake Tahoe the next day. We crashed at Ryan's friend's place in Tahoe for a few nights, then Ryan and I split ways. I still really liked him, but I could tell that he wasn't that into me anymore, so I just let it go. *You can never force someone into liking you.* Ryan continued hitchhiking and I stayed in California.

California 2012

I logged into Couchsurfing and found a crazy skier to stay with. His name was Jake and he was an absolute lunatic, but mostly in a good way. He was a stereotypical young American guy—didn't know much about the world, loved drinking, smoking, and parties, had tons of credit card debt and no job, but he was very outgoing and always ready to do anything. I spent a couple of weeks hanging out with him and his friends, snowboarding the last of the Tahoe spring slush, going to the beach on the beautiful mountain lake, kayaking, taking boat trips with friends, and just having fun.

I also met up with a few people that I knew from having worked in Tahoe back in 2008. One of these guys, Kevin, invited me to join him and his friends on a trip to Mammoth Lakes after the ski resorts in Tahoe closed down.

"Mammoth is so huge that the mountain doesn't close until June!" said Kevin. "Sometimes it even stays open until July! We're gonna go down there and camp for a couple of weeks. Come join us!"

"Well I've already chased the snow this far," I replied, "so I may as well keep chasing it!"

"I wouldn't even call it snow anymore," said Kevin. "It's spring slush! But it's super fun."

Kevin and I took off for Mammoth Lakes in May. Kevin had a truck, so we didn't have to worry about hitchhiking this time. We drove through the beautiful mountainous landscape of Northern California, past big lakes and lush pine forests, then to Mammoth Lakes, California. There, we met our two companions, Freddy and Mike.

Freddy was about forty years old but looked like he was twenty-something; he was French but grew up surfing big waves in Hawaii. He was a rocket engineer, an awesome skier, and absolutely full of life. Mike was closer to sixty years old, and was also very excited to be alive and to ski the last of the Californian spring slush.

I loved this lively crew of people! Kevin and I followed Freddy's truck to the outskirts of Mammoth Lakes, onto a dirt road and into a spectacular valley. The 360 degree view from this valley was out of this world. The valley was wide, flat, and dry. The ground was covered in light green grass and small shrubs, but there were no trees in sight. The wide open landscape unveiled a wall of immense snow-capped mountains surrounding the valley in the distance.

"Wow! This is incredible," I said as we drove down the dirt road.

"Wait till you see our camping spot," said Kevin.

After a few minutes, we stopped the truck next to a beautiful meandering river.

"Woo hoo!" yelled Freddy as we hopped out of the truck.

"Check it out!" he said. "The river is hot."

"Well, I wouldn't say hot," said Mike, "it's warm here. And very hot upstream."

"It's perfect!" said Kevin.

I touched the water. *It is warm!*

"We're standing on an ancient volcano," said Freddy. "The volcano exploded over seven hundred thousand years ago and created the huge basin we're in now. The warm water comes from the natural hot springs in the area. We'll check out the hot pools too, there are a bunch of really cool ones here. Perfect for après-ski dips!"

"This river is perfect for dips too!" yelled Kevin as he ran into the water.

"Totally!" I quickly put on a bikini and followed him into the river. It was shallow and there was a ton of seaweed, but the warm temperature of the water was pleasant. We hung onto the seaweed as the warm current pushed across our bodies.

After the swim, we set up our tents, made a fire, had a barbecue, and gazed at the stark bright Milky Way above our heads.

This is the life.

The next day, the four of us planned on going skiing and snow-boarding on Mammoth Mountain. The only problem was that neither Kevin or I had enough money to buy lift passes, since they cost about a hundred dollars per day, and by the year 2012, ski resorts like Mammoth already had pretty advanced security. The resort no longer just gave out stickers for day passes, now they printed plastic cards with photos and information. When you swiped the card to get onto a chairlift, a photo of your face would automatically pop up on the lift attendant's computer screen. The lift attendant also had access to your data—your gender, age, height, etc. Lift attendants were only paid about eight dollars an hour, and Mammoth Mountain gave them big rewards for ratting people out! Because of this, we could no longer wait around the parking lot and ask any random strangers for their day passes. Now we either had to find people who looked just like us or figure out a different strategy.

"What if we bribe the ski patrol guys with a bottle of Jack?" said Kevin.

"What do you mean?" I replied.

"Everyone that works for the mountain gets some complimentary passes for their friends and family. At the end of the season, there's always somebody that never used their comp passes. We can go into the ski patrol office with a bottle of whiskey and offer it to whoever still has these passes. If they agree, they can register our names on the passes as if we were their friends."

I chuckled. "Okay let's try it!"

Kevin and I bought a bottle of Jack Daniel's for about twenty dollars, then walked into the ski patrol hut and waved the bottle around.

"Hey guys!" I said. "Does anyone have complimentary passes they still haven't used?"

"I do!" said one older guy as he eyeballed the whiskey bottle.

"I do too!" said another guy.

"Perfect! We just need two passes today, but we'll need another two tomorrow!" I grinned.

"Sure thing! We'll be here," they said as we swapped the bottle for the two lift passes.

Kevin and I walked out of the ski patrol hut giggling like two little schoolkids. "High five!" He smacked my hand. "Let's head up the mountain!"

We took the chairlift up and met Freddy and Mike on the slopes. There wasn't much snow left on the mountain in May, but there was a lot of sunshine, a pretty good park, and fantastic views of the Sierra Nevada mountains. We spent the entire day riding around in T-shirts, swishing through the melting slush, hitting some big kickers, and having a lot of fun.

After snowboarding, we drove back to our camping spot, bathed in the warm river, made a fire, had a barbecue, gazed at the startling Milky Way, and chatted about life, the world, and the universe.

The next day, we'd go back to the shop, buy another bottle of whiskey, swap it for lift passes in the ski patrol hut, then ride the mountain all day and repeat the cycle all over again.

We did this over and over until the ski patrol guys ran out of complimentary lift tickets.

"Bummer!" said Kevin. "We'll have to figure something else out, I can't afford to buy passes."

"Yeah, me neither," I said. We drove away from the ski resort and walked around the little village of Mammoth Lakes.

"The best would be to get a season pass somehow," I said. A season pass for Mammoth Mountain usually costs about a thousand dollars and allows you to go up the mountain every day for the entire ski season (from November until June/July). Clearly, we weren't considering buying a season pass, but a new idea popped into my mind. "It's the end of May now. Most people that live here have season passes but don't use them anymore, since the season's almost over." I noticed a girl walk by. She was about my height and looked like she was around the same age as me.

"Heya!" I stopped her. "Um, sorry if this sounds weird, but do you happen to have a season pass for the mountain? I'm looking to buy a pass from somebody who's not using it anymore."

"Um, okay," she replied, smiling. "Yeah I'm not going up there anymore, is there still snow up there?"

"Well not really," I laughed, "just some slush."

She took the season pass out of her wallet and showed it to me. I examined the photo. "I think we look similar enough. Oh and we have almost the same birthday! I was born just one week before you! Same year!"

"Oh that's cool," she said.

"Will you take fifty?"

"Okay, sure!"

I handed her fifty dollars in cash and she gave me her 2012 Mammoth Mountain season pass.

"Sweet! Thanks a lot!" I was stoked.

"Lucky you!" said Kevin as he grabbed the season pass from my hand. "Yeah she looks just like you in that photo. The only difference is the hair color."

"Yeah, maybe I'll dye my hair brown, just to be on the safe side," I said.

We went to the supermarket and bought a five-dollar bottle of hair dye. I dyed my hair in a laundromat that night and went up the mountain with my new pass the next day.

It worked like a charm! And soon, we found a season pass for Kevin too.

After a week or two of snowboarding and camping by the warm river, I invited Jake, from Tahoe, to come and join us in Mammoth. He drove down in his fully loaded Subaru a few days later. Jake's Subaru was always stuffed with just about everything you could possibly need—a blow-up mattress, a barbecue grill, a very loud speaker, skis, a bike, sleeping bags, pillows, a cooler, two guitars, a shovel, paddles, all kinds of clothes, and a bunch of other random stuff.

When Kevin, Freddy, and Mike left Mammoth, Jake and I stayed for a few more weeks, snowboarding and living out of that Subaru. Since it never rained while we were in Mammoth, we never needed to sleep in a tent. We blew up Jake's big inflatable mattress anywhere we wanted and slept in a different spot each night.

We rode Mammoth Mountain every day and explored different hot springs every night. The hot spring pools in the Long Valley Caldera were absolutely spectacular. Some of the pools were built up with little footpaths, cobblestone walls, and small pipes and levers that controlled the temperature and water flow, other pools were just holes in the ground with natural spring water. Sometimes we had the pools to ourselves, other times we shared them with friendly visitors.

Each night, we'd take a dip in the warm water, cook food over a fire, blow up the mattress next to the hot pools, and fall asleep beneath the stars. Then we would wake up, take another dip in the warm water, eat breakfast, deflate the mattress, and ride up the mountain all over again.

This felt like true freedom, the only problem was that both Jake and I were running low on money. We didn't need much, just a little bit for food, gas, and drinks, so we came up with an idea.

"What if we sell hot dogs and beer in the Mammoth parking lot?" I proposed one day. "We can buy a big bag of hot dogs and a case of beer, grill the hot dogs out of the back of your car, and sell them to the people coming down from the mountain."

"Okay!" Jake agreed without batting an eyelid. Neither one of us even considered the heavy penalty we would have had to face had we been caught selling alcohol like this.

We snowboarded most of the day, came down the mountain an hour or so before closing, moved Jake's Subaru to a convenient location, blasted Creedence Clearwater Revival from Jake's powerful speaker, and began grilling.

I made a sign: 2 HOT DOGS + PBR= $5!

Once people came down from the slopes, they walked over to us and started buying! The first day, we sold more than half of our hot dogs and beer. We didn't make a huge profit, since we didn't charge much, but we did make enough to buy a tank of gas, and we got to have leftover hot dogs and beer for dinner.

Life was easy and sweet.

We did this "gig" several times and made just enough money to pay for our bare necessities. When Mammoth Mountain finally closed, Jake and I took some trips to Yosemite National Park to check out the raging waterfalls, towering granite cliffs, and beautiful mountain valleys.

Yosemite was a powerful sight. There were a bit too many tourists for my liking in Yosemite Valley, but the thousand-meter rock walls, herculean waterfalls, rivers, rainbows, and rounded-down mountaintops were out of this world.

We ran to the top of Yosemite Falls and admired the incredible view of Half Dome across the valley. Once we were up there, we snuck past the barrier and lay on top of a ledge to look down at the valley 1,647 meters beneath our bodies. As I gazed down, I felt like the great big rocks I was lying on were swaying from side to side. I got dizzy. *I've never been on such a high cliff before.* I closed my eyes for a moment, then crawled back to the safety zone.

Jake and I tried to climb up to Half Dome with our camping gear, but were stopped by rangers saying that we needed a permit. We weren't supposed to camp anywhere except the overcrowded designated camping spots, so we parked the car in a random place, made a sign saying, "Car Broke Down," and climbed to the top of a hidden boulder facing Half Dome in the distance. We camped there for the night and nobody bothered us.

When Jake decided to go back to Tahoe, I mailed my snowboard and winter gear to my mother's house, then bought a bus ticket to Los Angeles. I didn't like the pollution and busy streets of LA, so I left as quickly as possible, took a train to San Diego, then walked to Mexico.

19

Mexico, 2012

There was a busy footpath going through the border between San Diego and Tijuana. I followed the long line of people down the cement pavement and into a gray security building. I had my bag screened through metal detectors, my body patted down, then I waited in line some more and filled out some papers. Eventually, I presented myself to the border police people. I handed over my passport and the papers, got an "entry stamp" for Mexico, and was finally allowed through the border. I felt a sense of relief as soon as I walked out of that building.

They really make you feel like a criminal, I thought. *And for what? To separate people into tribes, that's all. US tribe on one side, Mexican tribe on the other.*

No wonder people have a hard time understanding that we're all human. According to these laws and regulations, we're not all humans on Planet Earth, we're either Mexicans, Americans, Russians, or whatever other tribe members from the "designated territories" that we establish and maintain through force.

And we consider ourselves to be "civilized." What a joke.

I walked to the nearest money exchange kiosk and changed my dollars into pesos, then had a look at the map.

Where should I go now?

I walked to the main bus station and checked the schedule. I noticed a cheap bus to Ensenada, a coastal city just one hundred kilometers away.

I can get there before dark, find a cheap place to stay, then figure out what to do next. It'll probably be safer than staying in Tijuana.

I didn't have much of a plan for Mexico. I came there to brush up on my Spanish language skills because I was considering going back to university in August. Since Spanish was one of my majors and I barely used the language for an entire year, I thought this would be useful.

I bought the bus ticket and arrived in Ensenada by late afternoon. I got off the bus, then walked around the neighborhood looking for a cheap room. The funny thing about being a white girl with a big backpack in a place like Mexico is that all kinds of random people offer you accommodation as soon as they see you. I talked to the locals and bargained for the cheapest possible price. Eventually, I found a room for about ten dollars a night.

That's still a bit expensive, I thought, *but it'll be okay for a night or two.* I found a WiFi connection and sent out a few couchsurfing requests in Spanish, then went wandering around the city. Ensenada seemed a bit strange at first. I noticed that there was one very colorful, nice-looking street by the seaside. It was only about five blocks long and one block deep. It was clean and there were dozens of souvenir shops, cafés, and restaurants clearly set up for the tourists that came off their giant cruise ships. As soon as I walked just one block away from the colorful street, I found myself in an impoverished ghetto.

So the giant cruise ship stops here, the tourists get out for an hour or two, consume as much as possible in the five colorful blocks that are designed specifically for them, then they get back into their cruise ship with bottles of tequila and Chinese-made sombreros, now claiming that they've "been to Mexico." I wonder if any of these tourists have even bothered to look just one block beyond the colorful street...

The next time I logged back into Couchsurfing, I noticed that my request was accepted by a guy named Alfredo. He seemed very nice, judging by his profile and the references that previous couchsurfers had left him. I told him where I was located and he offered to pick me up in his car the next day.

Perfect! I realized this would be the perfect opportunity not only to practice Spanish, but also to get to know the Mexican culture and the real Ensenada.

Alfredo showed up the next morning with a friend named Hector and a dog named Tropi.

"Hey, nice to meet you!" he said in fluent English.

"Hola! Nice to meet you too! Podemos hablar en Español?" I explained that I wanted to practice as much Spanish as possible while I was in Mexico.

"No problemo!" said Alfredo.

Alfredo seemed to know English much better than I knew Spanish, but Hector was relieved that we chose to speak his mother tongue. We went back to Alfredo's place, where there was an empty guest room just for me, then we dropped off my backpack and went for some great local tacos.

The three of us got along straight away. I enjoyed their nice company and they were amused by my travel stories. They showed me some beaches, some nicer parts of Ensenada, and a lot of great food. I spent one full day with Alfredo and Hector, then the next morning, Alfredo offered me his car for the day.

"I have to go to work," he said, "but if you want, you can drop me off at the office and take my car. I can point out some cool spots for you to check out. Feel free to take Tropi along too, if you wanna take her for a walk or something. Just don't forget to pick me back up from work!" He grinned.

"Oh okay, sure, thanks!" I couldn't believe how kind and trusting Alfredo was. Many people would hesitate to even let a friend or relative drive their car, let alone a random couchsurfer they met less than twenty-four hours ago.

I dropped Alfredo off at his office then drove around and checked out some local sights with Tropi. At 5:00 p.m., I picked him back up from work and cooked some dinner.

When Alfredo and Hector were off work, they gave me a fantastic tour of the city and the surrounding area, and they introduced me to some of the most delicious dishes in Mexico.

They showed me the best ceviche on the Baja California Peninsula —fresh fish, squid, shrimp, and other seafood cured in lemon juice and mixed with diced tomatoes, onions, cilantro, and delicious spicy sauces. They also showed me the best taco truck in town, the best quesadillas, sopes, flautas, chilaquiles, fajitas, and other tasty dishes that I can't remember the names of.

"*All* Mexicans are just a little bit chubby," said Alfredo. "Not fat. Just a little chubby."

Alfredo and Hector also took me out to a live ska band and to a traditional Mexican restaurant with a loud mariachi band. The three of us went on a small road trip down the coast to explore beautiful hills, ocean views, rocky cliffs, and a massive blow hole. One day, we even went ocean kayaking in a spectacular mountainous location.

This was a fantastic trip and I barely spent any money on it because I stayed with Alfredo for free and only ate local food, which Alfredo and Hector often didn't even let me pay for. The kayaks belonged to Hector and everything else was basically free.

While I was staying at Alfredo's place, I was contemplating what I should do next.

I have about fifteen hundred dollars in my bank account, I thought. *I can go back to Australia, do just three more semesters of university, and I'll be able to graduate! Just three semesters! My parents would be so happy. And then I'll be able to travel around the world without this stupid university burden.*

A flight to Australia was about eight hundred dollars. A student visa was around five hundred. *This means I'd have two hundred dollars left. But, I still have that lucky credit card...*

Enzo sent me a message saying that he was in Wanaka now, on the South Island of New Zealand, and suggested for me to get a layover flight to visit him on my way back to Sydney.

I wasn't sure what to think about Enzo at that point but I felt bad that he was now paralyzed. I knew that he was a different person in his letters than he was in reality, but I thought that perhaps I could give him a chance, at least to be his friend. He had, after all, admitted his mistakes and claimed that he had changed because of the accident.

Plus, the ski resorts in New Zealand are about to open up for the Southern Hemisphere's winter season...

I decided to spend over half of my money on a flight from Los Angeles to New Zealand, feeling reassured that I still had that credit card. I also asked my mother to ship my snowboarding gear to Enzo's place in Wanaka.

I can spend one and a half months snowboarding on the South Island, then I'll fly back to Sydney and finish those last three damn semesters of university!

The day before I left Ensenada, Alfredo and Hector bought me a big piñata stuffed with Mexican candy. "It's a Mexican tradition!" said Hector. "Now you have to hit the piñata blindfolded until the candy comes out! Then you can eat all the candy."

They covered my eyes with a bandana, spun me around, and handed me a bat. "Where's the piñata?" I laughed.

"Right in front of you!" said Hector.

I nudged it with the tip of the bat.

"Now smack it!" yelled Alfredo.

I hit the piñata and heard Tropi jumping around me and barking. *Smack! Smack!* "It's not breaking!"

"Hit it harder!" yelled Hector.

I swung the bat and missed!

"Not there!"

Four more swings and the candy finally dropped to the ground! I took off the blindfold and unwrapped the sugary treats. "You guys are just too much," I said. "I don't know how I could ever thank you enough for this whole experience."

The next day, I said goodbye to my two amigos and took a bus back to Tijuana. Once I was in Tijuana, I walked from the bus station back to the dreadful border crossing.

The border again... I looked at the long line of people. *It will be fine, just follow the line.* I had a bad feeling about this border crossing.

*What can happen? Really, I mean I'm a US citizen now—they **have** to let me in, right? And I'm not doing anything wrong at all. I* *have nothing on me—no drugs, no bongs, no alcohol, not even a single souvenir!* I tried to reassure myself that everything will be just fine.

I followed the long line of people down the cement pavement, from one gray building to another, through security, metal detectors, and pat downs, then I finally faced the US border police.

One police officer examined my passport for a while, then asked, "Why do you travel so much?"

"I just like to travel," I replied.

"What is your job?"

"I don't have a job."

"Where do you get all the money to travel so much?"

"I don't need a lot of money to travel."

I tried to tell them the truth but they didn't seem to believe me. They didn't think it was possible to live the way I did, and they probably thought I was doing something illegal. They sent me into an isolated room and several policemen questioned me for several hours. One policeman thoroughly searched through everything I had in my backpack. He found my diary, opened it up, and started reading.

"Oh that's just an old piece of writing," I said, waving it off.

He looked at me, put it down, and continued searching. Eventually he found my Russian passport, which was not illegal to have.

"What are you doing with this?" he barked.

"That's my other passport. You're allowed to have dual citizenship in the US," I said.

"We don't want to see this. Next time, leave it at home!"

"Okay, sir." This time I knew to be as nice and respectful as possible. *All these pigs really want is for you to bow down to them.*

After about four or five hours of intense interrogation, they finally gave me back my passports and let me into the "land of the free."

20

New Zealand, 2012

I made it to Los Angeles International Airport just on time for my flight to Christchurch, but the flight was delayed by about twelve hours. As a result, Air New Zealand put us up in a hotel. They rounded up all the passengers from this flight, and to my surprise, brought us all to a nice Hilton resort. They gave us vouchers for dinner and breakfast, and they gave me my own fancy hotel room. The resort had a big outdoor pool, hot tubs, a gym, and a bunch of nice restaurants. I felt very out of place, but in a fun way.

Well, I paid a lot for this flight, I thought, *so I may as well enjoy this hotel too!* I put my dirty old backpack in my glamorous hotel room, then hit the hot tub. I sat in the hot tub for a while, enjoying the fresh air and the warm bubbly water. Eventually, I started speaking to the people around me. It turned out they were all on vacation, spending lots of money on this nice hotel and their "adventure" in Disney Land. After a week or two, they would all go back to work and to their ordinary lives, which they didn't seem very excited about. They asked me where I was from and what I "do."

"I spent the last year backpacking around the world," I replied. "First, I traveled through the middle of Australia, then I backpacked through Indonesia for a couple of months. In Eastern Indonesia, I stayed with a tribe that sacrificed animals! Then I lived on a sail-boat in New Zealand for a couple of months, then flew to the US and lived in New Mexico. After that, I hitchhiked to California, lived on a blow-up mattress in the Long Valley Caldera for a month or so and snowboarded in Mammoth, then I spent a couple of weeks in Mexico. Now I'm on my way back to New Zealand to snowboard some more." I giggled. "But I'm from Russia, originally. And I don't have a job, so I guess I don't "do" anything."

They looked a bit shocked. "Um... Where do you get the money for all of this?" they asked.

"I worked as a bartender in Sydney and saved about five thousand dollars before I left. I also bartended in Jersey for four weeks and worked as a snowboarding instructor for two months in New Mexico. I probably spent six thousand or so dollars on that whole trip, maybe less. How much do you spend on your vacation?" I asked.

I think they spent a lot. And I don't think they really understood me, but that's okay. Few people ever do.

The next day, I flew to New Zealand. Luckily, the New Zealand border police were much nicer than the US border police, so they let me into their tribe without having to go through hours of interrogation. Once I walked out of the gated area, I spotted Enzo.

"Hey there, brown-eyed girl!" he said as he rolled up to me in a wheelchair.

He looked so skinny that it frightened me at first. I had never known anybody that had gotten paralyzed before and I wasn't sure how to react.

"Hey! Thanks so much for picking me up!" I gave him a hug.

Enzo's upper body was fully functional and one of his legs moved a bit, but both legs were extremely thin and his face and upper body had changed a lot. He had a lightweight wheelchair that he was fully in control of and a new car with hand controls.

"This is my new baby," he said as he showed me his car. "It's a gift from the New Zealand government!" He laughed. "I feel real real lucky that this accident happened to me here in New Zealand. The hospital gave me the best care for weeks and I didn't have to pay a dime for it. Now they've given me a car, a bunch of perks, and a monthly income!"

226

"Yeah if this happened to you in the States and you didn't have health insurance, you'd be absolutely screwed," I said. "Even with health insurance you might get screwed, depending on the insurance."

"Yeah I woulda been outta the hospital not only with a broken back but with a hundred-thousand-dollar bill to pay. Maybe even more! And then what? That's truly horrible. I'm so glad to be here in Aotearoa."

Enzo went to a doctor's appointment and visited some friends in Christchurch, then we drove the long and beautiful way to Wanaka. I was happy to see that he was fully independent and didn't seem to struggle to get around. He was able to hop from his wheelchair to the driver's seat of his car, disassemble the wheelchair, place it in the car, take it out, and basically go anywhere he needed to go. I helped him when I could, but he didn't really need my help.

Enzo told me that the worst thing about being paralyzed was not that he couldn't walk, but that his bowel and bladder no longer functioned properly. He had to trigger his bowel movements through digital stimulation and he had to use a long tube to extract urine from his bladder. If he didn't do this properly or on time, it could result in an accident. The entire process seemed painfully uncomfortable.

Everything seemed uncomfortable, actually. Enzo lived in a share house in Wanaka with two or three young snowboarders. As soon as we arrived, snow started coming down and it got very cold inside the house. It's always cold in New Zealand in winter because they don't make many winter houses with proper heating and insulation like in northern countries. Electricity is also extremely expensive in New Zealand so Enzo and his flatmates mostly tried to heat the house with their fireplace.

"In Russia and in many northern countries, lots of houses are heated with a masonry stove," I said to Enzo as we sat by the fire. "It's kind of like a fireplace, but much more efficient. As soon as you light the fire, your entire house heats up and stays warm for a while. Oftentimes, it even gets too hot. I wonder why they don't build these kinds of stoves here in New Zealand."

"Yeah here they have these British-style fireplaces. It takes like four hours just to heat up the living room with this thing!" Enzo laughed.

"Maybe they're just made for looks," I smirked.

I spent a couple of weeks in this cold house with Enzo. I wasn't really sure what I came there for, maybe I wanted to comfort Enzo or see how he really was. It felt a bit sad at first, especially to see him struggle to cope with his bowel and bladder problems.

I talked to Enzo for a while; he seemed calmer than before but he hadn't really changed like he claimed to have in his letters. He was still deeply disturbed by something and this accident didn't make that go away. He still acted like he was happy and "living the dream" in his writing and in public, but behind the curtains it was the same old story as on Selena. The only thing that changed was that he stopped talking about other girls and now he claimed to be in love with me.

This was disappointing but I still felt bad about the situation and I wanted to help him somehow. This time, I decided not to bubble up my thoughts, but to explain everything I wanted to say in an attempt to solve some of Enzo's psychological problems. Unfortunately, that didn't help. Actually, it made things much worse. We argued a lot and then I decided to leave.

I didn't leave on a very bad note, but I knew that I couldn't be with Enzo anymore and that I wasn't able to help him. I hitchhiked to Queenstown, where my old Whistler roommate, JB, happened to be living.

* * *

It was great to catch up with JB after so many years. I hung out with him a lot but couldn't stay at his place because he lived in a small flat shared by about ten people. I stayed in a hostel at first, then found a host through Couchsurfing. The host's name was Ricky, he was a nice Indonesian guy who worked as a chef in a fancy hotel. Ricky and his roommate Aziz had couchsurfers and friends over all the time.

"It's bloody cold here in New Zealand!" said Ricky. "We like to have people over to warm the place up." Like so many houses in New Zealand, Ricky's place was not insulated.

When I first came to their place, there were five other people staying in the living room. They slept on couches and sleeping mats, while I crashed in Ricky's hammock.

I introduced Ricky and Aziz to JB and they introduced me to their friends. All of us got along well and I ended up crashing in Ricky's hammock about half the time I was in Queenstown. The other half, I mostly spent in a hostel that I snuck into for free.

I used my credit card to buy a season pass for a resort called Remarkables, then went snowboarding every day. I made friends with some ski bums from Chile and Argentina, so I was able to continue to practice Spanish while I was on the slopes.

Soon, I realized that I was back down to negative money, so I did a few "illegal" snowboarding lessons for cash and I tried to think of new ways to make money without legal working rights.

I have a guitar, I thought. *I don't play it very well but I've been dragging it around the world for a long time, so maybe I should try to make some use of it.*

I thought perhaps if I sat in the corner of a busy street and strummed four chords over and over, maybe somebody would feel bad for me and throw me enough change for a loaf of bread or something. The day I had this idea, I met a Czech guy who was planning to busk as well. He said that he busked from time to time and that sometimes he would only make about five dollars, but other times he would get sixty dollars or more. I told him that I was considering busking too, so we decided to busk together.

We walked over to a busy street, chose a bench, and took out our instruments. I'm not sure why I thought this would be a good idea in the first place, since I didn't play guitar very well and I had no idea how to jam with other people, but this guy started playing and he was amazing!

Uh oh. What should I do? I tried to listen and quietly pick at one string to find a tone that didn't ruin his song. Eventually I found about four individual notes that seemed to match the chords he was strumming. He noticed this and gave me a solo moment, so I plucked the string louder and played something that (at best) sounded like "Mary Had a Little Lamb." Then another guy with a guitar showed up, and he was even better than the Czech guy! They played together, the new guy danced and sung, and was very interactive with the people on the street. He got people to circle around us and clap their hands.

As the crowd grew in size and excitement, I stopped attempting to play the guitar. I clapped my hands and slowly inched away from the musicians and into the circle of people, then continued clapping and ran away, up to JB's house for sympathy. *Better stick to snowboarding lessons for now!*

* * *

Enzo came to Queenstown for a visit and I introduced him to Ricky and JB. We also took a trip to Milford Sound, which was perhaps the most incredible place I'd ever seen. Sheer rock faces and 1,700-meter-high mountains towered over a mirror of water. Enzo and I approached the rocky shoreline silently, then sat and stared at the reflection of the colossal snowy peaks. Not a single ripple disturbed the stillness of the sound.

Later, we took an easy kayaking trip through Milford Sound and noticed a seal, a beautiful waterfall, and some stunning glacier-carved rock walls.

Enzo and I continued to argue throughout this trip and basically anytime we spent more than an hour together, but when I left New Zealand, he still wrote me long letters and claimed that he loved me. I didn't really get it. *Why does he want to be with me when all we do is disagree and argue about everything? What's the point?*

Part 4

21

Sydney, 2012

In August, I flew back to Sydney. I sat in the plane and did nothing but think. I thought about everything. So much had happened in just one year. It was both happy and sad, exciting, scary at times, and it was just *so much.* I felt saturated with life. Now I was off to a new beginning. I was motivated: *three more semesters of university and then I'll be free! After I finish university, **no one** is going to stop me from doing anything I want to do! I'm only twenty-three years old so my whole life is ahead of me.*

I put Enzo's problems to the side and concentrated on life in Sydney. Luckily, my amazing boss, James, took me straight back to work at Three Wise Monkeys. I wasn't expecting him to take me back after being away for an entire year. Actually, I didn't expect him to take me back after the first time I went away for three months, but as soon as I messaged him, he put me right back on the bartending schedule for the following week. This saved me because I had negative money at that point and I couldn't even afford to pay for a place to live.

I spent a week or two at my friend Dave's place, near Sydney's prettiest beachside suburb, Manly. Then I decided that if I had to live in Sydney, I would live in Manly. This meant that I would have to spend an hour and a half getting to Sydney University and an hour getting to work, but that my "home" would be surrounded by beautiful nature and a beach where I could surf. I was determined to learn to surf because I knew that I needed an extreme sport and the ocean as therapy from work and university.

I found a small room in a small apartment near the beach for 150 dollars per week. The room was "so cheap" because it was shared with another girl. I knew that sharing a room would make it difficult to study but I couldn't afford my own room at the time. I bought a bicycle for twenty dollars, took a ferry from Manly to Sydney, and then biked to Three Wise Monkeys and to Sydney University.

I had such a busy schedule that I didn't even meet the person I shared a room with until about a week after I had moved into this apartment. It turned out that my roommate was a tall and beautiful American girl who grew up in a trailer home in Texas. Her name was Rachel. In our room, there were two queen-sized beds that were basically attached to each other and took up more than half the space of the room, so it seemed like we had one big shared bed and not much else.

The night Rachel and I met, we stayed up talking for hours in our big long bed. She was really funny and loved to travel as well. It was a hard feat for her to leave her small trailer-park town in Texas and make it all the way to Australia. She had been in Sydney for over two years and was taking some bullshit college courses just to live legally in Australia under a student visa. She was also working about three jobs and saving up for a big trip to Southeast Asia.

I spent the semester studying a lot, working a lot, and surfing, running, or boxing for small breaks. That semester almost killed me, actually. I stressed so much that I was getting eye twitches and extreme back pain that I could not get rid of.

Rachel and others told me to take it easy. "It's just a course," they'd say, "don't take all of this so personally!"

But I couldn't do that. *It is a course, yes, but it is real. I am learning about the real world. The actual real world and how it functions, not the tunnel-vision, job-praising, bullshit "real world" that everybody tries to make you believe is real.*

Take climate change as just one example. This was one of the global topics we explored at the University of Sydney. It is very real, it is serious, it is happening, and there is basically no question that it will affect humanity and many other species in a very negative way.

In the following section, I will outline some basic information about the science of climate change and about the international and global actions taken to stop climate change. Remember, climate change is a global problem whether we like that or not, so the solution for it has to be global as well.

The following section is very fact-heavy, but it is important. That's why I included it.

Climate Change 101

To put it simply, the Earth receives energy (radiation) from the Sun —this is why we see light and feel heat in the daytime. Most of the energy that comes from the Sun to the Earth comes in the form of visible light, which travels in short wavelengths. The Earth's surfaces (like land and water) absorb some of this energy and then radiate back longer light waves. These longer light waves, called infrared, are not visible to the human eye but can be measured using special instruments.

Back in the 1800s, scientists figured out that if the Earth was absorbing the Sun's energy and then shooting it all back out to space, the Earth should actually be much cooler than it is today, so there must be something trapping some of this radiation on the Earth's surface. What they later figured out was that the atmosphere of the Earth, which is composed of a number of gasses (N_2, O_2, CO_2, H_2O, CH_4, and others), acts like a blanket by trapping heat within some of those gasses. They learned that gases like CO_2, H_2O, CH_4, and others absorb infrared radiation and then emit it in different directions. Some of this heat does go back out to space, but some of it comes back to Earth, thus, making the Earth much warmer than it would be without an atmosphere. This is called a "greenhouse effect," a term coined in the late nineteenth century, which implies that the Earth's atmosphere traps heat much like the glass of a greenhouse traps heat.

Take note that most of the radiation that comes directly from the Sun is not absorbed by greenhouse gases; it is either reflected by surfaces like ice, or absorbed by things like land, water, and living creatures.

The thicker the glass of a greenhouse, the better it will be able to trap in heat and the hotter it will get inside the green-house. The same thing applies to the Earth's atmosphere. The thicker the atmosphere (meaning more molecules of CO_2, CH_4, H_2O, etc.), the better it will be able to trap heat and the hotter the Earth will get. Scientists have known about this effect for over a century, but today's technology has allowed the scientific community to come to a general consensus that climate change is, in fact, happening, it is caused by the emissions of greenhouse gasses like CO_2, and it is very much something we need to be concerned about.

Some people may say, "Oh but climate change is still just a theory!" What they probably don't understand, however, is that in science, a *theory* is not by any means the same as a *theory* in our day-to-day language. For something to be considered a scientific theory, it first needs to go through an enormous number of scientific experiments made by many experts in many different fields. A scientific theory is not just something that scientists happen to "believe in"; it needs to be tested, observed, and evaluated over and over and over again before it is considered a theory.

In fact, there is a group of thousands of volunteer scientists from all over the world who are dedicated to studying climate change in order to provide an objective scientific understanding of this theory. This organization is called the Intergovernmental Panel on Climate Change (IPCC) and every scientist involved is an expert in their field and offers their time and knowledge for free.

What does the IPCC do, exactly? Well, for one, they write big reports. They gather information from thousands of scientific papers and many different fields of science in order to give us a thorough understanding of what is actually going on with the global climate of our planet. There have been six assessment reports written by the IPCC between 1988 and 2023. Each assessment report takes years to produce, it has to reach an agreement among hundreds of scientists, it is rigorously picked apart and questioned by governments and other agencies, and only indisputable facts are published. Here are a couple of quotes from the IPCC's sixth assessment report:

> "It is unequivocal that human influence has warmed the atmosphere, ocean and land. Widespread and rapid changes in the atmosphere, ocean, cryosphere and biosphere have occurred."

> "Climate change is already affecting every inhabited region across the globe, with human influence contributing to many observed changes in weather and climate extremes."

So yes, climate change is, in fact, caused by humans. Primarily by industrial activities such as burning fossil fuels. "Fossil fuels" are basically just a bunch of dead plants and animals that have been cooked and compressed under the ground for millions of years, eventually turning into things like coal, gas, or oil. Because this stuff was once alive, it contains stored energy (energy that it got from the Sun a long long time ago)—that's what makes it so great to burn! So when we burn this stuff, we release energy that's been stored for millions of years. This dead stuff also contains a lot of CO_2, so when we burn fossil fuels, we also release CO_2 that's been trapped under the ground for millions of years! The more we burn, the more CO_2 we release, the thicker that greenhouse glass will get, and the hotter it will get inside our greenhouse (meaning, on Earth). CO_2 accounts for about eighty percent of all greenhouse gases and the concentration of CO_2 in our atmosphere has increased by about forty-five percent since the start of the Industrial Revolution (from about 280 parts per million (ppm) in 1750 to about 420 ppm in 2023).

By studying ice cores, scientists can tell that we haven't seen such high levels of CO_2 in our atmosphere for over 800,000 years. *That's a long time.* So clearly, there has been an extremely fast jump in the concentration of CO_2 in our atmosphere in the last 150 or so years.

What does history tell us about such rapid changes in CO_2 levels?

You may know that life on Earth did flourish even when the global climate was much warmer and there were high levels of CO_2 in the atmosphere, such as during the Jurassic or Cretaceous period. However, it is important to understand that this flourishing life had *millions of years* to adapt to such warm climate. Abrupt changes in climate, on the other hand, have caused mass extinctions.

You see, Earth, in a way, is like an aquarium in the vast universe. Everywhere else we know of is too cold or too hot for us to walk around comfortably (plus, there's a bit of an issue with gravity, oxygen, pressure, intense radiation, and much more). *Think about fish in an aquarium.* They live just fine in their fish tank as long as the temperature and composition of their water is stable and they have enough to eat. If you very slowly increase or decrease the temperature of their water tank, the fish will probably survive, especially if they continue to reproduce and their offspring have enough time to adapt to these gradual changes. But if you pour a lot of very hot, very cold, or acidic water into their tank in a very short amount of time, they will probably die. They will also die if you stop feeding them and they don't find any other food to eat.

That's basically how mass extinctions work. Some kind of event (whether an asteroid, volcano, plant, and/or something else) triggers a change in the balance of our atmosphere and that quickly changes the composition of our Earth-aquarium. Life that isn't able to adapt to these changes fast enough dies out. When one species goes extinct, this affects other species who depend on that extinct species for food, habitat, or something else. So when a change in climate causes one species to go extinct, this can cause a domino effect that kills off many other species in the food web.

The most catastrophic mass extinction the Earth has seen so far, the Permian-Triassic extinction, happened about 250 million years ago and wiped out about ninety percent of all species. There are several hypotheses about why this extinction occurred, but it was most likely triggered by great volcanic eruptions that filled the atmosphere with ash, debris, and gasses such as an enormous amount of CO_2. This would have initially caused global cooling as ash and debris blocked sunlight from entering the atmosphere, and would have followed up with global warming as a result of the release of tons of CO_2. There is evidence that the global average temperature increased by at least 5°C, triggering a snowball effect when rising ocean temperatures caused the released of methane from the seabed into the atmosphere, raising the temperature even more, causing anoxia, the acidification of the ocean, and a runaway greenhouse effect. Methane is a powerful greenhouse gas that absorbs heat more than twenty-five times better than carbon dioxide.

*Note that the Permian-Triassic extinction probably happened in the course of about 100,000 years (which is considered extremely fast on a geological timescale) and it's possible that the runaway greenhouse effect that led to the extinction was triggered by only a **5°C** global average temperature rise.*

And guess what's going on today?

We've managed to imitate these gigantic volcanic eruptions by releasing 2.2 trillion tons of CO_2 into the atmosphere, raising the global average temperature by about 1°C in less than a century, and consequently setting off some of those "snowballs" that took off during the Permian-Triassic extinction. There's another name for this type of "snowball effect," actually, it's called a *positive feed-back loop* and we're already witnessing a number of these loops start to take effect today. I'll briefly mention just three (there are countless more).

Positive Feedback Loops:

1. Water vapor is a greenhouse gas, therefore, the more water molecules there are in the atmosphere, the better the atmosphere will be able to absorb heat; so adding more water to the atmosphere is kind of like adding more layers of glass to your greenhouse.

From basic physics, we know that when the temperature rises, more water evaporates. Since we've caused the global average temperature to rise by about 1°C, we've also caused more water molecules to evaporate from oceans, rivers, lakes, etc. into the Earth's atmosphere. Since these extra water molecules are able to absorb more heat, they will make the atmosphere hotter; when the atmosphere gets hotter, more water will evaporate; the additional water vapor will hold even more heat and will make the atmosphere even hotter, causing more water to evaporate, causing the atmosphere to absorb more heat and get even hotter, causing more water to evaporate... *You get why it's called a feedback loop?*

Studies show that water vapor feedback has the potential to double the amount of warming caused by CO_2.

2. You've probably heard about the ice caps melting, right? Well, this isn't only a problem for polar bears, it's pretty bad for us and many other living creatures as well. You see, ice reflects sunlight (the thing that heats up our planet), so the more ice there is on our planet, the more heat will be reflected back out to space, and the less will be absorbed by our oceans and atmosphere. But when ice melts, it leaves in its place either land or water, both of which absorb heat. So melted ice not only loses its capacity to reflect sunlight, but the land or water in its place will absorb heat instead. More heat absorbed by newly exposed land and water will lead to a hotter atmosphere, which will lead to more ice melt, which will lead to more exposed land and water that absorb more heat, leading to a hotter atmosphere, melting more ice, exposing more land and water that absorb more heat, leading to an even hotter atmosphere, melting more ice... *You get it?*

That's why warming in the Arctic is happening at least twice as fast as in the rest of the world, and why we've lost about seventy-five percent of Arctic sea ice in the last four decades. At our current rate of emissions, summer sea ice in the Arctic is projected to essentially disappear in the next twenty to twenty-five years.

3. Remember that thing I said about triggering a huge release of that super potent greenhouse gas, methane, during the Permian-Triassic extinction?

Well guess how much methane is in the atmosphere now?

Approximately five gigatons (billion tons).

And guess how much methane is trapped in the East Siberian Arctic Shelf?!

Probably somewhere between five hundred and five thousand gigatons. That's up to **one thousand times** the amount of methane that's in the atmosphere!

And guess what will happen when temperatures rise in the Arctic?

That's right, this methane will be released, and so will other enormous amounts of methane and CO_2 trapped in the permafrost (permanently frozen ground) that covers about twenty-five percent of the Northern Hemisphere's land area. This happens because when temperatures rise, permafrost thaws and the methane trapped in the permafrost gets released into the atmosphere. Once the methane is in the atmosphere, it will be able to trap heat much more efficiently than CO_2, so it will have the capacity to make the atmosphere much hotter, much quicker. A hotter atmosphere will cause more permafrost to thaw, releasing more methane and causing a dangerous positive feedback loop.

This is just starting to happen, and because climate models are not sophisticated enough to include abrupt permafrost thaw, the full potential release of methane is not included in our current predictions of climate change.

So what does all of this mean?

Are the seas going to boil up? Are we all going to die from heat strokes?

Well, not exactly. More likely, we'll experience fiercer, more frequent, and longer-lasting natural disasters such as hurricanes, snowstorms, and floods (fed by an increase of water in the atmosphere), heatwaves, droughts, and wildfires (when the average temperature is hotter, heatwaves will be even hotter, and droughts and wildfires will be stronger), and other unpleasant weather-related phenomena. Such natural disasters will devastate natural habitats and infrastructure, and will force millions of people to migrate. Living creatures that aren't able to migrate or adapt to the changes in their habitat fast enough will be wiped out; that includes many unique and threatened species of plants and animals. The extinction of one species can have a domino effect on other species, causing a dramatic impact on food chains and entire ecosystems.

Natural disasters and a general change in the climate of a particular area can also alter the area's crop-growing capabilities. *And what happens when lots of crops fail?*

Famine! Migration! And sometimes, war!

The number of climate-related disasters has already more than tripled since 1980 and will continue to rise and intensify as the global average temperature rises.

Another phenomenon that we're already experiencing, and will experience more and more of as the Earth warms, is sea level rise.

Sea level rises because when water gets hotter, it expands, and also because gigantic hunks of ice are melting from the land and going into the ocean. Sea level is currently rising at a rate of 3.4 millimeters per year, but since the rate of melting glaciers and ice sheets is accelerating, so is the rate of sea level rise. If this current pace continues, sea levels are projected to rise by 65 centimeters or more by the year 2100.

This will be destructive for many cities and coastal regions, causing habitat loss for many plants, fish, birds, and other creatures such as humans. Sea level rise can cause flooding, destructive erosion, powerful storm surges, salt contamination of aquifers and agricultural soil, and more. Cities such as Venice, Miami, Shanghai, Mumbai, and hundreds of others will be affected by sea level rise.

If all the ice from glaciers and ice sheets melted, the sea level would rise by over 65 meters (216 feet)! Some scientists say that it would take over five thousand years to melt all of our planet's ice, but if we continue to indiscriminately burn all of the Earth's fossil fuels, it very well could happen. This would wipe out London, New York, Tokyo, Hong Kong, Baghdad, Buenos Aires, Bangkok, thousands of other cities, the entire state of Florida, and entire countries like Bangladesh, the Maldives, and the Netherlands.

Speaking of the ocean, *did you know that about thirty percent of the CO_2 we pump into the atmosphere is absorbed by the ocean?* **And do you know what happens when the ocean absorbs a lot of CO_2?**

Due to a series of chemical reactions, ocean water becomes more acidic (you know, like lemon juice). When the ocean becomes more acidic, this affects marine life such as clams, oysters, crabs, coral reefs, many types of plankton, and other "calcifiers" because it makes it difficult for them to form shells and stony skeletons. With enough CO_2 in the ocean, the shells of these organisms can even dissolve. Since coral reefs provide habitat for a quarter of the world's fish and plankton are the food of many small fish that are eaten by medium-sized fish, that are eaten by large fish, that are eaten by seals, sharks, humans, and their cats, you can probably imagine that losing the foundation of this food web and ecosystem would be quite disastrous.

This will have a huge negative impact on entire ocean ecosystems as well as on the two billion people who eat seafood as their main source of protein, not to mention on all of those people who depend on the seafood industry to make a "living."

As of now, about sixty percent of the world's coral reefs are heavily threatened. If we somehow manage to halt global warming at a 1.5°C rise, we will probably lose about seventy to ninety percent of coral reefs by 2100. If we manage to halt global warming at a 2°C rise, we will probably lose more than ninety-nine percent of our reefs. Unfortunately, at the rate we're burning fossil fuels now, it's likely that the global average temperature will rise by 3.5°C or more by the end of the century.

The great thing about the ocean is not only that it has absorbed a lot of excess CO$_2$, but that it has also absorbed about ninety percent of the extra heat that's been trapped by human-generated greenhouse gasses.

As a result, the world's corals are also bleaching. Half of the Great Barrier Reef is already dead. And unfortunately, phytoplankton are also very sensitive to heat. Phytoplankton are incredibly important not only because they are the base of the marine food web, but also because they perform photosynthesis and absorb about as much CO$_2$ from the atmosphere as the world's forests, making the ocean a very important carbon sink. So the more phytoplankton we lose, the more CO$_2$ will remain in the atmosphere, the hotter it will get, and the more phytoplankton we will lose, the more CO$_2$ will remain in the atmosphere, the hotter it will get, and the more phytoplankton we will lose ... *Sound like a positive feedback or what?*

I'll mention just one more potential climate change disaster, and then I will move on to today's so-called "solutions."

Ever hear of the great conveyor belt of the ocean? (Technically termed the thermohaline circulation.) It's basically a giant circuit of currents that loops around our planet's oceans, bringing warm water to the colder parts of our planet and cold, nutrient-rich water to the warmer parts. This on-going oceanic circulation is very important because it regulates our planet's weather. This is actually the reason it is so warm on the west coast of Europe even though Europe is located at the same latitude as the northern US and Canada. The Gulf Stream (one part of the conveyor belt) brings warm water from the Gulf of Mexico, across the Atlantic Ocean, and toward Europe. Without this conveyor belt, weather would be much different in Western Europe and many other parts of the world.

Another thing that would be different without this conveyor belt is life in the ocean. These great ocean currents are critical to marine life because they circulate oxygen around the oceans and bring essential nutrients from the depths of the oceans to the surface. This happens because cold water absorbs nutrients better than warm water and because there are a lot of nutrients (from dead, sunken organisms) at the bottom of the ocean. So it's important that cold water currents bring these nutrients to the surface because living creatures like plankton depend on them. Without these nutrients, plankton and many other microorganisms wouldn't be able to survive in the great quantities they live in today. *And we already know what happens when a lot of plankton die, so let's not go back there again.*

Now that we know how important the thermohaline circulation is, let's go over how it functions. Basically, it works like this: wind currents drive surface water from the equator toward the poles. Once this warm water reaches higher latitudes, it cools down. At the poles, some of the water freezes and leaves behind salt (making non-frozen water saltier than before). Colder and saltier water is more dense than warmer, less-salty water, so it sinks—this drives the movement of deep water ocean currents. Once this water reaches lower latitudes, it gains heat and moves up toward the surface of the oceans, bringing nutrients with it. So in short, deep-water ocean currents are driven by differences in temperature and salinity. Without enough cold, salty water, the global ocean conveyor belt would shut down. If the conveyor belt shut down, it would cause a mass extinction in the ocean and crazy, unpredictable weather above the ocean.

Right now, scientists aren't exactly sure whether human-driven climate change will cause the thermohaline circulation to shut down, but what they do know is that the Arctic is warming two to three times faster than the world average, sea ice and ice shelves are melting at an alarming rate (diluting the dense salty water with light fresh water), and that the Atlantic meridional overturning circulation (one part of the conveyor belt) has slowed down by about fifteen percent since the mid 1900s.

In general, there are a lot of uncertainties about how fast some of these apocalyptic events might unfold, but what scientists are quite sure of is that the more greenhouse gasses we pump into the atmosphere, the faster these scenarios will approach us, and the worse they will get.

Today's "Solutions"

Now let's take a look at what humans are trying to do to solve this global climate change problem:

In 1992, some of our planet's tribes signed an international treaty called the United Nations Framework Convention on Climate Change (UNFCCC), which was an agreement that suggested greenhouse gas emission limits for every "country" that signed the treaty. The agreement was non-binding (not enforced by law) and did not include penalties. The objective was to "stabilize greenhouse gas concentrations at a level that would prevent dangerous anthropogenic (human induced) interference with the climate system" (UNFCCC). Today, there are 198 countries involved in this agreement, and each year, they get together for international climate change conferences to assess the world's "progress."

In 1997, some tribes signed another treaty called the Kyoto Protocol. This treaty was linked to the UNFCCC but this time the agreement was legally binding (with penalties) and established obligations for developed countries to reduce their greenhouse gas emissions between the years of 2008-2012. One part of the agreement included an emissions trading scheme. There were no binding targets or penalties for developing countries such as China and India, and the US chose not to participate in this agreement. Together, those three tribes make up for more than half of all global greenhouse gas emissions. Canada later withdrew from the agreement because restricting oil production posed a financial threat to their economy. Although a few countries did manage to reduce their emissions, many simply paid their penalty fines and continued "business as usual." Globally, greenhouse gas emissions increased by thirty-five percent from 1990 to 2010. The agreement was extended until 2020.

In 2010, during the annual United Nations Climate Change Conference, our great leaders created an agreement stating that we, humans, should limit global warming to less than 2°C relative to preindustrial levels. At this point climate models showed that going beyond 2°C could lead humanity into dangerous territory, possibly triggering changes in our global climate that are beyond our control. The IPCC's updated 2018 special report, *Global Warming of 1.5°C*, made it clear, however, that it would be much wiser for the human species to keep global warming below a 1.5°C rise, as opposed to 2°C. That report describes that even a 2°C rise can lead to disastrous consequences such as the extinction of over ninety-nine percent of coral reefs, the triggering of an irreversible loss of the Greenland ice sheet, and/or the destabilization of the Antarctic ice sheet, and much more.

In 2015, our planet's tribal leaders signed another major climate change agreement, called the "Paris Agreement." This is an international treaty in which each country can set their own goals and submit their own plan for how to lower emissions. It is basically a voluntary "pledge" and there are no penalties or enforcement mechanisms involved (apart from "social pressure"). The agreement urges humanity to keep the global average temperature well below 2°C above preindustrial levels, preferably limiting the increase to 1.5°C.

And in the following years, in the following international climate change meetings and agreements, world leaders continued to stress the importance of limiting global warming to 1.5°C.

According to the IPCC, such a goal is still be achievable, but in order for us to avoid a rise above 1.5°C, global greenhouse gas emissions have to PEAK by 2025, decrease by forty-three percent by 2030, and reach net zero by 2050. From a technical perspective, we have the means to do this—we've already developed renewable energy, we know how to plant forests, and we've developed negative emissions technologies. If we treated climate change as a global emergency, we could certainly solve this problem.

But what are the world's tribes doing today?

Instead of planting forests, switching to renewable energy, and heavily investing into negative emissions technologies, humans are instead cutting down forests at the rate of one football field per second and are planning to produce 120 percent more fossil fuels by 2030.

All of the biggest fossil fuel-producing nations—including the United States, China, Saudi Arabia, Russia, India, Brazil, Canada, Iran, the Emirates, Qatar, Norway, and Australia—plan to significantly increase production.

If all goes as planned, the US, Russia, and Saudi Arabia will all drill for more oil and gas in 2030 than ever before. The UK plans to open new oil and gas fields in the North Sea; Canada plans to open hundreds of new drilling wells; China, Indonesia, India, Vietnam, and Japan plan to construct over 600 new coal power units; while India plans to destroy thousands of hectares of dense, biodiverse forest to open dozens of new coal mines.

The US plans to build twenty-two new mega-projects, from drilling to fracking, which will have the potential to release four times more CO_2 than is released annually by the entire world. And of course, the biggest oil and gas companies plan to spend nearly a trillion US dollars developing new oil and gas fields by the end of 2030, while governments around the world spend more money on fossil fuel subsidies than they do on education.

Meanwhile, the last decade was the hottest on record and we're on track to hit the 1.5°C mark somewhere between 2030 and 2052. If "business as usual" continues, it's likely that we will hit the 2°C mark well before 2100 and by the end of the century, we'll be somewhere between 3.3° and 5.7°C above preindustrial levels (or up to 7.8°C if you include climate uncertainty). This would be absolutely disastrous.

As a result, millions of "young people" and "environmental activists" are screaming at their governments to do something about climate change, but *somehow*, "business as usual" overpowers their screams. Year after year, world leaders give evermore passionate speeches about the state of our planet, but *somehow*, every year, greenhouse gas emissions are higher than the year before, and the global average temperature continues to rise.

The Prisoner's Dilemma

In class, we did an exercise in which we simulated a series of international climate change conferences. We based this exercise on the iterated prisoner's dilemma of game theory. In the exercise, each student was assigned a country to represent in the conferences. Just like in the real world, some countries had more power, others had less. The countries that released the most CO_2 (like China, the US, and Russia) had the biggest impact on the climate change agreements. I was assigned Albania, a small country in Southeast Europe. *Not much power.*

In each round of simulated conferences, every country was given a choice: cooperate or defect from cooperation. "Cooperating" meant to agree to lower CO_2 emissions. Just like in the real world, lowering emissions came with an economic cost. The less fossil fuels you burn and/or sell, the worse off your economy will likely be. That's because our "economy" is based on the need to sell as much stuff as possible. The entire process of manufacturing, transporting, and selling goods requires energy, which, in today's world is primarily based on fossil fuels. So in order to lower our emissions, we have to decrease some "economic activity" or invest into renewable energy sources, which may be costly. In the long run, the disasters we will face as a result of climate change will do a lot more harm to the "economy" (and to life in general) but this threat is not *immediate*.

If every student chose to cooperate, the cumulative score would be the highest (we will have lowered global CO_2 emissions), but each individual country's score would be lower (because of the strain on their economy). If a particular country chose to defect from cooperation while others chose to cooperate, this would lead to the highest individual score for that country, but a "negative" score for those who chose to cooperate (because those who defected from cooperating will be rewarded economically, while those who cooperated will pay an economic cost and CO_2 emissions will continue to rise). If all (or most) countries decided to defect from cooperation, this would lead to a "low" score for individual countries and the lowest possible cumulative score. A low cumulative score meant that CO_2 emissions would continue to rise globally. The lower the cumulative score, the more emissions would increase, and the more natural disasters were thrown at us in the exercise. Each natural disaster led to additional economic costs to the country that was hit.

Every student was given a certain number of points that represented their country's "score." The more points, the better off their country was. If they lost all their points, it meant that their country went bankrupt and was in a very bad situation.*

I looked at my sixty points, then glanced at the person next to me. "How come the US has five hundred points and I only have sixty?"

"Five hundred?" said another student. "I only have twenty!"

The US grinned. "What country are you?"

"Somalia…"

"Well, that's why! Ha ha!"

"Welcome, everybody, to the 2012 International Conference on Climate Change!" said the teacher. "Our mission here is to negotiate an agreement to lower global CO_2 emissions. Our current level of atmospheric CO_2 is three hundred ninety parts per million. The Earth's global average temperature is almost one degree Celsius warmer than the pre-industrial average. An additional one-degree rise would likely lead to disastrous consequences, intensifying natural disasters, threatening our global food supply, melting ice caps, rising sea levels, bringing coral reefs to extinction, and possibly setting off crucial tipping points. If we warm the globe further beyond two degrees Celsius, we may be heading into uncharted territory that is beyond our control. Nations of the world, the future is in your hands!" She rang a bell. "Round one begins now. Negotiate!"

Everybody looked around for a bit, then Switzerland spoke, "All right guys, let's be smart about this. We all know that if we don't cooperate with each other, the consequences will eventually be bad for every one of us. Let's work together to solve this problem."

"Well, Switzerland," said Bangladesh, "you have so many points that it's easy for you to say that. But I only have twenty-five! I can't afford to lose any right now. I will have to strengthen my economy first and then I will be able to join the rest of you in the fight against climate change. You rich countries were the ones that created this problem in the first place and you're the ones who benefit from it, so you should pay the cost, not us developing countries."

"Well, if Bangladesh doesn't cooperate, then why should I?" said India. "I'm also a developing country and I also need to strengthen my economy!"

"Well, if India doesn't cooperate, then I won't!" said China.

"China?! Really? You're responsible for like a quarter of all emissions! If China doesn't cooperate, then I definitely won't!" said the US.

"What?! You can't do that, US," said Venezuela. "Historically, you are the most responsible, so you should take the greatest responsibility and help developing nations instead of making things worse!"

"If the US doesn't cooperate, then I'm not cooperating," said Russia.

"Do you want your entire state of Florida to drown completely?" said Mexico.

"Didn't Switzerland say we need to work together?!" yelled Canada.

"Guys! Guys! Calm down!" I yelled.

The bell rang. Round one was over. Many nations chose not to cooperate, so the cumulative score was low. After round one, Vietnam was hit with a cyclone that killed fifty thousand people, devastated the capital city, and cost the nation ten points.

"Round two!" said the teacher. "The year is 2022. We are at four hundred nineteen parts per million, with over a one-degree global average temperature rise. Let's negotiate smarter!" She rang the bell.

In round two, I created an alliance with my neighboring Southern European countries. We agreed to collectively lower emissions, hoping that our combined strength could make a difference. Unfortunately, neither the US or China agreed to cooperate in the second round, so our alliance was barely noticeable. Round two resulted in a low cumulative score and two big natural disasters: a huge hurricane in the US and the Caribbean, and devastating fires across Australia.

By round three (2032), we were almost at a 1.5°C rise. Our alliance carried on, but since most powerful nations still didn't cooperate, we felt like we were sacrificing ourselves for nothing. Six countries were hit by major natural disasters. By round four (2042), we were over a 1.5°C rise. Several countries in our alliance were hit with an influx of migrants that came from disaster-hit African and Middle Eastern countries. We tried to continue our alliance and pledge to reduce CO_2 emissions, but by round five (2052), I was almost out of points.

By round six (2062), we hit the 2°C mark. Major natural disasters struck many different regions of the world, rice and wheat crops failed, millions of humans were displaced, and dozens of countries lost all their points. Some countries were flooded by rising sea levels, others were devastated by droughts and fires, the Great Barrier Reef was dead, and there were warnings about a mass extinction in the ocean. The fewer points each country had, the less willing they were to cooperate. The less we cooperated, the lower the cumulative score was and the worse the situation became. By 2072, we were around a 2.5°C rise and by the end of the game, we basically destroyed ourselves.

I walked out of class a bit shocked that day. *It's just a game, right?* I tried to laugh it off. *It's not really funny though.*

As silly as this exercise may have appeared, it was actually very eye-opening. In the "real world," most of these countries may actually agree to cooperate *on paper*, but unfortunately, "pledging" to lower emissions without taking any serious action does nothing to actually stop climate change. This exercise showed me that as long as individual countries have a stake in this system (they gain money if they don't cooperate, and they lose money if they cooperate), then most countries simply will not cooperate. It's not in their immediate interest to do so.

Their values and this system are completely distorted, I thought. *They judge the well-being of their countries by how much shit they sell. The more you sell, the better!—That's the most important thing! Exactly what I learned in my business class. Climate change (or any other problem) will never be more important than the "economy" in this system, and as long as that is the case, we will ultimately destroy ourselves.*

I felt like all of these conferences, global organizations, and agreements were useless because they never dig to the roots of any global problem. They don't seem to ask questions like, *What is causing humans to emit greenhouse gasses? What is stopping them from putting an end to it? How could we change this behavior?* I mean, these people understand that *humans* are responsible for climate change, so how could they avoid questioning human behavior?

If they at least dared to question the structure of our society and its impact on human behavior then maybe they'd have something to work with. But as far as I could see, all these international organizations and global institutions do is write complicated papers to promote patchwork to a faulty system—and that's not going to solve the problem.

Fuck it. I finished my final essay then bought another flight out of Australia.

---

*I don't remember the exact points that were given to each student, or exactly which disaster hit when/which country, but this gives you a general idea of what went on in our classroom (which gave us a general idea of what goes on in the real world).

22

Southeast Asia, 2012

I probably would have quit university again after that depressing semester, but luckily, I had a three-month break ahead of me. I spent the first three weeks of my break backpacking through Thailand and Cambodia with Rachel. I didn't want to go there at first. I wanted to go to Russia to visit my family and then snowboard, but flights from Sydney to Moscow were cheaper via Thailand than they were straight to Moscow, so I decided to join Rachel for a portion of her big trip.

Rachel and I slept in cheap hotels and used public buses to get around Thailand and Cambodia. First we visited some spectacular places like the Temples of Angkor, Tonle Sap Lake, and Khao Sok National Park. Then we visited some typical tourist destinations like Ao Nang, Ko Samui, and Ko Pha-ngan. I had very mixed feelings about these mega tourist spots. On one hand, they were extremely beautiful. Ao Nang had a gorgeous white-sand beach surrounded by towering limestone cliffs—*a mecca for rock climbers.* In the distance, there were droplet-like lush green islands and enormous cliff faces. Both Ko Samui and Ko Pha-ngan were alluring tropical islands full of palm trees, white-sand beaches, crystal-clear water, beautiful coral reefs, the whole deal. But all of these places were insanely overrun by tourists and tourist-driven consumerism.

Everywhere we went, it was packed with people, bars, restaurants, souvenir shops, and tour companies. The huge flocks of tourists were accompanied by local merchants trying to sell them just about anything. As a result, there was no opportunity for any real cultural exchange. *How could you learn anything about the local culture if everyone around you is either a drunk tourist or a merchant desperately trying to sell you something?* Nor were there any opportunities for exploration or even much relaxation since everywhere we went was completely packed with crowds.

I felt shitty to be a part of this mass tourism, but I also felt like there was no escape. Rachel and I had planned to go to the infamous full moon party on Ko Pha-ngan, one of the biggest raves in the world. After that, I planned to fly out of the country, so I decided to make the best of it.

There was a big storm on the day of the party, so everyone was wet and muddy. Rachel and I hopped onto a ferry that was jam-packed with drunk, loud tourists. Once we got off the ferry, we followed a huge crowd of people to the party spot—an enormous beach set with many different stages, very loud music, lights, fire spinners, stalls, merchants, and craziness. Everywhere we went, tourists were drinking, dancing, and screaming, while local people were trying to sell them buckets of alcohol, glow sticks, and colorful ornaments.

The first thing Rachel and I did was go up to "Mushroom Mountain," a place we had heard you could buy magic mushroom shakes. We stood in line for a while and eventually bought a shake each. It was expensive and diluted, but what else do you do at a rave? I couldn't be there sober.

Mushroom Mountain was located at one edge of the beach and since the bar that sold mushroom shakes was on top of a hill, the place overlooked the entire party. There were *thousands* of people there. Each month, between ten and thirty thousand tourists come to this beach for this full moon party.

Rachel and I agreed that if we lost each other, we would meet back at Mushroom Mountain, which was easy to find. Then we walked back down the hill and hit the party. We went from one dance floor to another, to another. Each stage was pumping different electronic music. It was so loud that we could barely say a word to each other. Instead, we danced.

Soon, things got fuzzy. Rachel found a set of fire poi equipment on the ground and started spinning fire. She was great! Then we met a group of people with even more fire equipment. They were holding up fire sticks and moving through the festival. Rachel and I tagged along.

At one point, I found a slide and a trampoline that I managed to do some little flips on. As the night progressed, I lost Rachel. I looked around for a bit, then headed to Mushroom Mountain. *That was the agreement.* I stood there for hours and Rachel was nowhere to be found. Eventually I made new friends and had more mushroom shakes, then decided that Mushroom Mountain was the best place to be anyway.

At some point, there was a huge fireworks display that lit up the stormy clouds and the wild ocean beneath them. This was a dazzling sight. Every time a firework sparked, it illuminated the mighty powerful ocean. I watched silently as huge, choppy waves swirled, crashed, and churned under these bright bursts of light. Thunder and lightening accompanied the spectacle and dark ferocious clouds were exposed in color. I was in awe not particularly by the fireworks, but by the awesome power of nature above and below the sparkling lights.

As the sun came up a few hours later, I noticed how spectacular this beach actually was. It looked like an exotic wonderland. There was lush greenery, palm trees all around, soft beautiful sand, crystal-clear water, and beautiful hills in the distance. But as I looked down at the beach, I was devastated. *Look at what we did to this place.*

There were infinite straws. Infinite little pieces of plastic floating in the ocean as far as the eye could see. The straws formed a colorful layer that bobbed up and down as the waves gently hit the shore. The sand was covered in cups, buckets, hats, straws, clothes, bottles, broken glass, broken people, and garbage as far as the eye could see. A few locals were sorting through the trash.

Imagine growing up here, I thought, *in this tropical paradise. Watching it mutate over the course of just a few decades, changing from a quiet and special place, to an absolute disaster. Full of garbage, waste, and wasted people. And for what? Just to listen to some music and dance?*

I later read that the locals in Ko Pha-ngan constantly complained about noise pollution, freshwater shortages, waste, pollution, and a number of other problems due to these crazy full moon parties and the mass tourism.

I found Rachel at some point in the morning, smooching an English guy. I was relieved to see that she was fine. She seemed to have had a good night. I tried not to get angry at her for not meeting me where we had agreed. I was more upset at the sight of this beautiful ruined paradise, and at the fact that none of the tourists seemed to give a shit. I was ready to leave. This wasn't the kind of traveling I was after.

We took a ferry back to Ko Samui, then I said goodbye to Rachel and took a bus to Bangkok. I had left my snowboard and winter gear in a locker in the touristy area, so I had to go back there to get it. Once I was in Bangkok, I took a minibus from the main bus station to the tourist strip. On the minibus, I met an Italian guy who was traveling by himself. He said that he was also planning to spend just one night in Bangkok. The guy seemed harmless, so I asked if he wanted to split a room with me to save some money. He agreed, so we soon found a cheap hotel room with two single beds.

I was tired. I took a shower and went to bed. The guy did the same. Then after a few minutes of lying in bed with the lights turned off, he tapped me on the shoulder and casually asked, "Hey, do you want to have sex?"

Oh fuck, that's awkward, I thought. "No, thank you," I replied.

"Okay!" he said in a friendly tone, then went to sleep.

The next day, I got on a plane to Moscow.

23

Russia, 2013

It was January, 2013. I flew from Thailand, where it was around 30°C, to Moscow, Russia, where it was -10°C. My dad planned to meet me at the Moscow airport with a big warm jacket, since all I had was one flimsy snowboarding jacket and a pair of leggings. The problem, however, was that I also had a five-hour layover in Siberia, where it was -36°C! This was the first time I had ever experienced such a drastic temperature change—an entire sixty-six degrees.

Once I got off the plane and passed through security in Siberia, I had to go outside and walk from the international airport to the domestic one, which was a hundred or so meters away. I curled up into a ball inside my jacket and torpedoed through the fierce wind to the domestic terminal. The tops of my cheeks burned from the cold, but I was excited about the change. It felt great to be back in Russia and away from the mad tourism of Thailand.

After another six hour flight, I got to see my dad again. I hadn't seen him for at least two years. He looked underweight and perhaps a bit down, but he was happy to see me. I didn't have a very close relationship with him while I was growing up, since we lived in different countries, but as I got older and started traveling, we started to bond more and more. Back then, he was the only person in my family who accepted my lifestyle, and he was the first person to tell me that I was doing the right thing.

"I tell everyone that my daughter is the only person who knows how to live," he said. "She doesn't want to have a job, money, a house, or anything like that. But she travels around the world and enjoys her life. That's what should be important—enjoying life. Not gaining money and stuff." He smiled.

I thought it was ironic that my dad was an ex-millionaire. He told me that even when he was earning those millions, he never considered the possibility of changing his lifestyle. "I could have sold everything," he said, "quit work and just lived off my savings for the rest of my life. But that didn't even cross my mind! Back then, I just came to my office, worked all day from Monday to Saturday, just like everybody else. I continued to do that and eventually I started earning more and more money. Eventually, a lot of money started coming in, but it never occurred to me that I could stop going to the office. I just continued working and making more money, so I bought nicer things and sent you guys to the US. And now you're coming back to Russia!" He laughed. "My worst nightmare was for you to come back to Russia again. I worked so hard to get you out of here!"

"Don't worry, dad." I grinned. "I won't stay here long."

"I know, I'm only joking," he said. "You're doing the right thing."

* * *

While I was in Moscow, I visited my grandmother, my aunts, uncle, cousins, and some old childhood friends. I also got to spend some time with my father's youngest daughters, Dina and Sonya. After divorcing my mother, my father married a young woman in Russia and had two more children with her. Now the girls were five and seven years old.

My dad, his wife, and the two girls lived in a small apartment in Moscow. The apartment was newly renovated but only had one room and a small separate kitchen. My father and his wife slept on the couch, which they converted into a bed for the night, and the two girls slept in a bunk bed on the other side of the room. I slept in the kitchen whenever I came over.

I noticed that Dina and Sonya fought nonstop. They were extremely short-tempered and mean to each other. They reminded me of my brother and me after we had moved to America. My dad and his wife also fought nonstop. She clearly wasn't happy with their living situation. From what I could tell, she married my dad largely for his money (back when he had a lot of it). When they first met, my dad owned a big beautiful apartment in the center of Moscow. Pretty soon, however, his business collapsed and he lost almost everything. He sold that apartment and bought a big house and some land in Turkey, hoping to make a business there. Unfortunately, that business didn't work out, and after living in Turkey with their two daughters for several years, they moved back to Moscow. At that point my dad had lost most of his money, but managed to buy this small apartment and start another business—a small office that sells vacations to Russian tourists. This new business, however, was not very profitable, so my father could no longer satisfy his wife's desires (although he did buy her the new car she asked for when they came back to Moscow).*

While I was visiting them, my dad looked miserable. He was struggling financially. He and his wife seemed to be in a constant state of hostility. I noticed that his wife was dressing up and going out at night, while he tried to run his business and take care of the kids in the evenings. I had never seen my dad look so sad before.

Their daughters seemed to mirror their behavior. The more my dad and his wife fought, the more the girls would fight. They were constantly screaming at each other or nudging and hitting one another.

My dad's wife wanted a divorce and he seemed to have no say in this. They both agreed, however, that it would be better for their daughters to not see them fight all the time. None of this was my business, but after observing the situation for a while, I had to say something for the sake of the two little girls. I told my dad and his wife about my childhood and teenage years. I told them that I was hurt by my father leaving, and by the realization that we would never be a family again. This killed me and caused me to push away my brother, to defend myself by becoming mean and reckless.

I told my dad and his wife how I used to steal, do a lot of drugs, and get into some dangerous situations. I even told them that I was almost raped at age fifteen and that I sold drugs at age seventeen.

I spilled out everything to my dad and his wife. They were both in shock. My dad had no idea that any of this had happened; he thought he had brought us to a safe and happy place. We both cried a lot and he felt very sorry. He asked me to forgive him. Of course, I told him that I already had. I forgave him a long time ago, when I realized that he left us in the US because he genuinely believed it would be best for our future. The society pushed him to do this. I knew that none of this was malicious, and I also knew that I would have become a completely different person if I had grown up in Russia. I probably never would have ended up traveling the world.

After this long discussion and a lot of tears, my father and his wife agreed to split up, but to make sure they would both stay in the same city as their daughters and would both see them on a regular basis. My relationship with my dad also improved after this day. I finally felt like I had made peace with the problems I had built up as a teenager. I felt like I understood myself, my past, and my family better now. As a result, my father and I were able to become best friends.

* * *

After a couple of weeks in Moscow, I planned to go somewhere else to snowboard. My original idea was to take a train to Sochi, a city in the south of Russia where there were a few nearby ski resorts. However, my dad was very much against this idea. He kept on telling me how dangerous it was to travel through Russia alone, telling me stories about people waking up without their kidneys and things like that.

"Those guys that woke up without their kidneys got drunk with some random people the night before, right?" I said. "Don't worry, dad. I mean, I know bad things can happen, but I'll be careful. If I'm careful, it's very unlikely that something bad will happen. There's a much higher chance that I'll get into a car accident and die here in Moscow than of somebody stealing my kidneys in Sochi."

"It's still not a good idea," he said. "Look, I've looked at some cheap tours to Bulgaria. They include a flight from Moscow, an airport transfer to Bansko, and a hotel for two weeks. The entire package is less than two hundred dollars. I can buy it for your birthday. Bansko is a very popular ski town in Bulgaria, it's much better than Sochi! What do you say? Your flight and hotel will be included so all you'll have to pay for is food and lift tickets. Then after two weeks you can go wherever you want. But please don't go to Sochi."

I laughed. "Really? You want to buy me a tour to Bulgaria just so I don't go to Sochi?"

"Just consider it a birthday gift!" He smiled. "I'll book it for you tonight."

"Okay, Fazer. Thank you." *Bulgaria.* I never even considered snowboarding in Bulgaria before, but *why not?*

*Of course relationships are complicated and surely there was a lot more to this story, but that's what I understood from my limited observations.

24

Bulgaria, 2013

I flew to Bulgaria on January 31. I got off the plane, passed through security and immigration, then looked for the company that my dad had booked this package with. At the gate exit, I noticed someone with the company sign. I walked up to them, and what do you know —they had me on their list! It felt weird but somewhat comforting to have someone pick me up from a completely foreign airport and bring me all the way to my hotel room. It also felt a bit weird to be in a hotel room alone, since I was much more used to hostels, random people's couches, or shared rooms.

I arrived in Bansko after about a two-hour drive in a minivan. The hotel was small and cheap, but cozy and even included breakfast. I put down my backpack, had a shower, then walked around the little village.

At first, I felt like I was in South America. It was chilly, but not too cold. There were cute little cobblestone streets partially covered in crumpled snow. There were big mountains in the background and several street vendors selling colorful wool sweaters, hats, and blankets. The signs on the shops and restaurants, however, were written in Cyrillic. I walked into a small wooden restaurant and ordered a bowl of soup and some bread. The bread was fresh and warm and the soup was delicious—and cheap.

The next day, I woke up early, had breakfast, then hit the mountain. Bansko's mountain wasn't as impressive as I had expected. This was the biggest mountain resort in Bulgaria, but the mountain was more like what you would find on the East Coast of the US, rather than in Colorado or the Alps. The plus side was that it was a lot cheaper than most resorts in the US or Western Europe. I ended up buying a two-week pass for the mountain.

I took the chairlift up and spent the day riding around the slopes by myself. I went on every piste and kept an eye out for backcountry terrain. Unfortunately, the snow was wet and heavy, and there wasn't much of it. I went off-piste just a bit and scratched up the bottom of my board.

It's February and there's barely any snow on the mountain, I thought. *If it doesn't snow in the next two weeks, I'll definitely go somewhere else.*

I spent the next few days alone. This gave me time to think, which was important. I finally had the time to slow down and think through the last few months—my university work, the crazy tourism in Thailand, the trash, the plastic, the destruction of Ko Pha-ngan, the big emotional conversation I had with my dad, my past, everything. I needed this time alone and I was happy to have it.

I had breakfast alone, went snowboarding alone, walked around Bansko alone, and had dinner alone. I loved it. But after a week or so, it started snowing and I wanted to ride some of that off-piste terrain I'd been scoping out.

As the snow was coming down, I scanned the side of the mountain by the top of the highest chairlift. *Theoretically, this part of the mountain should lead back to the piste below.* There was a steep hill covered in fresh powdery snow. Farther down, it looked like there was a lot of untouched powder between sparsely scattered trees. *That looks like fun!* But I knew it would be a bad idea to go down there alone. *Who knows where this hill ends. There's not a single track down there.*

I need to make some friends! Once I came back to the hotel, I logged into Couchsurfing and searched for local ski bums. The weird thing about Bansko, though, was that there weren't many of those ski bums you would typically find in ski resort areas. Since Bulgaria was a pretty poor country, the locals didn't come there to ski or snowboard, they only came there to work. And the tourists only stayed for a week or two, so they didn't know the mountain well and most of them were more interested in getting drunk than they were in riding the mountain.

I talked to one Bulgarian girl who said it was her dream to try skiing or snowboarding. "I always wished to go up the mountain one day!" she told me.

"Why don't you?" I asked.

"I have to work every day. And I don't have enough money. It's expensive. But one day, I hope to try it." She seemed very sweet.

"How long have you been working in Bansko?" I asked.

"About ten years now."

"Ten years and you never got to try skiing or snowboarding?" I was shocked. I would have taken her up the mountain myself but she didn't have a single day off work the entire time I was there.

I realized that was how most local people lived in Bansko. They didn't come there just to ski (and work only to afford skiing) like typical seasonal workers do in richer countries, they came to Bansko to work their asses off just to earn money. They worked so much that they had no time to ski. And they earned so little that they couldn't afford it anyway, even though it was much cheaper to ski in Bulgaria than in most American resorts.

Soon, I realized that Bansko wasn't all that different from Thailand or any other tourist destination. It comes in a different package—Bansko's a cute little mountain town rather than a "beach paradise." In the souvenir shops they sell wool and pottery rather than bikinis and seashells, and the bars and restaurants look warm and cozy rather than cool and tropical. But both places revolve completely around tourism and in both cases the local people are exploited.

I thought about the other ski resorts I'd been to: Whistler, Lake Tahoe, Mammoth Lakes, Taos, a few resorts in Utah and Colorado, as well as a bunch on the East Coast of the US. Plus four resorts in New Zealand, one in Australia, and one in Switzerland. *It's true that all ski resorts are completely centered around tourism. Whistler, for example, is no different, and sure people get exploited there too. But the dynamic is so different! Most of the locals that live in Whistler have a lot of fun, most of them certainly ride the mountain as much as possible, regardless of whether they*

267

work as a snowboarding instructor, a dishwasher, or anything else. Here, they are so enslaved that they can't even enjoy the place. That's the sad part.

Eventually, I did find a snowboarding buddy through Couchsurfing. His name was Keith and he was from Northern California. He was a slim guy with long brown hair and a thick beard.

Keith and I got along pretty quickly. He was renting an apartment in Bansko for the entire winter season and he didn't have many snowboarding buddies either. He agreed with me that it was sad and weird that barely any Bulgarians were riding the mountain.

We took the chairlift up and skimmed around the side of the piste, then rode down some of those off-piste hillsides I had been scoping out. They turned out to be great—and they did lead back to the chairlift after only a short walk. The snow was very heavy, however, and we often hit stomps and lightly-covered debris, but this backcountry terrain was definitely the best part of Bansko mountain.

Keith and I chatted a lot as we sat on the chairlift. Keith had an interesting but traumatic past. He served in the US military right after he got out of high school and he went to war in Iraq.

"They trick you into joining the military when you're just a kid and you don't know anything about the world," he said. "They came to our school and convinced us that we'd be heroes if we joined the military."

"So you thought you'd be doing a good thing?" I asked.

"Yes, we genuinely thought we were going to save the world. They make it sound like the world is so fucked up, but America is there to help! To save people! And to make the world a better place. When you're a kid you just believe this bullshit. After so many years of pledging to the flag."

"Little did you know, you'd be sent to Iraq to destroy their country and steal their oil," I said.

"Yeah the first task we had to do once we got to Iraq was capture an oil rig. We were like, 'What the fuck? *Why* are we doing this?' And the answer we got was, 'We need to take this oil because we're gonna destroy this country and we need the money from oil in order to rebuild it.' That's what they actually said."

"I'm surprised you were even allowed to ask questions," I said.

"Yeah well, not many. You're just supposed to follow orders." Keith told me many horror stories about shooting people and being shot at, about bombs, explosives, and life-threatening situations, about people being tortured and killed. It was truly horrifying.

"I would have just run away," I said.

"Yeah." Keith laughed. "There was nowhere to run. It's not like you can quit after you've joined. Once you're there, you're stuck, you're fucked."

We talked about how fucked up war was and how it was a byproduct of this profit-driven system. Keith was familiar with Derrick Jensen, the writer of *The Culture of Make Believe.*

"Of course," I said, "there's a profit motive in every war. Whether that profit is made through taking oil, selling weapons, getting land, resources, power, or whatever else. So as long as we live in this profit-driven system, I doubt we'll be able to get rid of war."

Keith said most of his ex-military buddies were traumatized. Some were now activists, others were homeless. "Many ex-military guys want nothing to do with this system. So they end up on the streets, not even getting the support the government is supposed to give them. They just don't wanna deal with any of it."

"Yeah I get them. What about you? What do you want to do?" I asked.

"I receive some money from the government, monthly, because of my disability from the war. I live off this money and I won't have anything to do with this bullshit anymore. Sometimes I teach English if I need some extra money."

"Oh so you don't really have to work anymore then? At least that's positive."

"Yeah, it's not worth it though. Nothing is worth fucking up your physical and mental health. And destroying people's lives," said Keith.

I crashed on Keith's couch for a few days after my hotel reservation expired. I felt both sad and angry about the stories Keith told me. I wish I could have helped, but there wasn't much I could do.

After a few days at Keith's, I decided to move on. I didn't care to stay in Bansko much longer because the snow was already starting to melt and the snowboarding was just not that great. I considered going to the Alps.

Maybe I can afford to go to Austria, I thought. *It's not that far from here. Maybe if I knew somebody there... Hmm...* I remembered Chris, the Australian snowboarder I had a big crush on in Switzerland. *Has Chris lived in Austria? He's definitely lived in the French and Swiss Alps. And he knows a lot of people, maybe he has friends in Austria...*

I decided to send Chris a message to see if he had any advice or connections in the Austrian Alps. He replied straight away and told me that unfortunately, he didn't, but he also said that he was working in a surf camp in Morocco at the time, and he invited me to visit him there instead. He said that I could stay in the surf camp for free if I was willing to help out in the kitchen for a couple of weeks, so all I would have to pay for was the flight.

I wasn't expecting that. *Hmm... Surfing in Morocco.* I thought about it. *Hmm... Chris.* He was sexy. He looked like Brad Pitt in the movie *Fight Club,* but he also had an Aussie accent. *Hard to resist.* I looked at flights and found a relatively cheap one from Istanbul to Morocco and back. *Let's see...*

Istanbul is about six hundred kilometers away from Bansko. *I can take a bus to Istanbul. Maybe I can leave my snowboarding gear somewhere in Istanbul and then head to Morocco for a couple of weeks. Then I'll fly back to Istanbul and go from there back to Sydney; the cheapest flight to Sydney is from Istanbul anyway!*

I talked to Chris and decided to go with that plan. I took a bus from Bansko to the nearest large city, Plovdiv, and another bus from Plovdiv to Istanbul. I left my snowboard with a friend's family in Istanbul, then caught that flight to Morocco.

25

Morocco, 2013

I ended up in Agadir Al Massira Airport in the middle of the night. Luckily, I wasn't the only person from the surf camp on this flight and someone came to pick us up from the airport.

After a very bumpy two-hour drive, we made it to Aglou Beach, a small coastal fishing village with some nice waves. I couldn't make out the beach in the dark, but I could hear the waves breaking in the distance. The air felt salty and slightly humid, though I could sense that I was in the desert. The driver showed me Chris's room. Since I came to this surf camp as a friend/kitchen helper, the agreement was that I would sleep in his room, rather than in a dorm room with the other guests. I was happy about that.

I walked up to Chris's door and knocked quietly, feeling bad about waking him up at 3:00 a.m. He opened the door and... *Oh damn!* There he was—all six feet of him—tan, with thick sun-bleached hair, clear-cut six-pack abs, perfectly toned muscles, and a stunning smile—standing right in front of me in nothing but small multicolored underwear.

I stumbled toward him, trying to be all nonchalant and not drool. "Hey! It's so great to see you again!" I said. Chris was barely awake but we hugged and he showed me where to put my stuff. He said that we'd have to wake up in just a few hours to make breakfast, so we should get some sleep.

"You can sleep here on the couch if you want." He pointed to a very small and old sofa just below the bed. "Or share my bed. Whatever you want." His bed was big and spacious.

"Um... Probably in the bed, if you don't mind." I grinned inside.

"No problem, we can sleep for like three hours, then we'll get up to help Ang in the kitchen. Basically, you'll just have to help set up the buffet and dining room area before and after the guests come to eat. I work as an instructor here so they don't make me do kitchen work, but I'll help you out tomorrow."

We woke up the next morning to the sound of a prayer coming from a nearby mosque. There was a cool breeze and salty mist in the air. We walked from Chris's room to the balcony and dinning area that overlooked the endless coastline. The morning light was faintly brushing over the Atlantic Ocean as offshore winds shaped and curved the waves in the distance. There was sand and water as far as the eye could see. There were no trees or much greenery, just a few sandy hills, several small white buildings, one mosque, and a few camels on the beach.

Chris and I set up the food, drinks, and dishes, then ate with the guests once they arrived. There were about twelve guests at the surf camp, plus the two owners of the camp, Chris, me, and a local helping hand. It felt nice and cozy. Most of the guests were from Germany or Austria, since the owners were Austrian, but they all spoke English.

The hotel had a fun rooftop area with some beanbags, a slack-line, and a balance board. The mission at the camp, however, was not to eat and relax, it was to learn to surf! After breakfast, we went down to the beach for our first surfing lesson.

I hadn't had sex in weeks, perhaps even months at that point, and I was extremely turned on by just about everything Chris was doing. He showed us how to paddle for waves and pop up from our boards. He was shirtless. I could barely pay attention to what he was saying. Then he did some warmup exercises, stretched his muscles, put on his tight wetsuit, and led us into the water. I was so excited for him to teach me how to surf!

I did surf back in Sydney, but since surfing is such a difficult sport, I was still very much a beginner. Chris helped me catch some fun little waves. After surfing, we set up lunch, ate, then went surfing again. I loved it. After a second round of surfing, we relaxed a bit, surfed again, then prepared dinner. By dinnertime, everyone was absolutely exhausted and ready to hit the sack.

Chris and I went back to his room and ended up talking for hours. It had been several years since we last met and a lot had happened since then. He told me stories about traveling through Europe, surfing, camping on various beaches, and getting caught up in some funny situations.

"One time," he said, "I decided to camp in some sand dunes in Portugal. After a surf, I sat outside my tent reading a book. About five minutes into my book, some random guy came over to me and started making small talk. It was weird because I was in the middle of nowhere, camping in these dunes. I don't even know where the guy came from. He sat down right next to me and started asking questions. I didn't know what the culture was like in Portugal, but this felt pretty weird. He left after like twenty minutes. Then, like five minutes later, another guy came by! He was older, he kept on walking past my tent. He didn't say anything but he kept on looking over at me and walked by like ten times.

"I was like, 'What the fuck?' Then a younger guy came by and just sat right in front of me! Like less than a meter away and just eyed me down. I was like, 'WHAT do you want?' And the guy was shocked that I asked him that question. He said, 'Does this bother you?' And I'm like, 'YES! Of course it bothers me! What the fuck?'"

"Oh shit." I chuckled.

"That guy left," Chris continued. "Then a few minutes later he came back, almost in panic mode as if he had something really important to tell me. And he did! He told me that this sand dune was right in the middle of the gay area!"

"No way!" I said.

"Yep, so those sand dunes were where gay men get together to meet and have sex, and I pitched up a tent right in the middle of it. And sat outside, shirtless, as if I wanted to invite them in for tea and biscuits." We cracked up laughing.

Chris told me more crazy stories of gay men hitting on him and trying to touch his dick. I wasn't surprised. "Sometimes," he said, "I wish I was gay. Gay men have so much sex it's nuts. But no, I'm just not attracted to men, I could never go there."

Chris and I spent most of the night talking to each other. I told him all about my backpacking, sailing, and hitchhiking trips, he told me more about himself. I felt so comfortable with him, as if we had been best friends all of our lives.

Then one night, he kissed me. I could barely comprehend what was happening. I felt a million butterflies flooding in and fluttering inside me. I started to fall deeply in love with Chris.

As the days went by, we connected more and more. We had amazing sex, and so much of it. We just couldn't get enough of each other. We woke up in the morning and had sex. We had breakfast, went for a surf, then had sex again. After lunch, we had more sex. Another surf, then sex again.

Everything was orgasmic about those two weeks in Morocco. I felt like Chris's personality highlighted mine. I felt like I was really, fully, truly myself when I was with him. We had the same sense of humor and we laughed so much that my face muscles ached. I had never had this kind of connection with anybody before. I felt this strong sensation of missing him even when he was just a few meters away from me, even for just a few minutes. I'd spend all night wrapped up in his arms. While we were together, it felt like the whole world could just disappear and fall apart, yet everything would be just fine, as long as we were still together.

I talked to Chris about everything, from travel stories, to my university studies, to my current understanding of the state of the world. Chris seemed to be as interested in the world as I was. I told him how I thought it was all fucked up—the entire system; money, profit, capitalism, whatever you want to call it. This profit-driven system was causing climate change, exploiting people and the environment, creating pollution, destruction, deforestation, war, waste, and a billion other problems. He agreed.

"Have you heard of the Venus Project?" he asked.

"No, what's that?" I said.

"I can show you a video. Hour long documentary. You wanna see it?"

"Sure." He showed me a film called *Paradise or Oblivion*, made by the Venus Project. The first part of the documentary outlined some of today's global problems and explained that our current methods of solving these problems weren't working. War, hunger, poverty, homelessness, environmental destruction, and many other problems are *caused* by our current system and as long as we live in this system, these problems will perpetuate. They explained that in this system, we value profit over the well-being of humans, the environment, and basically anything else. *That's what I've been saying for years!*

The documentary stated that "War represents the supreme failure of nations to resolve their differences. From a strictly pragmatic standpoint it is the most inefficient waste of lives and resources ever conceived." Peace treaties won't work if you don't get rid of the underlying conditions that cause the problems in the first place. "There is no way to make this system just or equitable." The entire structure of our global society is harmful, unsustainable, and it needs to change—that was the premise of the documentary. *I agreed.*

The second part of the documentary described an alternative solution, something that has never been tried in the past—an idea that the Venus Project called a global resource-based economy (RBE). That is, an economy that would not be based on money, debt, credit, or servitude of any kind, but rather, on the carrying capacity of the Earth's resources. The Venus Project claimed that the Earth was abundant with resources. "There is not enough money to feed or house all people on this planet [...] but Earth has more than enough resources to meet the needs of all people, but *only* if managed intelligently."

The idea, as far as I understood, was to create a global, advanced society in which people had access to an abundance of goods and services. This project claimed that technically, it was already possible to create such an abundance, but our current means of distributing and managing resources stood in the way of this.

The Venus Project also demonstrated designs for a number of futuristic smart cities. These city-systems were meant to be an integral part of the project and idea. The founder of the Venus Project was an inventor and engineer who had spent decades developing these concepts and city designs. He seemed like a very passionate and ambitious person.

After we finished watching the documentary, I turned to Chris and said, "That sounds *really nice*... But you know this will *never* happen."

He turned back and said something like, "But Sasha, if even someone like you says it could never happen, then it definitely won't."

I grinned. *Maybe that's true. Maybe there would be a tiny tiny tiny chance for things to change if at least some of us kept an open mind. Most people don't even care about these things...*

"What's that guy's name again? In the video?" I asked.

"Jacque Fresco. He's a legend. He's like ninety-seven years old and he's still talking shit about humanity!"

"Oh wow. Ninety-seven? Well he looks pretty good." I was intrigued by this little old man. I liked his determination and charisma, and although I thought that his idea of a future society was too unrealistic, I enjoyed listening to his criticism of our current society and culture.

Chris and I ended up watching many more lectures and recordings of Jacque Fresco while we were still together. I discussed these ideas with Chris and I think this connected us even further. Few people care to talk about the world and its problems, let alone about an entirely different idea of how to organize society. Chris was my dream man.

Unfortunately, after those two weeks in paradise, I had to leave again. I would have loved to stay with Chris forever, but I couldn't drop university again. *I have to finish this damn course once and for all,* I thought. *I only have two semesters left!*

In the beginning of March, I flew from Morocco back to Istanbul, picked up my snowboard bag, then flew back to Australia. I missed Chris the minute I left. Without him, I felt utterly and totally heartbroken.

26

Sydney, 2013

I arrived in Sydney one week late for university, but I didn't care. I felt empty inside. I moved back into the small apartment in Manly with Rachel and my three other flatmates. I didn't do much homework or pay much attention to my classes. Instead, I walked along the beach, thought about Chris, and cried. I cried so much that I laughed at myself for crying, for being so weak, so girlish.

I was happy when Rachel came home. She was always giggly and friendly. I told her about the rest of my trip and how I fell in love with Chris. She told me how she backpacked through Thailand and Vietnam with a sexy British guy. It was great to see her again.

Soon, James put me back on the Three Wise Monkeys bartending schedule. I wasn't completely broke this time since I didn't spend much money in Asia, Russia, Bulgaria, or Morocco, but my savings were running low. I don't have an exact record of how much I had spent on that three-month trip, but it was probably somewhere between two and three thousand dollars. Accommodation was either free or about five dollars per night. Food was either free or cheap. The two-week ski pass in Bulgaria wasn't too expensive and surfing in Morocco was "free" in exchange for the work I did in the kitchen. I didn't buy anything else. My main expense, as always, was the airfare, which cost less than two thousand dollars for that trip (Sydney-Bangkok-Moscow-Istanbul-Morocco-Istanbul-Sydney).

If you earn twenty-five dollars an hour (which I did at Three Wise Monkeys), you only need to work 120 hours (or about three weeks) to make three thousand dollars. Of course, some of your earnings will have to go toward your living expenses, but I always kept my living expenses to an extreme minimum. I shared a room in a shared apartment to pay a bare minimum rent, I bought the cheapest possible groceries (usually rice, beans, and vegetables), I rarely went out to restaurants, I used a bicycle as much as possible for transportation. I would never even consider buying a car unless I absolutely needed one. If I needed clothes, I'd buy them from a second-hand shop, but usually people just gave me clothes. If I needed a haircut, I'd go to the hair school, where it was free. I never bought jewelry, makeup, fashionable items, useless electronics, ornaments, or any other useless or stupid things. Because of that, I was able to save money fast and then use this money to travel for months at a time.

For the next four months, I worked a lot, surfed as much as possible, and tried to pass my university classes. I also ended up talking to Chris almost every day. I didn't expect for that to happen, but it did. We texted and called each other every chance we had. Every time I talked to him, I felt those million butterflies again. We continued our investigation into the Venus Project together, sending each other new Jacque Fresco recordings on a daily basis.

The more I learned about the Venus Project, the more my appreciation grew for Jacque Fresco. Jacque talked about many different concepts—from human behavior, to language, to nations, nationalism, culture, religion, freedom, corruption, education, social change, resource management, technology, and much more. I wasn't particularly surprised by anything that Jacque said, but I liked what he talked about and how he explained pretty simple but important ideas in a very comprehensible way.

Jacque explained that we live in a dumb society with a false value system based on mindless consumerism, but he also said that this wasn't the fault of the people. "Our behavior and values are reflective of the culture we are exposed to," explained Jacque in one of his recordings. "If you were raised by the headhunters of the Amazon, you'd be a headhunter. If I said to you, 'Doesn't it bother you to have five shrunken heads?' you'd say, 'Yes, my brother has twenty.' Is he nuts? No, that's normal to his culture."

In the same way, it's normal in our culture to pay people one dollar per day to work in a sweatshop, it's normal for children to be enslaved in cocoa plantations and cobalt mines, and it's normal for big companies like Nestle, Apple, and Tesla to profit from slavery. In business terms, that's called "efficiency," as long as it makes your business more efficient at earning profit.

But rather than punishing those who commit such crimes and atrocities, Jacque stressed that we need to understand what *conditions* cause people to create these problems in the first place, and then work toward changing those conditions.

I realized that Jacque Fresco was one of very few people who actually thought outside of the box. It bothered me that organizations like the United Nations had so many "nice-sounding" goals (like ensuring sustainability and eradicating hunger and poverty), yet they never seemed to analyze human behavior or question our society. As a result, such organizations were only capable of temporary solutions to very few problems, while in the long run, most global problems would only get worse. Jacque, on the other hand, asked deeper questions, he wasn't afraid to criticize our society, and he emphasized the importance of studying human behavior.

Jacque was also genuinely concerned with global problem solving. He wasn't doing all of this research because it was a part of his "job" or "career"; this was his passion—the stuff he really cared about. Perhaps that's what inspired me the most. This little man had dedicated his entire life to figuring out how humans can live sustainably on this planet, and at age ninety-seven, he was still fighting for this cause. *What a legend.*

After watching many more recordings of Jacque Fresco, his idea of a resource-based economy started to make more sense to me. I was still skeptical about whether or not it was achievable, but after reading Jacque's book, *The Best That Money Can't Buy,* I decided that it was necessary. *We need to do something—anything —to at least try to make this happen!* I thought. *If we don't, we'll most likely bring ourselves and many other creatures to extinction in the not-so-far-away future.*

I tried to explain these ideas to the students in my International and Global Studies class, but most of them didn't seem to care. They were busy trying to pass their classes. The professors didn't seem to care either. They were busy doing their "jobs."

Everyone's too busy to even care, I thought. *And when they're not busy, all they care about is getting laid or getting a drink at the pub. No one really cares about "saving the world," whatever that means...*

Soon I got busy too. That semester was difficult and it pissed me off a lot. I took one "business ethics" course where we learned about all kinds of people being enslaved in sweatshops and factories all over the world. We learned about many "unethical" business decisions that caused the deaths and suffering of countless numbers of people. None of this was surprising to me. What was surprising, however, was that this "business ethics" course was *optional* for a business major. Therefore, most people who study business don't even get a glimpse of the atrocities caused by "efficient" businesses all over the world.

In my International and Global Studies course, we touched upon topics like inequality, global wealth distribution, and sustainability. We discussed global population growth, our ecological footprints, and a possible collapse of the system as a result of our limits to growth. I learned that free trade development hasn't alleviated poverty, nor has it decreased levels of environmental degradation. In fact, whenever "development" happens, the environment only gets more degraded and most of the money that is earned ends up in the hands of the rich and powerful. Those who are said to be in need of "development" only get the scraps, at most.

I was very stressed out by the end of the semester. I was so stressed that I developed extreme neck and back problems. The pain was so strong that I could barely move my neck from side to side and my back felt like it was covered in sores and bruises. I also became addicted to energy drinks. I wasn't able to concentrate on my assignments without this sugary substance. Rachel started to worry about my well-being.

"Maybe you should take it easy," she said.

"At least I don't smoke," I replied. "And when this semester's over, I won't touch these things again, I swear." I was getting jittery from the energy drinks. It was also difficult to manage my schedule and stay awake in class when I had to bartend until 4:00 or 5:00 a.m. several nights per week.

"Maybe you should take some time off work," said Rachel.

"Yeah I'll leave for a month when the semester's over. I'll be fine. I'd like to save up some more money till then," I said.

"Where do you want to go?"

"I don't know yet." I considered flying to Europe to see Chris, since he was working in Spain at the time, but he told me not to since the flight would have cost a fortune for such a short trip. He said that he'd come to Australia after he finished his contract in a few months. Then I sent Emma a message to see what she was up to. She wrote back:

I'm currently in the middle of the Northern Territory driving a massive dozer & grader. But I've scored a job in Kununurra WA, in the mines. Not sure on start date yet, I go there for a site visit next week and will find out when I start. Come up and we will go fishing and hunting.

That sounded like a great escape to me. I didn't care much for fishing and hunting but I knew that any time with Emma would be a good time.

At the end of the semester, I booked a flight to Darwin, where Emma said she'd meet me. I finished my final exams and essays, took some time off work, packed up my backpack, moved out of my apartment, and caught that flight.

27

Outback, 2013

Once I got to Darwin, Emma picked me up from the airport and we began our drive out west. Emma had to sort out some paperwork for her new job at the Argyle Diamond Mine, which was in Western Australia (WA), about a thousand kilometers away from Darwin. The drive was fantastic. I spent hours catching up with Emma and observing the dry shrubs and enormous boab trees scattered sparsely around the desert. Every once in a while I'd spot a kangaroo or a few wallabies. The farther we drove, the more relieved I felt.

"It's so great to be out of Sydney," I said. "Away from university and away from work!"

At night, when we got tired of driving, we simply stopped on the side of the road, took out Emma's swags, and slept outside beneath the universe. I stared at the brilliant starlit night and felt all the stress and pain of university melt away into the desert.

I was free again. For a short and temporary moment, I was free.

We got to a small country town called Kununurra the next day. This was the nearest town to Argyle Diamond Mine, which was another two hundred kilometers away. "They'll fly me out to the mine tonight," said Emma. "You can take my truck and drive around town, sleep in the back tonight, it's all set up." Emma's pickup truck had a lot of space in the back, along with a cooler, swags, and other camping gear. A swag is basically a thick sleeping bag with a waterproof shell. It zips up, provides a soft cushion to sleep on, and protects you from snakes and insects. *Best way to camp in the desert.*

I dropped Emma off at the local airport then roamed around town for a bit. There wasn't much to see in the town itself; there was just one pub, a couple of shops, and some residential areas. About five thousand people lived there but many more flew in to work in the mine or on nearby agricultural land.

That night I decided to go to the pub. I'm not going to lie, I was very horny that night. I hadn't had sex in months. And now that I was in Outback Australia, I had a big craving for an Aussie cowboy. I wasn't going in there to find a date though, I just thought I would have a beer and scope out the scene, just for fun.

Chris and I talked a lot at that point, but we weren't in a monogamous relationship. We had both agreed that there was nothing wrong with having sex with other people. I mean, we had only been intimate together for about two weeks, and that was four months ago.

As soon as I walked into the pub I felt like all the men in there could just smell that I was horny. Some were glancing over at me, others were staring me down like a Spanish bull targeting his matador. *Jesus Christ,* I thought. *I haven't even dressed up or anything, and I haven't showered today. I hope I smell okay...*

I had a beer and hung around for a few minutes, but I felt like the tension in that pub was too strong, so I decided to leave. As soon as I started going for the door, an older not-so-attractive man grabbed my hand and said, "I will eat your pussy so good! You won't regret it, come with me and I'll give you the best pleasure you've had in your life! I love eating pussy. I'll eat it so good!" Then he made the not-so-attractive side-to-side motion with his tongue, presumably showing me how he was planning on pleasuring me.

"Oh, thanks, but no thanks! I need to go *that* way!" I pointed to the door and tried to escape his charming hand grip. A split second later, a young guy grabbed my arm and helped me get away from the tongue man. This young guy was hot, blond, and from Perth. Not exactly a cowboy, but he sure was Aussie.

Somehow, I ended up at his place that night. He was sexy and rough. He ripped open the buttons on my shirt, grabbed my hair, and took control of me. I really liked him at first, but then he slapped me so hard in the face that he made my nose bleed! And it wasn't just a little bit of blood, it poured out of my nose like a waterfall! The blood spilled all over his room, down the hallway, and all over the bathroom floor. When I finally managed to stop the nosebleed, I realized that his hotel room looked like a crime scene. Blood was everywhere! I laughed, hoping his flatmate wouldn't come out of the other room.

I calmed down after that night. *That was enough fun for the next month or so,* I thought, *now I can relax.* I picked up Emma from the airport the next morning and told her what happened. "I wanted an Aussie cowboy," I said, "but all I got was a slap in the face!"

She laughed. "Oh those WA boys! Watch out for them! I had a feeling you'd tell me something crazy about last night."

"Yeah!" I cracked up.

"We'll go to the rodeo in Katherine next month, all the boys will be after you there. Watch out for them though, they're not as nice as those WA boys!"

"Cowboys are they?" I grinned.

"Yeah, not the nice kinda cowboys though," she laughed. "Let's get some coffee then head in that direction."

Soon we were back on the road. This time, we were only planning on a 530-kilometer drive from Kununurra to Katherine, Emma's hometown in the Northern Territory. A few of her family friends were expecting us there.

The drive was empty and beautiful. We stopped to admire a few more boab trees, some giant termite mounds, and a dead snake that was almost twice as long as my body. Once we got to Katherine, we stopped in a local shop to buy a few groceries. As we looked around the shop, I noticed something odd hanging in the fridge, and it was on sale! There was a big sign saying, "Kangaroo Tails 50% Off!"

"I gotta get a picture of that, Em!" I said.

I took out my camera, then all of a sudden, the lady in the shop started yelling, "There's no picture takin' in muay shop!" in a thick Aussie accent. "Get that camera outta my shop! Out! Out! Out!"

"Okay, sorry! I just wanted to photo the discounted kangaroo tails!" I said. *Jesus Christ.*

"OUT! OUT! OUT!" She was angry!

Emma was paying for the groceries with her credit card while all of this was happening, and said to the lady, "She's Russian," implying that I'm just a tourist and I mean no harm.

The lady replied back, "There's no rushin' this machine!" as Emma's credit card payment was processing.

"Um... Never mind." We chuckled and moved on.

We spent a few nights at Emma's friend's place in Katherine. It was very peaceful and quiet there, until Darius showed up. Darius was one of Emma's childhood friends, he was a *huge* guy, a bit ogre-like, with several scars on his head. He loved getting hammered and whenever he got drunk, he got very rowdy. He had been in jail several times for various reasons (once for nearly stabbing his girlfriend) and let's just say that he wasn't the sharpest knife in the shed, although he sure had a lot of sharp knives. Darius loved Emma like a sister though and respected her wholeheartedly. He also seemed to be quite fond of me, so he decided to stick around us as much as possible.

After a few nights in Katherine, Emma and I planned to drive to the Barkley Tableland, about a thousand kilometers away. Emma had been working on a cattle station there, driving a grader and bulldozer, and had a few more days of work to finish up. She told me that I could hang out at their work station while she finished the job. "The boys won't mind, I'm sure!" she laughed. Darius didn't have a job or much money at the time, so he decided to come with us too. He thought that if he showed up at this cattle station, he might be able to find some work.

The three of us took off and drove south, stopping at some tiny country towns and gas stations along the way. It felt great to be on the road going to the middle of nowhere again. We drove for hours and hours, past hundreds of kilometers of red sand, blue skies, and long dusty roads. When Emma got tired, I took over driving. One time, we decided to swap seats as we were on the road going about 120 kilometers per hour. Darius was in the back seat, sleeping. Emma looked over at me with a sneaky smile and asked, "You wanna swap?"

"Okay," I grinned. The road was long, straight, and completely empty. Emma kept the truck going straight, then took her foot off the gas and leaned back on the driver's seat. I squeezed in right in front of her, grabbed the wheel, and put my foot on the gas pedal. At the same time, Emma jumped over to the passenger seat. As she jumped, I jerked the wheel by accident, forcing the truck a bit to the left, then jerked it back to the right.

"WHAT THE HELL ARE YOU GIRLS DOING?" yelled Darius.

"You almost got us killed!" laughed Emma.

"What just happened? I almost flew out the back window here!" said Darius.

"Don't worry, Dar, you won't fit through the window!" We chuckled as I got the truck back on course.

"Gotta try everything once, right?" I said.

"Yep, just once!" said Emma.

That night we slept in a truck stop in the middle of nowhere. There wasn't a single town for hundreds of kilometers, but as with all truck stops in the middle of Australia, there was a pub. The pub was extremely expensive, but as far as I remember, Emma and I ordered a couple of drinks while Darius downed an entire bottle of whiskey. He didn't kill anybody that night, but he did piss off a few truck drivers. Some of the truckers were pretty annoying though, so maybe it wasn't all Darius's fault. One of them, an older, toothless fellow, started to bother Emma to the point that she was forced to beat him up. She slapped him around, hit him a bit, and forced him to go back into his truck, crying like a little girl. Then he drove away.

Emma and I slept in her truck, while Darius slept on the roof of the vehicle like a guard dog. The next day, we drove several hundred more kilometers to Brunette Downs, a massive cattle station on the border of Queensland and the Northern Territory. This place was spectacular. As far as the eye could see, there was nothing but red dirt, dirt roads, dry grass, cattle, termite mounds, and the odd kangaroo hopping around here or there.

Once we arrived at the site, I realized that this was a bit of an awkward situation. There were two trailers set up for the people who worked there, one was the kitchen and living room area, the other was a dorm room. There were three or four men living there, all of whom were working on the station full time, grading new roads and setting up water pipes. There was nothing else around. No stores, no houses, not even a single tree! And there I was—a college girl on my "vacation." And there was Darius—an "ogre" looking for work. Emma didn't tell her boss that Darius and I were coming to work with her, and once we were there, we couldn't exactly leave. The next town was like four hundred kilometers away!

Luckily, Emma's boss agreed to let me hang around the trailers and eat their food, and he even found some work for Darius. The rest of the week was very relaxing for me. We woke up around 5:00 or 6:00 a.m. each morning, watched the sunrise over the desert, had bacon and eggs for breakfast, then everyone left to do their jobs while I hung around the trailers. Many people would have been bored in my place, but I was so happy to sit around and just relax. I read books, played my guitar, and watched the horizon. I finally had time to just sit and think.

When Emma and the guys came back to the trailers, I heated up some precooked meals for them. The meals had been cooked and packed by the boss's wife, so all I had to do was stick them in the microwave. All of Emma's coworkers knew this, but for some reason, they were extremely thankful for these meals. Even the boss thanked me as if I had been cooking this food for them all day.

Sometimes Emma, Darius, and I jogged around the desert in the evenings and watched the sunset from different waterholes and sandy points. The sunsets were incredible and the night sky was just out of this world. I slept outside in a swag and watched the stars all night. This was the most brilliant sky I had ever seen. The Milky Way was crisp and clear. The air was dry. The desert, still and silent.

Just imagine, I thought. *Almost every dot, every sparkle, every twinkle—is another sun. Somewhere far, far away. A distance so vast that you could never really grasp it. And here I am. Spinning on a small speck of an Earth that you wouldn't even see from the vantage point of those distant stars. I am so small, yet I am part of it all. The atoms that make up my body, and everything on Earth— the carbon, the oxygen, the iron, the elements—were created inside the core of a giant collapsing star. Somewhere out there—in the universe.*

That's what happens inside of stars. Elements are formed through fusion—hydrogen atoms fuse together to form helium; helium atoms fuse together to form carbon and oxygen; carbon atoms fuse together to form bigger, heavier elements; then bigger, heavier elements fuse together to form even heavier elements; until eventually, the star explodes. As it explodes, it creates even more heavy elements. Then—it seeds the universe with all the ingredients it needs to form new stars, new planets, new moons, new oceans, new mountains, and life. That's where we truly come from—the elements of our bodies were crafted in the center of a dying star. *In this sense, Earth and everything on it truly is star dust. And we, humans, are recycled Earth stuff.*

How could we know this yet lack the understanding that we are one race, one species, one lifeform that evolved on this one unique and incredible planet?

How could we understand all of this yet not take care of our precious home?

How could we prioritize fictional entities like money, countries, and corporations over nonfictional wonders like oceans, forests, and earthlings?

But perhaps it's not our fault, I thought. *Perhaps we need to understand that we are all victims of our own culture and system. And to change ourselves collectively, we need to change the culture and the system. Only then could we truly cherish our pale blue dot —the only home we've ever known.*

I didn't get much sleep at night, but I loved every moment of it. I loved being in the middle of nowhere, far away from the world of cities and citizens.

* * *

After about a week, Emma finished the work that she had to do and Darius got fired, so we hit the road again. Our first stop was at a place called Devil's Marbles, about six hundred kilometers away. This was a pretty interesting sight. There were a bunch of big round and oval shaped rocks lying around in the middle of the desert. Some looked as if they had been split open with a giant knife. We climbed all around the rocks like a bunch of kids, then got back in the truck and kept on driving.

I never got tired of driving through the desert. The landscape didn't change much for thousands of kilometers, but it was so peaceful and beautiful just to be there. We stopped in several random spots, slept outside or in Emma's truck, and kept on driving. We laughed about driving thousands of kilometers just to see some rocks. The biggest rock, Uluru, was quite impressive though. This was a sacred and spiritual place for the local Aboriginal people. Unfortunately, it had now been turned into a major tourist attraction. The place was built up with neat little footpaths, tourist stops, and fenced off areas; and of course, there were a lot of tourists.

Uluru was much bigger and more colorful than I had expected. We drove around the entire rock formation, then watched the sunset from a distance. The evening rays immersed the rock in a colorful play of light. One minute, Uluru was bright red, the next minute, it was pink, then purple, then bluish. Eventually, it was gone and the night sky lit up like a crystal ball. We slept on the red sand in a quiet corner of the national park.

In the morning, the sky looked like it was on fire! Big, puffy clouds were bedazzled in bright red, pink, and orange colors. We watched the sunrise over Uluru before we took off for another long drive through the desert.

Next, we went to another big rock formation called Kata Tjuṯa, then to King's Canyon. Both sights were very impressive. The smooth and colorful rock walls of King's Canyon are over a hundred meters high and the creek at the bottom of the canyon looked like it was made of gold. After a long wander through the national parks, we got back on the road and made our way back up north.

One thousand five hundred kilometers later, we were back in Katherine, just on time for the rodeo. This yearly event was quite the spectacle. I had never been to a rodeo before, so I was amused. Emma and I had a few drinks, wandered around, and watched some strange events, like bull riding and horse racing. At some point, Emma and her friends convinced me to sign up to ride a small bull as well. Lucky for me, when the time of that event came, there were no small bulls available. Instead, I got into a boxing ring.

No other female volunteered to box me, so I ended up boxing Emma in front of a huge crowd of people. Emma is about a foot taller than me, so she easily knocked me down to the ground over and over again. I was so pumped up with whiskey and adrenaline that I forgot our agreement—I was supposed to stay on the ground and make it look like Emma was beating the shit out of me! That would have been funny! Instead, I kept on prancing back up and Emma kept on knocking me down again. It was funny anyway. After this event, all of Katherine knew us as the two boxers—the little Russian and the tall Aussie chick.

Once the rodeo was over, Emma and I drove another three hundred kilometers up to Darwin. We had some fun wandering around the markets and hanging out with Emma's friends, but after another day or two, we had to say our goodbyes. Emma had to go to work in the diamond mine and I had to go back to university. I hadn't booked a flight back to Sydney so I decided to save some money by hitchhiking. Sydney was about four thousand kilometers away from Darwin, but since most of the drive was down just one long road, I figured it would be pretty easy.

* * *

I was right. Emma dropped me off at a petrol station and I got a ride all the way to Adelaide (three thousand kilometers away) with the first drivers I talked to. They were two nice guys named Greg and John, and they were driving a gigantic vehicle called a road train. This was a truck with three full trailers attached to it—an enormous load! In fact, Australia's road-legal road trains are the longest and heaviest in the world, and this may have been one of them.

Inside the truck there were two comfortable seats, a small fridge, and a bunk bed. Since there were two drivers, this vehicle was legally allowed to go straight to Adelaide without a single long break. When Greg drove, John slept in his bed or relaxed in the passenger seat. When John drove, Greg did the same. This was perfect for me because it was the fastest possible way to get to South Australia for free.

I sat in the bunk bed or in the passenger seat and chatted with Greg and John for hours. They both lived in Adelaide but frequently made this trip up to Darwin, and they seemed to love it. Greg said that when he had time off work, he got into his car in South Australia and did road trips just for fun.

I loved staring out the window of this big truck, looking down at the wide open view of the red-sand desert. It was mesmerizing. I loved it all. I spent about two days in this truck and I never got bored. When I was tired, I slept in one of the bunk beds. When I was hungry, I ate. I brought enough food to last me several days. I had nuts, cereal bars, fruit, bread, cold cuts, and lettuce for sandwiches. Greg laughed at me for eating lettuce. He called it "rabbit food," but by the end of the trip he was eating it himself!

Two days later, we made it to Adelaide. I was actually sad to say goodbye to Greg and John. We swapped email addresses, then they dropped me off at a petrol station where I could catch a ride to Sydney.

Unfortunately, I didn't get as lucky with my second ride. I walked around the petrol station and talked to a few truck drivers. Eventually, one older, chubby truck driver agreed to take me to Sydney. "But I gotta load up first," he said. "If you don't mind waiting you can come with me."

I guess he means load the truck, I thought. This one was just a normal cargo truck, not a road train. *That can't take too long, right?*

"Sure, no problem," I said. "Thanks a lot!" I hopped in his truck and we drove to a farm outside of Adelaide where the truck was to be loaded with vegetables.

It was hot at this farm and we stood around for hours while the truck was being loaded. *What the hell is taking them so long?* I wondered. I walked around the big storage area. There were boxes of cabbage, tomatoes, carrots, and pretty much any vegetable you find in the supermarket. About half the day went by before we were actually able to get on the road. *And I thought I could get to Sydney by tonight...*

It took only two days to drive the three thousand kilometers from Darwin to Adelaide, and the drive from Adelaide to Sydney was less than half that distance, so I expected it to take about one day, but I was mistaken. First of all, I had no idea that loading up the truck would take half a day. I could have easily caught a different ride by the time they finished loading. That was the first mistake. The second mistake was that I didn't ask the driver which route he was planning to take. I didn't know until much later that he wasn't planning to go straight to Sydney. He needed to make a detour around Melbourne, which was a bit out of the way. Of course, it would have been nice for him to mention that before I hopped into his truck, but this driver wasn't as friendly as Greg or John. Actually, Fat Bob was quite annoying.

Bob was very unhappy with his life and he complained a lot. He was overweight and ate junk food, oily chips, and donuts all day. He told me stories of how his girlfriend left him and how nobody liked him. He also told me about his physical problems and how the doctor kept on telling him to quit truck driving. But he wouldn't. His attitude seemed quite harmful to himself.

I tried to be nice and helpful at first, but after so many hours, I just wanted to get out of Bob's truck. The problem was that I couldn't get out. I had nowhere to go! It had taken so long to load up the truck that we only made it about halfway to Melbourne by the time it got dark. There were also a ton of restrictions that Bob needed to follow. He needed to take fifteen-minute breaks every few hours and a seven-hour break after about twelve hours of driving. He wasn't happy about these rules but he said that his company was very strict and the penalties were huge.

I didn't know about that part either... I was sure that we would be able to make it to Sydney without stopping for an overnight sleep, but it turned out that that was against the law. So at some point in the middle of the night, Fat Bob stopped his truck at a rest stop, climbed into his bed behind the seats, and said, "Now we gotta sleep for seven hours."

All right, I guess I can't complain about a free lift, I thought. *It would have been nice if he had told me about this ahead of time though...* He sprawled his blubber out onto the narrow bed, scooted over just a bit, and said, "You can sleep here if you want," as he stroked the two-inch space between his floppy boobs and the back of the driver's seat.

"Oh, thanks, but I'm fine here!" I said awkwardly as I snugged into the passenger seat. "I'm very small so I fit here perfectly. It's very comfortable!"

"Okay," he said as his greasy body enveloped the bed. Luckily, he didn't try to make any sneaky moves on me in the middle of the night. I was ready to run away with my phone and wallet just in case. There was a twenty four hour petrol station nearby, so that made me feel a bit safer. Plus, I knew that I could outrun Fat Bob any day.

After spending the entire night in the passenger seat, thinking of escape plans and listening to the loud snores and snorts of Fat Bob, I was tired as hell. My body was sore and my brain was sick of Bob. *You should still be grateful for the free ride!* I tried to convince myself.

Bob and I spent another twelve or so hours in the truck together the next day, then we finally made it to Sydney! I was *so* relieved to get out of that truck! I thanked Bob, said goodbye, and hopped into the first train station I saw. I took a train to Sydney's city center then a bus to Manly. I didn't know where I would sleep that night, but it didn't matter. Somehow, I felt like I had made it home.

28

The Last Round

Before I left for the Northern Territory, Rachel and I moved out of our apartment because of a stupid fight we got into with our other flatmates. Looking back at the situation, I realized that that was an unnecessary bitch fight and a dumb mistake. I don't remember what the fight was about but I'm sure if we had stayed calm and rational, we could have come up with some solutions. Instead, Rachel and I created drama, made the situation worse, and then decided to move out of the apartment altogether. The only positive thing about this was that I didn't have to pay rent for the month I was traveling around Australia, so I saved about six hundred dollars.

Rachel and I assumed we would easily be able to find another place to live once I came back to Manly, but that was also a mistake. Manly was insanely expensive and there weren't many rooms or flats available. As a result, Rachel ended up staying on a friend's couch for a very long time and I ended up moving into a backpackers' hostel. This wasn't an ideal situation for me since I was still in university, but luckily, that semester was very easy. I only had to finish two more classes in order to get my degree—one business class and one Spanish class. I didn't care about either one of those classes, so I paid little attention to them.

The hostel was loud and messy, but I made a lot of new friends from all over the world, so the social aspect of it was fun. I shared a room with seven or eight random people, cooked food in a big shared kitchen, and showered with my sandals on. The worst part was that a bed in this hostel cost a lot more than the room I was renting before (in the nice quiet apartment) or any other accommodation I had previously paid for in Sydney. And this was the cheapest place in Manly! After a week or two, I realized that I could save money by cleaning the hostel in exchange for free accommodation.

So that's what I did for the next four months. I slept in a shared room, swept and mopped the hostel rooms, and made a bunch of new friends. I went to university two days per week and to work at Three Wise Monkeys three or four nights per week. This was probably the best time I had in Sydney. I met a girl named Ziva, who was extremely lively and always ready to do just about anything. We went surfing, sailing, paddleboarding, swimming, running, played beach volleyball, slacklined, went to free shows and concerts, and just had a lot of fun. I also had a buddy named Diego who was there for me through all of university. He was such a genuinely happy guy and just as excited as Ziva to have some fun Since Diego had a car, we also went on camping and surfing trips up and down the beautiful coast of New South Wales.

I had so much fun in Manly that it was easy to ignore all of the problems I was learning about before. I had already completed all of my International and Global Studies classes so I didn't feel like I was studying anything important anymore. I hated the business class and I didn't care too much for Spanish either. Diego was from Chile, so we practiced Spanish at the pub while I helped him pick up older women (that was his niche).

There was WiFi in the hostel but it was hard to do anything productive since there was absolutely no private space. Every once in a while, I went to the library or to the beach to talk to Chris, do some assignments, read a book, or watch more Fresco lectures.

* * *

At the end of November, the stunning jacaranda trees bloomed at Sydney University. Their bright purple flowers sprinkled the campus lawns and reminded the students that their final assignments were due. I handed in my very last essay and completed my last final exam. Then I rode my bicycle around the campus in disbelief that my struggle was finally over. *I finished university.*

This is it! It's over! I'm free! "I'm free!" I yelled. *I'm finally done with this stupid bullshit!* I took my business notebooks and dumped them into the trash bin. *I'll never have to take a university exam ever again! I'm done with essays! I'm done with stress!* I felt like I had just been released from prison.

I called both of my parents and told them the news. They were in as much disbelief as I was. Then I sat beneath a remarkable jacaranda tree and almost melted with relief. I thought about my degree. *Was it worth it?* It was not worth it to major in business or Spanish, that's for sure. But I did feel like I learned a lot in the core subject, International and Global Studies. I closed my eyes and thought about the crazy international and global world we live in. *All the problems we've created*—climate change, waste, pollution, deforestation, slavery, inequality, and a hell of a lot more.

This course should be taught to everybody, I thought, *but in a much simpler way. Actually, it should be taught in high school, to every young person, because they will all have to deal with this increasingly chaotic world. They will all have to deal with climate change, further environmental degradation, greater inequality, and a billion other problems. The least thing we could do as a species is to educate young people about these problems. Instead, kids are taught almost nothing relevant and almost nothing that will help them solve any problem.*

Fuck it. Fuck it all. At that point, I just wanted to forget about the problems of the world. *Chris comes here next week! That's all that matters now!* I rode my bike to Circular Quay, then took a ferry back to Manly. I went for a surf, watched the sunset, and calmed my mind.

Once I came back to the hostel, I accessed the internet and noticed a new message from Enzo. I hadn't talked to Enzo for a while, but it seemed like he had something important to tell me now. He said that he was planning a big sailing trip halfway across the world, from the Caribbean to New Zealand. He wrote:

The idea is to make a film...

Not to inspire the creation of more sailing bums or for people to reject society like Alexander Supertramp, but to inspire people that they do not need to follow a career and work an entire lifetime, simply for the sake of accruing money, in order to achieve something that burns intensely within them but will never get achieved.

People save for so long to do what they want that by the time they have enough they are either too afraid or disinterested...

The draft of the storyboard is so far: 2–5 people crossing half the world away, different misfits from diverse ends of the world, on a safe boat, with zero income and a budget that only allows for emergency boat repairs. Guidelines still to be set within the comfort zone of whoever's gonna be participating.

[...]

We'd be cruising around for 10 months, having fun in the best of company, across the most pristine waters of the Caribbean Sea and to the remotest cultures, villages and islands of the Pacific Ocean.

Suggestions?

Comments?

Wanna join??

You're certainly one of the cleverest traveling rats we know, hence why we'd love to have you aboard...

Feel free to bounce any ideas or questions off Ricky...

I think this is our chance to help start remodeling our world's rotten society!!!

Enzo planned to invite Ricky (my friend and couchsurfing host in Queenstown, NZ), me, and a guy named Will. Will was a young

British guy who grew up in Dubai and was hitchhiking around the world.

This message came as a bit of a surprise to me. On one hand, this trip sounded incredible. So far I had only dreamed of sailing around the world, but here was an opportunity to actually do it. And to do it for free! Or at least very cheap. *I may never get such an opportunity again...* On the other hand, there was Chris... I had spent eight months away from him, could I spend another ten months without him? Would he even accept this? And did Enzo have any hidden intentions?

I wrote back saying that I was interested in the idea but that I needed to sort some stuff out first. I also explained that I had a boyfriend and that I would only join the trip if Enzo and I could be friends—the kind that don't kiss or fuck.

Enzo replied back saying that he had no intentions of having a romantic relationship with me, and that he was planning this trip strictly for the film. He wrote, The film is EVERYTHING!!! He wanted me aboard strictly for my philosophical input and budget traveling expertise—the same reason that he wanted Will and Ricky aboard.

I thought about this more and more and decided that I couldn't miss out on such an opportunity. I loved sailing, I loved traveling, and I loved the idea of this film. How could I say no to a trip that would allow me to explore the islands of the Caribbean, Central America, the Pacific Islands, and the great Pacific Ocean? *If Chris truly loves me, then he'll understand*, I thought. It was December then and this sailing trip was meant to start in March, so Chris and I would still have a few months to spend together before my departure.

I decided to take a sailing course and participate in some sailing races near Manly to prepare for this trip. I also continued working at Three Wise Monkeys and saved as much money as possible.

Pretty soon, Chris arrived in Sydney. I was ecstatic to see him again! Luckily, at that point, Rachel finally managed to find an apartment to rent, so Chris and I didn't have to stay in that dirty hostel. Instead, we moved into Rachel's balcony. The balcony was closed off so it was almost like a separate room, except that we had to walk through Rachel's room to get in and out, and it was a bit chilly at times.

Once Chris arrived, I told him about my plan to sail across the world. At that point, I had basically made up my mind about this sailing trip, so he wouldn't have been able to talk me out of it. I think he knew that he either had to let me go or *let me go*. He wasn't too happy about the idea, but it seemed that he didn't want to end our relationship over it either. We agreed that from now on, we would be in a monogamous relationship.

Chris and I spent a few weeks in Manly together, trying to figure out what to do next. Since I had finally finished university, I now had to leave Australia because my student visa was going to expire.

Soon I came up with an idea. "Chris, what if we go to California together?" I said. "We can snowboard in Tahoe for the next three months and then I'll head to the Caribbean from there. You can go surf in Mexico after." I smiled. Since I would have to be in the Caribbean in March, it made the most sense for me to go to California, because flights between California and the Caribbean were relatively cheap. I had also been in touch with Keith from Bulgaria and he had recently moved to Lake Tahoe and was looking for flatmates to split the apartment he was renting.

"Um... I don't really have enough money for that," said Chris. "I don't even have enough for a flight or a pass."

"I have money," I said. "I saved up plenty from Three Wise Monkeys, and the pass to Squaw Valley is not that expensive. My friend Keith is living there now and looking for flatmates. The room is only like four hundred dollars a month, I can pay for it."

Chris wasn't extremely keen on this idea since he was pretty broke, but I somehow managed to talk him into it. He did love to snowboard after all. I bought our flights and season passes, confirmed with Keith that we'd rent his room, and just like that, Chris and I were off to California!

29

Lake Tahoe, 2014

Chris and I flew to Sacramento, California in January, 2014. My buddy Jake picked us up from the airport and drove us back to Tahoe. It was good to see this crazy guy again. He hadn't changed. It was also great to see Lake Tahoe again, and to be there with Chris. We spent a day or two with Jake, then made our way to a town called Truckee, just north of Lake Tahoe, where Keith was renting a flat.

It was great to see Keith too, it made me feel like this world was very small. He told me that the rest of the winter season in Bulgaria was pretty crappy and that unfortunately, this season in Tahoe was starting off the same way.

Chris and I unpacked our backpacks and moved into our new room. It was small but cozy, and the apartment itself was nice. It wasn't a fancy wooden chalet or anything like that, but it had everything we needed. Plus, Keith was a great housemate. He was neat and calm, and he loved to snowboard as much as we did. The three of us lived together for the next two or three months and went snowboarding almost every day.

I considered looking for a job in Truckee when we first arrived, but then quickly changed my mind. I had three or four thousand dollars left in savings even after having spent a ton of money on flights, rent, and season passes for the mountain. Enzo said that I wouldn't need much money for the sailing trip, so I didn't see any reason to waste my precious time working some bullshit job just to earn more of it. *If I have enough money, why should I work?* I thought. *Time with Chris is more valuable than any amount of money, so let's just make the most of the next three months.* Chris and I ended up spending almost every hour of every day together. We got into a few arguments over little things every once in a while, but most of the time we spent together was beautiful.

Unfortunately, the season was a bit disappointing. There was barely any snow when we arrived in January, it was extremely warm most of the time, and it didn't snow much at all that entire winter. In fact, it even rained once in February! Chris and I didn't let that get us down though. When there was no powder to ride, we hit the park. It turned out that all of that slacklining I did with Ziva in Manly came in handy. As soon as we started sliding on rails and boxes, I realized that my balance had improved a lot. I still wasn't great in the park, but I managed to learn a few little tricks.

When we weren't snowboarding, the three of us would be sitting around the living room reading books, watching videos or documentaries, or browsing the internet. Since my next plan was to sail halfway across the world, I decided that it would be a good idea to learn as much as possible about sailing. I read through *Sailing for Dummies* and another book that outlined the basics of sailing a boat, but after a little while, I realized that I shouldn't worry too much about knowing every detail of how to sail a sailboat. Enzo was the captain. He knew how to sail and I trusted him to be able to handle his boat. He had already sailed across the Caribbean once single-handed, as a paraplegic.

I'll learn more and more once we start sailing, I thought. I also realized that if shit really did hit the fan, it wouldn't really matter how well I knew how to sail, what would be more important is for me to know how to *survive*. Because of that, I decided to read a few survival stories while I was still in California. Enzo recommended three books to me:

1. *Adrift: Seventy-six Days Lost at Sea,* by Steven Callahan. This is an amazing story of a man who survived in a liferaft in the Atlantic Ocean by himself for seventy-six days. He almost died several times as he got caught in storms, attacked by sharks, was

constantly on the verge of dying from dehydration, and had to fix his deflating liferaft to save himself from drowning.

2. *Survive the Savage Sea,* by Dougal Robertson. Six people—husband, wife, three kids, and a crew member survived in a liferaft and dinghy for thirty-seven days in the Pacific Ocean in the 1970s.

3. *117 Days Adrift,* by Maurice and Maralyn Bailey. Wife and husband survived in their liferaft for 117 days in the Pacific Ocean, catching fish, seabirds, and turtles by hand and with safety pins to stay alive.

These are all true stories written by the survivors. I think these books impacted me far beyond what I had expected. Aside from learning that you have to have a very strong will to survive being lost at sea (and also be pretty damn lucky), I acquired an even more realistic perspective of what it means to live. *When you're lost out at sea, nothing matters but survival.* What do you need in order to survive?—Drinking water, food, a flotation device, and perhaps something to keep you warm. All three books described the devastating times when the survivors had about three drops of water to drink in a single day, and those times when they managed to collect large amounts of water. All three described how rich they felt when they had stored up water and food. All three described that the fish's eyeball was the best part of the fish because it holds the most water. *Water* is everything! And it's so underappreciated in our day-to-day lives.

I realized that if all these people managed to survive in the ocean for months with almost nothing at all, surely it can't be that hard to survive on *land*! On land, you don't even need a flotation device! All you need is food, water, and something to keep you warm. The rest is not all that important. But our society teaches us a different story—that we need "jobs," money, and stuff. *For what purpose?* Nobody really asks, they just do as they're told. They go to school, then university, then they get a "job," and they start accumulating things—cars, homes, gadgets, clothes, and thousands of useless items. Then they get trapped in this rat race. They buy "cool" stuff to make themselves feel better on the days they don't have to slave away. The more stuff they buy, the more trapped they become. *Mortgage? Car payments? Loans? Phones? Clothes?*

What else? Selfies and social media "likes"? Approval becomes important.

This rat race gives people very little time to actually enjoy their lives. Rather than enriching their minds, exploring the world, and following their passions, most people are busy working jobs that they hate, accumulating money and things they don't need, and getting approval for all of this in the form of "likes." As a result, our society is full of empty people, with empty heads and a lot of mental issues.

But it's not the people's fault. I remembered what Jacque Fresco used to say. *It's the culture and system that makes people this way.* ***So fuck this system!*** This realization made me furious at anybody who dared to tell me that I need to get a job. "I never want to take part in this rat race!" I'd say. "I'll work when I have to, just to make enough to survive in this bullshit society. But I'll spend most of my life doing what I love, and I don't need much money or anyone's approval for that."

This type of conversation usually ended in a fight. In March, I caught a flight from California to Sint Maarten via New York. The flight was less than four hundred dollars and allowed me to visit my mother and stepfather on my way to the Caribbean. At that point, my mother had basically accepted my lifestyle. She wasn't thrilled about it, but she was okay with it. Her husband, on the other hand, continued to argue with me about how I should be living.

"What is the point of being a snowboarding, surfing, sailing *bum*?" he asked.

"There is no point. What's the point of anything that you do?" I replied.

"Don't you want to make something of your life?"

"I am making something of my life. I'm enjoying it. You want me to stop enjoying my life and get a job instead? Why?"

"What about your future?" he asked. "You think you can just live like this all of your life? What about retirement?"

"You want me to waste my entire life just for the sake of having some money left over when I'm old? What's the point of that? When I'm old I'll barely even be able to enjoy my life. Maybe I'll be sick. Or who knows, maybe I won't even live to retirement age!"

"You'll probably live," he said, "but you could be sick and poor, with no health insurance. Doesn't that worry you?"

"Not really. I mean, I think the US healthcare system is really fucked up so hopefully I'll "retire" in a country that actually cares enough about its citizens to provide them with healthcare (like say Canada, Australia, Europe, or even Russia). But I'm not worried about what will happen to me when I'm like seventy years old, I'm more concerned about wasting the good, young and healthy years of my life—the next fifty or so years.

"Think about it! How many years of life will you have left after retirement? Ten years? Maybe twenty if you're lucky? Compare that to the forty or fifty years you have between the age of childhood and retirement. How sad would it be to trade fifty years of your young and healthy life just for ten or twenty years of happy "retirement"—when you're old and sick." Soon I realized that this whole "retirement" bullshit was just another trick in this system. Just like debt, the fear of having no retirement funds traps people and turns them into obedient little slaves. It keeps them working and working all their lives just to one day reach that carrot. If they ever manage to actually reach it, they'll see that the carrot's become old and shriveled, just like themselves. And they probably won't even enjoy it...

"Another things is," I went on, "even if I did slave my entire life, there's no hundred-percent guarantee that I'll actually get a nice retirement reward once I'm old. There could be an economic collapse, a natural disaster, inflation, who knows what else. So I just think it's not worth the investment."

"You know, you don't have to "slave" as you say." He never gave up. "You don't have to do something you hate. What about doing something useful with your life? Something that contributes to society?"

"I don't see any reason to contribute to a society that's based on infinite consumption," I said. "This is just not sustainable and it's stupid. Almost every job is based on selling something. *Selling more and more shit—that's how this system works.* This might be okay if we lived on a planet with infinite resources and if we weren't causing so many environmental problems and changing the world's climate, but unfortunately, that's not the case. I'm sorry but I just don't want to be a part of this idiocracy."

Our discussions went on for a long time and I don't think either one of us ever changed the other one's mind. After just four nights at my mother's place, I caught a flight to the Caribbean.

30

Caribbean, 2014

*The following chapter comes from a collection of journal entries I wrote during this sailing trip in 2014.

March 17, 2014
Day 1, St. Maarten

I arrived in St. Maarten after a short flight from New York. Excitement ran through me as I walked out the door and felt the heat and humidity of the Caribbean on my wintery white skin. Straight ahead I saw Enzo strolling toward me in his sporty little wheelchair. He looked quite well. He had gained a bit of weight on his upper body since I last saw him, grew some hair on his head, had a pretty dark tan, and a big smile on his face.

It was around midday when we drove out of the airport and onto the "airport beach" (about two hundred meters away), where people enjoyed the sun and the beautiful turquoise water while getting jet blasted by international airplanes. Enzo brought out a jug of homemade guavacoladas and we watched the ocean, the lush green hills, the tourists, and the giant steel birds as we discussed our new home, a thirty-eight-foot Bavarian yacht named Calypso.

After the jug went dry we slowly made our way to Calypso. It was great to finally see her in person. She was in decent shape but definitely still in need of some serious work. Calypso had one main cabin at the bow, a pretty snazzy L-shaped bench in our starboard "living room," a decent portside kitchen area across from the bench and table, a good-looking work station for the captain, and two smaller cabins at the back.

Enzo was planning for the two of us to share a cabin and said that he would let me choose which one I preferred. This was quite an easy decision but he still insisted that we try all of the cabins out together. This seemed like a bit of a scheme to get us to sleep in the same cabin(s) straight away when there were two completely unoccupied ones, but after seeing the condition of the cabin cushions and realizing that I had no sheets and that we were going to share a cabin anyway, I had to give him the benefit of a doubt.

I had talked to Enzo about Chris many times in the past and had made it clear long before my arrival that I was not interested in any sexual or romantic relations with him or any other person in the Caribbean. However, Enzo insisted on having a talk with me about "us." He wanted to make it clear that this trip was not about "us," it was all about the documentary. "Everything is about the documentary!" he said.

"Of course," I replied. *Why even bother mentioning this?*

March 18, 2014
Day 2, St. Maarten

This sailing trip was meant to be about filming a documentary. Enzo said, "It's all about the documentary!" but he seemed so surprised when I started filming a few video clips with my shitty little camera today. He didn't seem to be interested in filming at all. Also, he doesn't even have a camera! I mean, he has a couple of old GoPros, but that's all.

March 25, 2014
Day 9, St. Maarten

We have been working hard on Calypso for the past eight days and finally decided to take a day of complete rest (apart from putting up the mainsail). Ricky arrived five days ago and Will arrived yesterday. Since my first day in St. Maarten, we have replaced the stanchions and lifelines, Enzo fixed up the engine, the toilet, and the standing rigging, he also replaced all of the lining on the hatches. I replaced all of the lights with LED lights, cleaned out the bilge pump, most of the cabinets, and all of the kitchen appliances. Ricky cleaned some of the yacht's cushions (which were pretty rank), we put up both sails now and replaced some of the running rigging with new lines. We also did some additional petty work like blowing up the dinghy and screwing around with its outboard only to find out that it was a liability to our well-being. Enzo did a lot of work to the boat on the hard and in the water before my arrival and I would imagine that he hadn't had a day off in over a month. Not to mention that in the Caribbean sunshine any kind of work seems five times more difficult than in any temperate region as it involves constant perspiration.

The end of the day is always rewarding. We are tied to the end of a dock facing due west and the sunsets are spectacular, generally enjoyed with a nice cold Presidente (local beer) or guavacolada.

Last Friday night was the night of Ricky's arrival and the three of us strolled into the old-time legendary yachtie's pub, Lagoonies, for some Presidentes and live music. As soon as we showed up, there was a crowd of people surrounding Enzo, shaking hands, hugging, dancing, the whole deal! I think he's become a bit of a legend on this island, ever since he single-handed his last boat through the Caribbean as a paraplegic. As we were standing at the bar waiting to order Presidentes, there seemed to have been a line forming as people were waiting to talk to Enzo. The dancing and laughing went on into the night and once the band stopped playing, we (a group of ten or so drunk-o yachties) formed a drum circle led by Ricky banging on the wooden floorboards and my infamously loud tongue clicking. Enzo's friend Palain banged on a garbage can until the bar staff took it away from us to do their cleaning. I don't remember much about getting home but we must have somehow stumbled back to Calypso without falling off the dock.

The second messy night was last night, celebrating the arrival of our final companion, Will. The four of us managed to drink down a liter and a half of rum along with our remaining Presidentes. This time we stayed on Calypso and worked on our soon-to-be music band, "Calypso Crew." Surprisingly, our marina neighbors complemented us the next day instead of scolding us for their loss of sleep.

A few thoughts on this trip so far: I'm excited, but I'm really excited to start sailing!

March 30, 2014
Day 14, St. Maarten

We're still at the marina in St. Maarten. Really getting ready to get out of here… There are just a few major projects to do, most of them only Enzo can do (like properly setting up the liferaft and the new solar panel). Tomorrow we should be getting back our mainsail from the shop and hauling that up for the last time (since we have a roller furling mainsail).

We already did one big shop, bought a lot of beans and rice, and after we stuffed tons of food and supplies into the bilges, we realized that we have heaps of space left! This is great news because we now believe that we can stock up for our whole trip right here in St. Maarten, all eight months of it! The lot we already purchased only cost us three hundred dollars (although Enzo bought an additional two hundred dollars worth of food that he didn't want us to pitch in for). Either way, I believe that it's possible for us to spend less than five hundred dollars each on the purchase of food for the next eight months (not including Presidentes of course). This is important because we have been told that once we get past Panama the cost of everything, including food, will rise to extraordinary rates.

About the documentary—we still haven't filmed anything. And we still don't have any camera equipment besides those GoPros and my shitty little camera. Enzo isn't planning to buy a camera and he doesn't seem to be interested in filming. He doesn't even talk about the documentary.

April 3, 2014
Day 18, St. Maarten

I really want to trust Enzo as a friend and believe that he is genuine about his words and actions but there is something in the back of my mind that wants to be very cautious of his intentions.

We sleep in the same bed because it makes the most sense (right?), we are the closest friends and two guys sharing a berth would probably be less comfortable. Enzo also says that he wants to make sure that nothing dodgy happens on the boat during our long crossing. Although, ironically, I do believe that if there was any dodginess, it would come from him.

Last night he offered to give me a massage because my back and neck were in pain. I lay down on my stomach in our cabin, took off my shirt, and unclipped my bra. I had a small pair of shorts on, which he pulled down below my entire ass, exposing everything. When I asked him why he needed to do that, he gave me some "because of the muscle here and there" answer, then he laughed, ripped my shorts and underwear completely off my body, and threw them into the corner of the cabin. I cursed him out, then he laughed some more and said, "I respect you, there's nothing wrong with this."

Should I really trust Enzo?

April 5, 2014
Day 20, St. Maarten

Yesterday my mother sent me this email:

Could you send me the contact information of all of your crew members and their emergency contacts.

Also can you give them my email and phone.

I'm VERY worried about you maybe you could change your mind and not go?

I replied with their contact details as well as this message:

Please don't worry mother... I'm not going to change my mind out of nowhere, we have a really great harmony between the four of us and the boat is almost ready. We have taken a lot of effort to make sure this boat is safe and ready to go and we have all of the proper safety equipment. This boat has already sailed across the Atlantic. The path that we will take to New Zealand, "The Coconut Milk Run," is one of the safest routes across the world and is much safer than driving a car or even being a pedestrian in NYC.

I realize the risks of being lost or drowning at sea and I am willing to take those risks because I believe that the reward will be much greater than the risk itself. If I do die, for any crazy ambition before you do, I hope that you can understand that I would have died for my life; not just for sailing across the Pacific but also for driving across North America, for hitchhiking across Australia, for backpacking four different continents, for snowboarding all over the world, for meeting hundreds of amazing people, and for living out my dreams. I am willing to die for a life that is truly lived.

I hope that you can understand and accept this.

April 5, 2014
Day 20, St. Maarten
Last night we had a barbecue for Enzo's farewell. It was a great chance to meet and chat with some old sailors that have been living this life for dozens of years. I'm so ready to start sailing!

April 10, 2014
Day 25, St. Maarten
We're still here... Still haven't even gone for a sail. Still haven't filmed anything. Don't really know what we're still doing here, I have a feeling that Enzo got angry at us or at the situation and is now testing us. Well I definitely know that he is angry at me, mainly for expressing my opinion against his opinion way too much. I think the main argument was when he said he would prefer to support McDonald's instead of the local fisherman for a moral purpose (because he had recently seen a documentary on commercial fishing). I told him to consider where the local fisherman

sources his fish as opposed to where McDonald's sources their meat. He got very upset and told me that I couldn't talk to him like that (and tell him what to do) because he wasn't my boyfriend. I told him that I talk to all of my friends like this and jokingly added, "Maybe that's why I have so few."

I'm not sure exactly what happened but something changed in the past few days. Maybe we seemed too eager to get out of St. Maarten or maybe I offended Enzo with my comments but now it seems like he's stalling, not getting too much done, and doesn't seem to want to move quickly at all. We had a goodbye party last Sunday and now he seems to have scheduled another one for the following Sunday with one of the friends that we already said goodbye to last week.

We all basically agree that he's testing us now, so Will, Ricky, and (especially) I are going to calm down and act like we're fine to stay here another decade. Then maybe we'll leave.

April 12, 2014
Day 27, St. Maarten

We are now at anchorage in Philipsburg, St. Maarten. We went for our first sail today, just for about an hour but it was great fun. I was a little nervous being the helmswoman, especially when we were anchoring as I wasn't exactly sure where Enzo wanted to put the boat. It worked out well as I didn't hit any other boats or run Calypso aground.

After anchoring, we had dinner then Ricky and Will took the dinghy to check out the Philipsburg night life. While the two boys were out, Enzo had a long talk with me about everything that was bothering him about me.

He started off by saying that these past few weeks (from the beginning of my arrival) have been the worst in his life. One main problem was that the "gods"/ his surroundings were telling him not to do the documentary he was planning on. He mentioned that one reason was my careless opinion over whether he should buy Coke in a can or Coke in a bottle. This was the dilemma at the beginning of my arrival—Enzo's opinion is that you must be a "conscious shopper" in order to save the planet. I, however, had just been

313

reading the book, *Deep Green Resistance*, by Derrick Jensen, which, in a very powerful and effective way, explains that these kinds of individual choices are delusional and diverge from the underlying issues that are killing the planet. I tried to explain this to him and went on saying, "It's not just a matter of buying cans or bottles, it's a matter of the whole industry! In order to really save the planet we need to bring down this profit-driven industrial civilization, not just buy Coke in a can instead of a bottle." At the end of the conversation I also said, "But sure, in the meanwhile (while we're not bringing down civilization), it's good to make conscious choices while shopping and I do try to do this when I can. I usually don't buy Coke at all." Obviously these statements didn't register one bit because I have already heard him tell several people that all I said was "it doesn't matter."

So now he doesn't want to do the documentary at all, which doesn't surprise me one bit. I have had a slight suspicion from the very beginning that this entire trip was never actually based around a documentary, but I will probably never know the truth.

After this, he mentioned how I spoke out against him about the liferaft. The emergency liferaft comes in a big plastic box and weighs more than I do. Enzo's idea was to put it inside a compartment under the seat in the cockpit. At the time, I was very concerned about the liferaft being in a place that would be difficult to get to in an emergency situation. This liferaft is hard for two people to lift together and there is a chance that one person would need to access it on their own. The smallest and weakest person on this boat is me, this is why I said that we should make sure it's in a place where I can get it out on my own, because if I can do it, then everybody else would obviously be able to do it too. I never said that we should keep it where it already was (on the roof), I just said, "Let's think about what else we can do before throwing it under the seat." Anyway, I ended up tying two ropes around the handles to make it easier to pull out of the seat. Enzo, however, still seems to believe that I was yelling orders at him to leave it on the roof and that these orders were selfishly based around me being able to lift the raft. What I do understand from this discussion is that I need to explain myself in a much calmer and more comprehensible way, and I cannot rush my opinions or allow Enzo to think that I am making orders. I respect that he is the captain and the leader, and I trust him to make the best possible decisions regarding our safety.

One weird thing he mentioned was that he thought I was always looking at him when he was flirting with other girls. He said that Ricky "noticed" this as well. This is definitely not the case and I could care less about who he flirts with. Then he said that he would not like it if I had sex with someone in our cabin. I told him not to worry about this because I'm not planning to cheat on my boyfriend but that he could go right ahead and have sex with whoever he wants. I told him to just let me know if he wants the cabin and I can sleep on the couch, "Just please change the sheets the next day." He didn't hear this at all and continued to insist that I would care about "dirty sheets." Then he said that what he needs is affection, not sex, and if I can give him this, the sheets will stay dry…

After this, he asked me what I have done for society in my twenty-five years on this planet and went on implying that I've done nothing and that I'm a stubborn bitch. He said that I do nothing for him but that he still loves me, he doesn't know why, but he does. He also lectured me about why "I have so few friends."

He later went on to talk about the possibility of me being raped by either Ricky or Will while out at sea (which, by the way, is the last thing I'm concerned about). I'm pretty sure the point he was trying to make was that the only reason I would get raped by either one of my friends is because I led them on. Enzo stated that the pain he would feel knowing that "it was his fault" that I was raped and having to go to court for it would be worse than the pain I would feel while actually being raped… And this is why he wants to make sure I don't get raped. I don't have much else to say about these ridiculous statements.

He ended the discussion by saying that I was on "probation" from here to Aruba and from Aruba to Panama.

April 14, 2014
Day 29, St. Maarten

Yesterday we sailed back to Cole Bay and anchored next to Palain's boat to have some farewell drinks with him (even though we already had farewell drinks with him last Sunday at Enzo's farewell barbecue). Enzo seemed to be in a bad mood from the beginning of the day, not exactly sure why... I hope he hasn't snuck into this journal. I'm glad I wasn't the helmsperson then. It can be difficult to maneuver the boat when you have so little experience and don't know where Enzo wants you to go as he's yelling orders that are often not exactly clear. But anyway, Will did a good job at keeping it cool and Enzo wasn't half as angry as he used to be in New Zealand.

He seemed much more aggressive, though, after he returned from picking up beer with the dinghy. He got back on board and didn't say much but started re-anchoring the boat. Calypso was a bit too close to a different boat and needed to be moved, but Enzo certainly didn't need to move it alone. I was right in the cockpit when he started the process and the two boys were just inside. I wasn't going to interfere and make him angrier so I just watched as he pulled up the anchor, scurried to the wheel, moved the boat forward a bit, then scurried back to the anchor and lowered it down somewhat (if I had offered my help he probably would have just yelled at me). I was surprised when he didn't come back to the wheel to back up the boat and let the anchor settle in more.

Soon after this, we hopped onto Palain's boat for some drinks. Palain gave us a tour of his beautiful hand-built yacht, then we all sat in his cockpit and Palain gave Enzo some advice about anchoring. He told Enzo not to charge forward with the anchor just above the water, to let out more chain, and to back up the boat. Since Palain is a person that Enzo highly looks up to, this was extremely embarrassing for Enzo. In fact, I think this was a huge knock to his ego. After this talk, Enzo didn't say a word for nearly an hour. He sat in his seat and looked around awkwardly while strangely smiling to himself. After about an hour, he said just a few words then continued to sit quietly for almost the entire rest of the night, often with his head in between his knees, looking down at the floor.

April 17, 2014
Day 32, Sailing!

Sailing: 80% boredom, 20% terror. It began with the terror. We left around 4:00 p.m. from St. Maarten into deep swell and a dark, rough night just ahead of us. I had never been inside of a plastic boat in the open sea before and I never expected a yacht to make such frightening creaky sounds down below. The rocking of the hull and frequent crashing of waves was accompanied by noises that resembled that of an old wooden building on the verge of collapse during a hurricane. It wasn't exactly comforting to have Enzo explain that the hull of Calypso was made out of six millimeters of fiberglass followed by a few millimeters of foam and another six millimeters of fiberglass, although he did say that this was meant to make the boat flexible, and that the creaky sounds came from the walls and furniture as the hull expanded and contracted. Deciphering everything, I was still half-expecting the hull to break open on the next three-meter wave it bashed into.

Going down below was basically unbearable for more than a couple of minutes not only because of the fear of the hull breaking in pieces but even more so because of the queasiness. Calypso was rocking around like crazy, pots and pans banged inside their cabinets, and the sound of waves breaking against the hull was magnified twelvefold. Everybody was at least a little bit seasick, but Ricky had it worst. He threw up over the edge of the boat and was very queasy for the next four days. The positive side is that he owes us all a round of drinks for being the first to spew.

I gained a bit of confidence as the night went on (and as I stayed away from the inside of the boat). My shift was from 9:00 p.m. to midnight. At first I was quite uncomfortable being on watch when the only thing to watch was black water and dark gray skies, but once the full moon came up everything changed to magic. I remember the exact moment I realized that I had lost sight of land. It was absolutely exhilarating. The deep orange moonlight created a perfect path along the ocean and the water roamed wildly through it. Watching the water was enticing, almost bewitching. Numerous emotions ran through me—excitement, nervousness, and fear, but a good kind of fear, the kind that shakes you up and shows you that you're alive, perhaps a kind of respect to the ocean as well.

When my shift was over I went down below to try to sleep. I was very tired but could not take my mind off the thought of the boat shattering into pieces. All I could think of was whales ramming the boat or partially submerged steel containers smacking the boat and filling it up with water. I was literally shaking with fear.

April 18, 2014
Day 33, Sailing

Poor Ricky, sweating, panting, couldn't find his harness. He searched anxiously for it down below (where you couldn't stand up without holding onto a wall or piece of furniture), then came to my door around 6:00 a.m. to see if I had it. He was drenched in sweat and extremely distressed. It turned out that I did have it and as soon as he put it on he went outside and spewed straight over the lifelines.

I went back to sleep and was woken up into a consistently bigger swell around 8:00 a.m. This was when I was told that the autopilot had broken overnight. In a way this was good because the three of us (Ricky, Will, and I) needed to practice steering as we have not had much previous experience, but it was also pretty tiring and worrying at times, especially when three-meter waves were pushing the boat sideways. The concentration it takes to stare at one spot for hours, trying to keep the boat from swaying too far to either side of that spot, can be quite draining.

Not long into my shift, I overcame my fear of daytime sailing. I made peace with the creaking noises and was confident that I could see directly in front of me as well as hundreds of meters ahead. This shift went well and excitement ran through me again as I stood straight behind the wheel and bounced up and down with each wave we rolled over, giving my legs a bit of exercise.

Around 9:00 a.m. we saw dolphins! Enzo was in the cockpit with me and took the wheel, telling me to go ahead and get a better look at them. There were about thirty of them! They were brown on their top half and white or pinkish with brown spots on their bellies. They were quite small and very playful. It was amazing to see them swim speedily into a big wave and then fly out of the other side with such grace.

Enzo didn't want us to use the toilet (for good reason—it hardly flushes) so each time we needed to "go" we went on the back of the boat on the transom, with our harnesses hooked up to the backstay. This experience may have given me my first really memorable shit. I yelled, "Bye-bye little part of me!" as my food baby bounced over one wave and disappeared into the abyss. This reminded me of how important it was to hold on tight and make sure I do not fall off the boat. If the harness failed it would have taken less than five seconds for a head to disappear into the sea, with very little chance of ever being found again.

The rest of the day went by relatively fast and was quite monotonous. Most of us just sat in the cockpit and stared at the sea. Ricky slept a lot and tried not to spew. I ate one can of spaghetti that day and a few pieces of cabbage sprayed with vinegar.

At 3:00 a.m., I took over the steering while everybody was asleep. This may have been my most exciting shift. At first I was a bit spooked by the dark swell again, but once I turned on my MP3 player and Rage Against the Machine hit my ears, I was in complete control of the boat. I normally love Rage but that night I was *in love* with them. As emotions intensify out at sea so does music! I felt each beat and each instrument, paid attention to each lyric, and was in tune with the music and the sea. I danced with the waves behind the wheel.

My MP3 player was on shuffle and after Rage Against the Machine came up Vivaldi. It was magical, the sea metamorphosed into a peaceful state as I imagined its whole and entire beauty. Then I orchestrated the ocean.

April 19, 2014
Day 34, Sailing

Today I remembered why I cried the first time I got my period at age eleven. I remember saying, "*This* is going to happen *every* month?" in absolute horror. This time, it came unexpectedly on the third day of sailing, and it was heavy. Pads were out of the question because my butt was always wet while sailing, and there was no way in hell I would have even tried to change tampons on the back of the boat in that swell. I couldn't stand being in the little toilet even for a minute (and I also didn't want Enzo to think I was using it), so I went into the cabin, lay on the bed, put one leg on a wall, one on a shelf—trying to balance myself and not spew as the boat swayed up and down and side to side like a roller coaster ride— then I put pressure on the bed with one hand, held a tampon in the other, hoping that nobody walks in on me, all while trying very hard not to get blood on the bedsheets. Thankfully, I succeeded.

Today we also had our first real meal. Will was the least sick out of all of us and was able to cook up a pot of rice, add a can of chickpeas and a can of coconut cream while the boat bobbed in the swell. Although it was a very simple meal, it was absolutely delightful and we were very grateful for it. Enzo even said, "Will, I take back all of the bad things I ever said about you!"

Night came quickly once again and was magnificent. Will woke me up around 10:00 p.m. to see dolphins swimming through bioluminescent phytoplankton. This was incredible! They looked like underwater ghosts as they swam swiftly toward the boat, glowing in the bioluminescence, and then disappearing into the black ocean.

April 20, 2014
Day 35, Sailing

After sunset I was scheduled for my least favorite shift, about an hour after dusk, when it always seems to be much darker than the middle of the night. Around 8:00 p.m. it was pitch black, straight ahead was just black—black seas and black skies. It was almost deceiving, you could start to believe that the sea was calm until a big wave came up and knocked the boat sideways. Since I couldn't see the waves, I had to try to feel them coming. This was also a challenge. Closer to 9:00 p.m., however, I was beginning to see stars looking over my left shoulder. It seemed like every minute more and more would show up, until the sky was glittering.

About fifteen minutes before my shift was up, I looked over my left shoulder and it looked like there was a giant black hole in the sky! There was a deep dark perfectly round circle of what looked like black empty nothingness right in the middle of a remarkable array of sparkling shining stars. What a sight.

April 21, 2014
Day 36, Sailing

Enzo woke me up for my 6:00 a.m. shift. There wasn't much of a sunrise but the news that we were only eighteen nautical miles from Aruba was uplifting. We also had fresh bread that Enzo made in the pressure cooker the night before, it was delicious.

It took about three more hours to catch sight and smell of land. It was pretty interesting to smell land for the first time in five days. I suppose such a smell would vary from port to port, but Aruba smelled warm and hearty, with a slight scent of garbage. I could feel the air thicken as the smell flooded my nostrils.

When we approached the island, the wind grew stronger, almost to gale force. This was the first time that Will, Ricky, and I all sat at the edge of the yacht, trying to balance it out as it beat into the wind.

We anchored in a pretty open area about 150 meters from land. The first thing that Will, Ricky, and I did as soon as we dropped the anchor was get into our bathing suits and jump into the water. I never would have thought that after staring at only water for five days, the first thing you would want to do when you get to land is jump into the water! The three of us took out our sponges, soap, and shampoo and scrubbed ourselves down for about a half hour on the back of the boat. Rubbing shampoo and conditioner into my head had never felt so good!

As the three of us were having a blast bathing in the sea, Enzo was already starting to plunge back into his pathological state. His face grew dark red as he reorganized the boat in silence. We were so excited about being on a still boat that we didn't pay much attention to Enzo's behavior. Ricky cooked an amazing meal and the three of us chatted like a bunch of schoolgirls on vacation. Enzo sat and worked silently. After dinner, we played a game of cards. Enzo joined after a few games but we could tell that his mind was already bouncing around elsewhere as we played. Losing both games he played didn't help. Another thing that didn't help was that he offered to give me a massage at the end of the night and I said no.

April 23, 2014
Day 38, Aruba

The next day we took off to customs and immigration. At this point Enzo was furious. He asked me to steer through the channel and to immigration even though he yelled at me the day before for steering poorly. It was nerve-wracking. Once we got to the immigration port I told him I was nervous and did not want to be at the helm. He told me to be quiet and follow directions. Then he told me to go straight at the concrete wall where we would tie on. I was coming at this wall at a forty-five degree angle at what seemed like full speed for this yacht. I was in a dilemma because he yelled at me to follow orders but his orders appeared to have set me up to sink the boat. He took the wheel about six meters away from this concrete wall and managed to keep the boat afloat. The three of us came to the conclusion that Enzo sets people up to fail because this feeds his ego.

He was extremely angry when he got out of the boat to go to immigration and it was almost humorous that Will asked Enzo to do him a favor. All Will asked for is to tell the agent to stamp an old passport page, because he was running out of empty pages, but apparently that was too much for Enzo.

After customs, we went to the Renaissance Marina and settled in. Once we were settled, the three of us went to explore the island and gave Enzo some space.

April 26, 2014
Day 41, Aruba

Last night he was better again, seems to be that way because I was really friendly to him again when we were drunk. Before we went to sleep he kissed me on the cheek and said "I love you Sasha." I turned the other way and went to sleep.

Today we had a long talk. He started off by saying that I did a good job crewing his yacht, that I was the only one that gave a hundred percent on this sailing trip, and that all of the work I have done on the boat was "immaculate." Then he discussed the issues he has with Ricky and Will. The conclusion he made was that Ricky is his buddy and will stay on the boat no matter what, but that he has no trust and has had enough of Will. He doesn't like Will because Will is very young (he's twenty-two) and because he took a drag of a cigarette once or twice while we were out at the pub. So Will will probably be kicked off the boat.

After talking about the two boys, Enzo went on to talk about me. He said that I was valuable to him for the documentary, *that* was why he invited me. Now that we are no longer doing the documentary (because he can't manage it), I am no longer valuable. Now what he wants to do is have fun and party with Ricky. And the problem is that lately he hasn't been having any fun because he is stressed about the boat (he put all his money into it) and because he is still in love with me. Because he loves me and I obviously have zero interest in him, I am now in the way of him having fun with Ricky. So now he wants me off the boat too.

I am not exactly sure how I feel at this point, perhaps a bit angry and disappointed. And stupid. Stupid for being so eager to sail across the Pacific that I became naive. So naive that I actually believed Enzo would have honest intensions. The first thing I asked him before agreeing to go on this trip was whether we could just be friends. I made it clear that I wanted nothing more than friendship, I had also talked to him about Chris before I even flew to California. He said yes and that this trip had nothing to do with romance or sex, it was all about the documentary! But he never even bought a camera...

I wouldn't be so angry if Enzo had at least offered to buy me a flight back to Australia, or even let me sail to Panama. But he told me that he had no intention of buying me a flight and his justification was that life is unfair at times. After I asked him to at least take me to Panama he said he would consider it, but now I'm not sure if I even want to continue any part of this trip, especially if Will is kicked off for something so stupid.

This is how much money, time, and work I have put into this trip:

- I spent $600 on a sailing course.
- I flew (and persuaded Chris to come with me) to California because it was easy to get from there to St. Maarten. The flight cost around $1,000 from Australia.
- I spent $390 on a flight from California to St. Maarten.
- I spent a month in St. Maarten working on Enzo's boat. I probably spent about half of that time actually laboring. All of the work I did will add to the boat's value when Enzo sells it in New Zealand.
- In St. Maarten, I spent about $500, mainly on food as we stocked up for an eight-month journey across the world.

The money adds up to about 2,500 dollars. If I fly to Australia now, from anywhere in the Caribbean or South America, the flight will cost around 1,500 dollars for a one-way ticket. I want to go to Australia because that's where I came from and that's where my boyfriend is. A ticket to New Zealand would be fine as well, since that's where we were planning to sail to.

April 27, 2014
Day 42, Aruba

Enzo made it clear that I will not go to Panama with him. Will is off the boat too so it doesn't even matter, I wouldn't go anyway without our most peaceful companion. When I told Enzo that he should pay for my flight to Australia (big mistake to ask so quickly) he freaked out and said that he will pay for no flight at all. He gave me three hundred dollars for the canned food and said that that's all I'll get. Then he threatened to call the police on me to get me off the boat. I told him to calm down, then I walked away and searched for a police station.

I didn't find a station but I found a cop who explained the law to me. The policeman said that it was Enzo's choice whether I continue to Panama or not, however, him being the captain he is responsible for his crew and is therefore responsible to get me home safely. He is also not allowed to kick me off the boat without warning. Unfortunately, "home" means wherever my passport is from, which will only get me as far as the US or Russia, but flying to California would still be better than nothing (flights from LA to Sydney are eight hundred dollars).

I have not spoken to Enzo since our last argument but I did send him a nice email that complimented him and explained the situation from my perspective. It's been almost a day since I've sent it and he has not replied, nor has he said a word to me.

He's been sitting at his computer for hours, watching *Seinfeld* and *That '70s Show*. It may be important to point out that there's a lot of work to be done on the boat before Enzo's next sail, and he is paying around 180 dollars per week to be at this marina. I suppose he won't be able to get any work done until Will and I leave and his mental state improves a little bit.

April 28, 2014
Day 43, Aruba

Will and I spent most of yesterday cooking and hanging around the boat. Enzo didn't say a single word to me until the end of the day. When we finally went to "have a talk," Enzo started by saying, "I have lost all respect for you because you went to the police." I asked him why, and he said, "You didn't think I knew the law?!"

Enzo was dark red in the face and storming inside but not entirely surprisingly went on to invite me to sail to Panama. He told me that Will was off the boat and that was one problem solved, then he said he decided that I could continue to Panama under the condition that it would be Ricky's decision whether I get off the boat or not in Central America.

Little did he know, I am not a complete idiot and saw straight through his reason for "inviting me." If I had said "no," it would have been me refusing to continue the trip as opposed to him kicking me off the boat, and therefore he would no longer be responsible for purchasing my flight.

Naturally, I said "yes" and he went on telling me that he has no respect for me and that I will have to work my ass off during this trip for absolutely no pay. He also said that my letter to him was the most pathetic thing he had ever read and that it was ridiculous for

325

me to ask for so much money. I was never asking for all of the money I had spent on this trip, all I asked for was some consideration for everything I've done for him (which came in the form of a plane ticket). It wasn't long before we started yelling at each other and he kicked me off the boat again.

On my way back to the boat he yelled at me to go to the cops. I hopped into the boat and sat at the table with Will. Man was I thankful that Will was there! Then Enzo yelled some more and stormed out saying he was going to the police. An hour later he was back on the boat buying me a flight to Newark for the following day.

April 29, 2014
Day 44, Airplane
So that's it. A weight is now lifted and although I did not cross the Pacific Ocean or even get to Panama, I believe that I had a valuable learning experience. It was quite interesting to analyze the actions and thought processes of a psychopath and it was very valuable to listen to Will's philosophies about life. But perhaps the most valuable learning experience of all was analyzing my own behavior and listening to how others analyzed it. I constantly thought back to why I argued with Chris in Tahoe and what caused this sort of behavior, and I believe that next time we're together I can make it all better. Perhaps I gained a little piece of peace within myself in the midst of this pathological crisis.

Oh yeah and this morning I hid little pieces of sardines all over Enzo's cabin!

Part 5

31

Back to Aus, 2014

My mother picked me up from Newark Airport with a euphoric look on her face. I don't think I had ever seen her so happy to see me. She was extremely relieved that my plan to sail across the Pacific Ocean was cancelled. She spent the next few days treating me as if I had defeated some life-threatening disease or trauma.

After a few great days with my mother, I bought several flights to get back to Australia. I found a ticket from New York to Moscow for 384 dollars, another one from Moscow to Thailand for 360 dollars, and one more from Thailand to Sydney for 370 dollars. That meant that the total cost of getting from New York to Australia was about 1,100 dollars. *Expensive,* I know, but at least it allowed me to visit my family in Russia on the way.

My dad picked me up from the airport in Moscow. He looked a bit happier this time around. He was no longer living with his ex-wife. Instead, he was living with his sister, which he wasn't thrilled about, but I suppose it was better than the previous situation. His business wasn't doing so well, so he couldn't afford his own place at the time.

I spent a couple of weeks reconnecting with my dad and the rest of my family, then I caught my flight to Australia via Thailand.

In June, I finally arrived in Sydney! Chris met me at the airport. As soon as I saw him, I ran for his arms like a character in a slow-motion romance film. Then I melted as his lips touched mine. *I'll never leave him again, I swear,* I told myself. *Even if someone offers me the trip of a lifetime, I'll refuse it just to be with Chris.* He smiled and held me in his arms.

We left the airport and took a seven-hour train from Sydney to Chris's hometown, Moruya, on the South Coast of New South Wales. It was a charming and quiet little town. We stayed at Chris's mother's house, in the countryside surrounded by green hills and beautiful forest. I spent the whole night in his arms.

In the morning, we woke up early, had a sweet cup of coffee, and went surfing. We drove Chris's mom's car down a long dirt road, past the little town, and toward the coast. I gazed out the window as I watched big herds of kangaroos and wallabies hopping around the faintly lit grasslands. Soon, we arrived at a long and beautiful, nearly empty beach with crystal blue water and some great waves.

We put on our wetsuits and hit the water. It was cold. The waves smacked me in the face and almost knocked me off my board as I attempted to duck dive. Even after all those months of surfing in Manly, I was still a newb. Plus, the waves were a bit big for my liking. I managed to paddle out to the line-up after about ten or twenty minutes of fumbling around, then I stayed close to Chris. I felt safe with him by my side. He kept an eye on me and helped me catch a few waves. Once I got the hang of it, it was amazing. I loved the feeling of catching a wave and being pulled by the ocean, balancing and swerving through water, riding its energy.

After the surf, we drove back to Chris's mom's place, had a warm shower and a nice meal, then got to "work." At the time, Chris was taking a massage course, so he was busy learning all about muscles and rubbing techniques. Lucky for me, he also needed a body to practice on. Chris gave me one or two massages every day as part of his training. I felt like the luckiest girl alive. When I wasn't surfing or getting massaged, I would go for walks around the forest, read books, watch documentaries, or observe the wombats and kookaburras behind the house. I still had a bit of money left in savings and Enzo eventually transferred me the money I had spent on flights from New York to Sydney, so I didn't need to look for a job for the time being.

After a week or so in Moruya, my friend Alfie (from Whistler), sent me a message with an interesting proposal. Alfie said that he was living in Indonesia and working as a scuba diving instructor on Gili Trawangan, off the coast of Lombok. The dive shop he worked for was looking for somebody to do a three-month scuba diving internship. Out of curiosity, I asked for more info.

Alfie wrote:

They are looking for someone over busy season any time from now but def over July August and September. The training gear and everything is for free. They are planning to give away a free Rescue diver course and Divemaster course.. The value is probably around $1,200. You also get unlimited diving. You are probably looking at 70 to 100 dives in that time frame (that is a lot of diving). Could be more but it really depends. They are looking for someone who is already Open water advance diver. But they are flexible, it's more that they are looking for someone who likes diving and is going to stay. If you don't have any of that and you are interested, don't worry I can train you up for free. You just need to pay for your Padi Registration round about $70 per course. The same goes for the rest of the courses you just need to pay the registration fees to Padi, all and all it would be around $400 or so really not a lot for everything.

Living in Gili is not expensive. Rent will cost you around $170 per month, food another $200. It is the drinking thing that gets you but you can have a few good nights and still budget around $500 for the month everything included but that all depends on you. It is a really big party Island tho.

I thought it was almost comical that Alfie offered me this opportunity as soon as I finally decided to settle down with Chris. I would have jumped on it in an instance if I didn't feel so bad about dragging Chris around and having him wait for me while I went on these adventures. At first, I didn't even want to mention this to Chris. I mean, it sounded like a fantastic opportunity—*free scuba diving! Who the hell would say no to that?* But at the same time, I didn't want to ruin our relationship over it. I told Alfie that I'd think about it and that I'd only do it if Chris wanted to come with me.

July, 2014

A couple of weeks went by and it got very cold in Moruya. Not cold like Siberia, but worse—cold like *New Zealand*. The kind of cold that you can never get away from. It was cold outside at night and in the mornings, and it was cold inside the house *all the time*. Even when the sunshine warmed up the meadows and the kookaburras, inside the house was always cold. We often walked around the house with our hats and coats on.

In the mornings, Chris and I would often wake up before sunrise to catch the best surf. The bedroom was freezing. The bathroom was freezing. The kitchen was freezing. There was frost outside. I felt like I could never really warm up. Our wetsuits were rarely dry. I remember sleet coming down once as we were standing outside, putting on our cold and wet wetsuits to jump into the freezing cold water. I think it was after this surf that I told Chris about the diving opportunity in Indonesia.

"What if we could live on a warm, tropical island?" I said. "Maybe just for a few months while the winter passes here." I explained everything that Alfie had told me. "We would have to stay on Gili Trawangan for three months. All we need is about three hundred dollars each per month for the living expenses. That's only nine hundred dollars. Besides that, we just need flights." I didn't have enough money to support both of us this time, but Chris had been working as a surf instructor so he did have a little bit in savings.

After a few more very cold days and a bit of persuasion, I convinced Chris to come with me to Indonesia. Two weeks later, we were on a plane to Bali.

32

Gili Islands, 2014

We arrived in Bali on July 21. This place was familiar to me. The smells, the sounds, the people, the warm air. I loved it. Chris and I spent one night in a cheap and crappy hotel in Bali, then took a ferry to the neighboring island, Lombok. We made our way up the west coast of Lombok to a small fishing village with a busy port. It was loud, dirty, and everyone was out to sell us overpriced boat tickets. We ignored the noise, walked straight to the ticket booth and bought two tickets to Gili Trawangan for about three dollars. Less than an hour later, we were on Gili T.

The island was much busier than I had expected. "I was here just a few years ago," I said to Chris. "It was so quiet here back then. I remember just a few buildings on the main street but not much else. Now there's so much commotion!" There were hotels, bars, restaurants, and dive shops everywhere.

"At least they haven't built a proper road," said Chris.

"Yeah, they would absolutely destroy this island if they brought cars and motorbikes here." There were a lot of horse carriages and bicycles, but no paved roads or motor vehicles. "I mean, this island is like two by three kilometers long. It's not like anyone needs a car to get around it." I liked that the island was so small. We walked along the main, beachside dirt road and looked for a dive shop called Gili Scuba. Alfie said to find him there.

Twenty minutes later, I spotted him! Sitting in a chair with his big curly hair and big goofy smile. "Alfie, you crazy man!" I gave him a big hug. "You haven't changed at all!" I had kept in touch with Alfie over the years but I hadn't actually seen him in person since 2008! He looked just the same, even had the same hairstyle.

"Great to see you again, Sash! So this is the man?" He gawked over Chris. "I'm impressed," he whispered. I introduced Alfie to Chris, then Alfie introduced us to some of his friends, "This is Dragos, he's from Romania. This is Pedro and Hugo, both from Spain, and Mateas, from Kalimantan. Dragos is the manager here and he'll be your DM instructor. Pedro's also an instructor, and Hugo and Mateas are doing their divemasters." It turned out that since I had initially turned down this internship, they found someone else to do it—Hugo, but once I told Alfie that I wanted to come after all, he talked them into letting me do it as well.

"So you guys are lucky, we found a nice place for you!" said Alfie. "Dragos and his girlfriend Montez just moved into a house and they have an extra room. It's a super nice house, I think you'll like it." Alfie and Dragos walked us over to their new place. It was a beautiful little yellow house with a very cool garden.

"Oh bonsai!" I noticed over a dozen miniature little trees growing out of pots among several flowering plants in the front yard.

"Yeah, the owner's a big fan of bonsai. He comes over here to take care of the garden, don't mind him," said Dragos.

"That's nice," I said.

"I'll show you guys your room." There was a porch with some bamboo furniture, a sunny living room, two bedrooms, a bathroom, and a decent kitchen. Our bedroom had a big bed, a small cabinet, and a fan. That was basically everything we needed.

Dragos seemed like an interesting flatmate to have. He spoke Indonesian fluently and had been on several expeditions to native tribes deep in the jungles of Papua. He wasn't a big fan of Gili Trawangan or tourism in general, but he stayed on this island because it was one of few places in Indonesia where you can make some money as a diving instructor. His girlfriend, Montez, was also an interesting character. She was from Lombok and she didn't know English too well at the time but she was very friendly and quite funny. Montez worked as an accountant for a hotel and restaurant on the island, so she was often busy.

The next day, I began my scuba training! I started with theory and some beginner diving lessons in the pool. The first time I stuck my head underwater with full scuba gear on felt strange. It took me a few seconds to get used to the idea that you can actually breathe underwater. At first, I freaked out for a few seconds, then I calmed myself down, put my face in the water, and slowly breathed in and out. *It's just like snorkeling*, I told myself. *Just breathe.* After a few more seconds, I went a bit deeper and tried to keep myself calm.

Meanwhile, Alfie was about a meter away from me, signaling something. I tried to remember what he wanted. *Okay, calm down,* I thought. I gave him the "okay" sign then began my first few exercises. I calmly breathed in and out through the diving regulator, then I took the regulator out of my mouth while breathing out, put it back in again, and breathed in again, as Alfie demonstrated. Then I took the regulator out of my mouth again, dropped it, breathed out, picked it up, put it back in my mouth, breathed in, and continued to breathe calmly. Finally, I made a few signs and managed to clear my mask underwater.

"Whew! That was fun!" I said to Alfie once we came back up to the surface.

He laughed. "Wait till you get in the ocean!"

Next, we assembled all of our diving equipment and stacked it onto a long wooden boat. The captain brought us to a quiet, shallow dive spot, then Alfie showed me how to jump into the water with all this equipment on my back.

"First, make sure you do your buddy check," he said. "Your buddy should check that your tank is open, your regulator and alternate air source are working, your BCD is inflated, and everything is clipped up and in place. Also, double check the pressure gauge and make sure your buddy's weight belt is on the right way. Then stand up and scoot yourself up here." He moved to the side of the boat and gestured for me to do the same.

"Damn that's heavy!" I said. This stuff was bulkier than my backpack!

"All right, now put your regulator in your mouth, two fingers on your mask, one on the regulator, then lean back and just fall into the water. I'll go first to show you." Alfie splashed into the water like a frog. I followed him. *It was fun!* We bobbed around like two fat balloons at first, then we deflated our BCDs and descended into the ocean.

Wow this is amazing! I thought as I scanned the underwater world. There were hundreds of fish and dozens of different types of colorful corals. I also spotted turtles, sea snakes, and many other strange sea creatures. Alfie did a couple more exercises with me, then we went for a short dive. I loved it!

I came back to our yellow little house after the dive and told Chris all about it. I felt bad that Chris didn't get to dive, but he was still busy doing his massage course over the internet and this dive shop wouldn't take another intern. He did bring his surfboard with him though, and the Gili Islands did get some little waves every once in a while, so at least there was that. Chris also got along well with Dragos, Alfie, Hugo, and a few other friends of ours, so I hoped that it wasn't too boring for him.

I went diving once or twice per day, almost every day, for the next four months. After getting an Open Water certificate, I moved on to advanced diver specialties. I learned how to deep dive, drift dive, night dive, use NITROX, and do a bit of underwater photography. Soon, I fell in love with the underwater world. Every time I splashed into the ocean, the world above became irrelevant. The underwater world was so different. It seemed peaceful, quiet, yet colorful and alive. We explored remarkable landscapes and admired the vivid sea life—fish, coral, turtles, octopuses, eels, stingrays, nudibranchs, and much more.

My first night dive was with Pedro and one of his students. The three of us put our gear on after sunset, grabbed some dive torches and a few glow sticks, then walked into the water by our dive shop. It was amazing to see how different the ocean was at night. The fish were calm, many of them were resting in the corals. There were many strange-looking worms, sea slugs, and small crustaceans. Some were glowing in the dark! A few crabs and lobsters were actively walking around and the moray eels were out hunting.

At one point, Pedro gestured for us to turn off our torches. It was pitch black at first and a bit scary, but once we started waving our hands around the water, we noticed dozens of tiny shimmering lights. There was bioluminescent plankton all around us! It was magical. Then, once we turned our torches back on, we noticed a big blacktip shark coming straight toward us! The three of us froze. This was the first shark I had ever seen in the wild. Not knowing what to do, I stayed still and shined my light onto its body. *Oh man this thing is huge!* I thought. It moved closer. I held my breath. I don't know why. *You're not supposed to hold your breath while scuba diving! Breathe!* The shark came even closer. *What to do?* I looked at Pedro and the other guy. Nobody moved. It came closer. *Oh shit!* Then finally, it made a quick turn and swam away from us. *Whew. That was exciting! My first night dive and my first shark— all in one experience!*

I ended up diving with many more sharks after that night. Most of them were small and terrified of people, so I never felt threatened by them again. I loved observing sharks, eagle rays, cuttlefish, and other sea creatures, but my all-time favorite type of dive was a drift dive on a clear day. Perhaps this is the closest you can get to flying like Superman (or Superwoman). This happened once on a beautiful sunny day, when the visibility was crystal clear and the current was very strong. My dive buddy and I took off and let our bodies flow swiftly above an underwater canyon. We grabbed each other's hands as if we were skydiving, then let go, separated, flew apart, and then back together again. Since the current was so strong and the water was almost as clear as air, it truly felt like we were flying above the remarkable carved-out landscape beneath our bodies.

After a few weeks of diving, I felt strong, healthy, and excited, yet absolutely exhausted at the end of each day. I'd collapse into my bed and have deep, vivid dreams about the underwater world. Then I'd wake up and my dreams would merge with reality. I felt like I was in the movie *Avatar*, but it was real!

The funny part was that I barely had to do any work in exchange for all of this diving. The only "work" that was needed was for somebody to sit around the shop until about 8:00 p.m. and sign people up for dives. But since the shop was also our main hangout spot, most of us would be there anyway, so I never felt like I was obliged to do anything.

After finishing the Advanced Open Water Diver course, I also completed a Rescue Diver course and my final Divemaster training.

All of this was easy to do because there was no rush. The guys in the shop were very laid-back and I had about four months to complete my training. In the meanwhile, when we weren't diving, we would all hang out, watch sunsets, have a few drinks, and ride our bikes around the island. Back then, none of us owned a smartphone or shoes, so life was pretty sweet.

* * *

While we lived on Gili Trawangan, I made a lot of scuba diving friends and I also hosted couchsurfers. This was a fun way to get to know more travelers from around the world. Chris and I also found and raised two abandoned kittens while we were on the island. We named one Gremlin and the other Pirata because that's what they looked like—a gremlin and a pirate (Pirata was missing one eye). When we found them right outside of our house, they were so small that they fit in the palm of my hand. They were in such bad condition that I thought they would die immediately. Both were skinny as hell and Pirata was missing half of her face. Gremlin was digging through our rubbish bin looking for scraps of food while Pirata was barely breathing.

I gave them some food, then went diving and expected to see dead kittens when I came back. Surprisingly, they didn't die! They were in the same spot right outside our house when I came home for lunch. I gave them some more food and went diving again, expecting to see dead kittens when I came back in the evening. But again, they didn't die! Instead, they moved a little bit closer to our house. I fed them again, went to sleep, and expected to see dead kittens on my porch in the morning.

In the morning, I opened the front door and guess what? They were still alive! I fed them some more and they carried on living. Once they were on our porch (still alive), Chris and I decided to wash them. They looked a bit better once they were washed but they were still barely moving. Once they were clean, we allowed them to go inside our house and we continued feeding them. After just a few days, they started to look and behave more and more like real kittens! They started moving around and playing with each other, chasing cockroaches, and growling at each other whenever I gave them food. They were absolutely precious. I quickly fell in love with these two kittens and could not wait to come home and play with them.

After a few weeks, the hair on Pirata's face grew back and both kittens were gaining weight quickly. Unfortunately, Pirata's right eye never recovered, but eventually it oozed out and the eyelid shut the empty gap. She seemed to be fine without it. I watched the kittens chase each other around the house, jump, hunt, and play around like crazy. At night, they cuddled with me and purred as loud as little lions.

Watching Gremlin and Pirata grow up filled me with love and joy, but at times it also saddened me. I kind of felt like these kittens were my babies and I thought about the fact that all children should be playing around like this, in a loving and nurturing environment. *That's all they need,* I thought. *Food, water, shelter, and love. But so many children grow up in poverty—in the same condition that I found these little kittens.* I had seen so many young children begging for money and selling souvenirs, even crying over these things and going hungry. *Can we really call ourselves a "civilized" society when our own children suffer and go hungry while we trash forty percent of the food we produce? All children should be playing, eating, relaxing, learning, and growing. Not begging for money or selling stuff.*

Needless to say, I was very sad to leave Gremlin and Pirata when it was time for me to leave Indonesia. I would have stayed longer if it was possible, but unfortunately, I was down to my very last dollar by the end of my four months on Gili T. Also, Chris had gone back to Australia after just two months, so I missed him a lot. He went back early because of our money and visa situation. The problem was that most foreigners were only allowed to stay in Indonesia for one month on a tourist visa (and it's pretty much impossible to get a different visa if you don't have a ton of money). After one month, you're able to extend your visa for one more month by going to the immigration office and paying about thirty dollars. After your second month is up, you are required to leave the country. If you don't leave the country, you could get into big trouble.

Most people who want to stay longer end up doing "visa runs" every two months. They catch a cheap flight out of Indonesia (usually to Malaysia or Singapore), where they'll spend a day or two, then they'll fly back to Indonesia for another two-month stay. I did this once—I flew to Malaysia after two months, but I didn't have enough money to do this again after four months. Chris didn't have any money at all after the first two months, so he went back home to Moruya. I didn't really have a home, but since I still wanted to be with Chris, I bought a flight to Australia for November 20.

33

South Coast, 2014-15

It was warmer in Moruya this time around and I was so happy to see Chris again. I hated being away from him for so long. He was now finishing up his massage course and doing some surfing and skating lessons for money. He wasn't getting much from those lessons, but since he was staying at his mother's house, he didn't need a ton of money. Chris's mother was a very nice lady. She was kind and hard-working, and she never questioned us about "settling down" or getting a "real job." I felt slightly uncomfortable about staying at her place for too long, but I didn't have much of a choice since I had no more money left.

Clearly, I needed to find a job. I made a shiny new resume and started handing it out to the bars in town. Unfortunately, finding a job in Moruya was much more difficult than I had expected. Since I no longer had a student visa (because I had graduated university), I no longer had "permission" to work in Australia. Now, I was in Australia as a "tourist" and "tourists" are not allowed to work for money.

Since Moruya is a small country town, a lot of the locals were already not-so-welcoming to foreigners. I not only had to search for work as a foreigner, but I also had to explain that I didn't have a working visa if they asked for my documents. This was embarrassing as hell. I didn't even know what to say if they asked for my documents. "Um, I'm hoping to be paid in cash, if you don't mind" was the best I could come up with. Then I'd only hope their response wouldn't involve the police.

I spent almost every hour of every day looking for work. Day after day, week after week, and nobody wanted to hire me! Well, a few shops would have hired me, but only if I had the right papers. At first, I applied at every single bar, restaurant, café, and shop in Moruya, then I drove to other towns in the area and applied at every single place within a thirty kilometer radius of Moruya. I even put up ads for dog walking and babysitting. But nothing worked! I applied to work as a divemaster in the only dive shop around, about thirty kilometers away. They told me they would hire me, but only if I had "documents."

After about a month of nonstop job hunting, I was about to give up and go to Sydney. "Maybe I can find cash work in Manly," I said to Chris. "I can clean that stupid hostel again." Then right before I decided to leave, an ice cream shop agreed to hire me! They offered me fifteen dollars an hour and they didn't ask about any "documents." The owners were very nice and humble people. I had the feeling that they weren't even aware of these stupid rules and they paid cash just because it was easy.

My job was to make coffee and work the cash register. Of course, when I applied to work there, I told them I was an expert barista and I used to make coffee in Sydney, which wasn't exactly the truth. It wasn't a complete lie since I did make coffee once in a while at Three Wise Monkeys, but I definitely wasn't an expert. And Aussies are very snobby about their four-dollar coffees. Luckily, they didn't fire me once they realized I didn't really know how to make coffee; instead, they taught me. *Not like it's that fucking difficult...*

I spent the next few weeks working at this ice cream shop. At first I was only hired for the busy holiday season around Christmas, but since they liked me, they gave me a few shifts in January and February too. Thanks to this ice cream shop (and Chris's mom), I managed to save about three thousand dollars by the middle of February. Unfortunately, by this time I had a new problem: my visa. It was due to expire on February 20.

I would have loved to start a new adventure with Chris at this time, but since he didn't have much money saved, he wasn't ready for a big trip. Because of this, I decided to simply do a long visa run. "I'll leave the country for one month," I said to Chris, "so hopefully the immigration officers won't be suspicious. Then hopefully I'll be able to come back here for another three months. Then we'll see."

"Where do you want to go?" asked Chris.

"Well I would love to just stay here," I said, "but I don't want to be deported for overstaying my visa. I don't really know where to go. Every flight out of Aus is so damn expensive."

"Back to Indo?" he asked.

"That's an option, but I don't know. I'd like to see something new if I'm forced to leave."

I called my dad and talked to him about this problem. He told me to come to Russia, he even said that he had air miles he could give me for a free or discounted plane ticket. I told him that Russia was too far and that he should keep those air miles for himself. Then he said, "What if we meet somewhere in the middle and take a vacation together?"

I hated vacations but I loved my dad, so I agreed. He suggested to go to Sri Lanka, saying that he could fly there for free and then pay for our hotels.

"Do we have to stay in hotels, dad?" I asked.

"Where else do you want to stay?"

"Maybe we could couchsurf?" I said.

"Um, I don't know, let's see about that." He chuckled.

"Okay let's see about the flights and visa situation first." I learned that the maximum amount of time I could legally stay in Sri Lanka was thirty days, so I found a flight from February 16 to March 17. The cost was about 750 dollars for a round-trip ticket from Sydney. I knew it would have been cheaper to fly to Thailand or Bali instead, but Sri Lanka sounded a lot more interesting and I was sure it would be cheap once I got there.

If I couchsurf, take public transportation, and eat locally, I can probably manage a budget of 250 dollars for the entire month, I thought. *That way, I won't spend more than a thousand dollars and I'll still have two thousand dollars when I come back to Australia. Sounds like a plan!*

34
Sri Lanka, 2015

My dad wasn't very stoked about my plan for Sri Lanka. Since he was on "vacation," he was only planning to join me for the first ten days of my trip and he wanted a bit of "comfort." I didn't care much for comfort and since I knew that we were both pretty broke, I wanted to introduce him to my way of traveling. I wanted to show my dad that traveling on a very little budget can actually be a lot more fun and enriching than traveling like the average tourist. Unfortunately, I soon realized that not everyone had the same perception of "fun" as I had.

We made a compromise—I agreed to stay in hotels for the first week or so in Sri Lanka and my dad agreed to stay with one couchsurfing host for his last few days. My dad booked a few hotels in different cities close to some attractions in the center of Sri Lanka and I requested to stay with a host in the south of the country. We agreed to take public transportation as much as possible and to not splurge on food or anything fancy.

My dad and I arrived in Sri Lanka at different times of the day, so we agreed to meet at a hotel he had booked in a city called Negombo, close to the international airport. I finally owned a smartphone at that point, so I downloaded an offline map of Sri Lanka and found out how to get from the airport to this hotel using public transport. The directions said to leave the airport and walk southwest for about one kilometer, then take bus number 187 to a place called "Pettah." It said to get off the bus near the Katunayaka

South Railway Station and catch train number 3412 to a place called "Kattuwa," then walk one more kilometer to the hotel. I could have easily skipped all of this by taking a taxi or a tuk-tuk, but I didn't have any money to waste on overpriced airport taxis and I didn't mind going for a walk after my long flight. Since I arrived in the morning, I had all day to find this hotel.

Sri Lanka was sunny and hot. As soon as I walked out of the gate I was approached by dozens of taxi drivers. I ignored them as politely as possible and kept on walking. Some of them followed me. After saying "No thank you" about twenty times to each cab driver, they finally got the picture and left me alone.

I walked for about a kilometer as more and more taxi and tuk-tuk drivers stopped to offer me a lift. "No, thank you," I said, trying to be nice but firm. Soon I found an ATM and took out some cash for the bus and train. I walked into a grocery store to split the large bills into smaller ones and to get a sense of the prices in Sri Lanka. I knew that one US dollar was about 130 Sri Lankan rupees, but how much was a bus ticket? Or a meal? Or a bottle of water? It turned out that a bottle of water was about 30 rupees, so I figured a bus ticket shouldn't cost much more than that. I decided to keep about 200 rupees in a separate pocket away from my big bills and credit cards.

Soon I found the bus station and the right bus. *Bingo!* It was crowded and very chaotic but I managed to squeeze in with my backpack on. I kept my valuables under close watch in my front pockets. Then the bus driver took off like a madman! He was honking nonstop and almost running over pedestrians and little tuk-tuks. *I never knew that buses could drive so fast!* I could barely keep my balance as I swayed in the aisle, knocking people around with my big backpack. I got off the bus after a short ride and managed to find Katunayaka Railway Station thanks to my offline map. Once I was in the train, I felt safer and much more relaxed.

I gazed out the window and watched the chaos outside. There were a lot of people, a lot of tuk-tuks, and a lot of traffic and pollution. I noticed a cow eating a plastic bag on the side of the road. *Nothing out of the ordinary, right?* It chewed and swallowed the bag as if it were a big juicy leaf.

After a twenty-minute train ride and another twenty-minute walk, I made it to the hotel. I checked in, took a nice cold shower, found some local curry for lunch, and then waited for my dad to arrive. He came in on a taxi later that evening, a bit tired from his long flight from Moscow. It was great to see him again. We had a good rest and got ready to hit the road the next day.

Central Sri Lanka

I didn't want to come to Sri Lanka to see tourist attractions but since my dad was on "vacation," this was sort of his priority. He had a few temples and sights on his list. The first attractions were in a town called Dambulla, about 130 kilometers away from Negombo. That may sound pretty close, but on Sri Lankan roads with Sri Lankan traffic, it would have taken at least five hours for us to get there using public transportation. Since my dad was short on time, he convinced me to take a taxi and save some time and energy for those attractions.

Once we arrived in Dambulla, I convinced my dad to try the local food. I found a small eatery on a busy street where an entire meal of rice and curry cost about one dollar. The place was a bit cramped and it probably didn't follow the same sanitation standards as most northern countries, but the curry was delicious! And very spicy! Unfortunately, that didn't go down so well in my father's stomach though. He wasn't able to process spicy food as well as I could, and there was nothing on the local menu that wasn't extremely spicy.

Dambulla itself seemed a bit dirty and overcrowded. We stayed in a cheap hotel and visited the Dambulla cave temple and an ancient rock fortress called Sigiriya. Both the temple and the ancient rock looked impressive, but the tourism around them was crazy. There were big groups of people from all over the world scrambling around like herds of selfie-obsessed sheep with cameras. There were also a lot of poor locals scrambling around trying to feed off these sheep by selling them things or begging for money. I didn't like being a part of this mess.

I hated that this type of tourism was entirely based on consumption and that this consumption separated people. Most tourists came to these famous attractions to consume the shallow outer coat of Sri Lankan culture—to visit each sight as quickly as possible, to take some photos, taste some food, and perhaps watch a "traditional dance" or something similar. The locals catered to the tourists and attempted to get money from them. As a result, neither group of people were very interested in connecting with or understanding each another; instead, they just wanted to get something from one another. Money, souvenirs, food, a dance, a costume, a photo, a trade.

The people in charge of the famous tourist attractions made this separation even worse. Sigiriya, for example, cost fifty rupees (about thirty cents) for the locals to visit, but foreigners had to pay thirty US dollars each! *One hundred times the price.* They probably try to justify this price difference by saying that Sri Lanka is a poor country and this money goes toward "development," but judging by the amount of poverty in Dambulla, I really doubt that any of this money actually trickles down to the poor people. Most likely, a few already rich people and companies profit from these extremely inflated prices while the poor get nothing but scraps. Since the tourists paid a lot of money to go on "tours" and visit these places, this makes the separation even worse because foreigners end up treating the locals as if they are different, perhaps as if they are their servants or a spectacle, rather than a fellow human being with a different culture.

So instead of paying thirty dollars each to climb Sigiriya, my dad and I found a different mountain to climb. This place was better anyway because it gave us a great view of Sigiriya from a distance. After this, I convinced my dad to take a public bus to our next destination, Kandy, a city about seventy kilometers away from Dambulla.

Unfortunately, my dad was not very comfortable with the public bus ride. The bus was extremely overcrowded, loud, and uncomfortable. We had to stand for about two hours as more and more people packed in as tight as stuffed toys in a claw machine.

On the bright side, the bus was cheap and allowed me to meet a nice local girl. Her name was Chapa and she spoke English fluently. She told me that she was twenty-two years old and was studying at Kandy University. I chatted with Chapa for nearly an hour while we were on the bus and once we arrived in Kandy, she showed us around the city and helped me buy a local SIM card. Chapa and her friend also took my dad and me on a hike to a nearby mountain temple the following day—and this was one of the most beautiful places we saw in Sri Lanka!

I exchanged phone numbers with Chapa before we left and she invited me to visit her home village at the end of my trip. Next, my dad and I headed to the south, where we planned to couchsurf. This was going to be my dad's first time couchsurfing, so I was really hoping to share a unique and positive experience with him.

Southern Sri Lanka

Unfortunately, this ended up being my only slightly negative couchsurfing experience. We stayed with a family of four—a father, mother, and two children. The children were absolutely beautiful and the mother was kind, but it was clear that the father was trying to use Couchsurfing in order to get something out of the people he hosted. He got us to buy extremely overpriced tuk-tuk rides, he asked us to buy all kinds of stuff for his house, he signed us up for overpriced tours that he probably got a cut from, and eventually, he even asked my father for a large sum of money.

This was an extremely uncomfortable and disappointing situation. I wanted to show my dad that there were kind, honest, and genuine people out there—people who are willing to share their home with you without wanting anything in return, people who treat you no different to a friend or family member—but instead we stumbled upon a host who tried to get money from us. (And this host was very active on Couchsurfing—he had had dozens, if not hundreds of people stay with him in the past.) I told our host that we couldn't give him that large sum of money and that he should use Airbnb instead of Couchsurfing. "This is not what Couchsurfing is meant to be about," I said. He smiled, thanked us, and said no problem. We did the same, then left his house.

Long story short, I didn't manage to convince my father that budget traveling was the best thing to do on your ten-day vacation. He flew back to Moscow and I continued my journey through Sri Lanka alone.

Boossa

I still had hope that there were genuine people on Couchsurfing in Sri Lanka, so I contacted another host in a town called Boossa. The host's name was Malithy. He was about my age, he liked to surf, and he had a lot of positive references. I took a bus to the main town area then Malithy picked me up on his scooter and drove me to his place up the road. At his house, there were a bunch of local guys, a girl from England, and a couple from Austria. The house looked like a bit of a party house and Malithy seemed like a very chilled out Rasta dude.

At Malithy's place, I finally felt like I was human. Malithy and his friends were clearly genuine people. They weren't trying to sell tours or get their couchsurfers to buy stuff for them, they just liked meeting different people. At night, we all made a fire, had a barbecue, enjoyed some drinks, and played some acoustic music. I got along really well with Malithy and the Austrian couple, Paul and Bianca, because they were as excited as I was to surf in Sri Lanka.

We spent the next few days surfing at a beach called Dewata, which was in a pretty poor area but had some great waves. Sometimes we went there with Malithy and his extra boards, sometimes I went there on my own and rented a surfboard at the beach for about three dollars. The waves at this beach were absolutely perfect for me! They were long, easy to catch, and usually not too big. I also loved the culture around this beach. The local surfers were so nice that they even encouraged newcomers to catch the best waves. This was surprising because I was used to surfers fighting over the best waves on their local beaches. In Australia, I had been to places where the locals wouldn't let me catch a single wave on "their" beach. Every time I went for a wave, they would drop in on me to make sure I wouldn't come back there again and take "their" waves. But here in Sri Lanka, when the locals saw a good wave, they would point at me and say, "Go! Go! Go!" It was unbelievable! (And they did the same thing to Paul, so it wasn't about me being a girl.)

The great surf and friendly vibe on Dewata Beach made me want to come back every day, so that's what I did. When no one else at Malithy's house wanted to go surfing, I would take two buses to get to the beach. This took about an hour and was a bit of a hassle, but it only cost about ten cents so that was my preferred method of transport. Paul and Bianca laughed about this, telling me that a tuk-tuk all the way from Malithy's house to Dewata Beach only cost about a dollar and sixty cents.

"Sasha is the most frugal traveler I know," said Paul. "She goes through all of this trouble, taking one crowded bus, and then another crowded bus for like an hour, just to save a dollar and fifty cents!"

"Yeah but Paul," I said, grinning, "the difference is actually pretty big. The difference between a bus and a tuk-tuk isn't just a dollar fifty, it's like a thousand five hundred percent! The bus only costs ten cents. So I can go to the beach sixteen times by bus for the same amount of money I spend on one tuk-tuk ride. If you're short on cash and you keep this in mind for everything you spend money on, you can actually save a lot of money and then travel for a long, long time."

"That's great, Sasha." Paul chuckled and patted me on the back.

Tissamaharama

I stayed at Malithy's house and surfed at Dewata Beach for about a week, then I decided to travel on. Next, I contacted another couch-surfing host from a village called Tissamaharama, close to Yala National Park. The host's name was Ruchira; he was a safari guide and he had a detailed Couchsurfing profile with over twenty positive references. His profile included a lot of information about his life, philosophies, nature, and family.

I sent Ruchira a couchsurfing request and left him my phone number. To my surprise, he called me straight away! He told me that I could stay at his house for a few nights and that I could bring a friend if I wanted to. I didn't have a friend to bring but I told Ruchira that I'd head on over.

Ruchira picked me up from the bus station in Tissamaharama and brought me to his family's house. He seemed kind and knew English pretty well. The drive to his house was warm and beautiful. Once we got out of the town, we passed a luscious meadow with grazing water buffalo and yellow triangular-shaped mountains in the distance. Then we turned onto a dirt road which eventually led to his driveway. I walked into the house and met Ruchira's wife, mother, brother, grandmother, two daughters, and his very cute two-year-old son. Soon after, I also met Ruchira's eighteen-year-old cousin, Thiranjana. Thiranjana was visiting Ruchira from a different part of Sri Lanka.

I felt a little awkward there at first. Ruchira went outside to do some yard work while I sat around with his wife, mother, and a few other relatives. Nobody spoke English and I barely knew any Sinhala, so we couldn't really communicate. I also felt like the women were surprised by me, for some reason. In the back of my mind I was wondering if it was perhaps strange for them to see a lone female traveler. *Maybe that was why Ruchira told me I could bring a friend.* I had this feeling that perhaps the family was trying to figure out if I was a prostitute or something. *Because why would a woman be traveling alone?*

After sitting around in silence for a while, trying to not look like a whore, I started a bit of a conversation with Thiranjana. Thiranjana was very shy but he spoke more English than I had expected and he seemed excited to talk to me once I started the conversation. Soon, Thiranjana offered to show me around the neighborhood on the family's motorbike!

Thiranjana took me to a beautiful lake and a huge temple in a town called Kataragama, about twenty kilometers away. There was a massive ceremony going on in the temple when we arrived. Hundreds of people were walking around, lighting incense, praying, and offering fruit to the gods (or whoever). I noticed a line of people about three hundred meters long just to offer fruit. We walked around for a little while, went into a small room where a monk put ash on our foreheads, then left.

On our way back, Thiranjana and I got some chopped up noodles from a little stand. They were cheap and delicious! Once we were back in Tissamaharama, I told Ruchira that I would like to go on a safari with him if it was possible. I was ready to pay full price for the safari, but Ruchira gave me a nice discount. He told me to be ready at 4:00 a.m. the next day.

Yala National Park

It was still dark outside when we woke up the next morning. Ruchira, Thiranjana, and I hopped into a big jeep and drove to town to pick up a couple of Japanese guys who had signed up for the safari. They were nice guys; one was quiet, the other was loud and cheery. It was too early for me to make much of a conversation with them, but I learned that they had been traveling around Sri Lanka on bicycles. We had some breakfast then arrived at the gate of the national park just as the sun was rising. I was surprised to see so many jeeps at the entrance of the park. We waited about twenty minutes for Ruchira to submit some paperwork and pay the entrance fee, then we drove in following about a dozen other jeeps.

As soon as we got in, we saw a massive elephant with big tusks! He was beautiful. About fifteen jeeps surrounded him, all trying to get a closer look.

"I hope it's not gonna be like this the whole time," I said to the Japanese guys. We followed the other jeeps for a few more minutes then Ruchira took a small side road and lost sight of everybody else. This was great, he drove slowly and was extremely observant. As Ruchira was driving, he pointed out leopard prints, a toucan sitting far away on top of a tree, mongooses, monkeys, water buffaloes, hogs, many different birds, beautiful peacocks, and of course, more elephants. The animals didn't seem to be bothered by our jeep, they weren't even frightened when we drove close by. Ruchira explained that they were just very used to this.

This part of Yala National Park was a semi-dry forest. There were a lot of dry shrubs and small trees, as well as some beautiful rock features, hills, and waterholes. After a couple of hours of driving around and spotting animals, Ruchira parked his jeep on a beautiful rocky slope where he knew a leopard had been spotted. He looked around but couldn't see one. "There are less than a thousand Sri Lankan leopards left in the wild," he said. "They are endangered. But many of them are here in Yala, so I think we'll spot one."

"Why are there so few leopards?" I asked.

"Because of humans, of course," said Ruchira. "Mostly habitat destruction. The leopard used to live all over Sri Lanka, in all types of habitats, from dry grasslands to dense forests. Now there are people there, people everywhere. Not enough space for the leopard." He puffed on a cigarette and took a deep look at the forest. "Also, poaching. People kill for money."

Soon we drove on, moving deeper into the park. As Ruchira was driving, he noticed something moving on top of a rock over a hundred meters away. It took the rest of us quite a while to see this, but it turned out to be a leopard! It was so far away that I could barely tell it apart from the rock even while looking through binoculars. We stared at it for a while, then moved on to see peacocks flaunting their feathers and an elephant bathing in mud. Before the end of the safari, we were lucky enough to spot another leopard, this time only a few meters away from us! It was a truly beautiful sight.

After the safari, we dropped off the Japanese guys and came back to Ruchira's place for some delicious curry. I spent the rest of the day doing laundry in the river behind the house, reading books, and exchanging text messages with Chapa. In the evening, Ruchira's wife took me to the local market with her. It was a typical South Asian fruit and veggie market—lively, chaotic, and full of people. I offered to buy her some groceries, but she wouldn't let me. For dinner, we all ate a tasty spicy curry prepared by Ruchira's wife and mother. I started to feel more and more comfortable with the family then, and I felt like they enjoyed my company too. *Maybe they've realized that I'm just a little weird,* I thought, *but I'm definitely not a prostitute!*

At night, I went down to the river to clean off. Ruchira and his family didn't have running water in their house, so they used the river for all of their washing needs. I walked down the hill and into the darkness. It was peaceful and quiet. There was nobody around so I stripped off all my clothes and carefully climbed into the water. This river was magical. Frogs and crickets chirped rhythmically at my side as the running water washed all of the dust and sweat off my body. I dunked my head underwater and the sound was lost. I felt energy, excitement, and passion. But I also felt a deep sadness. I couldn't stop thinking about the national park. *All of those animals—they were so beautiful.*

Each time I dunked my head underwater, I saw vivid images of mongooses, elephants, peacocks, and leopards. *There was so much life in that park!* So many large mammals and beautiful birds. *This is what all of Sri Lanka used to look like.* Now, everywhere you go, all you see is roads, buildings, vehicles, farms, people, and garbage. Everywhere. The only bits of wildlife are in these tiny sectioned-off pockets we call "national parks" and they only exist because humans made an agreement not to destroy them. *And it's like this all over the world, not just in Sri Lanka.*

I couldn't help but wonder, once again, whether this rat race was really worth it. When human "development" endangers the lives of so many beautiful species of animals can it really be called "progress"?

Bundala National Park

The next morning, Ruchira woke me up at 4:00 a.m. and asked if I wanted to go on another safari. "I'm going to a different national park for a private tour," he said. "You can come for free if you want."

"Really, are you sure?" I asked.

"Yeah no problem, be ready in fifteen minutes."

"Okay, thanks a lot!" *Wow another safari!*

We hopped into Ruchira's jeep and picked up an older French couple from a hotel, then drove to Bundala National Park, about a half hour away from Tissamaharama. When we arrived at the entrance of the park it was still dark and there were only a few other jeeps in sight. I walked out of the jeep with Ruchira to get an entrance pass and he showed me an incredible birdwatching lookout built high above some lively marshlands. Light was just barely touching the scenery as dozens of different types of birds flew through a dark blue hazy mist.

I walked around and marveled at the fantastic view and freshness of the cool marshy air. Soon, the sky turned red and the sun peeked out from behind a beautiful tree full of lively macaques. We gazed at them for a little while then drove into the park and spotted a large male elephant. Ruchira stopped his jeep about fifteen meters away from him and we watched as the elephant stomped his enormous feet, picked up sand with his trunk, and sprayed it all over himself. After a few minutes, he walked right over to our jeep! He was so close that I could have touched him if I wasn't so intimidated.

"Be careful," said Ruchira. "This elephant is aggressive because he wasn't able to mate." He pointed out a cut in the elephant's trunk and some liquid on the elephant's legs. "This elephant is about sixty-five years old. He is old but very dangerous right now." I jumped to the other side of the jeep and Ruchira turned on the engine to scare him away. The elephant backed up a little bit and continued his sand throwing, this time only about a meter away from us.

We drove farther into the park and spotted a lot of different birds, including flamingos, storks, ibises, and many peacocks displaying their spectacular feathers. I was very impressed by Ruchira's knowledge of the wildlife. There were about two hundred species of birds in Bundala National Park and he seemed to know the names and characteristics of every one of them. Sometimes, he would point to a shadow of a bird somewhere in the far distance and tell us exactly what kind of bird it was and how he could tell.

We drove on to an estuary where we saw grazing water buffaloes and small crocodiles, then we made a loop around the national park and Ruchira pointed out monitor lizards, monkeys, mongooses, hogs, some interesting flora, and more colorful birds. I was so happy about this safari that I tried to give Ruchira some money for it when we came back to his house, but he wouldn't accept it.

"Keep it for yourself," he said. "Just don't write about this in a Couchsurfing review. Else all couchsurfers will expect a free safari." He chuckled.

"Okay." I smiled. "Thanks again, you're a really impressive guide!"

I decided to leave the next day because Chapa had invited me to visit her village near Kandy. I didn't really want to leave Ruchira's place so soon because I really liked his family and I felt like we had a great connection by the end of my stay, but I also didn't want to miss the opportunity to visit Chapa's village. Ruchira's family was concerned about me traveling through Sri Lanka alone, so Thiranjana offered to escort me all the way to Kandy. He said that he was planning to head to his hometown anyway, and that Kandy was on his way (though it was actually about two hundred kilometers out of his way, I later learned).

Kandy and Around

Judging by the map, I expected it to take several hours to get to Kandy by public transportation. At first, Thiranjana and I planned to take a bus to a town called Ella and then hop onto a train to Kandy. Unfortunately, we missed the last train and had to catch another two or three buses to get to Kandy. I was happy to have Thiranjana there with me. Not only was he translating everything and finding out bus schedules, but he was also saving me from having to walk around and switch buses by myself after dark. Plus, Thiranjana kept on trying to pay for everything! He paid for all the bus fares and some food that we got along the way. I tried to give him money for all of this but he refused.

We finally arrived in Kandy after 10:00 p.m. Chapa was worried about me getting in so late; she texted me every five minutes and said to meet her at her cousin's apartment behind a big hospital. She gave me the address and I took a tuk-tuk from the Kandy bus station to the apartment. Thiranjana accompanied me the entire way to make sure I got there safely. I thought this was a very sweet gesture and I felt awful about having to leave him there after I met Chapa. Unfortunately, there wasn't enough space for him in Chapa's cousin's apartment, but Thiranjana said he would be fine. After I met Chapa, he took a tuk-tuk back to the bus station and caught a night bus to his hometown, Ratnapura. Before he left, Thiranjana also invited me to visit him in his hometown.

After saying goodbye to Thiranjana, I met Chapa's cousin, his wife, and their three children. They didn't speak English but were very friendly. Chapa's cousin gave us some rice, curry, and a place to sleep.

The next day, Chapa and I did some sightseeing then made our way to her hometown in the countryside. It took several hours to get to her village by bus but the views were spectacular the entire way and her village was very picturesque. Chapa's house was down a dirt road that had rice fields on both sides and mountains in the distance. There were peacocks flaunting their feathers all over the place and a little stream running down one side of the road.

Chapa and I noticed that everywhere we went, people stopped and stared at me as if I were from another planet. Because of this, Chapa called me an "alien" and laughed about how silly this was. Ironically, while I was with Chapa, I really felt like I was human. I didn't feel like a "tourist," a "foreigner," an "alien," or a bag of money. I just felt like a friend, a fellow human. We chatted for hours as Chapa showed me her village, the nearby forest, and some beautiful lakes and temples.

After several days in Chapa's village, she went back to university in Kandy and I went traveling on. I only had a few days left in Sri Lanka, so I decided to visit Thiranjana in Ratnapura. Thiranjana told his family and friends about me, and his mother welcomed me into their home. Their house was big and the family even gave me my own room to stay in.

None of Thiranjana's friends or family knew English, but we got along just fine. His friends drove us around in their tuk-tuk and showed me some beautiful rivers and waterfalls. Here, again, I felt like I was human. Nobody wanted to sell me anything, in fact, all they ever wanted was to show me stuff and give me curry—and I love curry. I was very grateful to have met Ruchira, Thiranjana, and their lovely family, as well as Chapa, Malithy, and the many other kind and friendly people I came across in Sri Lanka.

* * *

After a few more days, my trip was coming to an end. I went back to the south, then took a train to the airport to catch my flight back to Australia. I felt like it had been a long month. I learned a lot. I learned, again, that I hate tourism and that I never want to go on "vacation," but I love to travel. I love to experience life as the locals do, everywhere in the world. I love to be accepted by the local people as a fellow human. Not as a tourist, not as a foreigner, not as a bag of money or a vagina, but just as a human. And vice versa is just as important. I hate when people are treated as servants, spectacles, or anything other than human. The sooner we learn to accept each other as human, the sooner we will be able to create a better world.

But perhaps it's not that simple... Perhaps it's more important to understand *why* it is so difficult for people to regard each other as human in the first place. Culture and upbringing definitely have an impact, but I think it's also this rat race that separates people. People can't see each other as human when they're so busy trading with each other—trading tours for money, money for hotel rooms, food for money, money for souvenirs, on and on. When these trades are the priority, there's no reason for people to regard each other as human. It's easier to separate people and tag each other as either a tourist, a local, a merchant, a guide, a dancer, a beggar, or whatever else. That way you can get what you need from them and move on. That's the kind of world we live in. If we want a better world, then perhaps *that's* what we need to change.

35

South Coast, 2015

As soon as I arrived at Sydney Airport, I got a huge metaphorical slap in the face. Right when I was reflecting on the idea that we all need to treat each other as one human species, the Australian immigration officer snatched my passport and told me to come with him to another room.

In the room, two officers examined my passport and interrogated me. "What do you plan to do in Australia?" they asked.

"I just want to see my boyfriend," I said. "He's Australian."

"How many times have you been to Australia in the past year?"

"Um, two or three times, I guess. I was studying at Sydney University before, I had a student visa."

"Now you don't have a student visa, right?"

"No, I graduated."

"So why are you traveling to Australia so often?"

"I just like Australia. And my boyfriend is here. We will leave soon though, I've never stayed longer than my visa allowance." I was nervous because I knew I would be screwed if they didn't let me into Australia. *Where would I go? And when would I see Chris again?* I missed him so much, it had been an entire month since I had seen him last.

"You're not supposed to come and go from Australia every three months on this tourist visa. That's not what this visa is for," they said. Then they searched me, asked me more questions, searched through every single item in my bag, and even took my phone and went through it. I wondered if that was even legal, but in the position that I was in, there was nothing I could do. Luckily, I still had that Sri Lankan SIM card in my phone, so there was no evidence of all those lattes and cappuccinos I made "illegally" in that Australian ice cream shop.

After about four hours of interrogation, they finally let me in. They said, "This will be the last time you will be allowed to enter Australia on this visa. Make sure you leave before your visa expires. If you want to come back to Australia again, you will need to get a different visa."

"Okay, officer." *Jesus Christ. A different visa like what?* The only visa I could have possibly been eligible for was a working holiday visa but the application for that visa cost about five hundred Australian dollars and you were supposed to have five thousand Australian dollars in your bank account. At that time, I had less than two thousand dollars, no job, no home, and absolutely no ambition to get a job just for a visa.

Once I met Chris, we discussed the possibility of getting a "partner visa" for me to legally stay in Australia, but when we looked into this painful bureaucratic process, we realized that the application for this visa cost 7,715 dollars! Plus, the processing time was about two years, so we agreed that it would be much easier to just leave Australia before my tourist visa expired.

We went back down to Moruya together and tried to figure out what to do next. Chris was now working as a masseuse part time, but he still wasn't making much money. I contacted the ice cream shop and asked if they could hire me again. They gave me a few more shifts during the Easter holidays, but unfortunately, they weren't very busy so they couldn't give me consistent work.

After about a month in Moruya, I still had about two thousand dollars in my bank account. There were no prospective jobs in sight and my tourist visa was supposed to expire in two months. Then one fine day, I accidentally rammed one of Chris's mother's cars into a concrete pillar in a parking garage. This was such a stupid mistake and it absolutely devastated me. The outcome was that the door had bent in and I had to pay a thousand dollars for the damage, even though the car itself cost only two or three thousand dollars. I sucked it up and spent half of my money on fixing this car.

Now I had only one thousand dollars in my bank account, no prospective job, and my tourist visa was due to expire in less than two months. *What to do now?* The most logical thing to do, in my mind, was go somewhere where I could work legally, make some money, then continue to travel around the world with Chris.

"I think we have to go to the US," I said to Chris as we sat around his mom's kitchen. "The only places where I can work legally are the US and Russia. You would need a visa to get into Russia, plus I can't make much money there. In the US, I can get a bartending job and work my ass off for like two or three months. If I find a good gig, I can save a few thousand dollars quickly and then we can take off again. Maybe we can go surf in South America or snowboard in the Alps after I make some money."

Chris didn't seem too happy about my plan. "I don't really have much money to spend on the States," he said.

"But what else can we do?" I said. "I have almost no money left. I basically just have enough for a flight and then I'm fucked. I have to make money somehow and I'm not gonna look for another illegal job here, I've had enough of this. Plus my visa expires soon! And also, the Australian dollar is going downhill, it's better to earn US dollars now." When I was studying at Sydney University, the Australian dollar was either stronger than or equivalent to the US dollar, but it started to lose value around 2014, and by 2015, one Australian dollar was worth only about seventy-five US cents. "So if I earn fifteen Australian dollars an hour that's only about eleven US dollars, which is pretty shit. I can make way more money than that bartending in the States."

"Okay where in the US?" asked Chris.

"I don't know. Let's look at flights." We spent the rest of the day looking at the prices of flights to different US cities, and we found out that the cheapest flight out of Sydney happened to land in Honolulu, Hawaii. Now Chris seemed a bit more optimistic about my plan.

"I have a friend in Honolulu," I said. "Chili, she's my best friend from high school. I'll send her a message and see if we can stay with her for a few days. What do you think?"

"Okay, I'm sure Hawaii's cool. Great waves." He smiled. "But I'm also sure it's super expensive there."

"Yeah probably, but if we managed to live in Switzerland with almost no money, I'm sure we could also manage Hawaii."

"Okay let's see," said Chris. "Maybe we can go there together and see how it is. Maybe I can find some massage work for cash. If it's too expensive and I can't find any work then I can fly to Central America and stay somewhere cheap."

"Sure, and when I finish working I can just meet you in Central America," I said.

"Okay."

Now I got excited! I contacted Chili and told her the news. She seemed excited too, she said that Hawaii was beautiful and that we would love it, especially if we surf. She also said that she could pick us up from the airport and we could stay at her place for a few days.

"Done!" We booked two one-way tickets from Sydney to Honolulu for a total of 771 Australian dollars. Three weeks later, Chris and I packed up our backpacks and surfboards, hitched up the coast, and were ready to take off on our new adventure.

36

Hawaii, 2015

I was very excited to go to Hawaii and experience a new life with Chris. I was tired of screwing around, having to go from one country to another just to avoid overstaying these stupid visas. All I really wanted was for Chris and me to enjoy our lives together. I thought that our plan for Hawaii was perfect—*Chris is allowed to stay in the US for three months under the "Visa Waiver Program." That's enough time for me to find a job and save some money. Then we'll fly to Central America or Europe and continue our lives together.*

Unfortunately, the people at the Sydney Airport check-in counter had different plans for us. The lady at the counter looked over our tickets and passports, then turned to Chris and asked, "Where is your return flight?"

"Um, I don't have one yet," replied Chris.

"We can't let you on this flight without a return or onward ticket," she said.

"Really?"

"Yes, you need a return or onward flight to enter the US."

"But isn't that up to the immigration officer to say, not the airline?" asked Chris.

"Like I said, we can't let you onto the flight without a return or onward ticket. You can purchase a ticket from our counter if you would like." She pointed to a little booth a few meters away from us.

"Okay." We left the counter.

"Fuck," I whispered. "We should've expected this. Okay so let's buy a ticket then. We have like twenty minutes before they close the check-in counter."

"Goddamn it," said Chris. "Okay, I guess we have no other option. Let's buy it online, not at their stupid little booth. They're probably just trying to make money off us."

"Yeah, bastards!" We tried not to panic as we scanned through flights on my phone. The situation was difficult because we had almost no more money left, we knew that Hawaii would be very expensive, and we didn't know how fast it would take me to find a job or whether Chris could find any cash work at all. Because of this stressful uncertainty, we ended up buying the cheapest possible flight from Honolulu to Central America. The flight was booked for just three weeks after our arrival in Hawaii because all of the other tickets were at least double the price. Since we had so little money left, we just couldn't spend any more money on flights.

"Okay so we'll have three weeks together in Hawaii, and then I'll fly to Nicaragua," said Chris. "When you're done with work, you can meet me there."

"Okay." I was devastated that we'd have to split apart again. *Again and again and again because of these bullshit visa laws.* We walked back to the check-in counter and showed the lady Chris's onward flight. She gave us a fake smile, checked in our bags, and printed our boarding passes.

"Gate number forty-six," she said. We passed through security and the rest of the airport bullshit, got patted down and searched again, and made it to the gate just on time to catch our flight. I felt a bit more relaxed once we were finally in the plane together.

Chris and I calmed down and discussed what we should do next. "So I have about a thousand dollars in cash and minus a few hundred on my credit card," I said. I had paid for my flight and a few other expenses on my credit card so that I would at least have some cash when we arrived in Hawaii. "With a thousand dollars I can probably either rent a room for one month or buy a car. If I rent a room then I'd probably have to get a job straight away so that I could pay rent the next month. But if I buy a car then maybe we can just live in it and check out the island while we're together."

"You think you can buy a car for a thousand dollars in Hawaii?" asked Chris.

"Yeah probably. I bought a car once for four hundred twenty dollars!"

"And how long did that car last?" He grinned.

"Long enough! I drove that car from Utah to Vegas, all around the Grand Canyon, to LA, San Diego, back to Utah, and then to Vancouver. And then I sold it for the same price." I giggled. "I bet we can find something good again."

"Okay, I'm keen," said Chris. "Then we can go up to the North Shore for some waves."

"Yep!"

Once we arrived at Honolulu International Airport, a big friendly immigration officer greeted us with a big friendly "Aloha," stamped our passports, and let us straight through the exit door. He never asked Chris for proof of a return or onward flight. We picked up our bags, walked out of the airport, and were greeted by Chili and her little dog.

"Hey, girl!" Chili ran up to me with a big smile and a flowery lei. "It's been so long!"

"Chili! It's so good to see you!" Chili looked great. She seemed happy and healthy. She told me she had been living in Hawaii for several years now, she had a boyfriend, a well-paying job, a cute dog, and she was getting into body boarding. We drove to her apartment in Honolulu and she told us all about Hawaii.

"You guys will love it here," said Chili. "There are so many great hikes, waterfalls, beautiful beaches, great waves, it's awesome! You guys should check out the North Shore once you get a car. It's dope."

"Planning on it!" Chris and I spent some time with Chili, her dog, and her boyfriend, then we got onto Craigslist to search for a car. Since Chris was so short on time, we were ready to buy one ASAP.

367

The Explorer

Chili lent us her car when she went to work, so Chris and I were able to drive to different parts of Oahu and search for a thousand-dollar car. The first vehicle we went to look at was located on the West Side, in a town called Waianae. We drove from Chili's place onto a big highway, then up a busy beachside road.

There were a lot more roads, highways, and traffic on Oahu than I had expected. It took about forty-five minutes to get to Waianae. At first sight, it looked very beautiful there. The West Side was dry and rugged. There were mountains to the right and crystal-clear ocean water to the left, but Waianae itself seemed a bit strange.

"I didn't expect to see so much poverty in Hawaii," I said. There were a lot of homeless people and tents on the beaches and public parks. When we drove around the neighborhood, we noticed that a lot of houses were in poor condition, but outside of those houses there were very expensive-looking cars, mostly fancy new pickup trucks. Dogs were barking nonstop on every corner of almost every street.

We found the address of a guy who had listed a 1995 Ford Explorer on Craigslist. He was an older gentleman with gray hair and a mustache. "Hey there!" he said with a friendly smile. "I'll show you the Explorer." He walked up to a bright blue SUV parked on the side of the road.

It didn't look bad for a thousand dollars. There was definitely enough space for both Chris and me to sleep in the back. We popped open the hood and everything seemed to look fine, although neither Chris or I knew what the hell we were looking at. Then I took the car for a test drive.

"It seems to drive well," I said. "Does the car have any problems?"

"No problems that I know of," said the guy.

"Why are you selling it?"

"I'm moving off island. Selling my house and everything in it too. Come back in a month or so if you need some furniture!"

"Okay. Where you going?"

"Back to the mainland, you know."

"Okay." I wasn't sure if I should trust this guy or not. The car seemed to drive fine, there were no warning lights, visible leaks, or funny noises, but neither Chris or I knew anything about mechanics, so how could we tell? "Will you take eight hundred?" I asked the guy.

"No. Sorry, I wrote no bargaining in the listing."

"Okay, we'll talk it over and let you know." I drove the car back to his house, then Chris and I walked away and had a chat. We realized that no matter who we bought a car from, we wouldn't really know if it had problems unless we got it checked. Unfortunately, we didn't have enough money to spend on a car inspection, so we basically had to trust whoever was selling the car. Since Chris had less than three weeks left in Hawaii, we really didn't want to waste time going from one place to another just to test drive different cars. Plus, we couldn't borrow Chili's car to do that every day.

"If I buy this car now then we can get it all set up tomorrow and we'll be ready to hit the road the day after," I said to Chris.

"Yeah, I don't know what to say, I guess it seems fine," said Chris. "Do what you think is right."

I called the guy back and handed him a thousand dollars in cash. That was all the rest of my money. We did the paperwork and that was it—Chris and I had a new home! And a car! We felt free and excited. We drove back to Chili's apartment and got back onto Craigslist to look for free stuff. The next step was to turn the Explorer into a mobile home!

Chris and I got a couple of foam mats, a container, and a cooler for free through Craigslist, then we bought a camping stove and bedsheets from a department store for about twenty dollars. We also bought one pot, one cutting board, two bowls, two spoons, two forks, a knife, and two cups for about five dollars from a second-hand store. Everything we bought from then on was purchased on my credit card, which now had a limit of two thousand dollars (at some point, the bank decided to decrease my limit). Luckily, we didn't need much, although car insurance cost about sixty dollars per month and I had to pay another thirty dollars per month for phone credit. Food was also a bit pricey on Oahu, but since the island was small, we didn't have to spend too much on fuel.

Once we set up the Explorer, we were stoked and ready to explore Oahu! We drove up Kamehameha Highway and gasped at the beautiful view of green rolling hills and the bright blue ocean ahead of us.

"Oh yeah!" said Chris.

"This is awesome!" I felt happy and free. "You know, I think I won't look for a job yet," I said. "You're only here for a short time, so let's just have fun while we're together. I'll find a job after you fly out."

"Fine by me. I hope you can pay back your credit card though," said Chris.

"Yeah don't worry, it's no big deal."

"Okay."

After about an hour of driving, I noticed something odd. The check engine light turned orange, then it turned red. "Uh-oh," I said. "That's not good." I stopped the car on the side of the road. "Goddamn it, I knew that guy was dodgy! *Fuck!*" I called the guy that I bought the car from and he said not to worry about that light. He said that it went on from time to time, but it wasn't a problem. I knew he was lying. I let the car cool down a bit, then drove it to a mechanic to see how bad it really was.

The Exploder

This was the report we received from the mechanic:

Both front window motors have slipping clutch. Break pads down to sensors front & back. Front sway bar links missing all bushings. ABS codes C1210 R/F dump/outlet valve coil circuit fault. C1202 rear dump outlet valve fault Eng. Codes: 335 EGR (DPFE) Signal out of range 336 exhaust press hi. Or EGR (PFE) Signal high 337 EGR (DPFE) Signal too high A/C inop low pressure & missing pressure switch.

KBB Value $761

The Explorer was in such bad condition that the mechanic said he would refuse to work on it if we wanted anything fixed. "I wouldn't want to take any responsibility for this vehicle," he said. "It can break down any minute. There's no point fixing anything here. My advice is to drive it till it breaks down, then scrape it and leave it. Just be very careful driving. Don't go too fast or too close to other cars, okay?" On the plus side, the mechanic seemed to feel bad for us and he didn't charge us any money for this car inspection.

"Okay, thanks for your honesty," I said. *Jesus Christ, the mechanic's advice is to drive it till it breaks, then scrape it and leave it! Wow.* I felt devastated and very stupid for having blown all of my money on this shitty car.

"At least it's still driving," said Chris. "Maybe it'll last a few more months."

"Yeah hopefully. I guess we should just take the mechanic's advice, right? Drive it carefully and hope that it doesn't explode on us." I was nervous about the situation but I felt like there was nothing I could do. Chris would fly out in less than three weeks, I had negative money, and we had already transformed this car into a living space. "Okay, let's take this Exploder to the beach then!"

Chris and I spent most of the next three weeks on the North Shore, keeping driving to a minimum. We spent our days surfing, climbing, and snorkeling, our evenings watching sunsets, and our nights getting eaten alive by mosquitoes. The Exploder wasn't the most comfortable place to sleep in since we didn't have a proper mattress and it was often very hot, but it was still worth it to be able to do whatever we wanted, whenever we wanted, and to not have to slave just yet.

Cooking was pretty easy and fun at times. We bought food from supermarkets or farmers markets and kept it cold in a big cooler with ice. Whenever we wanted a hot meal, we would just park the Exploder by a park with picnic tables and cook on our camping stove. We usually didn't cook any specific type of meals, we would just chop up some vegetables and mix them together with beans, rice, or pasta, all cooked in one pot. Chris called all the food that I cooked "mush." Fortunately, he was never a picky eater. We also made sandwiches and ate a lot of fresh tropical fruit from local markets, local trails, or people's front yards (mangoes and avocados often hung over fences).

After a few days of wandering around the North Shore, Chris and I met a friendly group of rock climbers. We noticed them climbing around the boulders at Waimea Bay, so we went up to them asking about the climbing spots on the island.

"There's a lot of climbing here!" said a girl named Wai. "Mostly bouldering, but some top roping too. We go climbing a few times a week, you guys can always join if you want."

I had a pair of climbing shoes with me, but I wasn't a very experienced climber. Chris, on the other hand, was very into the sport. We took down some phone numbers and stayed in contact with Wai and a few other climbers. After this, we started climbing almost every other day!

I never climbed much in the past, but I *loved* it now. Climbing was not only a very fun sport, but there was such a friendly, non-competitive atmosphere around it. Most of the people we climbed with were expert climbers, some were instructors, others were in climbing magazines, but nobody seemed to mind that I was a complete beginner. They showed me some easy routes, guided me with a lot of tips and advice, and they even cheered me on when I managed to not fall off the easiest routes! Chris was also stoked to climb as much as possible since the surfing season was coming to an end on the North Shore.

After each day of climbing, we were completely wrecked, but in a good way. Every single muscle ached, every little bit of every finger, and even muscles that I never even knew existed! I *loved* it. I'd lie down in the Exploder next to Chris after a day of climbing and instantly drift off to sleep, feeling as healthy and powerful as a lioness.

Every once in a while, Chris and I would meet our climbing friends at Kaena Point, the westernmost tip of Oahu. Kaena Point is a beautiful rugged area that can be reached either via a dead-end road on the North Shore or a dead-end road on the West Side. There are steep mountains on one side of the point and endless rocky views of the ocean on the other side. There are also naturally carved rock pools, small beaches, monk seals, and a beautiful seabird sanctuary at the end of the point. Down toward the West Side, there's also an arch that the guys liked to climb. It was too advanced of a climb for me, but Chris gave it a good shot. Sometimes we would stay by the arch for hours, climbing and chatting with our friends, then we'd watch the sunset over the ocean and walk back to the Exploder under moonlight. There was something magical about that place.

Before Chris flew out, we gained a bit of confidence in the Exploder and decided to take it for one spin around the island. We drove down the East Side, bought some coconuts, and climbed the Olomana Trail, a breathtaking hike with incredible views of the steep, tropical mountains and the open ocean. Then we drove down to the Lanai Lookout and to a few nice beaches on the South Side. A day later, I dropped Chris off at Honolulu Airport, then made my way back up to the North Shore.

Homeless and Alone

Once Chris left, I felt sad and alone. I tried to be strong but it was hard at times. I felt scared and empty without him. *We had such a great time together,* I thought. *And now I'm all by myself living in a car called "The Exploder." It might explode any day now. I have no money at all. I've almost maxed out my credit card. What if the car breaks down? Then what? What if somebody tries to break into it while I'm sleeping inside? What if the engine doesn't start while somebody's breaking in?*

I drove back to Kaena Point and walked around the bird sanctuary alone until it got dark. I thought perhaps this would be a safe place to sleep since theoretically, there should be nobody there. The road that led to Kaena Point stopped at a dead-end parking lot, so there would be no reason for people to go there in the middle of the night. *Right?* I came back to the Exploder after a long walk, had a dip in the ocean, rinsed myself with a bottle of fresh water, then got into the back of the car. There was one other car in the parking lot and nobody around. *Don't worry, it's safe to sleep here,* I told myself. *Just sleep.*

I couldn't sleep. After about an hour of lying on my foam mat, I noticed some lights on top of a mountain toward the end of Kaena Point. *That's definitely a flashlight. What the hell are they doing up there?* Soon I noticed another flashlight at the bottom of the mountain. The lights were going on and off at different speeds and pointing in different directions. Two people were clearly signaling something to each other. *That's weird. I hope they're okay.* It looked like both people were walking pretty fast, so I didn't think they were hurt, but I was a bit freaked out by their signals.

A few minutes later, two cars drove into the parking lot. *Fuck,* I thought. *Should I start the engine and leave? But then I'll give myself away. And what if the engine doesn't start? Maybe it's better to just stay here and hide. Fuck I hope they don't come up to my car!* I was terrified. *They're probably drug dealers. Who else would come here in the middle of the night?* I was afraid that somebody would shine their light into my car or try to break in. I didn't sleep at all. More and more cars came and left the parking lot as the night progressed, some people played music, others walked around chatting with each other. In the morning, I drove to a town called Haleiwa and decided to only sleep in nice-looking neighborhoods from then on.

Once I was in Haleiwa, I started having trouble with the Exploder's battery. Sometimes the car turned on, sometimes it didn't. *Okay that's it,* I thought. *The Exploder is exploding. I have no other option but to get a job ASAP!* I went to the local library and printed out a few shiny new resumes, then I brushed my hair, dressed up nicely, and went around to every bar and restaurant in Haleiwa. Luckily, a restaurant called Breakers accepted me straight away! *But* there was a catch...

I talked to a manager named Lo. She seemed like a pretty down-to-earth, honest person. "What we really, really need," she said, "is a hostess. If you can host for now, I can get you waitressing shifts in a few weeks. After that, we can move you up to bartender."

Fuck, I thought. *What does hosting make? Like seven dollars an hour? But I can't say no to a job! I need any job right now.* "Okay, no problem!" I said. "I'm ready to work straight away."

"You can come in and train tomorrow at eight a.m.," said Lo.

"Okay, great. Thank you!"

I drove to a second-hand store to buy some work clothes, but I didn't manage to leave the parking lot without getting a jump start. Now the Exploder was really going downhill. When I came back to Haleiwa, I parked next to Ali'i Beach Park, about a kilometer away from Breakers and the Haleiwa town center. It felt pretty safe there. There were some houses on one side of the street and a big grassy area with picnic tables on the other side. There was a group of homeless people living in some tents in one corner of the park, but they seemed to stay in that corner. *Who am I to judge homeless people now anyway?* I thought. Close by, there was a beautiful beach with lots of coral and sea turtles, a public bathroom, a changing room, and an outdoor shower. I was lucky to have parked in that spot because from that day on, the Exploder wouldn't start even with a jump. I sucked it up, slept in the Exploder, and went to my new job.

* * *

Breakers was a bit hectic. The hostesses had no idea what they were doing and everyone seemed to be in a panic as soon as it got busy. I tried to stay calm and keep things organized. Fortunately, the staff were friendly even when things got a little messy. The restaurant served "American food," meaning burgers, sandwiches, wings, things like that, so it wasn't too fancy. They also had a big bar that got busy on the weekends, sometimes they even had live music.

I spent the next few months working my ass off at Breakers. I was scheduled to work there full time, but I took any additional shift that was offered to me, so I often ended up with seven or eight shifts per week. I didn't get my first paycheck for a couple of weeks, so I continued to live in the exploded Exploder by Ali'i Beach Park.

I'd wake up each morning as soon as it got too hot inside the car, then I'd put on my bikini and go straight into the ocean. I'd swim with sea turtles and other fascinating creatures, then I'd take an outdoor shower, brush my hair, and change into my work clothes in the public changing room. I'd usually work all day, eat at work, and come back to Ali'i Beach Park after dark. Then I'd change back into my bikini, take another dip in the ocean, have another outdoor shower, and climb back into the Exploder and go to sleep. Sometimes I was scared that somebody would creep up on me as I was showering alone at night, but luckily that never happened. Sleeping in the Exploder was also a bit more frightening during this time because I knew that if somebody wanted to break in or rob me, I wouldn't be able to drive away. Because of that, I didn't tell anybody that I lived in my car.

Eventually, one guy I worked with realized that I lived in the Exploder, but I made him promise to keep it a secret. "It can put me in danger, you know, if people find out that I'm sleeping in there," I said to him as we were walking toward the park after work.

"Yeah I get you. Don't worry, your secret's safe with me." His name was Ben. He worked as a dishwasher at Breakers and he was homeless. He usually slept on the beach by Ali'i Park.

One night, I stayed up late having a long conversation with Ben about how unjust and awful this system was. We talked about how monopolies screw people over and harm the environment, how all people are forced to work like slaves, and how it's basically impossible to escape this trap. Then, to my surprise, Ben said, "But at least I'm free. Here in America, I'm free and nobody can take that away from me!"

"What do you mean you're free?" I asked.

"I mean, I can do whatever I want."

"But can you? What if you want to shoot the guy over there? Are you free to do that? Or what if you want to live in that house over there?" I pointed to a nice beachfront property. "Can you do that? Or even eat whatever food you want? Or sleep wherever you want?"

"Well, of course there are some restrictions, but I can still go here and there and do whatever I want with my time," said Ben.

"Well you can't exactly go 'here and there' if 'here and there' are owned by somebody else. And you can't exactly do *whatever* you want. You can only do whatever you can afford to do with your money. I mean no offense, but how can you consider yourself to be free when you work your ass off all day in that restaurant but you still can't even afford to live under a roof?"

I remembered being bombarded with this idea of "freedom" when I was in school. *That's a great way to brainwash people,* I thought. *Drill this idea into their heads when they're young to make them devoutly believe that they're "free," then train them to be obedient little worker slaves for the rest of their lives. Great plan!*

"I'd say you're only ever free to a limited extent," I went on. "In this society, your freedom is limited by laws and the amount of money you have. Actually, if you think about it, you never really get to choose what you do. You don't choose where you're born, but as soon as you're born, you're assigned a label that dictates what part of the Earth you can or can't live in and what rules you have to follow. From day one, you're taught how to behave and what to believe in, and you may or may not have access to food, healthcare, or whatever else, depending on your family's income and social status. Then you're thrown into school, taught to listen, memorize a bunch of crap, and conform to authority, and eventually get a "job" for the rest of your life. That doesn't sound like freedom to me, it sounds a lot more like slavery."

I think Ben dozed off to sleep as I was talking. I went back to the Exploder feeling angry that this "free" man had to sleep on the beach night after night. *I wish people would question more*, I thought. *Kids should never be taught that they are free, instead they should learn to question what it means to be free in the first place. How do you define this concept? And how could we apply it to our society?*

The Turning Point

After two or three weeks of working as a hostess, I was able to pick up server shifts. I absolutely hated serving tables but I put up with it because the money was good. The shifts were six to eight hours long and sometimes I made over two hundred dollars in tips. It was hard work since there were no bussers or food runners in Breakers, but that allowed me to make more money because I didn't have to split my tips with many people.

After about a month and a half of serving tables in Breakers, I started taking bartending shifts. This was when my Hawaiian slaving experience made a turning point. Now I started to earn *a lot* of money. Actually, it was hard to believe how much money I was making in tips. On an average night of bartending, I made three to four hundred dollars, but sometimes I'd walk away with over six hundred dollars in a single night. I was making so much money that I didn't know where to hide it when I came back to the Exploder and I got paranoid about people following me "home" and wanting to rob me. I ended up hiding cash in different corners of the car whenever I couldn't get to the bank on time.

Since I had spent many years bartending in Australia, I found the US tipping scheme to be extremely weird. In Australia, I was paid about twenty-five dollars an hour when I worked behind the bar. People tipped a little bit from time to time, but tips were not necessary at all. In the US, however, tips were *everything* because servers and bartenders were barely paid an hourly wage. This made my job confusing because at times people tipped me extraordinary amounts of money and I didn't know why. Sometimes my boss showed up at the bar and gave me something like a hundred-dollar tip on a thirty-dollar bill, or someone else would tip me fifty dollars on a fifty-dollar bill. I didn't know how I was supposed to respond to that. *Do I owe them something now?* I wondered. *Like should I buy them drinks? How many?*

I tried to figure out what the other bartenders did but I couldn't get a straight answer. The best answer I got was from a bartender named Francesca. "You are a drug dealer," she said. "Just think about it like that, because that's the truth. You make their drugs, they tip you well. That's all."

Once I started bartending, I also made a lot of new friends and I quickly became a "local." I ended up buying a van from a friend for five hundred dollars, then I bought a new battery for the Exploder and sold it in Honolulu for seven hundred dollars. (Yeah, I screwed someone else over, it's true. I regret that now, but at the time I thought it was fair enough—I sold it for the KBB value in this dog-eat-dog world.)

Once I lived in the van, I had a lot more fun. On my days off work, I'd drive to different parts of Oahu and hike to beautiful waterfalls and mountaintops. I met up with Chili from time to time, went climbing with Wai and the crew, and started getting into freediving and acroyoga. From time to time, I also went sea kayaking, surfing, or paddleboarding with friends. Soon, the North Shore started to feel like home. I loved the people, the laid-back atmosphere of the place, the sea turtles, and the incredible sunsets. The only thing that I was really missing was my boyfriend.

I talked to Chris every few days or so. He seemed to be having a pretty good time catching big waves in Nicaragua. He even managed to find some massage work in a hotel but he wasn't making much money. There was one part of me that wanted to quit now and just go to Nicaragua to be with Chris, but there was another part of me that said, *I'm making so much damn money and having so much fun in Hawaii! How could I quit now?*

Instead of quitting and leaving, I persuaded Chris to come back to Hawaii in September. Since I was making a lot of money, I told him I would buy his flights. "If you come back here then I can work just one more month and save a few thousand dollars," I said over the phone, "and afterwards we can go to the Alps together and do the next winter season in Austria." We had been talking about snowboarding in Austria for a while, and now I finally had enough money to make this happen. "I can buy the flights from Hawaii to Europe too."

"Okay my Small." That's what he called me back then. "I'll probably need a ticket out of the US in case they don't let me onto the flight to Hawaii again, so let's figure out where to go exactly."

"Yeah, so we should plan now," I said. "One problem is that I'll need to go to Russia before the end of the year because I need to renew my Russian passport. It expires in November. So I can fly to Moscow, get the passport bullshit done, then maybe take a bus or something to Europe. What do you think? You want to come?"

"Wouldn't I need a visa for Russia though?" he asked.

"Yeah. But it shouldn't be too hard to get, I think."

It turned out that it was hard to get. Once we got off the phone, we contacted a few tourist agents and found out that Chris wouldn't be able to get a visa to Russia while he was in the US or Nicaragua. The tourist agents said that he would need to be in his "home country" to apply for the visa. Plus, it was expensive.

Chris called me back. "I don't think it's gonna work with this Russian visa," he said. "How about I fly to the UK and then meet you in Austria when you're done with your passport stuff? I have some friends I can stay with over there."

"Okay," I said. "So you can fly back to Hawaii in the beginning of September, we'll spend September and some of October here, then you'll fly to the UK and I'll fly to Russia. And then in November or December we can meet in the Austrian Alps. Kinda like that?"

"Yeah kinda like that, you Small."

"Okay." We bought one flight from Nicaragua to Hawaii for about 400 dollars, two flights from Hawaii to New York for 600 dollars, one flight from New York to London for 288 dollars, and one flight from New York to Moscow for 345 dollars. Altogether, the flights added up to approximately 1,600 dollars. *Expensive,* I know. *But what else could we do?* We probably would have stayed in Hawaii longer if it wasn't for my passport and Chris's visa situation.

* * *

In September, Chris was back in Hawaii. It felt fantastic to be together again. I introduced him to my new friends and showed him some beautiful new places around Oahu. We lived in the van together for the next month and I continued to work my ass off at Breakers, taking both server and bartender shifts. I didn't mind bartending at the time, but I *hated* those server shifts. Serving tables was very stressful and it gave me headaches and horrible back pain. I withstood the pain and took a lot of shifts, knowing that this job game would be over soon.

At the end of the month, I quit. It felt so damn good to quit. I told myself that this would be the last time I *ever* serve tables again. Then I bought two round-trip flights to the neighboring island, Kauai, just to do one special hike with Chris before we flew away for good. The trek I had in mind was called the Kalalau Trail, located on Kauai's infamous Na Pali Coast.

The Kalalau

Chris and I borrowed a lightweight tent from Wai, packed up our camping gear, and flew to Kauai in October. Once we were on Kauai, we hitchhiked to the end of the road on the northern coastline and camped on Ke'e Beach, near the Kalalau trailhead. By law, you're supposed to get a permit to hike the Kalalau Trail, but since permits were very expensive and basically impossible to get last minute, we decided to risk it and do the trail without one. We had heard that many people did this and that we just needed to watch out for the park rangers.

Chris and I woke up at first light hoping that the rangers weren't out yet. We had a quick bite to eat, then packed up our backpacks and snuck onto the trail. The trailhead was easy to find since there was a clear entrance with information about the trail and a bunch of warning signs. "Falling rocks!" Chris read the signs. "Hazardous cliff! Steep drop-offs along cliffside! Flash flood!"

"Yeah I heard that a few people died trying to cross the rivers on this trail, but that was during a storm. Today it's supposed to be sunny!" I smiled.

"Great," said Chris. He didn't seem as stoked about the trail as I was. The trail was somewhat difficult because it was eighteen kilometers long and weaved up and down the steep coastal mountains. Some parts of the trail were muddy and slippery as hell, so I walked carefully, trying not to fall. I enjoyed the beautiful views of the Pacific Ocean, the rocky cliffs, and the mountains in the distance. Chris didn't seem very impressed at first. He didn't like the mud or the fact that I was walking so slowly.

Along the trail, there were tons of fruiting guava trees. This seemed great at first, since we were able to have a delicious fruity snack whenever we wanted, but after a while of stepping over piles and piles of overripe slippery guavas mixed with mud and hundreds of fruit flies, we lost our appetite for this juicy treat. Eventually, our association of the sweet smell of guava fruit changed from "delicious snack" to "slightly repulsive warning sign for a slippery surface." We moved on and tried not to fall into the pools of squashed guavas.

Luckily, it didn't rain much while we were hiking the Kalalau Trail. The rivers were safe to cross and the trail that ran along the most dangerous cliffside was relatively dry and stable. There were many waterfalls and beautiful lookouts along the trail, but nothing compared to our final destination, Kalalau Beach.

"Holy crap!" My jaw dropped as we caught sight of the beach. "This is insane!" Huge walls of green and red mountains towered over the bright blue Pacific Ocean. "There it is! That patch of sand!" Chris's spirit improved a bit now. We trekked on, faster and full of excitement. Once we arrived at Kalalau Beach, we were in absolute awe. We sat on the beach looking out at a thick rainbow that ran from the mountains to the ocean. The view was absolutely mind-blowing in every direction. There were big caves on one side of the beach, exotic fruit trees on the other side, and a beautiful waterfall streaming down the unbowed, staggering mountains right behind the beach. The only downside was that there were *a lot* of people around Kalalau Beach. A lot more than we had expected, anyway. Most people looked like they were only there for a few days, but it was obvious that some had been living in this place for a long time.

There were so many people camping by Kalalau Beach that Chris and I had trouble finding a camping spot at first. All the best spots looked like they were taken by long-term dwellers. Some had great setups with fantastic views of the beach, well-built fire pits, many cooking pots and pans, books, hammocks, and a bunch of other stuff. After walking around for a while, Chris and I settled in a quiet spot by some small bushy trees. We set up our tent, jumped into the ocean, rinsed off under the waterfall, watched the sunset, made a fire, ate some food, then drifted off to sleep.

In the morning, I felt exhausted yet jittery with excitement. Chris was also in a better mood now that we weren't slipping around rotting guava fruit. We had planned to spend a few nights in the Kalalau, so we had time to explore the nearby area and the trail that ran up Kalalau Valley. We spent most of our first day relaxing on the beach, walking around the caves, and exploring the coast.

We noticed a lot of opihi (a sea slug that's considered a delicacy) on the rocks by the caves. I had eaten opihi before on Oahu, so I knew it was tasty. We peeled a few of the bigger sea slugs off the rocks using a knife and collected them in a plastic bag. On the way back to our tent, we noticed a couple of guys smoking a joint on the main trail. "These guys definitely live here," said Chris. They both had long hair, no shirts, no shoes, and they looked a bit scruffy.

"Hey guys," Chris walked up to them. "You guys know where to get some bud?"

"Yeah sure," answered the one with a long ponytail. "But I'll have to go up the valley to get it. How much do you want?"

"Just a bit, maybe a twenty. So you guys live here?"

"Yeah." The guy took a puff then handed his joint to Chris. "Up in the valley. I've been here a few years."

"Must be nice."

"Yeah, I love it here." The guy called himself Mowgli and his friend Steve. "Steve's been here about a year." We talked for a bit and asked what they do in this place day after day for so long.

Steve said, "I kinda do the same thing I do back home. Drink coffee, talk shit, play music, read books, make pizza, you know."

"Pizza in the jungle?" I asked.

"Yeah we make pizza all the time. You guys can come up and try some tonight if you want," said Steve.

"Yeah we even have a hand-built pizza oven up in the valley," said Mowgli.

"No way, that's awesome!" I said. "Sure, we'll try some." We hung around for a while, then walked up the valley with them. Chris and I were stunned by their fancy campsites. Steve lived on a plateau with remarkable views of the mountains; he had a big tent with a full-sized bed, a mattress, and a hand-built cabinet. Steve also had a nice outdoor living area with wooden furniture, a sturdy fire pit, and a bunch of cooking utensils.

Mowgli explained that flour was the best ingredient to bring to the jungle. "All you need to do is mix it with water," he said, "and you can make bread, pizza, or whatever you want. You can find everything else you need here in the valley. We've got a garden, fishing gear, hunting gear, basically whatever you need."

"What about cheese?" asked Chris.

"We trek out once every couple of months or so to buy cheese and flour from Walmart," laughed Mowgli.

"Heh. It doesn't go bad out here?"

"No, you'd be surprised how long cheese can last out here!" Mowgli took out some flour, mixed it with water and sculpted it into a ball of dough. Then he stretched the dough out onto a cast-iron pan, added some homemade tomato sauce, mozzarella cheese, a bunch of fresh vegetables, and some kind of pepperoni. He covered the pan with a solid lid and threw some coals over the top. "Dutch oven," he said. "Great for baking."

Chris and I took out our opihi, grilled them over the fire and shared them with Steve and Mowgli. We also brought a bag of dried fruit and nuts to share. "Man I would love to live out here for a while like you guys," I said. "How is it with the rangers though? I guess you guys don't have permits?"

Steve and Mowgli cracked up laughing. "Let's see. Twenty dollars per night, three hundred sixty days... Nope I don't have that kinda money!"

"Hah. Is that how much it costs?"

"Yeah the rangers only come around by helicopter," said Mowgli. "They raid this place once in a while but you can hear them coming so we just hide till they leave."

"I see," I replied. "Isn't it crazy that there's basically no place on Earth where you can just live freely without participating in the system? Like, by law, you have no choice but to join society, get a job, and slave your life away. Even just to get your basic needs."

"Yeah," said Mowgli, "it's hard to believe that living in the jungle is against the law."

"Meanwhile, people devoutly believe that they're "free" in this society. As if they have any real choices," I said.

"Like George Carlin said, 'The only choices you have are Pepsi or Coke, cash or charge, paper or plastic.' When it comes down to the things that really matter, you don't really get to decide," said Mowgli.

"Yeah and I think this valley is the perfect example," I said. "It shows that there is no place you can escape to anymore, at least not legally. I feel like people have this impression that if you don't want to live in this society, then you can just go into the forest and survive on your own, but you can't even do that anymore! Every piece of land is already "owned" by somebody and you need permission to live there. Isn't that nuts?"

"Yeah and it's not like you wanna do something bad if you don't wanna be a part of society," said Steve. "Maybe all you want is to grow some vegetables and make a pizza every once in a while." He smiled, took the lid off the cast-iron pan, and checked the pizza. "Done!" He slid the pizza onto a wooden board and cut it up into pieces. It was delicious!

The four of us ate pizza and chatted for a while, then Chris and I went back to our tent for the night. We were stoked to have met Steve and Mowgli. They said they could find some shrooms for us the next day and show us some more of Kalalau Valley.

"This place is going to be *insane* on shrooms!" I said. "Can't wait!"

Chris and I woke up early the next day, rinsed off in the waterfall, had some breakfast, and walked back up to Steve's place. He was playing guitar by his fire pit. "Hey guys!" he said. "I found this stuff for you. Don't know how good it is, it's a bit gooey. The guy I got it from said it's mixed with some fruit and stuff." He handed us a bag with a gunky reddish-brown square.

I opened it up and had a whiff. "It smells a bit fruity. Okay, thanks!" Chris and I grabbed a couple of handfuls and chewed on the sticky goo. "Doesn't taste as good as it smells." Shrooms never taste good, so that was expected.

A few minutes later, Mowgli came by and the four of us took off to explore the valley. The shrooms started kicking in little by little as the guys showed us the biggest bush in the world, where we climbed around like macaques; a huge rope swing, which kicked my hallucinations up a few notches; and an ancient stone that marked the spot where Hawaiians used to meet to trade goods. The view from this spot was out of this world. Then just when we thought it couldn't get any better, the guys took us to some incredible cascading freshwater pools. The water was cold, crisp, and clean enough to drink without a filter. We took a dip and filled up our water bottles. It felt fantastic.

After the refreshing swim, the guys showed us the Kalalau garden. "Here you have banana trees," said Mowgli as we walked into this massive paradise. "Papayas, coconuts, mangoes." He was pointing in different directions. "Guavas, avocados. Here are the potatoes, sweet potatoes, yams, and a bunch of different carrots."

"Wow, this place is amazing!" I couldn't believe how big this garden was.

"Here are some zucchinis, pumpkins, and string beans," Mowgli continued. "Chestnuts over there. Also, some herbs and different berries in that corner. Ah and over there, that's Jamaican passion fruit! It's a string of lilikoi that's extra big and sweet." He picked some fruit off a big vine and handed it to Chris and me.

"Wow!" I said as I slurped the seeds into my mouth. "Delicious! So who takes care of this garden?"

"Right now it's basically me and one other guy. But of course a lot of different people were involved at different times. The next thing I wanna do is build an irrigation system for the garden."

"That's pretty awesome," said Chris. "So you grow all this stuff for everybody?"

"Yeah, I just really like the idea of anybody being able to come here and take anything they need for free," said Mowgli. "Sometimes we have so much extra food that we bring it down to the tourists on the beach."

"Amazing," I said. The view from the garden was incredible as well. We gazed out at steep, triangular-shaped mountains and the deep valley below. The shrooms were kicking in and I could barely speak now. I felt like I was in awe and falling in love with the Kalalau. *I'll definitely have to come back here and stay for a while one day,* I thought.

After taking some vegetables from the garden, we hopped around a river, climbed a little waterfall, and made our way toward Mowgli's campsite. "Try to step on the rocks and not leave any footprints, okay?" said Mowgli. "I don't want to give away my position." It turned out that Mowgli lived in a cave toward the back of the valley. It was a pretty impressive spot. He had his own little garden with herbs, strawberries, and some fruits and vegetables. He also had a pretty cozy bedroom, a big kitchen, and a black cat.

"She keeps the mice away," said Mowgli as he pet her behind the ears.

We made a fire and Mowgli cooked some kind of delicious vegetable concoction. The four of us chatted for a while and continued to eat food for the rest of the evening. I never imagined that I would have ended up eating so much food on this trip! At first I was worried that perhaps Chris and I didn't bring enough food with us, but thanks to Steve and Mowgli, we barely even touched the food we had brought.

Chris and I went back to our tent in the evening, spent one more day in the Kalalau, then packed up our backpacks and got ready to trek back to Ke'e Beach. Before leaving, we handed Steve and Mowgli all of the food we didn't get to eat. "It's been great, guys, thanks for everything!" said Chris.

"Later!" said Mowgli.

"Aloha!"

I felt revived and rejuvenated from the Kalalau. *What a mind-blowing place,* I thought. *And what cool people!* It was good to know that there were some smart people in this world who simply refuse to participate in the system. It was also good to know that there was an amazing place that you can run away to. Perhaps it was "illegal," but it was there, in the Kalalau.

Chris and I walked the eighteen-kilometer trek back with ease. I was excited about the present and the future. *Our next adventure awaits! — Russia, then the Austrian Alps!*

37

Europe, 2015-16

I sold my van for about a thousand dollars before I left Hawaii, then I flew to New York with Chris. We visited my mother for a few days in October, then I packed up my snowboarding gear and flew to Russia. Chris flew to England on the same day. I didn't want to split ways with Chris again, but we basically had no other option. I had to get a new passport from Russia and Chris couldn't get a visa to enter Russia. We decided to spend the next month or two apart and then meet in the middle, in the Austrian Alps, once I had my new passport.

Chris and I chose to live in the Austrian Alps next because we wanted to do another snowboarding season. We knew that snowboarding would be great anywhere in the Alps, but that the living expenses in the French or Swiss Alps would be very expensive. The Austrian Alps, on the other hand, were affordable. Also, Chris knew German and had a European passport, so we were hoping he would be able to find some work this time around. We didn't know exactly where to go, since the Austrian Alps are a big place, so I contacted several people through Airbnb to see if we could find a cheap room to rent.

After sending over a dozen messages to random people in the Austrian Alps, I received a positive reply from a guy named Arthur. Arthur said that Chris and I could live with his mother for 400 euros per month (around 440 US dollars) if we could help her with things like shoveling snow and bringing up wood for the fireplace.

Arthur's mother lived in a village called Taxenbach, just a few kilometers away from the Zell Am See, Kaprun, and Kitzsteinhorn ski areas. Arthur said that we would have our own bedroom and bathroom, and we could share the kitchen and living room with his mother. He also said that there was a sauna in the house.

Next, Chris and I checked the prices of season passes for the nearby ski resorts. Surprisingly, we found out that you could buy one season pass for all of the mountains in the entire state of Salzburg for about 600 euros. That meant we could snowboard every day from November until May and we would have access to 77 ski resorts, 926 ski lifts, and 2,750 kilometers of ski slopes. That is a pretty good deal when it comes to snowboarding. Chris and I agreed to buy this "Super Ski Card" and confirmed our living situation with Arthur and his mother, Stefanie.

Now I got excited! I was at my dad's apartment in Moscow while I was making all these plans. I had handed in my old passport and was now waiting for the new one to arrive. As soon as it came in the mail, I packed up my backpack and was ready to hit the road. I bought a bus ticket from Moscow to Minsk, Belarus, for December 1, and another one from Minsk to Warsaw, Poland, for the day after. I was able to leave Russia and Belarus using my new Russian passport, but I could only enter Europe with my American passport. *Lucky me.*

The immigration officers scanned through my American passport at the Polish border and let me into Europe without a question! I was stoked! Since the rest of the borders between Poland and Austria were open, I knew that I wouldn't have to go through any more passport checks after this. The only tricky part was that technically, I was not allowed to stay in Europe longer than three months after my arrival. That meant that I had to leave Europe by March 1.

I stayed in a cheap hostel in Warsaw for one or two nights, walked around the city, then used a carpooling app called BlaBlaCar to find a cheap ride to the south of Poland. I found a ride to Krakow, a beautiful historical city with a big castle, a medieval town square, and a very cozy vibe. I stayed in another cheap hostel in Krakow for a few nights, walked around the city center, stuffed my face with Polish dumplings, and joined some Couchsurfing meet-ups to meet some locals. I also decided to visit Auschwitz, the Nazi concentration camp where over a million people were killed during World War II. Auschwitz was now a museum that served to remind us of our brutal past.

This was a bit heavy. I saw the trains that were used to bring the inmates to the concentration camp, I saw where people were forced to get undressed. I felt the icy wind cut straight through my skin. I saw where the inmates slept, where they shat, and where they were tortured. I saw the gas chambers they were killed in. I saw hundreds of pictures of people's faces, hundreds of pieces of clothing, piles of glasses, shoes, kids' toys, and a room filled with human hair. The guide said that when the Soviet Army liberated Auschwitz, they found *seven tons* of human hair. This was appalling, but the worst part about it was that I knew that these types of atrocities were not merely history. According to the UN, there are over 40 million slaves in the world today, over 100 million people fleeing from war, persecution, and conflict, and over 800 million people suffering from hunger. Genocides are not a thing of the past, nor are human rights violations, abuse, or torture.

Sometimes I felt guilty for continuing my quest to have fun— to surf, snowboard, and travel for fun, while the rest of the world burnt up around me. *Climate change will result in genocide on a whole new level,* I thought. *But what can I do about these problems?* I felt powerless. I had learned that patchwork solutions don't solve global problems, so I had no desire to attempt to join the UN or any other big organization. I had no desire to settle down and find a "job" because I felt like that only contributed to the problems, *so what could I do?*

The only organization worth working for is the Venus Project, I thought. *Maybe I can do something to help them.* I wasn't sure how though.

I calmed my mind and found a cheap BlaBlaCar ride to Budapest. I spent one night in a hostel in Budapest, checked out some awesome thermal hot pools, then caught another lift to Slovenia the next day. This wasn't the most direct route to Austria, but my friend Ziva (the one I used to hang out with in Sydney) happened to be living in

Slovenia at the time, so I decided to visit her. I caught two rides to the city Ljubljana, then took a fifty-minute train to Ziva's hometown, Kamnik. Once I was in Kamnik, I felt at home. Ziva and her family greeted me warmly and invited me into their house. It was great to reconnect with Ziva and to explore a little bit of Slovenia with her.

Ziva had a broken leg while I was visiting her, but fortunately, that never stopped her from having fun. We borrowed Ziva's mother's car and drove to the Mediterranean Sea, to Italy, and back to Ljubljana. We also made a loop around the northwestern part of Slovenia, which was absolutely breathtaking. Ziva limped around on crutches as we visited incredible icy mountain lakes, forests, and stunning mountainous vistas.

After about a week with Ziva, I was ready to head to Austria. Chris was now on his way, on a bus from England, and I couldn't wait to meet him. I couldn't find any BlaBlaCar rides going in the right direction, so I decided to hitchhike instead. I caught four rides and made it all the way to Taxenbach in about seven hours. I met Chris in the town center, reunited, kissed, and wished to never be separated again.

Austria

Taxenbach is a cute little Austrian village nestled in a beautiful valley surrounded by mountains. Chris and I walked around the village and noticed only one main road, one grocery store, a couple of bakeries, and a few wooden houses and small hotels. Pretty soon, Arthur and Stefanie picked us up from the town center and drove us to their home, which was about four kilometers down the main road and another kilometer up a steep hill.

"So are you guys planning to buy a car?" asked Arthur as we drove up the winding road. Over the internet, he had explained that it might be difficult to get between his house and the ski resorts without a car.

"I don't think so," I said. "But I think we'll be able to hitch-hike from the main road down there. I just hitched from Slovenia without a problem."

"Okay." Arthur didn't seem to be used to this idea of hitchhiking. "If it helps, you can borrow my car when I'm here or when I go to Norway. I usually live in Salzburg, but sometimes I have to go to Oslo for work, so I can leave my car with you guys if you want to use it."

"Oh that's really nice of you. Okay, thanks!" I replied. "What do you do for work?"

"I teach computer science and mathematics." Arthur seemed like a very smart, friendly, and helpful guy. "Here we are!" he said as we approached a two-story wooden chalet. "Home sweet home!" The place looked nice. It was authentic in a way, very "Austrian." Stefanie seemed very nice as well. She was small, cute, and over eighty years old. Unfortunately, she didn't speak one word of English and I barely knew any German so we couldn't communicate very well. Chris knew some German, but it was difficult for him to understand her thick Austrian accent.

We took our backpacks and snowboards out of Arthur's car and brought them inside, then we went downstairs to a cozy little room with a double bed. "This is your room," said Arthur. "You can use this electric heater. I hope it's warm enough for you." There wasn't much furniture in the room but there was a sink, which I thought was odd. There were also two warm blankets with huge pictures of deer faces. "You can use this bathroom," said Arthur as he pointed across the hallway. "And down the hallway is the sauna. We use it a few times a week, you are welcome to use it too. Not every day though, please." He smiled.

Next, we went upstairs to the living room and kitchen. Arthur explained that they heat the house with a wood-burning stove. "My mother needs help carrying wood from the basement to the kitchen," he said as he pointed to a big ceramic stove in the kitchen. "If you could help her in the mornings and evenings that would be really great, since I'm usually not home. She'll make the fire and everything, you just need to carry the wood."

"Sure, no problem at all," I said. Arthur showed us the gigantic pile of wood in the basement and he also explained that we may need to help Stefanie shovel the driveway from time to time. Chris and I were both happy to help.

Once Chris and I were settled in, we felt somewhat at home. It was cozy in our own little room and it was so great to be together again. We laughed, talked, and cuddled beneath the deer-faced blanket. In the morning, Arthur went back to Salzburg and Stefanie treated us with some delicious Austrian cheese and fresh bread. We helped her with the wood, then Chris and I walked down the hill toward the main road and hitchhiked to Zell Am See, the closest big town and ski area. We were ready to start snowboarding!

Unfortunately, this snowboarding season was off to another bad start. Even though it was already the middle of December, there was barely any snow on the mountains. Luckily, our season passes included a mountain called Kitzsteinhorn, which was over three thousand meters high and featured a glacier. Chris and I spent most of the next two months snowboarding there. The views were absolutely incredible from the top of this mountain and once it started snowing, the boarding was great too. The only downside was that it was difficult to get to this place without a car. The base of Kitzsteinhorn was only about twenty kilometers away from our new home, but hitchhiking wasn't always easy. Sometimes we waited in one spot for over an hour, sometimes it got cold, sometimes we got grumpy, sometimes we got hungry. But we always made it back one way or another.

When we weren't snowboarding, Chris and I would be cooking food, watching documentaries, or learning German. I used a phone app to learn new words and simple sentences in German, then I put everything I learned into practice while hitchhiking to and from the mountain. Most people who picked us up hitchhiking didn't speak English but were very friendly, so this was the perfect way to learn a new language.

Chris also tried to find a job as a masseuse while we lived in Taxenbach. This was a bit challenging since he didn't know German extremely well and he was new to the area, but he was accepted to work for two different hotels from time to time. Unfortunately, he wasn't able to find any consistent work. This bothered me because I knew that if he wasn't able to support us in Austria, then all the rest of my savings would dwindle away quickly and I would have to go back to the US to slave again; and most likely, Chris and I would have to separate again.

At one point, I got into a fight with Chris over this problem. "I can't handle being torn apart like this all the time," I said. "Being together for two months, then in different countries for three months, then together again for three months, then apart again for two month, over and over. I hate being away from you for so long, all the time! If we want to stay together, then we have to both *try* to make it work. If you can't support us this winter, then all of my savings will disappear and we'll have to leave each other again! I don't know how much more of this I can handle, honestly."

"I am trying hard to find a job," said Chris. "It's not as easy as you make it sound."

"I know it's not easy," I said, "but I did it last time, didn't I? Can't you find some other type of work? I mean, I worked in a fucking ice cream shop in Australia to be with you there, not like I wanted to do that job. And I worked my ass off in Hawaii. I worked overtime almost every week, doing something I fucking hated!"

"I'm not like you," he said. "I'll look for more massage work but don't expect me to be like you." Then he told me that he felt like he was following me around the world, as if I was forcing him into this situation.

I broke down crying. I had no idea that Chris felt this way. This whole time, I thought we were on this journey together. I thought we were just two humans on a beautiful planet, spinning around a star, living, learning, and exploring the world together, and doing whatever we could to keep ourselves together in this fucked up society. But it turned out that he was *following* me... *I would never want that, for either one of us.*

I walked away and thought about our relationship. *Was he really following me around the world?* I wondered. *We started our relationship at the end of 2013, when he came to Sydney. It was my idea to go to Lake Tahoe after that, sure. Then we split ways when I went to the Caribbean. After the Caribbean, I came back to Australia to be with him. Then I convinced Chris to come to Indonesia with me, but afterwards I came back to Australia for him. Then I had to leave because of my visa, I went to Sri Lanka, then I came back to be with him in Australia again. That was when the immigration officer told me that I could no longer come back to Australia after my visa expired. So once I ran out of money, I convinced Chris to come to Hawaii with me. What else could I have done at that point? I was broke as hell and desperately needed a job. I made a bunch of money in Hawaii, then I thought we had both decided to go to Europe together.*

I thought it over. *Maybe I was a bit pushy sometimes, but fuck it's difficult to survive in this bullshit society.* Eventually, Chris and I talked it out and agreed that we're in this together and we'll do what we can to make our relationship work. Our biggest challenge was simply to exist in one country at the same time, for a decent amount of time. This was only a big challenge because Chris and I had different passports. Actually, we had four different passports between the two of us, but none of these passports allowed us to live and work in the same place.

Chris is a citizen of both Australia and the Netherlands, so he was able to live and work in Australia and Europe, but I could only stay in either Australia or Europe for three months at a time. I'm a citizen of the US and Russia, so I was able to live and work in the US and Russia, but Chris was only allowed to enter the US for three months at a time, and he could not enter Russia without a visa. In fact, there was no place on Earth where both Chris and I could live together indefinitely and work legally (besides Svalbard, a very cold and expensive place in the Arctic Circle).

Speaking of this problem, soon I also had to worry about the expiration date of my European visa, which was March 1. In an attempt to solve this visa issue, Chris and I considered getting "married." Neither Chris or I believed in this idea of "marriage" but we were willing to give it a try if it allowed me to stay in Europe for the rest of the snowboarding season. We looked up the requirements for this ritual and soon realized that this would be a very expensive and perhaps impossible task. In order to get married, we needed original birth certificates, official translations of those birth certificates, some official papers from our embassies, translations of those papers, and a lot more. All of this would cost a ton of money and would take a long time to process. *Surely, my visa will expire before I even receive my birth certificate, let alone its official*

German translation and all the rest of these bullshit documents, I thought.

Before completely giving up on the idea, Chris and I also looked into what it takes to get married in nearby countries like Italy, Spain, Hungary, and Slovenia. Unfortunately, this stupid bureaucratic procedure was just as complicated in every country we looked into, so eventually we gave up. *Fuck it,* I thought. *Marriage is a bullshit religion anyway.* I never understood why two people needed a piece of paper or a big party to confirm that they love each other. *If you truly love each other, you should be able to be together and trust each other without any rings, papers, or parties.*

"Why don't you just do a visa run?" asked Chris as we were sipping coffee at the kitchen table.

"It's not so easy with Europe," I said. "The law says that I can only stay in the Schengen Area for three months out of every six months." The Schengen Area included Austria, Switzerland, France, Spain, Germany, Italy, Slovenia, Hungary, Poland, and several other European countries.

"So after three months in Europe you basically have to leave for an entire three months before you can come back again?" asked Chris.

"Yeah exactly, and those three months are up in like two weeks." I took a big slurp of coffee then pulled out my laptop. "I read something about Poland though. Like that maybe there was an old agreement between Poland and the US that bypasses this rule. I'll see if I can find some more info." I searched the internet and didn't find any official information about this rule, but I did read a few blogs that sounded promising. They explained that according to this old rule, US citizens are allowed to enter Poland and stay for three months, then they could leave the country (say to Ukraine or Belarus) and come back into Poland straight away and stay for another three months. Technically, they shouldn't be leaving Poland to travel to other countries in the Schengen Area after those first three months, but since the borders are open, who could tell?

"Back to Poland it is then!" I closed my laptop. This seemed like a very "gray area" rule, so I wasn't entirely sure that it would work, but I didn't have many other options so it was worth a shot. *In the worst-case scenario, I'll go back to Russia,* I thought.

Hitchhiking Europe

At the end of February, I packed just a few items of clothing into my backpack and hit the road. My plan was to hitchhike from Austria to Poland, take a bus from Poland to Ukraine, stay in Ukraine for a night or two, then take another bus back to Poland, and hopefully get a new entry stamp for another three-month stay in Europe. Chris didn't come with me because we didn't have much money left and he had found some work in Austria.

I wrote some notes on my phone while I was on this two-thousand-kilometer journey:

Hitchhiking. February 22, 2016

The first three rides were super cool. I was picked up by a Dutch security guard, then an art school teacher and musician. The teacher was really nice, happy to practice English and seemed like a really genuine person. Then I caught a ride with Richard, a super nice Austrian guy who only spoke German with me, for like two hours! He drove me out of his way a little bit to get me to a rest stop with a lot of people and then gave me a bottle of nice wine and a bottle of the best homemade apricot juice I have ever had. His family makes wine somewhere close to Vienna.

Then I was picked up by a mom and her two kids who just got back from holidays in Thailand. They were really nice, even gave me a tasty biscuit and an apple. They dropped me off at a rest stop outside of Linz where I was then picked up by an old Turkish man who creeped the shit out of me.

He stopped as I was holding my thumb out at the exit of the rest stop. I hadn't waited too long, in fact, the whole day at that point I hadn't even waited five minutes to get a lift. I didn't think too much of him, he was just a little old guy, quite short and skinny with short gray hair, darker skin, and light-colored eyes, maybe blue or green. He seemed nice and I didn't get any bad vibes from him at first. He told me he was going to Kaplice, a small Czech town just north of the border. He didn't speak a word of English but he did know some German so we were able to communicate at kindergarten level. When I asked him what he did for work, he told me that he wasn't working today.

We drove up the highway for about 20 minutes half in silence, half in me making awkward conversation in German. For example, I told him that I usually work in bars and restaurants, and he replied with, "And nightclubs?" then gave me a cheeky giggle, surely thinking about a strip club. Then, all of a sudden, he turned off the highway onto a dirt road that headed east. I checked the GPS on my phone and confirmed that there is no other way to get to Kaplice but the highway that we had just turned off of. He noticed this and told me that he needed to stop by his work.

I was getting a little weirded out thinking I really really hope this is not turning into a horror film scenario. We drove about 15 minutes out of the way on a thin gravel road in the beautiful north-Austrian countryside. There were a few houses and people around but it seemed like we were driving farther and farther into the middle of nowhere. He pointed to a big pile of granite and said that that was where he worked. Then we drove onto a different dirt road toward that pile of rocks and I felt relieved to see an actual building and a few people working there.

This creepy guy said hi to his coworkers, then parked his car and told me to wait while he went inside the office and got what looked like a bag of clothes. He also handed me a small bottle of crappy red wine. I didn't accept it and told him, "No thanks, I don't drink!" Then he drove farther into this granite mine and freaked me out some more. He said hi to a few coworkers in this place and seemed to make some pretty loud and exciting conversations with them. I didn't catch any of it but it made me feel better that there were people around, even if they were random miner guys. Eventually, he made a U-turn and drove back onto the dirt road. I think that he probably just wanted to show me off to his coworkers and will probably tell them later that we had sex or something like that.

Next, he drove back toward the highway and asked a few questions that I felt happy not to understand, then he laughed and touched my leg for a second. Then, he fiercely grabbed my leg and asked if I want to go to a hotel and have sex. I couldn't understand most of what he was saying but this part was clear. It's funny that the words *sex* and *hotel* are pretty much the same in so many languages. When I said no and plucked his hand off my leg, he tried to convince me that this was legal so we should do it. Hah. Once he understood that this was a definite *NO*, he said that he would drive me to the Czech border and drop me off there.

I was relieved to leave his car as soon as possible, even if it was earlier than we had initially planned. He parked the car just past the border and I quickly said bye and ran away. *What a creep-o!*

After being so creeped out, I wanted to be careful about who I got a lift with next, but I also just wanted to get out of there as quickly as possible. The next guy who pulled up was a younger-looking Czech guy, for some reason I wanted to trust him just because he was playing some Czech music that sounded similar to Rage Against the Machine. He dropped me off 10 kilometers up the road in Kaplice, where the creepy guy initially said he was going. This guy didn't speak anything but Czech so there wasn't much communication between us. He dropped me off at a really good spot where I was picked up in less than five minutes by a very sweet guy. This guy was about my age, he seemed really warm and genuine, and spoke probably the same amount of German as I do, so we were able to half-communicate. I was actually really surprised how far my recently learned German skills were able to take me on this trip. Hitchhiking really is the best way to practice speaking a new language!

So this guy dropped me off at a petrol station in a city called Ceske Budejovice. It was really sweet because he pointed out that Brno was straight ahead, I could find a bus station on the right and I could find him on the left, if I needed anything.

I was out of cardboard at that point and needed to make a sign for Brno. I probably spent about 20 minutes getting a new sign together and all I could find were two pieces of normal paper from a school behind the petrol station. This was really crappy because it was windy outside and really hard to keep the two pieces of paper together with the only object that would half-do the job—a bobby pin. I stood at this crappy spot for over a half hour before a nice lady told me that I was standing in the wrong place to get to Brno. She drove me to the right place, which was a roundabout that led to a highway.

This roundabout had pedestrian crosswalks before the entrance to the highway, so I figured this would not be a bad spot, since people would have to stop for someone crossing the street anyway. But these drivers were not impressed! I stood there for over an hour while people shook their heads at me, some honked signaling that there was nowhere to stop, and two cars stopped just to let me cross the road but did not want to give me a ride.

Eventually, I walked to another spot up the road. I probably stood there for another hour or so and finally caught a ride just as it was getting dark. The last guy who picked me up was extremely nice and genuine, he laughed and smiled a lot as he spoke pretty broken English. He drove me to Jindrichuv Hradec, about 60 km from where we were, then he dropped me off at the bus station and looked up the bus and train schedule for me.

The next bus to Brno was in an hour, so I walked around and found WiFi at a gas station, then booked a hostel in Brno for 7 euros. I also looked up how to get from the Brno station to the hostel. Everything went well from then on, I even managed to swap 7 euros for 200 Czech koruna with a nice man so I could pay for the bus and at least some of the hostel bed that night. Once I got to Brno, I walked to the hostel, had a nice glass of Austrian wine and some good sleep.

Now I'm on the bus from Brno to Krakow!

I kept in touch with my family while I was on this trip. I didn't tell them about the scary hitchhiking moments, but I did tell my dad that I was planning to go to Ukraine. He didn't like this at all. He told me all about the conflict between Ukraine and Russia, he said that it was very dangerous in Ukraine and that Russians were not welcome there, especially in the west, where I was planning to go. I told him not to worry because the conflict zone was in eastern Ukraine and I was only planning on going to one city in the west. "I'll go there as an American tourist," I said, "and I won't even tell anybody that I'm Russian!" If I had more money, I would have gone to Belarus instead, but since my savings were running low and Belarus was an extra four hundred kilometers out of the way, I decided to take the risk and go to Ukraine. *How bad could it be, really?*

Next, I took an overnight bus from Poland to Lviv, Ukraine. It seemed like a normal bus with normal people, nothing scary. According to the bus schedule, we were meant to arrive in Lviv at 6:00 a.m., so I would have plenty of daylight to find a safe hostel to stay in. I sat in the bus, gazed out the window, then took a long nap.

At around 3:00 a.m., the bus stopped, the driver turned the lights on and told everyone to take out their passports. *We're at the border*, I thought. I took out my US passport and kept the Russian one hidden deep within my belongings. Next, a Ukrainian immigration officer came onto the bus and checked everyone's passports, one by one. When he came up to me, he looked surprised and a bit unsettled. He stared at my passport photo intensely, then stared at my face, then back at the passport photo, then at my face again; he repeated this several times, then I laughed and said, "It's me," in English. He took my passport and moved on.

After about twenty minutes, I was called off the bus. It was cold, dark, and sleeting outside. The officer gestured for me to go into a small room for further questioning. I stood in this room for several minutes while two officers continued to examine my passport. At first, they stared at my passport photo and compared it to my face again, then they asked me to sign a piece of paper several times and compared my signature to the one in my passport. After this, they started asking me questions in Russian.

I didn't know how to respond to their questions. *If they know I speak Russian fluently they might search me and find my Russian passport,* I thought. *But I can't lie to them completely because on my US passport, it says that my last name is "Davletshina" and that I was born in Russia.* I decided to pretend like I understood just a little bit of Russian, but I did not speak it.

I spoke to the officers in English. "I was born in Russia," I said, "but I grew up in the United States. I am American." I showed them my US driver's license, a bunch of American bank cards, and anything else I could find. One officer squinted his eyes, then asked if I understood Russian. I replied with, "Very little," and pretended not to understand his other questions.

Then this big angry officer turned to his coworker and screamed (in Russian), "She understands *everything!*"

Oh fuck! I thought. *I'll pretend like I didn't understand **that**! This is a bit scary. Okay, just keep on faking it, I guess, there's no turning back now!* After another half hour of them looking over my documents and asking me questions that I pretended not to understand, they finally let me through the border. Now I wasn't sure if that was a good thing or not.

I got back in the bus thinking that maybe I should have listened to my dad this time. *Well, it's too late now!* I thought. *I'm already in Ukraine.*

Ukraine

It was still dark outside when the bus arrived in Lviv. I stepped off the bus and felt the sleet and cold wind hit my face. I didn't know exactly where I was or what I should do next. I was terrified to speak to anybody because I was afraid they might find out that I was Russian. I took out my phone and tried to figure out my exact location, but my GPS didn't work.

Eventually, I asked one lady where the city center was and whether I could walk there. I didn't want to walk in this terrible weather but I didn't have any Ukrainian money and the ATM at the bus station was broken. This kind lady said that the city center was too far away, then she offered to give me some change for the bus. She spoke a little bit of English and showed me the right bus to take.

It took about an hour to get to the city center by bus. It was no longer dark once I arrived, but it was very cold and gloomy. Soon, I noticed that there were soldiers with huge machine guns walking around almost every corner of every street. *Okay, let's go inside somewhere, NOW!* I thought. I walked into the first café I spotted. It was warm and cozy, it had WiFi, and the staff were very nice. They even spoke English! The funny part was that technically, I could have spoken Russian to everybody. Most Ukrainian people speak (or at least understand) Russian. I could also understand a lot of Ukrainian, since it is similar to Russian, but I was terrified to give myself away, so I pretended not to know the language at all.

I ordered a warm drink and used the WiFi to find a hostel. There was one located just two blocks away from the café and it only cost three euros per night. *Perfect.* I booked a bed, then walked over and checked in. Once I was in the hostel, I felt much safer.

The hostel was clean, cozy, and everybody there was friendly. I checked in with my American passport and didn't tell anyone that I spoke Russian. In a way, I felt like a spy, even though I wasn't trying to spy on anybody. After a shower and a bite to eat, I started talking to the people around me. I made friends with a local Ukrainian guy, a guy from Turkey, and a guy from Jamaica who was living in Kiev. The Jamaican guy's name was Nick, he seemed pretty cool. He told me that he was a doctor and he also played in a Ukrainian folk reggae band back in Kiev. Nick seemed to love the city Lviv, so he gave me a big list of places to see while I was there. He also said that he could join me for some sightseeing after about 4:00 p.m.

"Go check out the city!" said Nick. "Have fun!" This made me feel safe, so I left my Russian passport in the hostel and spent the rest of the day walking around the city. Lviv was a beautiful place. There were a lot of historical buildings, a big market square, a tower with a great view, a few big parks, and a lot more. The weather improved as I was walking around and it turned into a beautiful sunny day.

Once I was tired of walking, I decided to check out a restaurant that Nick had recommended. It was called "Kryivka" and was supposed to be located in the center of the city. I went to the address Nick had written down, but I couldn't find any restaurant there. I walked into what looked like an apartment building. On the first floor, there was one big wooden door with a closed window and nothing written on or around it. I walked upstairs and only found more closed doors. Once I came back downstairs, I noticed that the wooden door was open and two men were walking in. I asked them, "Is this Kryivka?"

Then a man dressed in leather towered over me and replied, "KRYIVKA!" pronouncing this word in a different, more Ukrainian, accent. "WHERE YOU FROM?" he barked in Russian.

Oh shit! I thought. "Oh okay, thank you! I'm from America, Bye!" I said as I walked away as quickly as possible. *I guess I forgot to put on an American accent when I said the word "Kryivka."*

Once I got away from this scary man, I got a phone call from Nick, saying that he could show me around the city. I told him that I couldn't find the restaurant he had recommended, so he offered to take me there. A few minutes later, Nick and I were back at the same big wooden door. I felt much safer now that I was with Nick though. *He's a black Jamaican guy, I'm American, we're clearly tourists, not spies!* I thought. *It's all good!* I didn't even tell Nick that I was secretly Russian.

We knocked on the big wooden door, then a security guard dressed in military clothes opened the small window and asked for a password. Nick said, "Slava Ukraine!" then chuckled, telling me this means "glory to Ukraine." The security guard opened the door, forced us to drink two shots of honey vodka, then let us in. On the other side of the door, there was an old bookshelf, a man with a gun from World War II, and a restaurant in the theme of an underground bunker.

"Fun place!" I said as I sidestepped the gunman. We walked through a small museum of military equipment and Ukrainian patriotic art, then went down to a cozy-looking restaurant. We ordered some drinks, some delicious Ukrainian dumplings, and a few other snacks. Then, Nick showed me the highlight of the restaurant. To the left of the bar, there was an area with a long hallway where you could shoot a BB gun at a target of Vladimir Putin's face!

"This is hilarious!" I said. I gave it a shot and got him right in the bullseye.

After this, Nick showed me a few more museums and themed restaurants. As the evening progressed, I felt more and more like this entire scary Ukrainian military vibe was just a gimmick. I mean, sure, the military was real and scary at times, and nationalistic anti-Russian Ukrainians do exist, but most Ukrainian citizens are just ordinary people. They are kind, friendly, harmless, and they like to laugh. By the end of the night, I felt so comfortable that I even told Nick and a few people at the hostel that I spoke Russian. They were surprised, but not offended or upset.

I had such a great time in Lviv that I didn't even want to leave so soon. Unfortunately, I had already booked my bus back to Poland, so I took off the next day. I took another overnight bus to Krakow, crossed the border without a problem and got a brand new stamp in my passport. I didn't want to hitchhike too much after that last incident, so I took buses and BlaBlaCar rides back to Austria. I was relieved to make it back without a problem.

Saalbach-Hinterglemm

Once I came back to Austria, Chris and I moved out of Stefanie's house and into our own apartment in a town called Saalbach-Hinterglemm. It was a cheap and crappy apartment but it was in a great location, right next to one of Austria's best ski resorts. Once we moved to this place, we no longer had to hitchhike to get to the mountain and Chris was able to find a bit more massage work. I spent the rest of the winter doing an online English teaching course, meeting new friends, and of course, snowboarding.

In a way, I felt like I had it all back then. I had a great boyfriend, a few good friends, I was traveling around the world, and now I was snowboarding every day. Although the visa and money situation was difficult at times, I enjoyed the adventures that traveling on a budget brought me into. The best part was that I felt like I had figured out what this world was all about. *Life can be easy, simple, and extraordinary,* I thought. *But people make it complicated. They tell you that you need to work like a slave all your life, when you don't. They tell you that you need shiny cars, new phones, and trendy clothes, when you don't. They tell you that you need so many bullshit things to have a great life, when in reality, you don't need much at all. Most people believe all of this and get trapped in jobs, debt, and misery.* I felt like I had escaped this trap and I finally understood what it was all about. *You have one life! It's short and beautiful, like a flower that blooms, withers, and dies. So enjoy it! Live it! Make the most of it and don't let anyone tell you how to live your life.*

Snowboarding alone in the Alps gave me ample time to think about the world and my place in it. I felt happy about my own life, but as time went on, I felt more and more concerned about the state of the world. As much as I would have liked to ignore all of the global problems I had learned about, I simply couldn't. CO_2 levels were now over 400 parts per million, glaciers were disappearing right before my eyes, and corals were going through another mass bleaching event. *Almost all coral will go extinct in my lifetime.* The world spent more than twice as much money on advertising as it did on renewable energy. Deforestation was at a scary, all-time high, as was biodiversity loss. *It's possible that the Amazon Rainforest could turn into a savanna within my lifetime. This would have catastrophic effects on the world's climate, not to mention on its incredible biodiversity.*

There were more tigers in captivity in the US than there were tigers in the wild in the entire world. The Great Pacific garbage patch was growing rapidly, microplastics were showing up in the Arctic, and over one-third of the world's fish stocks were overfished. *We are causing a sixth mass extinction!* Hundreds of millions of people went hungry, nine million people died of hunger each year, billions of people lacked safe drinking water and sanitation, meanwhile, the richest one percent of the humans on this planet owned the same amount of wealth as *all the rest.* NINE INDIVIDUAL PEOPLE owned as much wealth as HALF of the

ENTIRE HUMAN POPULATION. Around two million children were forced into the "child sex tourism" industry, millions of other children were enslaved in cocoa plantations, dangerous mines, and textile factories. Two in five healthcare facilities had no soap and water or alcohol-based hand rub. Over 1.4 billion people did not have electricity—and this was just the tip of the iceberg.

On top of all of this, even "privileged" people from rich countries seemed miserable. Any time I talked to a "normal" person, they didn't seem to enjoy their lives much at all. They hated their jobs and their lifestyles, they spent most of their free time on soul-sucking social media platforms, many were on antidepressants or drank a lot of alcohol (or both), and they would often say things like, "Oh Sasha, I wish I could live like you! But I don't have enough money!" *WHAT FUCKING MONEY? I have almost no money! And you don't wish you could live like me, you have no idea what that means. You wish you could live a fulfilling life without having to be a SLAVE. That's what you really wish for. But most likely, you defend the same bullshit system that enslaves you in the first place.*

I felt like the only people who truly shared my point of view were the ones involved in the Venus Project. Jacque Fresco talked about many of the issues that concerned me and he was one of very few people who were bold enough to say that these issues were a direct result of the structure of our society. *CO_2 emissions are rising because companies make money from burning fossil fuels. Deforestation is a problem because people want to sell more and more shit to each other—more meat, more palm oil, more furniture, more and more—because they want to make money. Overfishing— they want to sell more fish. Pollution, microplastics, climate change, and other environmental problems are just side effects of people seeking for profit over everything else. Why are millions of people dying of hunger while the world throws away thirty to fifty percent of the food it produces? Simply because food distribution is based on profit-making. Those who can't afford to contribute to the system go hungry.*

Why is there such a huge gap in inequality? Well, what do you expect when you play the Monopoly game? That's exactly what we're doing here on Earth. We're told that the point of our lives is

411

to acquire as much as possible. To acquire wealth, property, houses, and more. We're told that that's what makes you "successful." The entire structure of our society is just like a big, complicated game of Monopoly. The ones who are "winning" the game can easily acquire more and more and more, while the rest get screwed. What's even worse is that in our real life Monopoly game, nobody gets an equal start. Some players start with a lot of money, houses, and properties, others start with nothing. Two-thirds of the wealth of billionaires is inherited. If it wasn't, the game would still end up unfair.

Jacque Fresco claimed that we could do better than this. In fact, he had dedicated his entire life to developing and demonstrating such an idea.

"I would love to meet Fresco," I said to Chris as we were discussing some of this. "Before it's too late... You know he's a hundred years old now!"

"Yeah, he's getting old," said Chris. "I think he still does seminars in Florida though. Maybe you can go there and meet him."

"Hm, maybe. Isn't it crazy that he's still doing these things at his age? Would you want to come with me to Florida?"

"I don't think I have enough money," said Chris. "I have just enough for a flight to Nicaragua and that's basically it. But you can go to Florida and then meet me in Nicaragua after if you want." Chris and I were planning to go from Europe to Nicaragua after the snowboarding season was over.

"Okay. I don't have much money either, but after I get my tax return I'll probably have enough," I said.

"Do what you think is right." Chris was always very supportive of anything I wanted to do. I loved him for that.

Once I received my tax return, I had enough money to pay for a tour of the Venus Project's research center (which included Jacque's seminar) and a flight from Moscow to Nicaragua via Florida. I bought the flight then hitchhiked to Vienna, caught a BlaBlaCar ride back to Poland, and another ride from Poland all the way to Moscow. I got through the border without a problem this time. Chris took a bus to the Netherlands then flew to Nicaragua. I dropped my snowboarding gear off at my grandmother's house, packed lightly, and caught that flight to Florida.

38
Florida, 2016

I arrived in Miami at the end of April, 2016. I rented a car then drove about two hundred kilometers toward a little town called Venus. The Venus Project tour was supposed to start the next day. Once I was in Central Florida, I drove around a few random towns, got some greasy food for dinner, then looked for a safe place to park the car. I didn't have enough money for a hotel room, so I planned to sleep in the back of the rental car that night. I was sure I would be comfortable enough since it was warm in Florida and the rental car was spacious, but the problem was that everywhere I went, it looked ghetto as hell! I had no idea where to park safely.

After a while of driving around, I settled for a spot in front of a small park in a residential area. *It looks pretty quiet here,* I thought. *I'm sure it's safe enough.* I parked the car, put the back seats down, then climbed into the back and covered myself with a towel and some clothes. *Just sleep,* I thought.

Once I fell asleep, I had vivid nightmares about zombies trying to break into my car while I was sleeping in it. The zombies surrounded my rental car, banged on it, and tried to break the door open. Then, all of a sudden, I woke up to the sound of somebody yanking the door handle!

"What the fuck?!" I sprang up, expecting zombies.

"Are you all right in there?" asked a middle-aged man as he knocked on my car door. It was about 7:00 a.m. and the sun was out, so I didn't feel threatened once I realized that he wasn't a zombie.

"Oh, hello!" I said as I jumped into the front seat and rolled down the window. "Yes, I'm fine, I was just taking a nap."

"All right, just making sure you're okay. We get a lot of drug addicts coming to this park, that's all."

"Oh okay. Don't worry, I'm not doing drugs. I'll get on my way." I drove to a nearby town and got some coffee and breakfast at a local diner. I was a bit tired from the lack of sleep, but I was extremely excited to meet Jacque Fresco!

After breakfast, I drove to the Venus Project's research center. It was located down a long country road, surrounded by farmland. I recognized the entrance as soon as I saw it—there was a white gate with a black "Venus Project" sign. I drove in and parked the rental car by a white dome-shaped building, a pond, and some palm trees.

"Hello there!" A tall young guy came out of the building. "Be careful, don't go too close to the water! There are alligators in there," he said.

"Okay, sure," I replied. The guy's name was Saso. He was a volunteer and he seemed quite friendly. He escorted me into the building, where I met Jacque Fresco and his partner, Roxanne Meadows.

I felt a bit shocked when I first saw Jacque. He was so small, frail, and skinny. He didn't seem well. *I guess I should have expected this,* I thought. *I mean, the man is one hundred years old.* Roxanne greeted me and Jacque smiled softly as he sat on the couch. Then two local Floridian women came into the building to join the tour.

Roxanne led the seminar and explained several concepts about human behavior, the flaws of our current system, and the proposals of the Venus Project, all concepts that I was very familiar with. Jacque tuned in every once in a while and went on a bit of a rant.

"During the Great Depression I saw that there were still products in all of the stores," said Jacque, "but people didn't have the money to access those products. So I realized that there must be something wrong with the rules of the game we play—the way that society operates. I realized that these rules were old, inadequate, so I began to work on the redesign of society." Jacque was explaining

414

what I had heard him say in his recorded lectures, but it seemed like this was difficult for him. Unfortunately, Jacque had Parkinson's disease, his hearing and vision were very poor, and he seemed like he was in a lot of physical pain. It was very sad to see him in this condition but it was also inspiring to see that despite all of this, Jacque was still going at it—he was still talking to people about what he thought was important and even in his weak and fragile state, he was still determined to change the world. Seeing this inspired me even more, and made me want to fight for him and his ideas.

After talking for a little while, Roxanne gave us a tour of the research center's property. She showed us some more unique-looking buildings and many of Jacque's models and renderings. There were models of different houses, apartment buildings, aircraft, boats, transportation systems, bridges, circular cities, cities on the sea, megastructures that could house an entire city, and more. The city and megastructure designs included integrated transportation systems, agriculture, services, and prefabricated modular homes, some in the form of plug-in capsules.

Roxanne explained the concept behind each of Jacque's designs. "A lot of the buildings are dome-shaped because this type of design is very efficient. It uses a minimum amount of resources and has maximum strength and stability. You can see that there are no weak corners in this building," she said as she pointed to the walls and ceiling of the building we were standing in. "You see, the Venus Project isn't just about pretty buildings and advanced technology or automation, it's about an integrated systems approach to problem solving. Each building is designed for a specific function. Each city is designed for maximum efficiency. Not the kind of efficiency that you hear business people talking about, but true efficiency. Efficiency in terms of resource and energy use, waste, and other aspects of living systems."

"So clean energy, recycling, things like that?" asked one of the Floridian women.

"Yes," said Roxanne, "the city would use clean energy and will be in harmony with the local ecology. The aim would be to provide all people with the highest possible standard of living while protecting our natural environment. The city will also be able to change, grow, and adapt to people's needs as our technology advances and our needs change. It should function more like an evolving integrated organism rather than a static structure."

I walked around and admired the little models. I liked the idea of these cities but I never took them too literally. I had always regarded Jacque's designs as an example of what could be achieved if we put our minds toward global problem solving. I never thought that building such efficient cities would provide us with solutions to our problems, but rather, I thought that solutions to the structure of our society could provide us with such efficient cities and a different type of life.

To me, the most important aspect of the Venus Project was the idea that the environment shapes human behavior and that our human environment is largely determined by the structure of our society. Jacque and Roxanne explained that our society was structured around money. Most people wake up and go to work in order to get money. They use this money to get access to housing, food, clothes, and almost everything else that they need and want. Because money is such an integral part of this society, people are pushed to prioritize money over almost everything else, and this leads to destructive problems.

But can there be another way? Perhaps there could be. There is no cosmic law that forces humans to trade with each other in order to get access to everything they need. Jacque Fresco claimed that we have the resources, we have the technology, and we might even have the brains to provide all people with what they need and want without the use of money, debt, barter, servitude, or any other kind of trade. In order to do this, we need to automate as many jobs as possible, create an abundance of goods and services, and give people free access to this abundance. This was one of the main concepts behind the Venus Project's idea of a resource-based economy.

"But if people had access to everything they needed and wanted, wouldn't they go crazy and start accumulating too much stuff?" asked the Floridian woman as we walked out of the building.

"That's why education is so important," I said. "People's values need to change. Think about this—imagine you took some people from a primitive tribe in the jungle and you dropped them off in New York City without teaching them how to behave there. Without any kind of guidance, the tribal people would behave the only way they know—they would probably poop behind a bush, kill squirrels for dinner, and cook them over a fire in Central Park. In the same way, if you took people from today's culture and dropped them off in a place where they had access to everything they wanted, they would probably hoard a lot of stuff, take selfies with all of this stuff, and then post about it on Instagram to get "likes." I think today's people don't realize how primitive they are."

"People's values and ways of thinking need to change before we can make any significant changes to the social system," said Roxanne. "Today's people aren't ready for this kind of thinking."

"I would love to help you somehow," I said to Roxanne. "I've known about the Venus Project for a while now and I really appreciate all the work you do." I told Roxanne a bit about my background and education as Saso walked up to join our conversation.

"So you speak Russian?" asked Saso.

"Yeah," I said.

"You know, the Russian-speaking team is actually the biggest activism team we have, but we have some communication issues with them. We could use a good Russian-English link."

"Oh, well I can definitely help with that!" *Wow, I could be the missing link!* I thought, jokingly.

"We can get you into the next orientation process to become a point of contact, if you're interested," said Saso. "That'll involve going over some educational material and meeting online once a week for group discussions with volunteers. We can also get you in touch with the Russian-speaking team then."

"So is that kind of like a course?" I asked. "Does it cost any money?"

"We don't like to call it a course, since the orientation process is not an official course. You would have to watch some lectures, read some material, and take some notes though. That will allow you to go over just some of the basic topics that we talk about here at the Venus Project, but of course you won't be an expert on these subjects just from completing the orientation process. Oh and no, it

417

doesn't cost any money. It's run by volunteers and we don't feel the need to charge for it."

"Oh okay. Super, I'd love that!" I said.

"The only thing is, the next orientation process might not start for a few months. We have one going now, so we'll start the next session once this one is over," said Saso.

"Okay, no problem at all. That sounds great!" I gave my contact details to Saso and Roxanne at the end of the tour, then I hopped into my rental car and drove back to Miami.

I didn't know where I would sleep that night but it didn't really matter. I was so excited that I didn't want to sleep anyway. I drove around Miami for a while, parked by the beach, took a little nap, and then caught my flight to Nicaragua the next morning.

39

Nicaragua, 2016

Chris and I planned to go to Nicaragua next because we had agreed to work at a new surf camp in a place called Playa Maderas, on the southwest coast of the country. The idea behind this surf camp was to provide a "packaged vacation" that included accommodation, meals, transportation, and surfing lessons; so the camp needed a few different staff members.

Chris found this gig last time he was in Nicaragua, when he met two German brothers who were building this camp. Now that the brothers had finished building the infrastructure, they invited Chris to work as their lead surfing instructor. Chris was meant to give surfing lessons to the guests and also teach the local surfers how to teach surfing. Chris also convinced the brothers to hire me as a bartender. Since the bar was newly built, I was meant to set it up with the right equipment, create a drink menu, and teach the staff how to make drinks. The agreement was that Chris and I would get food and accommodation in exchange for the work we did, rather than money.

Once I arrived in Nicaragua, I took some local buses to get to a coastal town called San Juan del Sur. It was hot, dirty, and humid in the Nicaraguan cities and bus stations, but it felt great to be on a new adventure. I managed to get around without a problem because I still remembered some basic Spanish. Once I was in San Juan del Sur, I found WiFi, texted Chris, and soon I was back in his arms. It was great to see him again, he already had a sexy tan. I also met the two German brothers, Max and Lucas. They were both quite young. Lucas was twenty-five years old and Max was only twenty-two. We hopped into their four-wheel drive pickup truck and made our way to the camp.

"It's gonna be a bit of a bumpy ride," said Lucas as we drove off the paved road.

"No problem!" We drove through a dense jungle and onto a crazy dirt road that went up a mountainous slope.

"We built this road for the camp," said Max as he maneuvered the truck over big rocks, holes, and bumps. "We'll try to improve it later." He smirked.

We arrived at the camp after about twenty minutes of bouncing around like crazy. I hopped out of the truck and looked around. "Very cool spot!" There were two yellow buildings, an empty bar, a big patio with comfy-looking couches, and a beautiful infinity pool that overlooked the jungle and the Pacific Ocean. The sound of birds, insects, and other jungle creatures was mesmerizing. We walked through the property and heard the deep, scary growls of howler monkeys, one of the loudest land animals on Earth.

The only downside was that Chris and I had to sleep in a dorm room with a bunch of other people. Also, Chris wasn't very happy about one of our coworkers. "It would be nicer here if I didn't have to hear Celine's voice all the time," he said. "Fuck she's annoying!" Celine seemed nice to me but she did have a very high-pitched voice and a thick Swiss accent. She helped in the kitchen in exchange for food and accommodation.

Since this camp was newly built and the guests hadn't arrived yet, there wasn't much work for any of us to do at first. Chris wrote out a bunch of surf theory lessons and I made a list of the bottles and bar equipment that the brothers needed to buy. In order to do the rest, I needed the equipment and Chris needed guests.

After a few days, another girl from Switzerland showed up. She was also meant to help out in the surf camp in exchange for food and accommodation. So now there was a group of about six people who were staying at the camp and getting free food, but since there were no guests, there wasn't much work for anybody to do. The brothers also paid a salary to a few local people who worked on the property and in the kitchen.

After a week or two, Max and Lucas started to get stressed about money. Chris told me that they were able to invest into this surf camp because they had received a big inheritance from their father, but now this money was running low. They also started to drink a lot. Every night, there was at least one bottle of rum or a case of beer in the bar, and every morning it was empty.

* * *

Eventually, our first guest showed up, followed by another guest, and then a group of four guys from Switzerland. Unfortunately, the brothers continued to stress out about money and drink a lot. After a few weeks, the situation turned ugly. I don't remember exactly what happened, but there was a lot of drama. *Stupid, unnecessary, human drama.* Somebody called someone else a bitch. Someone borrowed money from somebody else and didn't return it. Someone stole somebody else's car. That person threatened to come to the surf camp and shoot everyone. He had a gun. Someone else threatened to call the cops. The cops came and brought them both to jail. Jail looked very scary. Someone else bailed them out. Somebody didn't want to pay back the bail money. Someone was in love with somebody else, that somebody didn't love them back. Someone wanted to steal someone else's gold. Someone brought a very young kitten to the camp, the camp's dog almost killed the kitten, we all fought over this. *Drama, drama, drama.* Unsurprisingly, the brothers' drinking habit made all of this drama even worse.

After a few weeks, Chris and I decided to leave. This just wasn't fun anymore. We packed up our backpacks and stayed in a bamboo hut by the beach for a few nights. It was quiet, peaceful, and cozy. There were tropical plants, birds, and howler monkeys all around us. It was just Chris and me again.

"Now what do we do?" I asked.

"I don't know," said Chris. We were in a shitty situation. Both of us were almost completely out of money again and now we had to pay for our own food and accommodation.

"I guess I'll have to go back to slavery now," I said. "And we'll have to separate again…"

"Didn't you apply for some English teaching jobs?" asked Chris.

"Yeah." I had applied to work as an English teacher in different schools in Central America while we were still at the camp. "I got an email today. I was accepted to teach at a school in Honduras for four hundred dollars a month. I'd have to sign a nine-month contract and live in the capital city."

"Oh," he said. "Sounds like slavery."

"I don't think there's any point of working for such a low wage. I can get four hundred a night bartending in the States." I knew it would be much easier to just go back to the US, work in a bar for a couple of months, save money, quit, and then travel around the world without being tied down to a job. The problem was that we didn't have enough money for two flights to the US, nor did we have enough money to sustain both of our lives in the US. Plus, Chris's visa would only allow him to stay in the US for three months and he would probably need an onward flight just to get into the country.

Soon I became angry. I noticed my own behavior change as the last bits of my savings trickled away. I became harsh, jealous, and controlling. I hated this but I felt like I couldn't help it. I was upset that Chris hadn't been able to save any money in Austria, while I had worked so hard in Hawaii. I had bought so many flights and paid for so much of our food, accommodation, and lives together, while Chris had barely managed to pay for one month of rent. But I also knew that I shouldn't be mad at him for this. I could never fully get over what Chris had told me in Austria, that he felt like he was *following* me around the world. This killed me. I didn't want him to follow me. I didn't want to force him to work or to come to the US with me. I didn't want to force him to do anything he didn't want to do. But now that we were out of money, I knew that he would either have to follow me or we would have to split ways again.

"I don't think I can handle this anymore," I said as I broke down crying. "I told you in Austria that I couldn't handle it anymore. I love you so much but I can't stand being torn apart like this all the time. I'm so tired of all these bullshit visa laws, they're killing me! I put so much energy into our relationship, just to keep the two of us together in this bullshit society." Streams of tears rolled down my face. "I think I need to be on my own for a while." I never, ever thought I would break up with Chris, ever. But somehow, I felt like this was what I needed to do now. "I want to do something else with my life. I want to put my energy into something more important, like the Venus Project. I want to at least *try* to do something about the world's problems, but in order to do that I can't spend all of my energy on making money and getting around visa laws just to keep us together. I think I need to go on my own path for a while. I'm sorry."

Chris didn't say much. He was upset but he didn't try to convince me to stay with him. He also had some deep-rooted psychological problems that ultimately I realized I couldn't help him with. I thought that perhaps this breakup would be best for both of us. *Maybe he can overcome his problems on his own,* I thought. *I only make things worse for him when I behave like a controlling bitch.*

I continued to cry as he held me in his arms. I cried all night. I cried when we kissed, I cried when we made breakfast in the morning, and I cried as I bought a flight to Hawaii. Now we had just a few days left together. We packed up our backpacks and took a bus to a town called Popoyo. It was a small, broken-down coastal town with a few crappy hotels and some great surf. I cried as I watched Chris surf big, powerful waves. In the evening, I tried not to cry.

As the fading light caressed the ocean, Chris and I took a long stroll up a steep grassy hill. We watched the sky turn orange, then pink and purple, as we spun, like two small dots entangled in the bending light. He held me by the hips and kissed me, then walked me down the hill and to a little beach bar. We sat on wooden stools by a fire pit and listened to a live acoustic band. I was mesmerized. I stared at the stars and into the fire, clenched the sand in my hands, and listened to the band play "Wicked Game." The singer was phenomenal. When we came back to the hotel, Chris and I made love for the last time and I cried again.

The next day, I packed up my backpack, got on a bus to Costa Rica, caught a flight to Mexico, and then another flight all the way to Hawaii. Once I was on the North Shore, I met an old friend who cheered me up.

"You know, Sasha," said my friend Niv, "life is like a ride, or a long walk. There are ups and downs, challenges, and beautiful times. Sometimes the walk is easy, sometimes it's fun, sometimes it's rough. Sometimes you walk alone, sometimes, people may join you. Some people may walk with you all of your life, others may come and go all the time. Some may walk right by your side for a very long time, then split ways forever. Some may return. Some are there just for the good times, others are there only for the uphill battles. But in the end, it's your walk, so don't stress. Be grateful for each step, for each companion, and for each moment that you spend alone."

"Thanks, Niv," I said. I took a deep breath and gazed at the deep blue ocean. "I guess it's not so easy to share your walk with others when all you want to do is trek off the beaten path!" I smirked.

40

The End & the Beginning

The first thing I needed to do in Hawaii was fix my money situation. I stayed at a friend's house on the North Shore of Oahu, borrowed some money to buy a van to live in, and applied for work in every bar and restaurant I could find. I would have liked to have worked at Breaker's again, but unfortunately, they didn't want to take me back. Instead, I found a job as a waitress at a new restaurant called Roy's, in Turtle Bay.

I worked at Roy's for the next seven months, saved about twenty thousand dollars, quit, then traveled around all of the accessible Hawaiian Islands for another three months. I traveled with Emma at first, then with a friend named Aaron. We slept on different beaches almost every night, bathed under waterfalls, and spent our days trekking through forests, mountains, and volcanoes. We also kayaked up the Na Pali Coast; swam with dolphins, turtles, and manta rays; and watched the Kīlauea lava pour into the open ocean. I had such a great time on the Hawaiian Islands that I almost forgot what I had come there for. My mission was supposed to be to make some money and then move on with my life—to travel on, to volunteer for the Venus Project, and to try to do something important in this world. *In Hawaii, it's easy to forget about the problems of the world, but that doesn't make them go away.*

* * *

Jacque Fresco passed away on May 18, 2017. This was sad to hear, but not surprising. I only hoped that he didn't suffer too much. A few weeks later, I finally joined the Venus Project. *Jacque may have died,* I thought, *but his ideas can live on through us.*

In order to become a volunteer for the Venus Project, I had to take a quiz, pass an interview with an admin, and then go through a five-month orientation process. I was told that after I finished all of that, I would become a point of contact (PoC) for the Russian-speaking Venus Project team.

I wasn't sure why I needed to go through all of that just to be a volunteer translator/communicator between the teams, but I was very excited to get involved so it didn't bother me. The quiz was extremely easy, sometimes in a comical way, and the interview went well. After I passed the quiz and interview, I left Hawaii and caught a flight to New Jersey to visit my mother.

Once I was in New Jersey, I began the orientation process and I was added to the online chat of the Russian-speaking Venus Project team. What happened next, I did not expect at all.

It turned out that there were big BIG problems between the teams (not only communication problems) and I was thrown right into the middle of a huge mess. I was introduced to problems upon problems upon problems. All internal issues, having to do with bureaucracy, laws, rules, trust, and so on.

I ended up spending almost every minute of every day writing and translating messages, contacting different people from the Venus Project, and digging into as much information about the organization as possible. At the time, I felt like this was the most important thing in the world. I felt like the Venus Project was the most important organization in the world and that solving these problems was absolutely crucial. Because of that, I flew to Florida a second time to talk to Roxanne Meadows about these problems in person.

I bought a round-trip flight from Newark to Florida, rented a car, drove 220 kilometers from Miami to Venus, spent an entire day discussing these problems with Roxanne, and then flew back. Unfortunately, that didn't solve anything, so then I wrote and translated a twenty-two-page document to better explain what the Russian-speaking team wanted to communicate. Unfortunately, that still didn't solve much. Then, I got into a series of long conversations with Roxanne and other Venus Project admins about even more problems.

I couldn't stay at my mother's house for too long, so in August, I decided to go to Russia. I flew to Moscow then took the Trans-Siberian Railway across Russia with my friend Maricruz. I continued to volunteer for the Venus Project while I was on this trip. Whenever I had free time, I continued writing, reading, and translating messages. Wherever I found WiFi, I continued communicating with the teams and doing my work for the orientation process.

Once Maricruz and I got to Irkutsk and I caught a glimpse of Lake Baikal, I decided to settle down for a while. Maricruz traveled on to India but I decided to stay there in Siberia. I wanted to slow it down. I wanted to read, to learn, to write, and to watch the seasons change. I searched through the local classified ads and found an old one-bedroom apartment next to a riverside park in Irkutsk. The rent cost 250 dollars per month for the entire place. No roommates, no bills. *Perfect.*

I unpacked my backpack, set up the internet, and took out my laptop. Then I put all of my time and effort into attempting to solve the Venus Project's internal problems. I kept in touch with the teams every single day, I wrote and translated over one hundred pages of texts and documents, I talked to dozens of people, and I put a ton of effort into this organization. But nothing worked. I tried harder and harder, but it still didn't work.

Eventually, I realized that it wasn't going to work. I realized that the Venus Project was not what I had expected it to be, and that this wasn't going to change because of me. I realized that Jacque Fresco's ideas and the organization that he had founded were two very different things.

I realized that Jacque was now gone and that the people running the main (English-speaking) Venus Project organization were incompetent and were even contradicting what Jacque used to talk about. I realized that the people behind the Venus Project were just "normal" people with "normal" lives and "normal" values, emotions, and ways of communicating. I realized that the whole organization was a strict hierarchy, with Roxanne at the top, and barely anything could be done without her permission. I realized that the Venus Project was stagnating because of all of this.

Jacque used to tell people to always question everything and everyone, to take in new information, to keep yourself updated, to let experts make decisions, to arrive at decisions through research, and so on, I thought, *but it seems that no one dares to question Roxanne or any idea behind the Venus Project.* I felt like Roxanne's word was the final word, regardless of whether she was an expert on the subject or not, while other people's advice and opinions were rarely considered. Eventually, I found blogs and resignation letters from past volunteers that all told a similar story. They confirmed that my experience with the Venus Project was not unique.

In reality, the problems I was trying to solve were stupid. They had to do with things like changing the name of the team's social media pages, sharing information, posting on social media, getting permission to translate Jacque's lectures, having "official status" in social media, blocking "imposters," and so on. I realized that if the Venus Project wasn't able to overcome these little problems, there was absolutely no way in hell they were ever going to change the world, no matter how great Jacque's ideas were.

Eventually, I kind of gave up. I finished the orientation process and became a point of contact at the end of 2017, but I stopped going out of my way to help the Venus Project. Once I was a PoC, I was added to a group chat with all of the other PoCs from around the world. There were a few dozen volunteers in that chat, but there wasn't much going on in there; it was mainly about chit-chat. I stayed in the PoC chat for a while because I still valued Jacque's work, but I no longer bothered trying to fix the ongoing problems between the Venus Project and the Russian-speaking team.

2017-2019

At the end of 2017, I decided to start my own blog and I also found out about the TROM project, which I was extremely impressed by. The project's website, tromsite.com, included a fourteen-hour documentary, dozens of fascinating e-books and videos, as well as a ton of curated material like documentaries, news, and podcasts. I learned that most of the TROM books were originally written for the Venus Project. They used to be called *TVP Magazine* and the person writing them used to be highly involved in the Venus Project. I learned that this person's name was Tio. He used to be as passionate as I was about the Venus Project, but a number of internal problems caused him to move away from the organization and focus on his own project. I contacted Tio and offered to help with TROM.

I spent the next two years in Siberia, learning more and more about the Venus Project, TROM, our society, and our world. I wrote many blogs and hosted weekly meet-ups based on the TROM documentary. I also got a part-time job as a hiking guide for a group called Syberia Top, so I got to explore some of the most spectacular natural places in Siberia. I climbed steep mountains, crossed wild rivers, and got to see frozen waterfalls, plateaus, boulders, hot springs, and the world's deepest lake in all of its beauty. I swam in Lake Baikal in the summer, watched the surface water freeze in the fall, and hiked on top of its crystal-clear two-meter-thick ice in winter. I also got to dive beneath its icy crust. *This was spectacular.* In the spring, the ice broke up and melted, then the cycle repeated itself.

In 2018, I hitchhiked to Mongolia, camped along the steppe, and explored Khuvsgul Lake, Gorkhi-Terelj National Park, and the Gobi Desert. The vast desert was astounding. The experience, priceless.

In 2019, I isolated myself in a small village by Lake Baikal and forced myself to work on this book. I rented a little house by the lake for about five dollars per night and acquired a bike with spiked tires for about the same price. The house was old and didn't have running water, but it was in a breathtaking location right across from Olkhon Island. I guess nobody wanted to live there during winter as it got down to -37°C at one point, but I absolutely loved it. I'd spend my mornings writing and sipping hot tea, then I'd take a break by riding my bicycle on top of the frozen lake.

The bike allowed me to explore every corner of the southern end of Olkhon Island on Lake Baikal. I rode over crystal-clear, cracked, and sometimes bubbly meter-thick ice, I found enormous icicles, biked to beautiful windswept islands, climbed mountains, and watched sunsets over the frozen lake. Then I'd come home and write some more.

I didn't manage to finish my book by the time I left this village, but I did make some progress. In the meanwhile, Tio wrote a book that made me reevaluate the entire perspective I had on solving the world's problems. His new book was called *The Origin of Most Problems*. A discovery it was.

A Realization

Eventually I not only realized that the Venus Project wasn't going to save the world, but I also realized that perhaps Jacque Fresco's idea of a resource-based economy wasn't all that special or important after all. Don't get me wrong, I still felt that this idea was inspirational, perhaps it really was the best idea about how to organize our society, but unfortunately, that's all it was—*an idea about how to organize our society.*

There have been many great ideas about how to better organize our society. The idea behind communism, for example, was to create a technologically advanced society with common ownership of the means of production and free access to the goods and services that were produced. The goal was to eliminate scarcity, automate jobs, end the exploitation of labor, and to create an equal society with no social classes, state, or money. The so-called attempted implementation of this idea, however, was an entirely different ballgame. Almost every time a country tried to "implement" communism or socialism on a large scale, it turned into a huge disaster. It was so bad that most people now associate the word "communism" with an oppressive dictatorship rather than with an equal society based on abundance.

Technocracy was another interesting idea that advocated for a world without money. The technocracy movement emerged in the US in the early 1900s. The proponents of this idea claimed that our problems were technical, and that everything had a mechanistic nature to it, including our own behavior. Therefore, if we applied the scientific method to the social system and allowed experts to arrive at decisions based on science (rather than profit), we could create a sustainable society. They claimed that we no longer lived in a state of actual scarcity, as we had the technology to produce abundance for everyone (in North America). They claimed that the "price system" kept us in a state of artificial scarcity and perpetual inefficiency.

Technocracy proposed to conduct a survey of the resources in North America, to measure everything in energy units, and to produce things for practical use, rather than for profit. Technocracy criticized the price system, which not only included capitalism, but any system in which goods and services were exchanged, bought, or sold. As early as the 1930s, they claimed that North America was capable of producing such an abundance that people would no longer need to work for wages or trade for the goods and services produced, and they wrote detailed articles to showcase how this was possible. Technocracy also advocated to automate jobs; to give people free access to all public services including housing, transportation, healthcare, and education; and to allow people to have more free time to pursue their creative desires. After the early 1930s, however, people started to lose interest in this movement and there was no attempted implementation of this idea.

There were also some interesting architectural movements that highly resembled Jacque Fresco's designs. Metabolism was a movement created by a group of Japanese architects and engineers in 1928. Their idea was to gear architecture toward solving problems like population growth and resource management. Metabolism wanted architecture to be able to change, grow, and adapt to people's needs and technological advancements. The group's members developed ideas such as the creation of "megastructures" that would be able to house an entire city or parts of a city. Such megastructures would contain transportation, services, and prefabricated modular homes in the form of plug-in capsules. Each capsule was meant to be a separate unit that could easily be removed, updated, or replaced as the megastructure evolved.

Metabolism also proposed an "Ocean City" project as a response to the scarcity of land in densely populated areas. The idea was to build floating cities on the sea which would include residential towers, agriculture, aquaculture farming, as well as industry and entertainment facilities. Metabolism envisioned that such a city would expand and multiply organically, almost as if it were undergoing cell division. The Metabolism movement gained international recognition in the 1960s, but unfortunately, only a few of their designs were ever put into practice. As a result, many of their ideas remain largely theoretical.

I'll also mention Buckminster Fuller. Fuller was born in the US in 1895. He was an architect, inventor, systems theorist, author, and futurist. He popularized the geodesic dome, explaining that such a structure was very efficient because it used minimum resources and had maximum strength and stability. He claimed that the geodesic dome could easily be mass produced and transported almost anywhere in the world, so it was possible to house all of the world's people using this design. When people asked him why they should live in a dome, he replied with, "You've been living in a dome all your life—your head!" Fuller also popularized concepts such as "Spaceship Earth," warning people that we need to live sustainably—within the carrying capacity of the planet's resources —and take care of our one and only home, the Earth.

Eventually, I realized that many people have had brilliant ideas about how to better organize our society, but these grand ideas never changed society all that much. Sure there have been revolutions and government take-overs inspired by ideas, but this usually led to deaths and dictatorships rather than to the great society that was originally envisioned. After such revolutions, the core structure of the society never changed all that much. There have also been groups of people who wanted to create change through building communities, but I have never heard of a community that managed to have a significant impact on the structure of the larger global society. Usually, when small communities aim to lead by example and change the world, the world winds up changing them instead.

With time, I realized that our society and culture is too complex and dynamic to change with any kind of "grand plan" of how to re-organize itself, regardless of how brilliant that plan may be. I realized that ideas like technocracy or a resource-based economy may be inspirational, but they should not be taken too literally. Unfortunately, society doesn't change by envisioning a better way to organize itself, and then demoing and "implementing" this idea. I honestly wish this wasn't the case because that would make it much easier to change the world, but if we truly want to make a difference, then we have to be realistic. Big societal changes almost always happen gradually, through the development of knowledge, needs, culture, infrastructure, and technology. This change is often driven by *problem solving*.

Let's take an example: *the problem of transportation—how to get from point A to point B quickly and efficiently*. People didn't need to envision an entire world of airplanes, trains, and self-driving cars in order to create change. Instead, people took this problem and gradually came up with different solutions—horses, bikes, trains, cars, airplanes, and more. With time, the solutions evolved, as did our society. If somebody had tried to create and implement a holistic plan for the future of transportation, it is very unlikely that they will have succeeded, even if their plan was really great.

Another problem: *infectious diseases*. In order to solve this problem, we didn't need to envision an entire world that was free of infectious diseases. Instead, we needed to study the problem and figure out what caused it in the first place. Once people understood that tiny organisms caused infectious diseases, they were able to come up with many different solutions to this problem. Over time, these solutions evolved and this changed our society.

One more example: *communication—how to connect people over long distances*. People used pigeons, postal services, the telegraph, telephone, radio, television, the internet, and a lot more. Even a few decades ago, nobody could have envisioned exactly what the internet would have evolved into today. If anybody did try to create such a vision, it is extremely unlikely that it would have turned out as they had imagined, even if they tried really hard to make that happen. Society is a lot more complicated than the internet, so imagine how difficult it would be to plan every aspect of how our society should function, and how impossible it would be to implement that plan.

A Problem

Eventually, I realized that if we want to make the world a better place, then we have to focus on problem solving, not on envisioning a better world. The problem, however, is that most people who try to address global problems do this in a very shallow way. They don't question the structure of our society, they don't analyze human behavior, and they don't look for the root cause of these problems.

This is how humans try to solve problems today:

Some humans are concerned about climate change, so they create agreements in which countries and businesses "promise" to emit less CO_2, but this doesn't work. Some promises are too weak, other promises are broken because some humans are given very large incentives to extract, sell, and burn fossil fuels. *Any promise will be broken if the incentive is large enough to break it.* Other humans protest their government's lack of action, some use civil disobedience, and some strike from school, but greenhouse gas emissions continue to skyrocket. Unfortunately, protests don't take away the *incentive* for people to extract, sell, and burn fossil fuels.

Other humans are concerned that we're destroying the forests that our survival depends on, so they make petitions and put laws in place to make some of this logging "illegal." Unfortunately, this doesn't work. *Any law will be broken if the incentive is large enough to break it.* Some humans claim that the best way to solve this deforestation problem is to stop eating meat, so they "go vegan" and tell everyone else to do that too. Unfortunately, this hasn't solved the problem. The consumption of meat has only been increasing in recent years, as "development" increases. Companies will continue to sell and advertise beef if they are given the *incentive* to do so.

Other humans are concerned about inequality so they try to tax the rich, but that doesn't work. Billionaires have figured out very "smart" ways to move their money around the globe so they can avoid paying most of their taxes. They've also figured out very "smart" ways to make the right connections, create monopolies, and take as much money for themselves as possible. As long as the *incentive* is there, these people will continue to move their money around and get what they want. Rules and laws won't stop them.

Other humans are concerned about plastic pollution, so they tell everyone to recycle and stop using single-use plastics, but this *doesn't work.* Companies will continue to create, sell, and advertise infinite products wrapped in or made of plastic—if the *incentive* is large enough to do that. People will continue to buy these products because they have little to no choice.

Other humans are concerned that whaling is driving whale populations toward extinction, so they take matters into their own hands—they go into the sea and physically stop fishing boats from catching whales. As much as I admire those people's ambition, I cannot see this as a long-term solution. Powerful fishing companies will do whatever it takes to catch those whales and the very last bluefin tuna—if the *incentive* is large enough to do so. The same story repeats everywhere—if the short-term incentive is large enough, people will do whatever it takes to get that reward, regardless of what rules and laws are in place and regardless of how catastrophic the long-term consequences will be. In the long run, this *incentive* will cause us to destroy ourselves and the environment that we depend on for survival.

With that being said, I propose to re-analyze how we go about problem solving. If we understand that that *incentive* is driving global problems, then perhaps we should target that incentive as the problem, rather than all of the bi-product problems that result from it. In other words, if we want to stop climate change, we shouldn't just tell people to "promise" to switch to renewable energy, but rather, we need to understand *why* they're burning fossil fuels in the first place, and then change *that.*

Perhaps we need to ask simpler questions. For example: *what is the incentive that's causing all of these problems?* Many would say that the answer is simple: *money. Money, money, money. Money causes corruption, abuse, destruction, waste, exploitation, and a ton of other problems.* Money is the incentive behind selling fossil fuels, cutting down forests, selling beef, cheating on taxes, exploiting people, killing whales, and a billion other problems. We can observe that when people do whatever it takes to gain money, this causes problems.

How about another simple question: *what is money?* As an objective reality, money is not much at all—it's just some pieces of paper, coins, or numbers on a computer screen. It is our powerful collective imagination that gives it value.

Another simple question: *value for what?* The imaginary value that we assign to money is used to access goods and services. *How?* Through trade. In order to get access to food, shelter, and almost everything else, humans have to trade. Money is simply a medium that we use to trade goods and services.

If you take an objective outlook on our civilization, you will notice that the entire structure of our global society is actually based on trades. You go to work not to get money, but to get access to whatever money can get you (food, houses, boats, cars, clothes, gadgets, etc.). You might store some of that money, but again, you only store it so that you can later get access to all kinds of stuff. The only way you get access to this stuff is to *trade* for it. This constant need to trade gives people the incentive to continuously seek out more and more money. As a result, companies do whatever it takes to cut costs and grow profits. If this means polluting the environment, lying, exploiting people, or destroying ecosystems, they will do that.

Since humans don't have any other means of getting their basic needs met, everyone is forced into this rat race. Everyone is forced to trade—to sell something, someone, or themselves. Some people sell coal, others sell logs, others sell cattle, palm oil, fish, cobalt, clothes, cocaine, ivory, pangolins, phones, diamonds, dildos, or rubber duckies. Others make ads, *because if you make a lot of stuff, you also need to convince people to buy it!* As a result, we have a ton of excess crap and a simple-minded population that values sales and consumerism. Obviously, creating all of this crap requires energy, resources, and labor. As a bi-product, it creates problems.

So perhaps we don't need a "grand plan" to change the structure of our society, but we do need to take some steps to address the deeper problem at the core of our society. This problem, I would argue, is trade. Or "the need to trade," as that is the incentive that's driving most of our global problems.

How could we possibly solve a problem like "the need to trade"? Perhaps we need to start small. Perhaps by providing people with their basic needs as trade-free. Perhaps by sharing, giving, and getting people out of the rat race. You don't need a holistic global vision to do this, but perhaps you do need an open mind.

---

*Take note that trades don't only come in the form of sales or money. Cryptocurrencies can be used to represent trades. You may trade your personal data to use platforms like Facebook, YouTube, and others. You may be an "influencer" and trade ads for physical products. If you live in China, you probably trade your freedom for a social credit score. If you behave like a "good" Chinese citizen (say you have a full-time job, you buy stuff from Alibaba, you're not Muslim, and you don't talk shit about the government), you may get a good score. With a good social credit score, you get perks. If you get a bad social credit score, however, you might be punished. You might not be able to buy a house, use long-distance transportation, or leave your city. You could even be placed into a detention camp. In the future, I wouldn't be surprised if China (or other countries) fully replaced money with social credits within their country. I don't know about you, but I wouldn't want to live in that kind of trade-based dystopian future, even if it was free of money.

An Escape

If I think back to my own life, I can see that this rat race was exactly what I've been trying to escape this whole time. Most people trade their entire lives away. They spend their entire day doing something they don't enjoy, five days a week, fifty weeks a year, just so they can trade for a nice place to live, some fancy gadgets, and whatever else. I never wanted that type of life or any of that stuff. All I really wanted was to be free. Free from trading my time and energy to a meaningless job, free to roam around the world and to live a life of adventures. Free to explore, and to wander at our remarkable universe.

The more free time I had, the more I learned about the world, the more stubborn I became. I learned to understand that I am just a living creature, a human being, on a remarkable planet, orbiting one of hundreds of billions of stars, in one of hundreds of billions of galaxies. *Isn't that astonishing? What the fuck is a job?!* I realized that human beings have created billions of problems and that "jobs" weren't going to solve those problems. In fact, jobs only make the problems worse. I saw no reason to conform to society, no reason to trade my life away.

I realized that the trick to traveling around the world was to trade as little as possible. To work for the shortest possible amount of time, to save as much money as possible, then to quit, travel, and trade only when I really had to. The less money I spent, the longer I was able to travel without returning to the job game. Unfortunately, I never figured out a way to fully escape the game, but I have minimized my participation. That is how I freed up my time to explore the world.

You see, exploration isn't only about having a good time. It's also about expanding your mind, learning about the world, and doing something unique with your life. People like Isaac Newton, Charles Darwin, Marie Curie, Nikola Tesla, and Albert Einstein weren't driven by their "jobs," they were driven by their curiosity and fascination of the world. Every person has the potential to be the next great innovator, but they need a proper environment to nourish and grow that potential. In other words, they need free time, information, and trade-free access to their needs. The more free time people have and the less trapped they are by consumerism, the more they will be able to focus on exploration and problem solving. The two go hand-in-hand and both are necessary for our society to evolve into something saner.

Thus, if you want to free up your own time and get a chance to explore the world, the first thing you have to do is escape this trap. Escape the notion that you have to consume endlessly and reject the idea that you have to work all the time. Remember that the less stuff you want, the less you have to trade in this society. The less you trade, the more time you have to explore the world, to live, learn, and to simply be a human. Don't forget that you *are* human, and you only get one life, so don't waste it. Don't trade your life away and don't listen to anyone who tells you to do so. *Your life is yours —in the end, that's all you'll ever have.*

And lastly, if you do care to solve our global problems, then consider targeting *trade* as the cause of these problems. Consider the trade-based structure of our society and its effect on human behavior. Ask simple questions, learn about the world, and don't be afraid to think outside of the box. If the key to societal change is problem solving, then our first step is to *understand the problem*. Only then can we find real solutions.

* * *

As for my story, I left the Venus Project in 2019, and I also left Siberia. I packed up my backpack, took the railway back across Russia, hitchhiked across Europe, and began a new adventure with Tio TROM.

This book is trade-free at
www.bigworldsmallsasha.com/book

You can find photos from most chapters of this book at
www.bigworldsmallsasha.com/photos

And find my latest posts and whereabouts at
www.bigworldsmallsasha.com

Thanks for reading!

This book was written, formatted, and designed
using trade-free, open-source software.

Thank you to the people who contributed to
LibreOffice, Krita, Inkscape,
and TROM-Jaro.

Acknowledgments

I've gone through many challenges in my life, but nothing compared to the challenge of writing this book. I would like to thank everyone who helped me overcome this challenge. (I will stick to first names and pseudonyms to avoid revealing some identities, but you know who you are.)

First and foremost, thank you to Tio for supporting me throughout my seemingly never-ending writing endeavor. Thank you for giving me feedback on the contents of this book and for helping me immensely with the cover design, among many other things. I don't think I could have done it without you.

Thank you to Roma, for your financial and emotional support. Your contributions not only helped me survive while focusing on writing, but re-inspired me and pushed me to keep on working.

Thank you to Aaron, Seb, Guillaume, and the many people who have been supporting TROM. Since I've been living with Tio while writing, your contributions helped feed and shelter me while working on this book.

Thank you to Melissa for helping me with feedback and proof-reading.

Thank you to Maria, Gigi, and Georgi for housing me while I finished the last parts of the book.

To my mother, father, and brother—I don't really think you should read this book (and I'm kind of hoping you haven't), but just in case you did (or you're reading this part of it), I would like to thank you as well. Thank you for all of the love and support you've given me throughout my life. I'm sorry for my awful behavior as a teenager. I hope you can forgive me. Thank you for being such kind, caring, and wonderful people, and accepting me as your daughter/sister despite my recklessness.

Thank you to the rest of my family as well, Baba Zoya, Tetya Lira, Yolochka, Tim, Masha, Sasha, Ksyusha, Varya, Vanya, Lyova, Pasha, and Sima. And my little sisters, Dina and Sonya. You are all dear to me.

Thank you to my friend Ziva, for encouraging me to write a book, for contributing to my fundraiser, and for inspiring me and so many other people with your courage and infinite positive energy.

Thank you to everyone who contributed to the fundraiser I made for this book. That helped keep me fed and sheltered for a few extra months.

Thank you to Chris, for being such an important part of my life.

Thank you to Emma, for being such an awesome travel buddy and overall great person. Thank you to all of my friends, in fact, and everyone in this book (friend and foe alike). I will list some of you here (in order of appearance in the book):

Thank you to Aaron from Oahu. Thank you to Mike and Lauren from Molokai, and Mel from Kauai. Thank you to Maricruz. Thank you to Chili, and to Dan. Thank you to PL, Tom, Scott, Max, Sean, and 34. Also British Tom. Thank you to Clark. Thank you to the police officer who let me through the Canadian border. Thank you to the nice ladies from the Squamish gem shop.

Thank you to Alfie, Danny, JB, Toby, and Jeremy. Thank you to Alex and to my flatmates in Kirkwood. Thank you to Rome from Naples. Thank you to the Three Wise Monkeys staff, especially James. Thank you to Sam and Ana from Seville, Spain. Thank you to Fernando and all of my other friends from Granada.

Thank you to Enzo. Thank you to all of the people who picked me up hitchhiking in New Zealand and all around the world. Thank you to Mike (the hitchhiker I met in NZ). Thank you to Jacob and Steve from Australia, and Erik from Belgium.

Thank you to Kristina and Manu—you are both very special to me. Thank you to Moza and all of the beautiful people I met in Indonesia. Thank you to Asry and her wonderful family in Malanuza and across Flores, Indonesia.

Thank you to Bubba, from Mayor Island. Thank you to Derrick Jensen. Thank you to Stu from Whangarei. Thank you to everyone at Castle Billiards. Thank you to Collin from Jacksonville and Dean from Taos. Thank you—and sorry—to the female ski instructor from Taos. Thank you to Ryan. Thank you to Jake, Kevin, Freddy, and Mike from California. Thank you to Alfredo and Hector from Mexico. Thank you to Ricky and Aziz from New Zealand.

Thank you to Dave from Balgowlah. Thank you to Rachel.

Thank you to Pablo for inspiring me to include a detailed chapter on climate change.

Thank you to Keith and the nice people I met in Bulgaria.

Thank you to Emma's friends in Katherine, including Damian. Thank you to Greg, John, and the other truck drivers who've picked me up hitchhiking. Thank you to my buddy Diego.

Thank you to Will. Thank you to Robert. Thank you to Marijke.

Thank you to Dragos, Montez, Pedro, and Hugo. Thank you to the people from the ice cream shop in the South Coast of Australia.

Thank you to Chapa, Thusitha, Malithy, Paul, Bianca, Ruchira and his family, Thiranjana, and all of the other wonderful people I met in Sri Lanka.

Thank you to Wai, Matt, Nancy, and the other friendly climbers on Oahu. Thank you to Lo and all of the people I worked with in Breakers. Thank you to Mowgli and Steve.

Thank you to Arthur and Stefanie. Thank you to Nick and the nice people I met in Lviv. Thank you to the people from the surf camp in Nicaragua.

Thank you to Niv and all the wonderful people I got to know in Hawaii. Thank you to everyone I worked with at Roy's.

Thank you to Katya, Artem, and Dima from Syberia Top. Thank you to everyone who came to my meet-ups in Irkutsk. Thank you to Felix.

Thank you to all of the people who volunteer(/ed) for the Venus Project, and a special thanks to the Russian-speaking team.

Thank you to those who volunteer for TROM.

If I didn't mention you, it doesn't mean I don't appreciate you. I appreciate you very much. Thank you to everyone who has been a part of my life. Without you, I would not be the me I am today.

Mahalo to the big world.

Bibliography

Chapter 2. The Hawaiian Islands:

Breitha, Olivia Robello. *Olivia: My Life of Exile in Kalaupapa*. Arizona Memorial Museum Assn, 1988.

Chapter 3. The Russian Railway:

UNESCO World Heritage Convention. "Lake Baikal." *UNESCO World Heritage Centre,* https://whc.unesco.org/en/list/754/.

Chapter 11. Turkey:

Heller, Chris. "Turkey's 'Fairy Chimneys' Were Millions of Years in the Making." *Smithsonian Magazine*, 21 Sept. 2015, https://www.smithsonianmag.com/travel/fairy-chimneys-turkey-180956654/.

Chapter 14. New Zealand:

"Life Of The Northern Royal." *Royal Albatross Centre,* https://albatross.org.nz/royal-albatross/.

Chapter 16. Indonesia:

Barry, Carolyn. "Komodo Dragons Kill With Venom, Researchers Find." *National Geographic*, 18 May 2009, https://news.nationalgeographic.com/news/2009/05/komodo-dragon-venom/.

Chapter 17. Sailing NZ:

Jensen, Derrick. *The Culture of Make Believe*. Chelsea Green Publishing, 2004.

"Poverty and Shared Prosperity 2018." *World Bank*, https://www.worldbank.org/en/publication/poverty-and-shared-prosperity. Accessed 14 Aug. 2020.

Chapter 21. Climate Change:

Ambrose, Jillian. "Five Asian Countries Account for 80% of New Coal Power Investment." *The Guardian*, 30 June 2021, https://www.theguardian.com/environment/2021/jun/30/five-asian-countries-80-percent-new-coal-power-investment.

Benton, Michael J. *When Life Nearly Died: The Greatest Mass Extinction of All Time (Revised Edition).* Thames & Hudson, 2015.

Biskaborn, Boris K., et al. "Permafrost Is Warming at a Global Scale." *Nature Communications* **10,** 264 (2019). https://doi.org/10.1038/s41467-018-08240-4

Borunda, Alejandra. "High Stakes for the Planet as Carbon Emissions Rise Again." *National Geographic*, 5 Dec. 2018, https://www.nationalgeographic.com/environment/article/climate-geoengineering-series-intro.

---. "Oceans and Ice Are Absorbing the Brunt of Climate Change." *National Geographic*, 25 Sept. 2019, https://www.nationalgeographic.com/environment/article/ipcc-report-climate-change-affecting-ocean-ice.

---. "Past Decade Was the Hottest on Record." *National Geographic*, 15 Jan. 2020, https://www.nationalgeographic.com/science/article/the-decade-we-finally-woke-up-to-climate-change.

Caesar, L., et al. "Observed Fingerprint of a Weakening Atlantic Ocean Overturning Circulation." *Nature* **556**, 191–196 (2018). https://doi.org/10.1038/s41586-018-0006-5

Carrington, Damian. "'Insanity': Petrostates Planning Huge Expansion of Fossil Fuels, Says UN Report." *The Guardian*, 8 Nov. 2023, https://www.theguardian.com/environment/2023/nov/08/insanity-petrostates-planning-huge-expansion-of-fossil-fuels-says-un-report.

---. "IPCC Report's Verdict on Climate Crimes of Humanity: Guilty as Hell." *The Guardian*, 9 Aug. 2021, https://www.theguardian.com/environment/2021/aug/09/ipcc-reports-verdict-on-climate-crimes-of-humanity-guilty-as-hell.

---. "One Football Pitch of Forest Lost Every Second in 2017, Data Reveals." *The Guardian*, 27 June 2018, https://www.theguardian.com/environment/ng-interactive/2018/jun/27/one-football-pitch-of-forest-lost-every-second-in-2017-data-reveals.

Carrington, Damian, and Matthew Taylor. "Revealed: The 'Carbon Bombs' Set to Trigger Catastrophic Climate Breakdown." *The Guardian*, 11 May 2022, https://www.theguardian.com/environment/ng-interactive/2022/may/11/fossil-fuel-carbon-bombs-climate-breakdown-oil-gas.

Catastrophic Feedback Loops - Runaway Climate Change.
GlobalClimateNews, 23 Apr. 2018, https://www.youtube.com/watch?
v=O8oMpbiDXhQ.

Cecco, Leyland. "Canada Oil and Gas Firms to Drill 8% More Wells next Year
as Emissions Target Slips." *The Guardian*, 24 Nov. 2023,
https://www.theguardian.com/world/2023/nov/24/canada-oil-gas-more-wells-
trans-mountain.

Champine, Riley D., and Ryan Morris. "The Melting Arctic Is Now Open for
Business." *National Geographic*,
https://www.nationalgeographic.com/environment/graphics/map-shows-how-
ships-navigate-melting-arctic-feature.

"Climate Change: Atmospheric Carbon Dioxide." *NOAA Climate.Gov*,
https://www.climate.gov/news-features/understanding-climate/climate-change-
atmospheric-carbon-dioxide.

"Climate Change Indicators: Global Greenhouse Gas Emissions." *US EPA*, 27
June 2016, https://www.epa.gov/climate-indicators/climate-change-indicators-
global-greenhouse-gas-emissions.

Demystifying Ocean Acidification and Biodiversity Impacts. California
Academy of Sciences, 30 June 2014, https://www.youtube.com/watch?
v=GL7qJYKzcsk.

Derouin, Sarah. "Deforestation: Facts, Causes & Effects ." *Live Science*, 28
Apr. 2023, https://www.livescience.com/27692-deforestation.html.

Ellis-Petersen, Hannah. "India Plans to Fell Ancient Forest to Create 40 New
Coalfields." *The Guardian*, 8 Aug. 2020,
https://www.theguardian.com/world/2020/aug/08/india-prime-minister-
narendra-modi-plans-to-fell-ancient-forest-to-create-40-new-coal-fields.

---. "India's Energy Conundrum: Committed to Renewables but Still
Expanding Coal." *The Guardian*, 15 Nov. 2022,
https://www.theguardian.com/world/2022/nov/15/india-committed-to-clean-
energy-but-continues-to-boost-coal-production.

Extreme Weather. *National Climate Assessment*,
https://nca2014.globalchange.gov/highlights/report-findings/extreme-weather.
Accessed 11 Feb. 2020.

Fleeing Climate Change — the Real Environmental Disaster. DW
Documentary, 1 May 2019, https://www.youtube.com/watch?v=cl4Uv9_7KJE.

"Global Temperature." Global Climate Change: Vital Signs of the Planet, *Earth Science Communications Team at NASA's Jet Propulsion Laboratory,* https://climate.nasa.gov/vital-signs/global-temperature/. Accessed 11 Feb. 2020.

Greshko, Michael. "What Are Mass Extinctions, and What Causes Them?" *National Geographic,* 26 Sept. 2019, https://www.nationalgeographic.com/science/prehistoric-world/mass-extinction/.

Hansen, Kathryn. "Water Vapor Confirmed as Major Player in Climate Change." *NASA,* https://www.nasa.gov/topics/earth/features/vapor_warming.html.

Harvey, Fiona. "No New Oil, Gas or Coal Development If World Is to Reach Net Zero by 2050, Says World Energy Body." *The Guardian,* 18 May 2021, https://www.theguardian.com/environment/2021/may/18/no-new-investment-in-fossil-fuels-demands-top-energy-economist.

---. "US behind More than a Third of Global Oil and Gas Expansion Plans, Report Finds." *The Guardian,* 12 Sept. 2023, https://www.theguardian.com/environment/2023/sep/12/us-behind-more-than-a-third-of-global-oil-and-gas-expansion-plans-report-finds.

Hawkins, Amy. "China's Coal Addiction Puts Spotlight on Its Climate Ambitions before Cop28." *The Guardian,* 27 Nov. 2023, https://www.theguardian.com/world/2023/nov/27/china-coal-addiction-spotlight-climate-ambitions-cop28.

Hoffman, Hillel J. "The Permian Extinction—When Life Nearly Came to an End." *National Geographic,* 2 Dec. 2009, https://www.nationalgeographic.com/science/article/permian-extinction.

How a Warmer Arctic Could Intensify Extreme Weather. Vox, 17 Apr. 2018, https://www.youtube.com/watch?v=yQliow4ghtU.

"Importance of Phytoplankton." *NASA Earth Observatory,* https://earthobservatory.nasa.gov/features/Phytoplankton/page2.php.

IPCC, 2018: Summary for Policymakers. In: *Global Warming of 1.5°C. An IPCC Special Report on the impacts of global warming of 1.5°C above pre-industrial levels and related global greenhouse gas emission pathways, in the context of strengthening the global response to the threat of climate change, sustainable development, and efforts to eradicate poverty* [Masson-Delmotte, V., P. Zhai, H.-O. Pörtner, D. Roberts, J. Skea, P.R. Shukla, A. Pirani, W. Moufouma-Okia, C. Péan, R. Pidcock, S. Connors, J.B.R. Matthews, Y. Chen, X. Zhou, M.I. Gomis, E. Lonnoy, T. Maycock, M. Tignor, and T. Waterfield (eds.)]. Cambridge University Press, Cambridge, UK and New York, NY, USA, pp. 3-24. https://doi.org/10.1017/9781009157940.001.

IPCC, 2019: Summary for Policymakers. In: *Climate Change and Land: an IPCC special report on climate change, desertification, land degradation, sustainable land management, food security, and greenhouse gas fluxes in terrestrial ecosystems* [P.R. Shukla, J. Skea, E. Calvo Buendia, V. Masson-Delmotte, H.- O. Pörtner, D. C. Roberts, P. Zhai, R. Slade, S. Connors, R. van Diemen, M. Ferrat, E. Haughey, S. Luz, S. Neogi, M. Pathak, J. Petzold, J. Portugal Pereira, P. Vyas, E. Huntley, K. Kissick, M. Belkacemi, J. Malley, (eds.)]. https://doi.org/10.1017/9781009157988.001.

IPCC, 2019: Summary for Policymakers. In: *IPCC Special Report on the Ocean and Cryosphere in a Changing Climate* [H.-O. Pörtner, D.C. Roberts, V. Masson-Delmotte, P. Zhai, M. Tignor, E. Poloczanska, K. Mintenbeck, A. Alegría, M. Nicolai, A. Okem, J. Petzold, B. Rama, N.M. Weyer (eds.)]. Cambridge University Press, Cambridge, UK and New York, NY, USA, pp. 3–35. https://doi.org/10.1017/9781009157964.001.

IPCC, 2021: Summary for Policymakers. In: *Climate Change 2021: The Physical Science Basis. Contribution of Working Group I to the Sixth Assessment Report of the Intergovernmental Panel on Climate Change* [Masson-Delmotte, V., P. Zhai, A. Pirani, S.L. Connors, C. Péan, S. Berger, N. Caud, Y. Chen, L. Goldfarb, M.I. Gomis, M. Huang, K. Leitzell, E. Lonnoy, J.B.R. Matthews, T.K. Maycock, T. Waterfield, O. Yelekçi, R. Yu, and B. Zhou (eds.)]. Cambridge University Press, Cambridge, United Kingdom and New York, NY, USA, pp. 3–32, doi:10.1017/9781009157896.001.

IPCC, 2014: *Climate Change 2014: Synthesis Report. Contribution of Working Groups I, II and III to the Fifth Assessment Report of the Intergovernmental Panel on Climate Change* [Core Writing Team, R.K. Pachauri and L.A. Meyer (eds.)]. IPCC, Geneva, Switzerland, 151 pp.

IPCC, 2023: Summary for Policymakers. In: *Climate Change 2023: Synthesis Report. Contribution of Working Groups I, II and III to the Sixth Assessment Report of the Intergovernmental Panel on Climate Change* [Core Writing Team, H. Lee and J. Romero (eds.)]. IPCC, Geneva, Switzerland, pp. 1-34, doi: 10.59327/IPCC/AR6-9789291691647.001

"It's Official: July 2023 Was the Warmest Month Ever Recorded." *UN News*, United Nations, 8 Aug. 2023, https://news.un.org/en/story/2023/08/1139527.

Jamail, Dahr. "The World Is on the Brink of Widespread Water Wars." *Truthout*, 11 Feb. 2019, https://truthout.org/articles/the-world-is-on-the-brink-of-widespread-water-wars/.

James, Lauren E. "Half of the Great Barrier Reef Is Dead." *National Geographic,* 7 Aug. 2018, https://www.nationalgeographic.com/magazine/article/explore-atlas-great-barrier-reef-coral-bleaching-map-climate-change.

Katz, Cheryl. "Warming at the Poles Will Soon Be Felt Globally in Rising Seas, Extreme Weather." *National Geographic*, 4 Dec. 2019, https://www.nationalgeographic.com/science/article/arctic.

Kent, Sarah, and Timothy Puko. "U.S. Will Be the World's Largest Oil Producer by 2023, Says IEA." *WSJ*, The Wall Street Journal, 5 Mar. 2018, https://www.wsj.com/articles/u-s-will-be-the-worlds-largest-oil-producer-by-2023-says-iea-1520236810.

Leahy, Stephen. "Dangerous Levels of Warming Locked in by Planned Jump in Fossil Fuels Output." *National Geographic*, 20 Nov. 2019, https://www.nationalgeographic.com/science/article/world-fossil-fuel-production-rise-guarantees-missing-paris-climate-goals.

Lindsey, Rebecca, and LuAnn Dahlma. "Climate Change: Ocean Heat Content." *NOAA Climate.gov,* 17 Aug. 2020, https://www.climate.gov/news-features/understanding-climate/climate-change-ocean-heat-content.

Lynch, Patrick, and Katie Weeman. "New Study Finds Sea Level Rise Accelerating." *Climate Change: Vital Signs of the Planet*, NASA, 13 Feb. 2018, https://climate.nasa.gov/news/2680/new-study-finds-sea-level-rise-accelerating/.

Milman, Oliver, and Nina Lakhani. "US Fracking Boom Could Tip World to Edge of Climate Disaster." *The Guardian*, 11 May 2022, https://www.theguardian.com/environment/2022/may/11/us-fracking-climate-fossil-fuel-gases.

Niiler, Eric. "The Ocean Is Getting More Acidic—What That Actually Means." *National Geographic,* 15 June 2018, https://www.nationalgeographic.com/science/article/ocean-acidification-underwater-drones-gliders-science-environment.

Nunez, Christina. "Sea Level Rise, Explained." *National Geographic*, 15 Feb. 2022, https://www.nationalgeographic.com/environment/article/sea-level-rise-1.

"Ocean Acidification." *National Oceanic and Atmospheric Administration,* https://www.noaa.gov/education/resource-collections/ocean-coasts/ocean-acidification. Accessed 12 Feb. 2020.

"Overview of Greenhouse Gases." *US EPA*,
https://www.epa.gov/ghgemissions/overview-greenhouse-gases. Accessed 11
Feb. 2020.

Parker, Laura. "Florida's Coral Reef Is Disintegrating." *National Geographic*,
2 May 2016, https://www.nationalgeographic.com/animals/article/160502-reef-
florida-acidification-fish-miami.

---. "Sea Level Rise Will Flood Hundreds of Cities in the Near Future."
National Geographic, 12 July 2017,
https://www.nationalgeographic.com/pages/article/sea-level-rise-flood-global-
warming-science.

"Seven Things to Know About Climate Change." *National Geographic*,
https://www.nationalgeographic.com/magazine/graphics/seven-things-to-
know-about-climate-change. Accessed 12 Feb. 2020.

Stankovic, Tatjana, et al. "The Paris Agreement's Inherent Tension between
Ambition and Compliance." *Humanities and Social Sciences Communications*
10, 550 (2023). https://doi.org/10.1057/s41599-023-02054-6

Tabuchi, Hiroko. "Nations That Vowed to Halt Warming Are Expanding
Fossil Fuels, Report Finds." *The New York Times*, 8 Nov. 2023,
https://www.nytimes.com/2023/11/08/climate/fossil-fuels-expanding.html

The Race for the Arctic Is Ramping up. Here's Why. DW Planet A, 25 Nov.
2022, https://www.youtube.com/watch?v=hvRzWzQW2go.

UNFCCC. "What Is the United Nations Framework Convention on Climate
Change?" United Nations Climate Change, https://unfccc.int/process-and-
meetings/what-is-the-united-nations-framework-convention-on-climate-
change.

Walker, Peter. "New North Sea Oil and Gas Licences Will Send 'Wrecking
Ball' through Climate Commitments." *The Guardian*, 31 July 2023,
https://www.theguardian.com/environment/2023/jul/31/rishi-sunak-approval-
100-new-north-sea-oil-and-gas-licences-fossil-fuel-climate-crisis.

Watts, Jonathan. "We Have 12 Years to Limit Climate Change Catastrophe,
Warns UN." *The Guardian*, 8 Oct. 2018,
https://www.theguardian.com/environment/2018/oct/08/global-warming-must-
not-exceed-15c-warns-landmark-un-report.

Welch, Craig. "Arctic Permafrost Is Thawing Fast. That Affects Us All."
National Geographic, 13 Aug. 2019,
https://www.nationalgeographic.com/environment/article/arctic-permafrost-is-
thawing-it-could-speed-up-climate-change-feature.

"What a 'Sobering' Report on Arctic Ice Loss Means for Global Sea Levels." *PBS NewsHour*, 10 Dec. 2019, https://www.pbs.org/newshour/show/what-a-sobering-report-on-arctic-ice-loss-means-for-global-sea-levels.

"What Is Coral Bleaching?" NOAA's National Ocean Service, *National Oceanic and Atmospheric Administration,* https://oceanservice.noaa.gov/facts/coral_bleach.html. Accessed 12 Feb. 2020.

"What Is Ocean Acidification?" NOAA's National Ocean Service, *National Oceanic and Atmospheric Administration,* https://oceanservice.noaa.gov/facts/acidification.html. Accessed 12 Feb. 2020.

"What the World Would Look Like If All the Ice Melted." *National Geographic,* 1 Sept. 2013, https://www.nationalgeographic.com/magazine/article/rising-seas-ice-melt-new-shoreline-maps.

"World's Biggest Fossil Fuel Firms Projected to Spend Almost a Trillion Dollars on New Oil and Gas Fields by 2030." *Global Witness,* 12 Apr. 2022, https://www.globalwitness.org/en/press-releases/worlds-biggest-fossil-fuel-firms-projected-to-spend-almost-a-trillion-dollars-on-new-oil-and-gas-fields-by-2030/.

Chapter 25. Morocco; Chapter 26. Sydney:

Fresco, Jacque. *The Best That Money Can't Buy*. Global Cyber Visions, 2002.

Paradise or Oblivion. The Venus Project, 30 Mar. 2012, https://www.youtube.com/watch?v=KphWsnhZ4Ag.

Chapter 29. Lake Tahoe:

Callahan, Steven. *Adrift*. HarperCollins, 2002.

Robertson, Dougal. *Survive the Savage Sea*. Sheridan House, Inc., 1994.

Bailey, Maurice, and Maralyn Bailey. *117 Days Adrift*. Sheridan House, Inc., 1992.

Chapter 30. Caribbean:

Jensen, Derrick, et al. *Deep Green Resistance*. Seven Stories Press, 2011.

Chapter 37. Europe:

Hoare, Philip. "More Tigers Live in US Back Yards than in the Wild. Is This a Catastrophe?" *The Guardian*, 20 June 2018, https://www.theguardian.com/environment/shortcuts/2018/jun/20/more-tigers-live-in-us-back-yards-than-in-the-wild-is-this-a-catastrophe.

"Just 8 Men Own Same Wealth as Half the World." *Oxfam International*, 16 Jan. 2017, https://www.oxfam.org/en/press-releases/just-8-men-own-same-wealth-half-world.

"Over 40 Million People Still Victims of Slavery." *UN News*, United Nations, 2 Dec. 2018, https://news.un.org/en/story/2018/12/1027271.

Secretariat of the Convention on Biological Diversity (2020) Global Biodiversity Outlook 5 – Summary for Policy Makers. Montréal.

The Sustainable Development Goals Report 2020. *United Nations Statistics Division, https://unstats.un.org/sdgs/report/2020/.*

"UNHCR: A Record 100 Million People Forcibly Displaced Worldwide." *UN News*, United Nations, 22 May 2022, https://news.un.org/en/story/2022/05/1118772.

"World Is Moving Backwards on Eliminating Hunger and Malnutrition, UN Report Reveals." *UN News*, United Nations, 6 July 2022, https://news.un.org/en/story/2022/07/1122032.

Chapter 38. Florida:

"What Kind of Change Do You Expect in Architecture?" *The Venus Project*, https://www.thevenusproject.com/faq/what-kind-of-change-do-you-expect-in-architecture/. Accessed 6 Apr. 2021.

Chapter 40. The End & the Beginning:

Buckminster Fuller: Thinking Out Loud, PBS American Masters, 1996.

"Metabolism (Architecture)." *Wikipedia*, Wikimedia Foundation, Inc., https://en.wikipedia.org/wiki/Metabolism_(architecture).

Technocracy In Plain Terms. Technocracy Inc, 1939, pp. 8-9. https://archive.org/details/TechnocracyInPlainTerms/mode/2up.